Mormon Convert,

Mormon Defector

Peter McAuslan and Agnes McAuslin McAuslan,
circa 1867, Marysville, California.

Mormon Convert, Mormon Defector

A Scottish Immigrant in
the American West, 1848–1861

by
POLLY AIRD

Foreword by William P. MacKinnon

UNIVERSITY OF OKLAHOMA PRESS
NORMAN

Library of Congress Cataloging-in-Publication Data

Aird, Polly.

Mormon convert, Mormon defector : a Scottish immigrant in the American West, 1848–1861 / Polly Aird ; foreword by William P. MacKinnon.

p. cm.

Includes bibliographical references and index.

ISBN 978-0-87062-369-1 (hardcover)
ISBN 978-0-8061-9212-3 (paper)

1. McAuslan, Peter, 1824–1908. 2. Mormon converts—Scotland—Biography. 3. Ex-church members—United States—Biography. 4. Ex-church members—Church of Jesus Christ of Latter-day Saints—Biography. I. Title.

BX8695.M257A37 2009
289.3092—dc22
[B]

2008043141

The paper in this book meets the guidelines for permanence and durability of the Committee on Production Guidelines for Book Longevity of the Council on Library Resources, Inc. ∞

Copyright © 2009 by the University of Oklahoma Press, Norman, Publishing Division of the University. Paperback published 2023. Manufactured in the U.S.A.

For my daughters,
DEANNA MCLEAN DAVIS
and
MARY MCPHERSON DAVIS

※

THE WORLD IS PARTLY DEPENDENT ON UNHISTORIC
acts; and that things are not so ill with you and me as they
might have been, is half owing to the number who lived faithfully a hidden life, and rest in unvisited tombs.

—*George Eliot*, Middlemarch

Contents

Illustrations

MAPS

Foreword

In becoming the biographer of Peter McAuslan, her Scottish-born great-great-uncle, Polly Aird has done so as a daughter of the American West—one born and educated in California, residing in Washington State, and long immersed in the history of territorial Utah. As such she is well suited by her background alone to advance the theme of many of the Arthur H. Clark Company's groundbreaking books about the Mormon experience of the nineteenth century—the concept that it was a regional (western), if not international, phenomenon rather than a Utah story alone. Accordingly, Aird takes *Mormon Convert, Mormon Defector* from Peter McAuslan's Presbyterian origins in the Scottish Lowlands of the 1820s to his 1848 conversion to Mormonism, 1854 migration to and across the United States, 1858 excommunication, and 1859 flight from Utah, and subsequent fifty years of religious thought and writing in agricultural California.

In the process of presenting this sweeping tale, Aird fills a gap in our understanding of the nineteenth-century Scottish diaspora to North America, a story that has usually focused exclusively on a few of the economically powerful or outrageously colorful people among McAuslan's emigrant contemporaries, such as Andrew Carnegie. Except for the hardscrabble Scottish origins common to all of these stories, Peter McAuslan's life fell outside the mold of these atypical examples. He was essentially a man of unexceptional attainments, a person whose major accomplishment was to survive life's buffeting in a series of trans-Atlantic economies best described as Darwinian. In effect, then, Aird presents the life of a rarely chronicled type: an ordinary Scottish emigrant rather than a Celtic captain of industry or a transplanted lord of the frontier. Nonetheless Peter McAuslan was a man with an extraordinary experience—that of first loving and then leaving Mormonism, a religion that has usually chronicled the adventures of the faithful rather than shedding light on those it labels "gentile" or "apostate." Studying Peter McAuslan's story is therefore eminently worthwhile, for it provides a glimpse into both a pilgrim's progress through economic adversity and his jarring service as an ultimately disillusioned foot soldier in the world of militant Utah Mormonism.

Aird, a non-Mormon, limns this view deftly and in balanced fashion while avoiding the grinding of anti-LDS axes, a tone not always achieved by historians and biographers surveying the world built by a rough-hewn Brigham Young. Aird's is a judicious approach worthy of Peter McAuslan's own unembittered post-Utah attitude. Even from the distance of California and with the passage of decades, McAuslan was consistently positive about the Mormon people and usually respectful of the religion he left behind until his death in 1908.

If in most ways McAuslan's life story in Scotland and the United States is that of an unexceptional person, this is not to say that it is an uninteresting one. If anything, readers might well view Polly Aird's McAuslan as something of a nineteenth-century Forrest Gump—an Everyman who was a ubiquitous witness to many of the seminal events in British, Mormon, and western American life of the period. Thus we see him as part of a Scottish family recently bereft of a centuries-old landed baronetcy, a post-Napoleonic loss that triggered descent into the world of tenant farmers whom the notorious Highland Clearances and Enclosure Acts soon drove into the horrors of factory work in the fetid mill towns surrounding Glasgow. Peter McAuslan was born in 1824 to such a downwardly mobile clan, managed to acquire a few years of common-school education, and at age eight followed his father and other family members into the textile industry to engage in the elaborate printing of calico shawls and handkerchiefs for the British colonial trade. From this vantage point McAuslan experienced the upheavals flowing from the 1848 revolutions of Continental Europe; the rise of Chartism and its demand for British political and economic reforms; the spreading impact of the Irish potato famine; a constant quest for work; an unprecedented religious fervor, with accompanying challenges to the established churches of both Scotland and England; the arrival in the British Isles of Mormonism and a covey of its most distinguished apostles; the stunned reaction by both Latter-day Saints and non-Mormons to the 1852 polygamy announcement; cholera outbreaks of unprecedented destruction; and Great Britain's disastrous lurch into the bloodbath of the Crimean War.

With McAuslan's 1854 migration to America from Liverpool, a year behind most of his large family but with a shipload of other Mormon converts that included his new wife, he became witness-participant to even greater upheaval. Much of this change constituted the landmark events of the LDS experience at midcentury: the cholera epidemics sweeping emigrant ranks between New Orleans and the Great Plains; the 1854 Grattan Massacre near Fort Laramie, catalyst to forty-five years of unremitting Sioux warfare; Brigham Young's espousal of the controversial Adam-God theory and public humiliation of Apostle Orson Pratt, McAuslan's personal hero; the 1854–55 sojourn of the U.S. Army's Steptoe Expedition in Salt Lake City; the drought and locust plagues of 1855; the devastating winter and famine of 1855–56; the Willie-Martin handcart disaster of 1856, the worst loss of life in the entire overland trails experience; the Reformation of 1856–57; and the Utah War of 1857–58, the nation's most extensive and expensive military involvement during the period between the Mexican and Civil wars. Throughout all of these events, with the help of his new wife, parents, maternal grandmother, siblings, uncles, and cousins, McAuslan worked hard to make the daunting transition from urban textile worker to desert farmer. He did so first in Salt Lake City and then in the milder climate of Spanish Fork, a community whose leaders soon called him to minor but increasingly responsible church roles as well as to that of a sergeant in the territorial militia (Nauvoo Legion). But by 1859 McAuslan had had enough. In that year he, about half his extended family, and a caravan of other disaffected Latter-day Saints left Utah forever, migrating from Camp Floyd to California on the northern route under the protection of a U.S. Army escort.

What went wrong for Peter McAuslan in Utah Territory? When so many others—some from his own family—chose to remain in both the Great Basin and their adopted religion, why did he court excommunication, migrate at substantial personal and economic risk to the Sacramento Valley, and abandon organized religion for a personal philosophy that he ultimately described as spiritualism? An understanding of the answer to this question constitutes the heart of Aird's book, and so is more properly found in the chapters that follow rather than here. Suffice it to say, though, that in Utah McAuslan chafed and eventually bristled when confronted by the rigorous demands of church discipline as imposed by authoritarian leaders whose ecclesiastical legitimacy and practical competence he could not accept. In a sense, McAuslan had heeded the call to gather to Zion with expectations that he would find a supreme leader of Joseph Smith's qualities. Instead he was disillusioned to discover Utah and Mormonism led by a quite different Brigham Young, a man who in McAuslan's view thrived on authoritarianism and presided over a society beset by appalling acts of violence. Perhaps most telling, McAuslan came to view Brigham Young as simply unprophetic.

But it was the violence rather than doctrinal differences that pushed McAuslan over the edge. In tiny, isolated Spanish Fork he was a mere six miles from Bishop Aaron Johnson's Springville, perhaps the roughest town in provincial Utah during the run-up to the Utah War and that which followed. From this vantage point McAuslan was soon aware of most, if not all, of the bloodshed that flowed in Springville, Payson, and neighboring districts to the south: the Santa Clara ambush, the Parrish-Potter murders, the slaughter of the Aiken Party, the assassination of Henry Forbes, the murder of Henry Jones and his mother, and, of course, the Mountain Meadows massacre, the greatest incident of organized mass murder of unarmed civilians in American history until the 1995 Oklahoma City bombing.

From her earlier research on the Parrish-Potter and other murders, Aird is unusually qualified to address the scene in Springville. From her indefatigable pursuit of McAuslan family documents—some held by distant relatives heretofore unknown to her—she is also uniquely suited to the task of assembling Peter McAuslan's own explanation of the impact of such unsettling events on his religious beliefs and his decision to move on to California. Here, then, is an account of a former Mormon's interior life and decision making rarely encountered in the published record bearing on territorial Utah. The comments of "apostates"—a label accepted

by neither McAuslan nor his biographer—are simply not valued or collected in any systematic way. That Peter McAuslan's story has now welled
up under Polly Aird's determined tutelage to shed light on an ordinary
but fiercely independent Scottish emigrant of the American West is to
our great good fortune. It is a special bonus that Aird has done so with a
narrative felicity that turns even such gritty events as the locust plague of
1855 and the padding of Utah's 1856 census into happenings described with
verve and drama.

WILLIAM P. MACKINNON
Santa Barbara, California
2008

Preface

THE MAJORITY OF ACCOUNTS WRITTEN ABOUT EARLY MORMON converts, their arduous journey to Utah by covered wagon or handcart, and their settling in the valley of the Great Salt Lake portray a heroic people: "Saints" led by the hand of God away from their persecutors, and faithful pioneers making the desert bloom in the Promised Land. This story does not fit that pattern.

This is a history of Peter McAuslan, who, with his parents, siblings, grandmother, aunts, and uncles, converted to Mormonism in Scotland in the 1840s, became fully absorbed in his newfound faith, and longed to "gather to Zion." Most of the immediate family sailed to New Orleans in 1853; Peter and his new wife, Agnes, came the next year. In Utah the families set about learning to farm and construct adobe homes, the men worked on the foundations of the temple, and all attended religious meetings. In everything they did, they were helping to build the new Zion, the place where God's people would live together in harmony and purity, ready to usher in the millennial reign of Christ. But within five years, Peter and his wife, his parents, and his brothers had become disillusioned and turned against the faith that had brought them to Utah. Believing that the once-persecuted Saints were now the persecutors, they set their sights on escaping to California at the first opportunity.

Peter McAuslan was my great-great-uncle. I grew up hearing about the family's hopes of helping to build a new society in Utah, about their walking more than a thousand miles to Salt Lake City, about cricket and locust plagues, drought, and an incredibly cold winter, and especially about what they came to see as the oppressive hand of the Mormon church. Years later I began to wonder about those stories. What had attracted the family to Mormonism? What led to their disillusionment? Did they fill the spiritual vacuum in their lives with something else?

In seeking answers to these questions, I turned first to the account my grandmother had written when she was in her eighties, which was based on what her parents had told her many years before. Her family history is filled with interesting stories. One of the most intriguing is about Davy, a young man the McAuslans befriended during their voyage and whom they helped outfit for the plains. Having a big heart, he turned his wagon over to the sick, and on their long trek west, it became known as "Davy's hospital." When they arrived in Salt Lake City, Davy helped the family build a sturdy barn. But when the bishop and his counselors came to requisition it to house new immigrants for the winter, Davy, upset and angry, failed to mind his tongue. "They took him away. Poor honest Davy. He was one of many," wrote Grandmother.

My father believed that the family had converted to Mormonism because of their great interest in education and desire to build a new society based on hard work and dedication. He discounted the sincerity of their belief in Mormonism and thought that the religion had been misrepresented in Scotland. The McAuslans had thought, he said, that the new faith was taking part in the grand American experiment: in Utah they would find a land of liberty, where one would be free of the tyranny of an established church and an inflexible class system.

As I began to explore these stories, I found that the mysterious Davy as well as my father's rationalization of the family's conversion had little basis in fact but had become family legends. What I found underneath, however, was a much more fascinating story. What emerged was not only the picture of a man truly sincere in his belief—who had a vision to confirm the truth of Mormonism—but also a picture that spoke to the larger human condition. Besides his hidden, faithful life, for which George Eliot's *Middlemarch* quotation given as this book's epigraph serves as an apt description, Peter McAuslan's experiences opened onto larger themes of major significance: the economy, society, and religious climate in Scotland at the beginning of the modern era; the remarkable missionary movement and immigration system established by the Mormons; the overseas and overland travel under that system, with its initiation into "practical Mormonism"; a theocracy in Utah and its violent overtones such as the Utah War and the Mountain Meadows massacre; and a risky flight to California that divided the family. Here was something much more momentous than one man's *Middlemarch* life. Besides new insights into these broad motifs, I found a very human man who had faced difficult choices: he changed the direction of his life to support his new belief but then came to doubt its truth.

Peter McAuslan was the first in his immediate family to convert to Mormonism and the first to lose his faith. William James in his *Varieties of Religious Experience* describes conversion as either a sudden event or the result of a gradual conscious and subconscious process. Disillusionment follows similar patterns. For Peter, both conversion and loss of faith were multifaceted and reached in stages. Peter was a Mormon for ten years: five years in Scotland, seven months on the journey, and almost five years in Utah. Understanding his conversion and disaffection necessitated looking not only at his character and the events of his life but also at his place in the larger historical and cultural context that influenced him.

The research and writing has taken eighteen years. Peter left a partial trip journal, a few bundles of letters, some jotted notes, and a number of books. A few letters written by his wife survive. Besides the usual genealogical records of censuses, immigration, land ownership, and naturalization, I found records of his baptism, membership, church offices, priesthood meetings, and tithing in the Archives of the Church of Jesus Christ of Latter-day Saints. There and in other Utah libraries I also found journals kept by his contemporaries in Scotland, on the journey, and in Utah. They filled out the picture of his activities and occasionally mentioned him. The National Archives and Records Administration had letters that referred to him, and the local newspapers in California recorded life events there and even some of his thinking. The more I learned about Peter McAuslan, the more I began to realize that his narrative was not very different from that of other British working-class converts who gathered to the Mormon Zion in the 1840s and 1850s. And yet, once Peter was there, his story changed: He did not persevere as most did. He became one of the minority, and his history illustrates the consequences of losing faith among the faithful.

Thus this account is about a foot soldier of the Mormon kingdom, a man who never wielded religious, political, or economic power. But the story is also about one man's search for God, a man who followed his beliefs, suffered profound disillusionment, and did not shrink from where that led him even when it put him and those he loved in danger. His search and the paths he chose were affected by events and forces in both Scotland and Utah at a particularly dramatic time. I became increasingly intrigued and wanted to comprehend what had happened to this man so long ago.

Acknowledgments

FIRST AND FOREMOST, I WOULD LIKE TO THANK DONNA MILLER Forguson of Live Oak, California. Great-great-granddaughter of Peter McAuslan, she unstintingly shared the contents of Peter's trunk, which contained his writings, drawings, books, and other mementos. In addition, Donna transcribed Peter's letters and notes with care and accuracy—not an easy task, as some were badly faded, had been chewed by mice, or were falling apart. Likewise, I want to thank Ada Redd Rigby of Blanding, Utah, a great-granddaughter of Peter McAuslan's sister Janet. Ada had in her possession several letters by Peter. She freely shared these and old photographs. Jean Williston Heilmann, Peter's great-granddaughter from Grass Valley, California, offered the photograph of him that appears in the last chapter. Helen Truman Clegg of Provo, Utah, sent me copies of letters written by Peter's wife, Agnes McAuslin McAuslan, to her sister, Elizabeth McAuslin Maxwell, in Peoa, Utah. Another cousin, J. Brady Allan, added Denny, Stirlingshire, to his itinerary on a visit to Scotland so as to bring back information and pictures. Without their generosity, this book could not have been written.

I would like also to thank those who read the various stages of the manuscript. Gary Topping, professor at Salt Lake Community College, gave me steady encouragement and read several versions of the early chapters. He later read the entire manuscript and suggested a number of significant changes. Lavina Fielding Anderson, editor of the *Journal of Mormon History*, early on had confidence in my abilities and at the end read the finished manuscript, to its benefit throughout. William P. MacKinnon, author of *At Sword's Point, Part 1: A Documentary History of the Utah War to 1858*, read the completed manuscript before writing his foreword, a substantial contribution to the book. Bill found a few items that needed to be corrected, and in addition, throughout my research and writing, he offered valued suggestions and interpretations, especially for the Utah War period. Ian D. Whyte, professor at Lancaster University in England, consented to read my Scottish chapters and corrected some inaccuracies in interpretation. Ronald O. Barney, senior historian for the LDS church, kindly read the Utah chapters and suggested structural changes so that they more accurately reflected Peter's experiences. Richard E. Turley, Jr., assistant church historian for the LDS church, reviewed my account of the Mountain Meadows massacre and offered several improvements. And finally, historian Doris Pieroth of Seattle read the manuscript as someone unfamiliar with Mormon history, which led to the clarification of several points.

Many gave generously of their time to assist my research. Will Bagley regularly sent me items that he thought would be useful. Val Holley shares my interest in and helped me track down some of the obscure and forgotten people in Utah. The staff of the LDS Church History Library and Archives—particularly Ronald G. Watt, Ronald O. Barney, and W. Randall Dixon—contributed substantially to the depth of my work by permitting me access to almost everything of interest and explaining much about Mormon history, organization, and practices. The staffs of the Utah State Historical Society, the L. Tom Perry Special Collections of the Harold B. Lee Library at Brigham Young University, and the Huntington Library in San Marino, California, helped me track down valuable information.

In Scotland, Graham Hopner and Arthur F. Jones, local-studies librarians at Dumbarton Public Library, led me to information about the family background. Alistair McIntyre from Garelochhead, Dunbartonshire, who is the author of a manuscript of local Gaelic place-names, taught me about early farming practices and the Clearances in the southern Highlands; he went so far as to hike to Stuckiedow, where Peter McAuslan's ancestors had lived, to take pictures of the remains of the farm. Friends Lydia Burnet, Naira Stoker, and Hazel Lloyd likewise tramped through the mud to photograph the farm and surrounding glens.

There is not room to thank all who aided me, but I would like to mention in particular Leonard J. Arrington, for believing early on that the story was worth pursuing; William G. Hartley, who kept me straight about priesthood quorums and overland travels; Frederick S. Buchanan, for his friendship and research on Scottish Mormons; David L. Bigler, for his insights to the religious thinking of this period; and Mario S. De Pillis, for our discussions on visions. In addition, I owe a great debt to Robert A. Clark, my publisher, for helping me to sharpen my writing and maintain a judicious tone. Likewise I would like to thank Steven B. Baker, managing editor of the University of Oklahoma Press, and Rosemary Wetherold, copy editor, for their meticulous attention to detail and help in finding a title for the book. Mapmaker William L. Nelson produced clear and exacting maps that add greatly to understanding where Peter McAuslan's story took place.

I would like to thank my daughters, Deanna and Mary, and my brothers, Johnny and Bruce, who took a great interest in this work. Deanna and Johnny critiqued many of the chapters. My special friends David and Ruth Ann Getchell, Sandy Sylvester, Hazel Lloyd, and Donna Miksys put up with my incessant absorption in this history and only moderately teased me about how long it was taking.

I have had companions on the road: my father explored family sites in Scotland with me; my daughters and I camped along the McAuslans' trail from the Missouri River to Fort Laramie; my friend Don Weir went with me on a steamboat from New Orleans to Memphis, and another time by car along the McAuslans' route from Fort Laramie to Live Oak, California.

Three spirited teachers were instrumental in spurring my interest in history and teaching me the fundamentals of the historical method: Betty Goerke, my high school history teacher at the Branson School in Ross, California; Professor Gordon Wright at Stanford University; and Lorraine McConaghy at the University of Washington.

I owe a fundamental debt my grandmother, Emily McAuslan Aird, for passing on her family history; to my father, Robert B. Aird, M.D., who first inspired my interest in history as a child and started me on the research for this project; and to my aunt, Margaret Hill Collins, who believed in the importance of this work and helped financially so I could pursue it.

The research and writing of this book has been a grand adventure. I have made many new friends along the way and discovered fascinating byways of history. My heartfelt thanks and appreciation go to all who have made it so rewarding.

Editorial Procedures

I HAVE USED ORIGINAL SOURCE MATERIAL WHERE POSSIBLE. When these were holographs, I have tried to keep true to the author in retaining the original spelling and syntax. But as these writings often lack punctuation, initial capitals in sentences, apostrophes, and paragraph divisions, I have added them in places for clarity.

Peter McAuslan's writings contained additional problems, as they consist of draft letters, notes, and essays. Because of their hurried style meant only for himself, I have felt it helpful to occasionally make further corrections. When the spelling of a word is so obviously a mistake and it becomes a distraction from what he is saying, I have corrected it. For instance, Peter wrote "the Angle of the Lord" for "the Angel of the Lord." Making such changes appeared to be a better choice than inserting a succession of bracketed corrections that would interrupt the flow. In some instances, I have added dashes where a phrase needed to be set off to make the sentence clear. Where he had crossed out something, I have left a line through the words. My aim throughout has been to retain the flavor of his expressions and turn of phrase while not losing his ideas in a mass of editorial marks.

Throughout the book I make reference to the "Peter McAuslan Papers." These are copies of original source materials and consist of Peter's draft letters, notes, essays, and drawings; early letters received by him or his father; marriage and naturalization papers, land deeds, and his will; and a few other items. These came from descendants of Peter or his sisters Agnes McAuslan Allan and Janet McAuslan Allan Racklebush. I arranged these in chronological order, placed undated items at the back, and numbered them. Thus one will find such references as "#55 McAuslan Papers." Later I received copies of letters from a descendant of Elizabeth McAuslin Maxwell, the only sister of Peter's wife, Agnes. The letters were written by Agnes to her sister, who was still in Utah. These I integrated into the chronological order but did not assign numbers, so as not to change the whole system; thus they are identified by date only. Eventually I plan to donate this collection to the Utah State Historical Society.

Mormon Convert,
Mormon Defector

Prologue: Turning Informer

JUST WEST OF THE TOWN OF SPANISH FORK IN UTAH TERRITORY
lay an Indian farm where U.S. Indian agent Garland Hurt was attempting to teach techniques of agriculture to the Utes as a way of survival, now
that the lands where they had traditionally hunted and gathered had been
appropriated by Mormon settlers. On the last day of April 1859, the young
peach trees in the town had just come into blossom after a late spring and
created a bright tracery that contrasted starkly with the drab crudeness of
the adobe houses. In the morning, from one of these small homes William
McAuslan stepped cautiously out into the dirt street and quietly walked
the two miles to the farm. Going into the fields where Hurt was working
and where the two could not be overheard, William reported to the agent
that fifty or more armed Mormon men had left Spanish Fork on "secret
maneuvers" the night before, destined, he thought, for Salt Lake City.

That evening, during a warm spring shower, William's brother Peter
and another man surreptitiously made their way to Hurt's home. When
Hurt came out at about 9 P.M., they emerged from the shadows and in a
hushed voice asked him to step away from the house so they could speak
to him in private. They then proceeded to substantiate William's story.
After hearing their accounts, Hurt asked if they could supply names. And
so the following evening they came again, this time with the names of
fourteen of their nearest neighbors who had left, and told of additional
armed men setting out late the previous night, making a total of perhaps
one hundred men altogether. "They insist that there must be some secret
military service on foot [afoot], but they seem to be afraid to inquire into
the matter. They say there is no security for them if they are known to
expose the Mormons except in the immediate vicinity of the Army," wrote

Hurt to General Albert Sidney Johnston of the U.S. Army, who was stationed at Camp Floyd, approximately forty miles away.[1]

A month later three McAuslan families with at least four other families started on the two- or three-day journey that would take them to the protection of Camp Floyd. In the McAuslan group were Peter and his wife, Agnes, with their little daughter and a baby less than two months old; William and his wife, Mary, who was pregnant, and their two toddlers; and Peter's parents, who were nearly sixty, with their youngest sons, Frank, aged twenty-two, and David, sixteen.

Some weeks before, the McAuslans and other disaffected Mormons had applied for and been promised an army escort to see them safely out of Utah. On June 12, 1859, a detachment of 162 mounted and foot soldiers left dusty Camp Floyd with the families of former Mormons to began the weary trek on foot and by covered wagon of more than 950 miles over desert and mountain to California. It was the final break from Mormonism, but also a major breaking up of the family: Peter and William and their younger brothers left behind five sisters, all married and with children; two uncles, an aunt, and their families; Peter's wife's sister and her family; Mary's parents, three siblings, and their families; and many Scottish friends. They were also leaving their dead: in the Salt Lake City Cemetery lay their grandmother who had crossed the plains in 1848 at age sixty-six and, particularly wrenching for Peter and Agnes, their eighteen-month-old son, Peter Alexander.

Why did the McAuslans lose the faith that once had framed their every action and filled their lives with such intense feelings of belonging and joy? What motivated Peter and William to approach the U.S. authorities with information about the military movements of their former Mormon brothers and then flee with their young families at great perceived risk to themselves? What caused the terrible split among the family members, with all their sisters and other relatives remaining in Utah?

The answers to these questions are found not solely in Peter McAuslan's conversion, crossing of the plains, or settling in Utah, for Peter was already thirty when he left Scotland, and those earlier years had in large part shaped him. Thus we must turn first to this background to begin to discover the man that he became.

---

[1] Garland Hurt to A. S. Johnston, May 1, 1859, Letters Sent, Letters Received, 1859–61. Hurt wrote a similar letter to F. J. Porter, the assistant adjutant to General Johnston, and a shorter one the next day also to Porter. In the letters, he spelled McAuslan as "McCoslin." The weather for April 30 is from the entry for May 1, 1859, in the journal of Spanish Fork resident Henry Hamilton.

I

From the Glens of Loch Lomond

"[MY GRANDFATHER] WAS EITHER A SON OR A SON'S SON OF HIM who was called Baron McAuslan who owned an estate called 'Stookadoo' at Luss, which he sold to a man named Calhoon while he was under the influence of liquor," wrote Peter McAuslan to his daughter. A former farm called Stuckiedow, which is pronounced nearly as Peter wrote it, lies in Glen Fruin, one of the valleys not far from the village of Luss on Loch Lomond in Scotland. Only a few piles of stones remain on the farm to indicate where cottages once stood. Just twenty miles north of Glasgow, this area belongs to the southern Highlands. As one travels north out of the metropolitan area, the land suddenly changes from gentle rolling hills to increasingly steep mountains and isolated valleys opening onto Loch Lomond. The area, now part of Scotland's first national park, retains an aura of tranquillity and wildness.[1]

In Glen Fruin and two other nearby glens on the west side of the lake, the McAuslans owned small farms for at least three hundred years. The head of the family was a minor baron, the title being linked to the land. From the late 1300s, records survive that mention the McAuslans of Callanach. The latter, a now-abandoned farm north of Glen Fruin, was the ancestral home of the Baron McAuslans.[2]

Little farm settlements once lay like beads on a string along each glen, with perhaps as many as three to four hundred people living in Glen Fruin alone. A short growing season, poor and sodden soils, and unreliable

---

[1] Peter McAuslan to Margaret M. Day, April 14, 1905 (#55 McAuslan Papers); McIntyre, "Place Names: Row Parish" and "Place Names: Luss Parish."

[2] William Fraser, *Chiefs of Colquhoun*, 2:281. A minor baron is in contrast to a great baron, who received extensive judicial and territorial powers from the king in return for services.

weather presented continual challenges. The farmers worked cooperatively, growing barley, oats, peas, and flax for linen and raising a hardy breed of sheep and Highland cattle with cocked horns and shaggy black coats. The soggy land prevented travel by wheeled vehicle, and few if any Highlanders had a cart before the 1750s.[3]

One Baron McAuslan succeeded another down to Alexander, the last baron. In 1664, Alexander inherited the lands of Callanach and three other farms, but within fourteen years he began to mortgage his estates. According to descendants who emigrated to Australia, he had "became involved in difficulties with a neighbouring Baron and after mortgaging his Estates one after the other . . . left his family in pecuniary difficulties." Or perhaps, as in Peter's version, Alexander lost them when he was "under the influence of liquor." Alexander had married and had a daughter, Janet. She married, but after her husband's death, she sold the family lands to the Laird of Luss, the largest landowner in the area. By sometime in the early 1700s the McAuslans had become only tenants, having lost their land and the title of baron.[4]

By the mid-1700s, influenced by the success of large sheep farms in southern Scotland and realizing that the hilly nature of their land did not lend itself to crops, the large landowners began to turn to sheep. In the Lowlands, textile trades were being mechanized, creating a demand for wool for the looms. Sheep did not require the labor that raising grain did, nor were they compatible with tenants living on the land and cultivating crops. Few of the big estate owners wanted to remove their tenants from the land; they just wanted to relocate them—the start of a process that came to be known as the Clearances. But the new land that was typically allocated to the tenants was even less fertile. Forced to abandon their homes, people headed for the Lowlands to find jobs around Glasgow or fled to America with the hope of discovering a better life. Glen Fruin and the neighboring valleys did not suffer the wholesale evictions that happened in the nineteenth century in the northern and western Highlands.

---

[3] Laurie, "Parish of Row," 8:76; Allan, "Parish of Row," 9:125. Today the glens are almost empty, although the population of Scotland is now at least four times what it was in the middle of the eighteenth century.

[4] The surname of the Laird of Luss was Colquhoun, which is similar to Peter's "Calhoon" in pronunciation. Particular Registers of Sasines for May 21, 1678 (RS 10/1 fol. 256), June 10, 1690 (RS 10/2 fol. 273), and March 4, 1692 (RS 10/2 fol. 330). Jennette McAusland to Mrs. Thomas Harding, October 15, 1866; I am grateful to John Guest of Melbourne for a photocopy of this letter. Buchanan of Auchmar, *Historical and Genealogical Essay*, 275.

Instead, landlords drove their tenants off the land by raising rents. The exodus was steady and dramatic. Without a future on the land, the McAuslans and others had no option but to go to work in the bleach-fields or other textile operations in the Vale of Leven, the industrializing area just south of Loch Lomond.[5]

Highly prized by the early textile finishing industries, this river valley offered clean, soft, and reliable water; labor readily available from the Highlands; and easy transport by river. But by the early 1800s, the Vale of Leven had begun to lose its pastoral character. James Barr, a young contemporary of the McAuslans there, wrote: "Huge brick erections, with their multitudes of tall chimneys, vomiting clouds of smoke and vapor that obscure the skies, are not well calculated to awaken the poetic afflatus." The fish, he added, "which still occasionally attempt to make their way to the lake, are frequently poisoned by the chemical compounds that escape from the factories." Here Peter's grandfather, the first to leave the Highlands, became a dyer in one of the plants.[6]

During this period of industrialization, the Scottish Enlightenment was winding down. Begun in Edinburgh in the latter half of the eighteenth century by men of the middle and upper classes, it was characterized by its interest in education, philosophy, art, architecture, and literature, as well as science, technology, and the social sciences, such as economics and history. In spite of a profound gulf between the life of the literati in Edinburgh and that of urban laborers, ideas percolated down and up. Most important for understanding the McAuslans' world was the "common sense" philosophy first developed by Thomas Reid of Aberdeen, which held that even ordinary persons had innate rationality. This democratization of the intellect soon caught the attention of revolutionary leaders in America and France. Thomas Paine was so influenced by it that he titled his famous pamphlet *Common Sense.*[7]

This philosophy and the growing intellectual life of the laboring classes produced other ideas. These included the importance of one's ideas and one's skill in articulating and discussing them, the right to state one's views without persecution, the responsibility for one's own intellectual development, and the right to resist tyrannical rulers. In their home, the McAus-

---

[5] MacPhail, introduction to *Statistical Account of Scotland*, 9:xxvii–xxix.

[6] Barr, *Balloch and Around*, 8; Peter McAuslan to Agnes McAuslan Allan, 1898; original in possession of Ada Redd Rigby, Blanding, Utah (#49 McAuslan Papers), 1.

[7] Smith, "Manners, Morals and Mentalities," 29, 49.

lans would have had a Bible, most likely a volume of Robert Burns's poems, and cheap chapbook editions of John Bunyan's *Pilgrim's Progress* and Daniel Defoe's *Robinson Crusoe*. The latter two, along with stories from the Old Testament, were seen as thrilling tales of leaving home, journeys, and difficulties overcome with the help of God. The typical working-class individual believed them—and anything in print—to be literally true.[8]

Robert Burns was beloved by the common people for his poetry, which, besides its romantic sentiments, attacked hypocrisy and placed value on independent thinking and on ordinary folk, no matter how poor. In addition to Burns, Defoe's *Robinson Crusoe* was a favorite. Readers liked Crusoe's self-determination and resourcefulness in surviving a shipwreck and overcoming the straits in which he found himself, including isolation, fear, and despair.

Such stories made many in the working classes discontent with their own hard lots of constricted routine. They longed for a chance to start on their own journey, usually imagined as being to America. The minister of one parish wrote in the 1790s that some who had gone to America had fed these yearnings by their letters home. These described "a wholesome and pleasant country, . . . a country provided by divine providence, to afford a comfortable habitation to those who are ill used at home; where the land is good in its quality, cheap, and gratuitously bestowed; and the passage to it unexpensive, and made in a few weeks."[9]

Peter's father, Peter McAuslan, Sr., apprenticed to become a hand-block calico printer, work that required more skill and offered better pay than that of a dyer. In 1820 when he married, he was working as a calico printer twenty miles from the Vale of Leven in Milncroft, a town four miles east of Glasgow. The city of Glasgow had grown by 94 percent between 1801 and 1821, becoming industrialized and losing its rural charm as the population exploded. Industrial pollution and coal-fire smoke was transforming it into a "semi-asphyxiated city."[10]

The senior Peter's move was most likely precipitated by the "big strike" among the calico printers in the Vale of Leven around 1815—just when he would have been starting his apprenticeship. The catalyst for the strike

---

[8] Devine, *Scottish Nation*, chapter 10; Rose, *Intellectual Life*, 12–17, 35, 93–96, 108, and 111.

[9] Quoted in Rose, *Intellectual Life*, 353.

[10] Burns, "Parish of Barony of Glasgow," 7:339; Cage, "Population and Employment Characteristics," 10. The "semi-asphyxiated city" is from J. B. Russell, Glasgow's first full-time medical officer in the 1870s, as quoted in Crowther, "Poverty, Health and Welfare," 285.

was the hiring of women for a lighter type of print work. The journeyman printers feared that their own skills would be downgraded or even replaced and that the women represented a foot in the door for mechanization. Perhaps as many as a thousand printers went on strike for several months. The factory owners called in the military to keep order, and without income, the families of the men suffered greatly. In the end the strikers lost and the number of female workers increased.[11]

Although Milncroft Printworks, where the senior Peter worked, avoided the Vale's labor strife, he did not escape the major economic depression that started in 1819. Unemployment spread widely throughout western Scotland, primarily the result of mechanization in textile occupations. The toll on handloom weavers was particularly hard, their real wages having dropped drastically since the Napoleonic Wars. Hand-block printing was also threatened, as calicos were increasingly printed with steam-powered engraved copper plates or large cylinder machines. Cylinder printing, however, was used when a design repeated from one end of the yardage to the other. This exempted the primary products of the firm where the elder Peter worked: cotton bandanna handkerchiefs and shawls, which typically had a single large floral design inside a border. For these the hand-block printer still used a block of wood on which part of the pattern was engraved. At the corners were brass pins that allowed him to line up the impression with the one previously made. At a side table, his young assistant, known as a "tearer" and often one of the printer's own children, spread dye paste onto a piece of wool stretched on a frame. The printer pressed his woodblock onto the dye-saturated wool to take up the dye and then positioned the block on the cotton cloth and struck the back of the block with a mallet. Several colors could be printed by changing the blocks and dyes.[12]

The depression of 1819–20 aroused radical sentiments. With both Highlanders and rural Lowlanders streaming into Glasgow and its surrounding towns in search of jobs, social conditions quickly deteriorated. Many workers became convinced that conditions could be changed only by parliamentary reform, and some thought that a drastic alteration to the entire system was necessary. The ideas of Tom Paine had taken hold among the Scottish working classes, and in 1816 bitter trade disputes had

---

[11] Neill, *Records and Reminiscences*, 240–41.
[12] Bremner, *Industries of Scotland*, 302–303.

A block printer and tearer.
From "The Manufacture of Woven Goods," part 3,
"Calico Printing," in Useful Arts and Manufactures of Great Britain, *8.*

led forty thousand people to hold a mass meeting on the east edge of Glasgow in a field called Thrushgrove—the largest political gathering in the history of Scotland to that time. But when their efforts to effect change through petition went nowhere, small groups of frustrated people began to meet in secret societies with the intent of forcing more radical changes in government.

The specter of the French Revolution made merchants and industrialists fear the movement, especially because their own interests depended on docile, cheap labor. Current intellectual thought conveniently supported such interests. Combining Enlightenment ideas of scientific study with evangelical Presbyterianism, middle-class writers and educators promoted the concept that the sublime order among the stars and planets should be reflected in social life on earth: just as each heavenly body had its fixed role in the heavens, so too on earth there existed a hierarchy of beings from the lowest animal up through the ranks of humans, to angels and finally to God. An immutable order designed by God, the system would descend into chaos if any part—such as the working classes—tried to change it.

The workers' underground ferment soon collided with these intellectual strictures. In February 1820 the government arrested twenty-seven members of a radical committee in Glasgow, charging that they were planning uprisings in Scotland and England. Then, on April 1, notices appeared in and around Glasgow calling for workers to strike until "their rights as free men were recovered" and to bear arms in a rebellion. Some sixty thousand men of all occupations in the west of Scotland went on strike for several days, Peter McAuslan, Sr., among them. The strike was a success, but the armed rebellion—a march of fewer than a hundred men to an ironworks near Falkirk—was a fiasco. In spite of calling themselves radicals, most workers were not willing to resort to violence to change the government. This "Radical War" ended in an abandonment of mass political action and a shift toward trade unions. Nevertheless, the Radical War represented the first time that workers in industrializing Scotland began to see themselves as having interests that transcended their particular occupation.[13]

During this period of unrest, Peter met Betsy Adamson. They married in December 1820 when they were both nineteen. Betsy was the oldest of eleven children of a family of coal miners. Her parents, William and Agnes Baird Adamson, had two more sons born just after the births of Betsy and Peter's first two children, making the uncles close in age to their niece and nephew. Years later these two Adamson boys, along with an older brother, would be the first in the family to hear of Mormonism and the first to convert. The McAuslans would learn of the new faith through them.[14]

Peter and Betsy had a daughter in 1821 whom they named Agnes, for Betsy's mother. Two years later the little family moved to Strathblane, a town eleven miles to the northwest. The move was probably precipitated by Peter's finishing his apprenticeship and finding an opening for a journeyman printer. Strathblane, situated on the Blane Water, is in

---

[13] For a summary of the Radical War, see Devine, *Scottish Nation*, 224–30.
[14] Old Parish Registers (OPR), Barony, Lanarkshire, vol. 622/16 Marriages, December 18, 1820.

the northwest corner of Stirlingshire. When Peter and Betsy arrived, the
population for the whole parish numbered about eight hundred, almost
all of it rural. Only a few small mills and factories had been built, including Blanefield Printworks, where Peter began work. On January 30, 1824,
Peter and Betsy had their second child, a boy. They named him Peter
for his grandfather. The local minister of the Church of Scotland christened him on March 14, 1824.[15]

The McAuslans' stay in Strathblane lasted only two years, for in 1825
the Blanefield Printworks went bankrupt. From there they moved southeast eight miles to Kirkintilloch, where the elder Peter began work at
Bellfield Printworks. Kirkintilloch had and still retains a jumbled appearance. Lying seven miles north of Glasgow in the eastern part of Dunbartonshire, it was "an irregularly built, strangely arranged, confused looking little town, conveying by its aspect the idea of such entire devotement
to trade and manufacture as precludes nearly all attention to the graces
of exterior appearance." This helter-skelter appearance derived in good
part from Kirkintilloch's being a transportation crossroads with a river,
a stream, a canal, an aqueduct, a turnpike, and a railroad intersecting
within a single square mile. Midway across Scotland, Kirkintilloch was
the first inland harbor for the Forth and Clyde Canal, which traversed
the town's center. One could commonly see the masts of canal ships moving among the houses. By 1826 nine out of ten industrial workers in Scotland worked in textiles, and the population in Kirkintilloch was no different, with the majority being handloom weavers. In 1831, Kirkintilloch
had a population of just under six thousand, most of whom—men,
women, and children—worked at looms. A visitor wrote that "the monot-
onous sound of the shuttle . . . greets the ear at every turn."[16]

The McAuslan family moved into a house on Kerr Street; the senior
Peter could walk east along a cinder path the quarter of a mile to Bellfield Printworks. In comparison with Milncroft and Blanefield, this plant
was small, with only eight journeymen block printers and thirteen apprentices. Records from the late 1820s show there were eighteen hundred journeymen countrywide and almost eight hundred apprentices, the latter fig-

[15] OPR, Barony, Lanarkshire, vol. 622/8 Births/Baptisms, November 12, 1821; H. Buchanan, "Parish
of Strathblane," 8:72; OPR, Strathblane, Stirlingshire, vol. 491/3 Births/Baptisms, March 14, 1824.
[16] *Topographical, Statistical, and Historical Gazetteer*, 2:181; Forman, "Parish of Kirkintilloch," 8:168–211;
Knox, *Industrial Nation*, 34. The quotation is from MacDonald, *Rambles Round Glasgow*, 421.

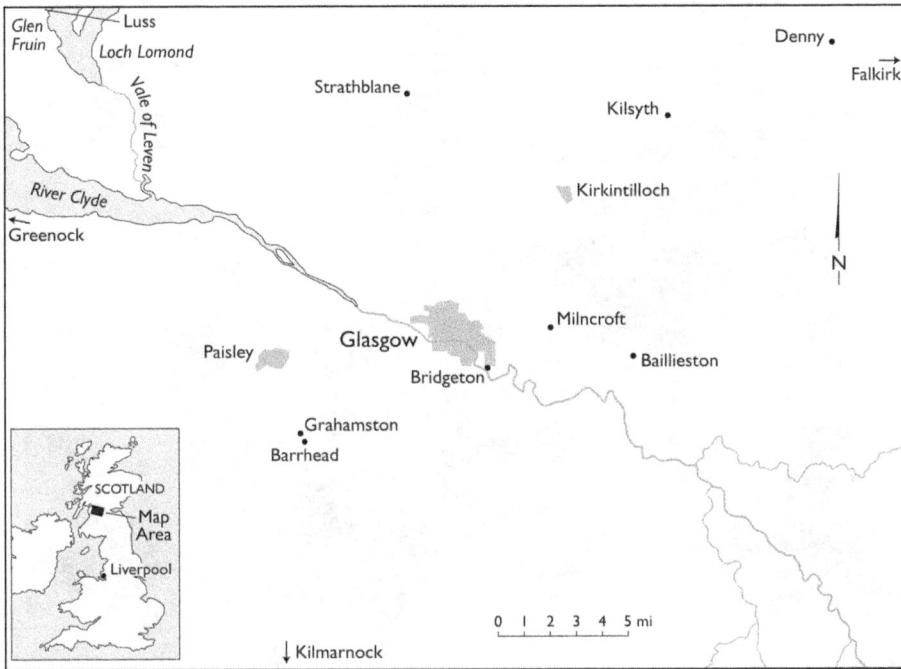

Glen Fruin · Luss · Loch Lomond · Denny · Falkirk · Strathblane · Kilsyth · Vale of Leven · River Clyde · Greenock · Kirkintilloch · N · Milncroft · Glasgow · Paisley · Baillieston · Bridgeton · Grahamston · Barrhead · SCOTLAND · Map Area · Liverpool · Kilmarnock · 0 1 2 3 4 5 mi

Glasgow area.
McAuslans were associated with the places named, 1800–54.
Map by Bill Nelson.

ure an indication that hand-block printing still offered a promising trade with job opportunities in spite of increased mechanization. All three plants in which Peter had worked specialized in calico shawls and bandanna handkerchiefs destined primarily for West Indian and South American markets.[17]

The McAuslans had another son during the first year they lived in Kirkintilloch, but he did not live long. Children now followed each other at two-year intervals; by 1838 the couple had eight living children, and

---

[17] McAuslan, miscellaneous note, [ca. 1907] (#56 McAuslan Papers), 1; 1841 Scotland Census, Kirkintilloch, Dunbartonshire, Enumeration District 7 (498), 17; "Odds and Ends about Kirkintilloch," 24. Information on the calico printing industry is from Turnbull, *History of the Calico Printing Industry*, 92, 104, 133, 195, 202–204, 421–22, 430.

Kirkintilloch, a "strangely arranged, confused looking little town."
In the center and left background the masts of ships on the Forth and
Clyde Canal can be seen. Photograph taken about 1878.
Courtesy of Ada Redd Rigby, Blanding, Utah.

two more would be born in the 1840s. Their father worked the typical
twelve to fifteen hours a day in the poorly lit, badly ventilated, hot and
humid plant, where cotton dust and fumes from the fabrics and dyes were
inescapable. Betsy struggled to keep their small home clean and to shop,
cook, sew, wash, and look after so many children. Their water had to be
drawn from a well, there were no provisions for sewage, and the whole
idea of public health had not yet been born. The menace of disease was
constant and erupted into epidemics of typhus and cholera. Carried by
lice, typhus was endemic among the very poor, and 1832 brought cholera's
first appearance in Scotland. Believed to have arrived from India via
Egypt, it indiscriminately attacked all classes. It first surfaced in the west

of Scotland in Kirkintilloch itself, and before it retreated at the end of 1832, it had killed nearly three thousand countrywide.[18]

At age four, the McAuslans' son Peter started school, walking the three or four blocks with his sister Agnes to the parish school in the old town hall. Scotland had been famous for its educated populace, but with rapid urbanization and industrialization the system deteriorated quickly. The parish schools could not handle the numbers of children, and working-class people could not afford to build or pay for private ones. "At school I learned the shorter cattachism [*sic*] and read in the Bible," wrote Peter. This typical but restrictive curriculum fit with the generally supported purpose of education, which promised the "formation of right principles, dispositions and habits." One historian summed this up succinctly: "The inculcation of pious habits was commonly thought to be fostered by requiring children to learn by rote, at a precocious age, large chunks of the Bible or the Shorter Catechism."[19]

Peter's full-time education lasted only until he turned eight, when he went to work at Bellfield Printworks for his father. From that time until he was about twenty, he attended night school. At the calico plant he worked as a tearer, spreading the dye paste on the taut wool pad so that his father's hand block would take up the color. It meant standing at the tray in the humid atmosphere from 6 A.M. to 6 P.M. on weekdays and from 6 A.M. to 3 P.M. on Saturdays, a total of sixty-nine hours a week. Twice a day the workers were allowed half an hour for meals. During the high seasons of spring and fall when work became particularly busy, extra hours were added. Child labor was an economic necessity for most families. In periods of unemployment, which became increasingly common between the 1830s and 1850s, often only children could find jobs.[20]

The calico shawls and bandannas that Peter helped his father produce were subject to the whims of fashion as well as general economic cycles. The boom year when the McAuslans arrived in Kirkintilloch became a

[18] OPR, Kirkintilloch, Dunbartonshire, vol. 498/4 Births/Baptisms, December 11, 1825; March 12, 1828; April 17, 1830; April 15, 1832; June 16, 1834; July 5, 1836; July 17, 1838; December 11, 1840; and January 28, 1843. Forman, "Parish of Kirkintilloch," 186. Horne, "Health," 5:476.

[19] McAuslan, miscellaneous note (#56 McAuslan Papers), 1. The quotation on the purpose of education is from Andrew MacGeorge, meeting of the Glasgow Educational Association, October 2, 1834, as quoted in Withrington, "'Scotland a Half-Educated Nation'?" 62; Smith, "Manners, Morals and Mentalities," 39.

[20] McAuslan, miscellaneous note (#56 McAuslan Papers), 1.

crisis the next. The handloom weavers took the brunt. At least three thousand in the Glasgow area and twelve thousand around Paisley lost their jobs. Modest growth occurred in 1828 but reversed in 1829. According to the *Glasgow Herald*, some twenty thousand Glasgow-area weavers met on the Glasgow Green that April to discuss their "present destitute and pitiable condition." The next year saw a temporary recovery, but trade fell again in the fall of 1831. In Kirkintilloch many left their looms for work on the railways and roads or in nearby quarries. Each downturn in the economy pushed wages lower, and they never fully recovered in the upturns.[21]

Fortunately for young Peter and his father, calico printing did not suffer the extremes in fluctuation that handloom weaving did. Nevertheless by 1831 journeymen calico printers in Scotland were being paid only 50 to 60 percent of what printers in Lancashire, England, were earning, and even there real wages declined by 30 percent between 1839 and 1849. The downward pressure on wages, the gradual introduction of much less well-paid women to do some work, and periods of unemployment due to sudden changes in fashion gave them little confidence in the future.[22]

Along with the middle class, the laboring classes fought hard for passage of the Reform Bill of 1832, which pushed to extend the right to vote. After stops and starts and the help of King William IV, the bill finally passed in both the House of Commons and the House of Lords. In Glasgow the people celebrated its passage with the tolling of city bells, bonfires, gun salutes, a gaslight display in the shape of Britannia with the word "Reform," two hundred bands, and a great procession of people carrying five hundred flags though the city. Participants and spectators numbered more than eighty thousand. Banners carried by the various trade groups showed the importance of the bill to the working classes: Dyers—"We live to dye, and we dye to live. Reform for ever." Laborers and quarriers—"We stand firm as a rock to the cause of Reform." Bakers—"Pure bread is the staff of life, and pure representation is the staff and safety of pure government." Slaters—"We are ready with our ladders to mount and unroof the strong battlements of corruption." "If the Reform Bill had not passed," wrote the editor of the *Reformer's Gazette*, "there would have been a sure and certain *Revolution* in this country."[23]

---

[21] *Glasgow Herald*, April 20, 1829, as quoted in N. Murray, *Scottish Hand Loom Weavers*, 55.

[22] Cameron, "Calico Printing in Campsie," 25; Turnbull, *History of the Calico Printing Industry*, 193, 212.

[23] Quoted in Mackenzie, *Reminiscences of Glasgow*, 2:243–51, 254, 257, 259–61, emphasis his; Cameron, "Calico Printing in Campsie," 16.

And yet after the banners were folded and put away and the streets swept, the laboring classes found they were not better off, for the act extended the vote only to the property-owning middle classes. Although an important step in breaking the ancient landowners' exclusive right to suffrage, the Reform Act nevertheless did not bring representative government to the people. As a result, the working classes felt bitter and increasingly alienated from the industrialists who controlled their lives.

In spite of not gaining the right to vote, calico printers had achieved considerable independence relative to that in many other artisan trades by limiting their numbers through apprenticeships and by attaining a high level of skill. They regulated much of what went on in their workplace and instituted a system of rituals that reinforced solidarity and pride in their craft. They were the "labor aristocrats." To protect their position, the printers in Kirkintilloch joined with those in Scotland's largest printworks in Lennoxtown and others in nearby towns to form a union, which by 1834 had accumulated over six thousand pounds.[24]

The printworks owners, however, continually strove to drive down costs by loosening worker control over calico printing. Starting in 1833, the owners in adjoining counties joined together to break the union, force wages lower, and introduce more women, children, and even some destitute handloom weavers to take over some jobs. The printers went to their union meeting: "Heat and temper got into the discussions. Strong speeches were made on behalf of the men, and the flourishing state of the funds was dwelt on."[25] In 1834 the hand-block printers voted to strike. For Peter McAuslan, Sr., this "great strike" must have recalled the "big strike" in the Vale of Leven just when he started his apprenticeship, for the issues of the admission of women and reduced wages were the same.

The employers stood firm and recruited strikebreakers, marching them to the plants with guards. As the strike became protracted, the union used up the funds that had seemed so ample. Riots threatened, and the owners called in the military to protect their factories. Disaffected workers threatened to burn down nearby Lennoxmill Printworks. In Strathblane and the Vale of Leven, where a sister strike was occurring, enraged hand-block printers dragged the strikebreakers out of the plants. Finally the strike collapsed. With the union broken, the discouraged men went

---

[24] For the calico printers' union and strike, see Cameron, "Calico Printing in Campsie," 27–31; and Johnston, *History of the Working Classes*, 306.

[25] Cameron, "Calico Printing in Campsie," 27.

back to work at lower wages and alongside more women. Employers felt they owed thanks to the strikebreakers and kept them on, leaving fewer jobs for the old hands, many of whom had to move away to look for work elsewhere. The rioters who had been caught were convicted and sentenced to between fourteen days and twelve months of hard labor.

In 1837 the cotton spinners, one of the largest segments of Scottish workers, went on strike against the introduction of machinery and a reduction in pay. The strike lasted four months. Other trades—stonemasons, carpenters, coal miners, and ironworkers—joined in walkouts of their own. But because these strikes occurred during an economic depression, a large pool of unemployed handloom weavers and Irish immigrants were more than willing to work at the lower wages. When the strikes collapsed, morale fell all across the industrial belt of Scotland. Unions were crippled and nearly ceased to exist. The next year, the leaders of the cotton spinners' strike were sentenced to seven years "transportation" (i.e., banishment) to Australia, and in the following years wages across the board dropped sharply.

This succession of strikes made a lasting impression on young Peter. The writings of his later years frequently dwell on the injustices of the capitalist system. Whether these were his thoughts while he was still in Scotland or whether they solidified later is unknown. It is easy to believe from what he wrote that he held these views from an early age. They portray socialist leanings that emerged from witnessing and partaking in labor struggles in Scotland. About strikes, he wrote, "As far as I can perceive, there is more harm as the result of strikes than good as long as the present system exists of capital being the employer of labor and the owener [sic] of both land and machinery. . . . As a general thing God's store house is shut against labor. . . . It cannot be denied [that] labor produces all wealth. The parasites who extract the honey from labor live in palaces, and labor in the cellar. To be cognizant [sic] of that fact you have got to be informed how the producers of wealth live in the congested populous cities where clothing is made, and sweat shops abound. God have mercy on Labor."[26]

---

[26] McAuslan, undated notes on labor (#60 McAuslan Papers).

2

Calico Flowers

THE GREAT CALICO PRINTERS' STRIKE OF 1834 DETERMINED THE direction of young Peter McAuslan's life. When he began his apprenticeship in 1838 at age fourteen, he did not follow his father into hand-block printing, for he had seen his father increasingly hurt by lowered wages and the introduction of less-skilled workers. Instead, Peter decided to become a pattern designer for calicos. Whether printed by hand or machine, the designs themselves would still need to be drawn, and being highly skilled work, it paid well. The future looked bright.

As Peter started his apprenticeship, Kirkintilloch continued to grow. Besides the primary industry of weaving and the calico printing plant at Bellfield where he and his father worked, there was now a silk hat factory, an iron foundry, three distilleries, and, in response to the growing threat of railways, seven iron "swift" boats that carried nearly two thousand passengers a month between Glasgow and Edinburgh on the Forth and Clyde Canal. In 1839 a gasworks with a fifty-foot-tall square stack was built, and gas lamps lighted the streets for the first time. Two libraries and nine schools supported learning; a branch of the West Bank of Scotland and a savings bank served the thrifty; and forty inns and alehouses catered to those seeking escape or indulgence.[1] The effects of the Industrial Revolution were thus mixed; although life was harder for laborers, it brought some amenities never before available.

Close to collapsing, St. Mary's Parish Church, the "Auld Kirk" where the McAuslans worshipped, was finally repaired in 1840. A second Church

---

[1] Sources for Kirkintilloch in this period include Forman, "Parish of Kirkintilloch"; and Lewis, *Topographical Dictionary of Scotland*, 2:108–109.

of Scotland, St. David's, had been built in 1837 to accommodate the growing population. Four other denominations—the United Secession, the Original Burghers, the Methodists, and the Catholics—had churches in the town. There were smaller congregations too, including the Unitarians, who had a meetinghouse on Kerr Street near the McAuslans' home.[2]

By the time Peter began his apprenticeship, the McAuslan family had grown substantially. The sisters closest to Peter in age—Agnes, then seventeen, and Jane, ten—worked in Robert Allan's weaving shop.[3] Work for girls was considered temporary and a means to save for marriage. At home were four younger children: Betsy, eight; William, six; Ann, four; and Frank (Francis), two. A new baby, Christina, was born in July. Life for Peter's mother, Betsy, as for other women of her class, centered around domestic duties.

Bellfield Printworks now had 120 workers, of whom 10 were journeymen printers like Peter McAuslan, Sr. Block printing continued to dominate the trade in spite of the new discharge press, which was more efficient, but not as precise for fine products.[4] The printers, with their high level of skill, still maintained considerable independence from their employers. The owners tried hiring managers or foremen to supervise them and indirectly controlled them by paying by the piece. Nevertheless, for a long period workmen such as the elder Peter retained their autonomy in the factories and took personal pride in their work. These artisans looked upon their skills as acquired assets, equivalent to private property for the bourgeois.[5]

At the upper end of the working-class hierarchy, calico printers lived well when times were good. In contrast, the sixty men, women, and children working in Robert Allan's handloom weaving shop—including Peter's sisters—earned very little. The country had witnessed a drastic decline in handloom weaving as machines took over and cheap labor multiplied. Even skilled weavers found life increasingly hard. They were forced to extend their hours at the loom to seventy a week just to make ends meet—"a maintenance and a starvation."[6]

---

[2] Forman, "Parish of Kirkintilloch," 8:205; Sunter, "Ecclesiastical History," 135–36.

[3] 1841 Scotland Census, Kirkintilloch, Dunbartonshire, Enumeration District 12 (498), 17.

[4] For calico printing in this period, see Cameron, "Calico Printing in Campsie"; and Turnbull, *History of the Calico Printing Industry*, 92, 115, 133, 142, 202–209.

[5] Knox, "Political and Workplace Culture," 143, 146.

[6] Forman, "Parish of Kirkintilloch," 8:199–200; and Martin, "Industrial Advancement," 170–72. The quotation is from *Topographical, Statistical, and Historical Gazetteer of Scotland*, 2:181.

One of Robert Allan's sons, John, entered his father's shop at a young age to learn the weaver's trade. But he quickly decided that such a sedentary occupation as sitting at a loom all day was not for him. Instead he apprenticed himself to a printer at Bellfield; although still confined indoors, the men stood at the printing table and moved from the tearer's dye pad to the different parts of the fabric. The higher wages of a calico printer and "half holidays" on Saturdays influenced his decision. John was four months older than Peter, and they probably began their apprenticeships at about the same time, John as a hand-block printer and Peter as a pattern drawer. The two families were close, and Peter's sister Agnes became good friends with Anne Allan.[7]

Relentless downward pressure on earnings was only one result of the Industrial Revolution on workers and their families, including even the relatively well-off McAuslans. Change came quickly and produced a new range of occupations with different standards of living, subcultures, and even religious beliefs. Moving to find work, often away from family and friends, and trying to adapt to new conditions left people feeling dislocated. Rapid urbanization and industrialization caused psychological trauma—depression and the feeling that one had lost control, that life was nothing more than a desperate struggle for survival. Such stresses were compounded by disease and hunger, with typhoid and typhus outbreaks in 1837–39, and in 1838 the worst harvest in over twenty years. Caught in a "long dark night of despondency," people sought relief and escape in different directions: some turned to drink and rowdy songs while others embraced evangelical religious movements with their messianic message.[8]

As the demand for hand-block printing shrank, the factory owners hired teenagers and women to operate the new machines for small wages, leaving the highly skilled printers with no place to go. In contrast, pattern drawing not only offered better pay and stability but gave the artisan extensive training in design and allowed him considerable artistic initiative. Peter specialized in flowers for the center of bandannas or shawls, with the border of the item, usually done on a flat press, serving as a frame for his work. Kirkintilloch calico prints acquired fame and were sought after "in almost every commercial mart in the world." One historian wrote that Bellfield prints were highly esteemed and well known not only in Scotland but also in London and Manchester, the center of

---

[7] Peter Allan, "John Allan," 1–2.
[8] Whatley, "Crucible of the Modern World," 182.

Calico pattern designed by Peter McAuslan.
Courtesy of Donna Miller Forguson, Live Oak, California.

the cotton industry. Peter's apprenticeship, if typical, was for seven years, until he turned twenty-one in 1845.[9]

The world of calico artisans usually centered on the home. Their values resembled those of the middle class and included the prevailing belief that God had a plan for society, that everyone had his proper place, and that hard work and thrift brought material well-being and thus were their own reward. Presbyterianism additionally taught that each person was his or her own priest and was thus not dependent on the clergy for interpreting the scriptures. To further this concept, the church emphasized literacy, which gave people self-esteem and an interest in learning. Artisans, who needed to read plans and carry out written orders, were particularly concerned with self-improvement and often joined Mechanics' Institutes, subscription libraries, debating clubs, or scientific societies.[10] Peter's friend John Allan, for instance, exemplified the artisan and the Enlightenment's encouragement of scientific study. Having an avid interest in birds, John developed a friendship with a gamekeeper on a large nearby estate. As a result, he learned to stuff birds and became a skilled taxidermist. He gained an extensive knowledge of birds from both taxidermy and observation.[11]

In contrast to the world of calico artisans, that of less skilled laborers centered in the pub. Alcohol pervaded almost every dimension of Scottish social and economic life. One went to the pub to drink with work colleagues, to meet a potential employer, to collect wages, or to attend a friendly society meeting. Some pubs were "free and easies"; besides alcohol, they had entertainments that made them precursors to music halls. A Glasgow printer of temperance pamphlets wrote that whisky had "struck its fibrous roots into everything so deeply, that to tear up the spirit-drinking practices is like tearing up the whole social system of society." Drinking became more prevalent and insidious as the stresses of industrialization mounted and the standard of living declined, providing a temporary escape from "a drab life in a drab climate."[12]

---

[9] Wilson, *Imperial Gazetteer of Scotland*, 1:755; Martin, "Industrial Advancement," 191.

[10] Smith, "Manners, Morals and Mentalities," 33; Knox, *Industrial Nation*, 43, 46.

[11] Allan, "John Allan," 1. Probably in the 1870s or 1880s, Allan bought a set of John James Audubon's *Birds of America*.

[12] Friendly societies offered members various types of insurance. The temperance printer's quotation is from King, *Scotland Sober and Free*, 6. The "drab life" quotation is from Levitt and Smout, *State of the Scottish Working-Class*, 128.

To counter the omnipresence of alcohol, artisans and others aspiring to respectability began to embrace temperance—the avoidance of distilled liquor but not ale—or teetotalism, the swearing off of all alcohol. A Temperance Society was started in Kirkintilloch in 1830, followed by the Kirkintilloch Total Abstinence Society in 1835. Sometime in the 1840s, John Allan became treasurer of the temperance group. Temperance, combined with religion, became a mark of social worth. Protestant and Catholic temperance organizations led parades to Glasgow Green. One of the most notable, held in July 1841, was led by the Rechabites (a friendly society emphasizing temperance), whose "full colour silk and satin sashes, aprons, ribbons and banners" made them particularly impressive. The following year Father Theobald Mathew, a Catholic priest from Ireland and a famous temperance speaker, came to Glasgow and addressed fifty thousand Catholics and Protestants on Glasgow Green. Later, at a banquet held in his honor, he said he had done what he could to unite the two religions, for temperance "was the cause of their common humanity, the cause of their country, and the cause of God." Some forty thousand pledged teetotalism that day.[13]

As an alternative to the allure of the free and easies, temperance societies offered teetotal concerts with tea and pastries. They opened coffeehouses, tearooms, and temperance hotels and organized excursions by steamboat on the River Clyde or by train to the coast. Those active in temperance movements, including the McAuslans and the Allans, were taking a stand against the customs of the day and were often outspoken in their criticism of society and in their assertion of independence.[14]

Many who were involved in temperance were also attracted to Chartism, a political movement that continued the struggles started with the Radical War in 1820 but was now generally nonrevolutionary. Chartism emerged after the passage of the first Reform Act in 1832, when it became apparent that the act had failed to extend suffrage to the working classes. In 1838 it published its "People's Charter," which outlined six objectives: to extend the franchise, to end property qualifications for voters, to elect an annual Parliament, to institute a secret ballot, to distribute the seats in Parliament more equitably, and to pay the members of Parliament. Chartism appealed to the middle class as well as the laboring classes—

---

[13] Allan, "John Allan," 3. The 1841 parade quotation is from King, *Scotland Sober and Free*, 14. Father Theobald Mathew's words are from Winskill, *Temperance Movement*, 1:74–76.

[14] King, *Scotland Sober and Free*, 11–12; King, "Popular Culture in Glasgow," 163.

especially artisans and weavers whose lowered wages meant they were losing their former status. Whether the McAuslans became Chartists is not known, but certainly they would have agreed with its goals.

Although Chartism flourished throughout Great Britain, the Scottish movement had distinctive aspects, including a strong press, which published such newspapers as the *True Scotsman*, the *Scottish Patriot*, and the *Chartist Circular*, and at least twenty-three women's groups (including women who worked in textile factories around Glasgow). The organization emphasized education and morality and even formed churches. By the beginning of 1839 there were 160 Chartist groups in Scotland. A year later, 20 Chartist churches had been organized. They eliminated pew rents and promoted a social gospel: "Their Christ was a working man who had been crucified on the social rack like they; their mission [was] to win back the rights God had given, but which the rich and powerful, the priesthood among them, had taken away."[15] Although it is impossible to know if Peter held similar sentiments at the time, his later writings echoed them:

> Jesus being a carpenter himself, he [k]new how to sympise [sympathize] with his fellow laborering man. . . . Hear the sound of the master's voice pleading, yes he is pleading for the widows and the orphants that justice might be done, that the children might have bread. And this pleader was a man of sorrow that had nowhare to lay his head. He accused the Scribes and Pharisees of his day of binding heavy burdens greavious to be born[e] on men's sholders. . . . The Scribes and Pharisees of to day, who profess to speak for Christ, display . . . the same characteristics.[16]

Along with Chartism, many in the working classes joined the Anti–Corn Law League. The Corn Laws of 1815 protected British farmers against the importation of foreign grain ("corn") until homegrown crops reached a certain price. These laws sparked protest meetings all over the Glasgow area, including Kirkintilloch. In spite of a revision to the laws in 1828, agitation continued and led to the formation of the league. It advocated removing tariffs on grain and allowing free trade and the importation of cheaper foodstuffs. The appeal among the working classes was immediate, for people were desperate. In Kirkintilloch in 1840, the *Scottish Patriot* reported that the cotton weavers were forced

---

[15] McCaffrey, *Scotland in the Nineteenth Century*, 45–6; Clark, *The Struggle for the Breeches*, 228. The quotation on the Chartist social gospel is given in Knox, *Industrial Nation*, 68.

[16] Peter McAuslan to Rev. W. S. Kress, [1904] (#54 McAuslan Papers).

to work fourteen hours a day because of low wages and the high price of bread. Even with the strictest economy, they remained in "a very low state of privation and distress." In 1843, during the investigation by the Scottish Poor Law Commission—a royal deputation charged with learning the state of the poor—another weaver in Kirkintilloch, who had eleven children, said that sending his nine-year-old son to work at the loom for more than twelve hours a day was "a distressing thing for a father, . . . but the thing must be done, or he must starve."[17]

Paisley, a great weaving center, suffered what one historian has called "perhaps the greatest distress ever experienced in a large British town."[18] With bad harvests in 1841–42, followed by a potato blight first in Ireland in 1845 and then in the Highlands in 1846, the period became known as the Hungry Forties. One unemployed weaver in Paisley, Andrew Sproul, who had a wife and three young children, suffered greatly in this period. Everything of value in the house had been seized because he owed thirty shillings of back rent. The sheriff had come and said they were to be evicted in four days. He had only one pair of trousers, and as they had just been washed, he was housebound until they dried, which prevented him from attending his Sunday religious meeting. He wrote,

> Poverty is in upon us like a fiend. Scarcety of labour, idleness for fore [four] & five weeks together. Nothing to depend upon for my family but my own labour. Dearth of food, part of the last & this year, has reduced us to want, & I could gither my fameley around me down before the Lord & in the naime of Jesus pray give us this day our dayley bread. All our clothes pledged, except our every day appeeal, to purchase a little food. Up to the mouth in debt & deep water besides. My wife & children to keep [in] the house as if hiding from a mad being. Thinley clad & the wether long, cold & frostey & all of us suffering a degree of ill helth.[19]

It is hardly a wonder that working people began to turn ever more fervently to God. The government and the well-off seemed uninterested or impotent to help. It would take a higher power to intervene and bring relief.

---

[17] Murray, *Scottish Hand Loom Weavers*, 234. The quotations are from Treble, *Urban Poverty in Britain*, 23–24; and Levitt and Smout, *The State of the Scottish Working-Class*, 106.
[18] Whatley, *Industrial Revolution in Scotland*, 85.
[19] Sproul, Diary, entry for January 31, 1847, 98–99.

3

Mormon Missionaries

THE 1830S AND 1840S IN SCOTLAND HAVE BEEN DESCRIBED AS "AN age remarkable for religious earnestness." Besides attending church, families worshipped at home. A leader in one weaving village wrote, "At this hour, this hour of Sabbath evening quiet, it may be said that almost every dwelling has become a family sanctuary, every hearth an altar, every home a temple of praise. Pass along that long range of thatched dwellings, and your ear will often catch the evening song of devotion, as it rises from poor and humble men to the throne of the Eternal." Similarly, a nineteenth-century Scottish poet observed that in the days before Sunday schools existed, private ones were held in every house: "No householder was accounted respectable who did not engage in the duty of family worship once a day, at least, and twice on Sabbath."[1]

The Church of Scotland, once the only voice for religious and morality matters, no longer reigned supreme. An 1836 ecclesiastical survey in Kirkintilloch showed that membership in the church had dropped to 70 percent of the population. In the years that followed, the church increasingly had to vie for members with other denominations and sects, ones that often reflected new social divisions. No longer having a single authority in religion, individuals were forced to rely on their own judgment as to which was the "true" church.[2]

In the Church of Scotland, the years between 1833 and 1843 were marked by continual argument and debate. Known as the Ten Years'

---

[1] James Taylor, *The Annals of Fenwick*, as quoted in C. G. Brown, *Religion and Society*, 79–80; Hamilton, *Poems, Essays, and Sketches*, 443.

[2] Lewis, *Topographical Dictionary of Scotland*, 2:180; C. G. Brown, *Religion and Society*, 6; Bullert, "Ethical Individualism," 4, 54, 80–81, 120–21, 131–33.

Conflict, the dispute centered on religious freedom. The "Moderates" declared that the right to choose the minister belonged, as it always had, to the patrons—large landowners, the Crown, universities, and town councils. The "Evangelicals" asserted that only the congregation of a parish had that right, for ultimately Christ should be the head of the church, not the Crown.[3]

In spite of their disputes, the Moderates and the Evangelicals—both of them from the middle and upper classes—agreed upon the divine order of society, in which the aristocracy, industry leaders, and the working poor each had their place and responsibility. For the working classes, that meant accepting the free enterprise system by submitting to those above them and to the laws of supply and demand that determined their wages. They were obligated to endure with patience and to be grateful for God's mercies. The Moderates believed that problems such as poverty came from spiritual or moral failings, and improvement would come through reforming the inner person. They emphasized "the plain duties of daily life"— moral restraint, good works, and sincere prayer—and found it "pleasantest to let sleeping dogmas lie." Evangelicals, on the other hand, believed that change could be brought about only by adhering to the stern dogmas leading to personal salvation through Jesus Christ.[4]

The Ten Years' Conflict came to a head on May 18, 1843, in Edinburgh when, in a spectacular act, 37 percent of the clergy walked out of the Church of Scotland's highest governing board, the General Assembly. This act became known as the Disruption. Those who "went out" were Evangelicals, and in taking this stand against patronage, they left behind their churches, homes, salaries, and status, an enormous sacrifice at a time when most had large families and were used to a comfortable life. With fervent feelings, almost half the congregation of the Church of Scotland followed their clergymen to form the new Free Church of Scotland. The next Sunday they held services in fields, farmyards, graveyards, barns, public halls, or wherever they could find a spot to assemble. Those going out compared themselves "to the Israelites leaving the bondage of Egypt and trusting God to bring them to a better land." Many historians consider

---

[3] An excellent source for the Ten Years' Conflict and the Disruption is the collection of papers in S. J. Brown and Fry, *Scotland in the Age of the Disruption.*

[4] Cheyne, *Transforming of the Kirk*, 111–18; Brown, "Ten Years' Conflict," 9; Graham, *The Social Life of Scotland*, 2:100 (the quotations are on 2:98, 150).

St. Mary's Parish Church (Auld Kirk), Kirkintilloch,
where the McAuslans and Allans worshipped. Photograph circa 1904.
Courtesy of East Dunbartonshire Information and Archives.

the Disruption as the most important event in Scotland in the nineteenth century, marking the beginning of the modern era, and as "the ultimate statement of social and religious self-determination."[5]

Members of the middle class and aspiring artisans were among those who left the Established Church. Yet the McAuslans and the Allans did not join them. One might have expected these families to have been against patronage and for those who stood up for principle. Nevertheless, many in the working class stayed with the Church of Scotland. Robert Allan, as an elder in the Auld Kirk, had a reason to stay. It seems likely that both families felt loyalty to their minister, Adam Forman, who had presided since the McAuslans first came to Kirkintilloch.[6]

---

[5] Brown, "Ten Years' Conflict," 1–2, 24 (the comparison to the Israelites is on page 1); McCaffrey, *Scotland in the Nineteenth Century*, 38; C. G. Brown, *Religion and Society*, 25. The "ultimate statement" comes from S. J. Brown and Fry, *Scotland in the Age of the Disruption*, viii.

[6] Hillis, "Sociology of the Disruption," 51; Allan, "John Allan," 2.

Besides the Church of Scotland and the new Free Church, Kirkintilloch had many other denominations and little "sects of Brethren, each
... claiming an infallibility of interpretation that is theirs alone." A visitor would have found Kirkintilloch to be a "churchy" town.[7] With more
places of worship, more residents went to church, generating more religious enthusiasm and more debate of religious ideas. Followers of the
many secessionist Presbyterian and other denominations and sects
enjoyed arguing over Christian truths and moral issues.

Peter McAuslan wrote of disputes he heard among a Catholic, a Unitarian, and a Presbyterian when he was a tearer at Bellfield Printworks:

> During the time I was at the Terring untill I was 12, I heard the men who
> belonged to the different religions of that time discuss. Each seemed to
> think that he was right and the others wrong. I remember well of an old
> man the name of James Gallaher. He maintained with emphasis that there
> was only one true Church and that was the Catholic, for Christ give the
> keyes to Peter to bind and loose on Earth, and it would be bound and
> loosed in heaven, and [tha]t athority was handed down through the Popes
> of Rome [to thi]s day, and he declared that the gates of hell would [not]
> prevale against it.[8]

Peter added that the Unitarian "maintained [that] no God was ever
born on Earth by a virgain and that men are libal to make mistakes, but
that Jesus was a [good] man and he rebuked the Scribes and Pharisees
of his day." This Unitarian also pointed out many contradictions in the
Bible. The third, a Presbyterian, "maintained that the Bible was the word
of God, and it contained all that was essential for man's salvation. He
proved from history that the Church of Rome was intolerant and maintained a murderous institution called the Inquisition and sold Indul-
gences to the rich, which gave rise to the Protestant reformation." Peter's
memories of this conflict demonstrate his interest in religion from an
early age and, more importantly, reveal his belief that each person has
the right to evaluate religious teachings for himself. Claiming authority
to judge for himself was a trait Peter carried throughout life.

In that period, many religious groups shared a belief in an imminent millennium, when Christ would return to earth. In preparation,

---

[7] Sunter, "Ecclesiastical History," 135, 136. See also C. G. Brown, *Religion and Society*, 39.

[8] McAuslan, miscellaneous note, [ca. 1907] (#56 McAuslan Papers). The edge of one page is torn;
probable words are in brackets.

evangelicals distributed tracts and conducted revivals, Bible classes, prayer meetings, and open-air preaching. The Scottish revivals were heavily influenced by their counterparts in America. Letters and published accounts of American experiences made their way regularly to Great Britain, and a revival society in Glasgow printed many of them: "British and American evangelicals . . . saw themselves as branches of the same closely knit family. The contagious element in revivalism, seen so clearly locally, operated at a transatlantic level, too."[9]

The most famous Scottish revival of this period took place in the summer of 1839 in Kilsyth, just five miles from Kirkintilloch and the McAuslans. The parish minister, William Chalmers Burns, soon had the whole community entranced. Although all denominations and trades came, the handloom weavers in particular responded. One historian described the event: "The web became nothing to a weaver, nor the forge to the blacksmith, nor his bench to the carpenter. . . . They forsook all to crowd the church and prayer meetings. There were nightly sermons in every church, household meetings for prayer in every street, twos and threes in earnest conversation on every road, and single wrestlers with God in the solitary places of the field and glen." Crowds came from all over the Glasgow area; in September, ten to twelve thousand traveled to Kilsyth, partly out of curiosity and partly to experience the religious enthusiasm. Over the course of the next year, revivals spread across the industrial belt.[10]

In the midst of this religious fervor, two Mormon missionaries appeared on the scene to take their place in the mix. Born in Scotland, Samuel Mulliner and Alexander Wright had each emigrated to Canada in the early 1830s, where they converted to Mormonism. They had moved to Mormon settlements in Illinois and Ohio, but in 1839 Joseph Smith, the founder of Mormonism, called them to go on a mission to Scotland. They arrived that December; Mulliner stayed for eight months and Wright for a year and a half. By the end of their assignments, others, including the Mormon apostle Orson Pratt, had arrived and several branches of the church had been established. At the British Mission conference held in Manchester, England, in October 1840, less than a year after the first missionaries arrived, Pratt and Wright reported 193 members baptized in the

[9] Carwardine, *Trans-atlantic Revivalism*, 59, 94–95; the quotation is on page 198.

[10] J. Hutchinson, *Weavers, Miners and the Open Book: A History of Kilsyth*, as quoted in C. G. Brown, "Religion, Class and Church Growth," 324; Carwardine, *Trans-atlantic Revivalism*, 97.

Glasgow area and 43 in Edinburgh. Betsy McAuslan's family, the Adamsons, became telling examples of the appeal of Mormonism. The first of the Adamsons to convert was Betsy's brother James in September 1843, four months after the Disruption. He was followed by her two youngest brothers, Alexander ("Sandy") and Dougal, and other members of the family soon thereafter.[11]

Mormonism's particular appeal to coal miners is explained in good part by the social and economic dislocations they had suffered, which were more severe than in any other group except handloom weavers. In the early 1840s the number of miners boomed in response to the growth of the iron industry, which needed coal for hot-blast furnaces. The new miners came from those who had been forced out of their traditional trades and from Irish immigrants who were flooding into Scotland. They were ready to work for any wage and in conditions much beneath those the traditional miners had won over years of successive strikes. To accommodate the new workers and their families, existing houses were divided, and rows of "single-ends"—one-room cottages twelve to thirteen feet square, usually with dirt floors—were built. Disease, drunkenness, and petty but sometimes vicious crime were rife. The miners went on strike in 1842 and 1843 but eventually were forced to accept lower wages. For many, emigration was the only way to survive, and starting in the 1830s, a great number of Scottish miners sailed to America to find better-paid work in the coal pits there.[12]

A declining standard of living, crowded conditions, poor sanitation, and hunger pushed the death rate in the Glasgow area to new heights in the 1840s. The Adamsons lost three family members during this period.[13] Studies of Scotland have shown that, during the first half of the nineteenth century, infectious diseases accounted for 60 percent of all deaths, the single largest killer being tuberculosis. There were epidemics of typhus

---

[11] "Minutes of the General Conference," *Millennial Star* 1 (October 1840): 166. LDS baptisms are from the Record of Members, Glasgow Branch: James Adamson, September 29, 1843; Alexander and Dougal Adamson, November 23, 1843; Mrs. Elizabeth Adamson (wife of James), January 21, 1844; Agnes Baird Adamson, July 24, 1844.

[12] By the 1860s, colliers' unions organized systematic emigration when several Maryland coal companies sought to hire six hundred Scottish miners to supplement their own workforce. A. B. Campbell, *Lanarkshire Miners*, 268.

[13] Betsy's sister Margaret died August 10, 1844, and her father, William, on November 14, 1844 (Ancestral File, Family History Library, Salt Lake City). Brother James died May 20, 1846 (Record of Members, Glasgow Branch, on the same line as his baptism registration).

in 1837 and 1847 and cholera in 1832 and 1848–49. Most people in Scotland, whatever their religious leanings, believed that disease, suffering, and death were part of God's unknowable plan and that one must humbly accept such personal tragedies.[14] But here the Mormons offered hope. The missionaries, in addition to their fundamental beliefs, taught that their priests could cure the sick—if it was God's will—by the laying on of hands. Convert diaries and reminiscences from this period give many examples.

Even the deaths of Joseph Smith, the Mormon founder and prophet, and his brother Hyrum in June 1844 did not discourage new converts. The two leaders had been killed by a mob in Carthage, Illinois, where they had been jailed after destroying an anti-Mormon press. The reaction of the members in Scotland to this tragedy is given in the report of the general conference held in Glasgow in August 1844:

> President [John] Cairns then rose and said that the circumstances which had called them together were well known, and . . . referred to the death of our Brethren Joseph & Hyrum Smith . . . who had suffered under the violence of Mobocracy in the land of America. . . . It was universally stated that the Saints felt keenly at the loss of our worthy brethren Joseph and Hyrum Smith. It was a stimulus to them to be closer to God and to accelerate his work by every possible exertion in their power to share in common with their brethren the persecutions and trials of Zion that they also may share in her blessings.[15]

In a period when missionaries of various denominations and sects visited homes and left tracts, what was it about Mormonism that caught the attention of the Adamsons and eventually the McAuslans? Undoubtedly a number of factors contributed. Besides the backdrop of increasingly difficult and tumultuous times, there was something about these missionaries from America that was especially refreshing and appealing: they were from the "land of opportunity," they were young, they were working-class, they spoke and read the Bible in plain terms, and they did not say that one had to accept one's lot in life as part of a God-given order. They brought a message that God had not forgotten his people on earth, but instead had sent a modern-day prophet (Joseph Smith), revealed a new testament (the Book of Mormon), and established the

---

[14] Cage, "Health in Glasgow," 57–62; MacLaren, "Bourgeois Ideology," 42–43, 49.
[15] "Glasgow 1844," Record of Members, Glasgow Branch.

true church once more on earth. Perhaps most striking was their notion of sacred time; they preached that people could once more live in God's time and be part of God's plan, rather than being weighed down by their daily struggles. They said that all the distresses of their lives were but signs of the coming millennium; that God would gather his people from the sinful nations to America, the new land God had set apart for his true church; and that there the chosen could begin to build the Kingdom of God in preparation for Christ's coming. Scots responded to this message, and by January 1847 there were more than a thousand Mormon members in the Glasgow area.[16]

Although the McAuslans knew that Betsy's family had joined the Mormon religion, they did not feel an immediate need to follow in their footsteps, perhaps because artisans aspired to religious as well as social respectability, which did not include Mormonism. By 1847 Peter had finished his apprenticeship and was working as a journeyman pattern designer at Bellfield Printworks. The hard times, however, had not let up. In 1845 the collapse of wild speculation in railways brought economic panic. A commercial depression followed, with mill closings and high unemployment. Then typhus broke out in January 1847. By the spring the situation in Scotland was so dire that Queen Victoria, with the approval of the Privy Council, issued a proclamation on March 9, 1847, calling on the people to turn to God with "contrition and penitence of heart" and to join a public fast throughout Scotland on March 26.[17]

Around the time that typhus began to abate in late spring 1847, the McAuslans left Kirkintilloch, their home for more than twenty years. The impetus for their move was probably that Bellfield's lease expired and the two managers left. The family moved to Denny, about thirteen miles to the northeast, not far from Falkirk. Three years earlier a firm in Denny had enlarged its calico printing capacity and was employing well over two hundred printers. This expansion most likely meant that Peter and his father found jobs there. The McAuslans in 1847 consisted of the parents, Peter and Betsy, and their ten children: Agnes, twenty-five; Peter, twenty-three; Jane, nineteen; Betsy, seventeen; William, fifteen (now a pattern-drawer apprentice); Ann, thirteen; Frank, eleven;

---

[16] Polly Aird, "Why Did the Scots Convert?" 91–122; "Minutes of the Glasgow Conference," *Millennial Star* 9 (February 1, 1847): 34–35.

[17] Mackenzie, *Reminiscences of Glasgow*, 3:527–28.

Christina, nine; Janet, almost seven; and David, four. The only one who did not move was daughter Betsy, who had a job in Kirkintilloch as a domestic servant for a family with five young children.[18]

When an artisan was unemployed, as both Peter and his father may have been before they moved, he faced a dilemma, not knowing whether the situation would be short-term or long-term. If the cause was a downturn in the trade cycle that proved to be short-lived, he might be able to ride it out on the strength of his savings and insurance payments from his friendly society. But if the unemployment stretched into weeks or months, he might deplete his savings and fall into a state of destitution from which he could never again rise.[19] As the large McAuslan family crossed the bridge on the road out of Kirkintilloch, they must have looked back with nostalgia to easier days in the past, but also forward with hope.

---

[18] Cameron, "Calico Printing in Campsie," 51; *Stirling Journal and Advertiser*, February 16, 1844, 4; 1851 Scotland Census, Kirkintilloch, Dunbartonshire, Enumeration District 6 (498), 9.

[19] Levitt and Smout, *State of the Scottish Working-Class*, 110–11.

East Borland Road, Denny, Stirlingshire, where Peter McAuslan lived.
Photograph circa 1910. *Courtesy of Falkirk Council Archives.*

4

Fires of Faith: A Vision

DENNY, WHERE THE MCAUSLANS STARTED THEIR NEW LIFE, WAS perhaps a third smaller than Kirkintilloch.[1] The town is on the road from Glasgow to Stirling, and five miles from Falkirk, the local center of commerce. Although Denny was a manufacturing town, its location on the northern edge of the great industrial belt of Scotland saved it from the chronic air pollution of the "black country." An easy walk took one to pastoral scenes. The family settled in a house on East Borland Road, just outside the main part of town. Young Peter, now twenty-three, shared a room with Robert Salmon, a hand-block printer and an old family friend.[2] From the house, a short walk by footpath and then by pedestrian bridge across the River Carron took them to the Denovan Printworks.

The abundant water supply in the area had given rise to a variety of waterwheel-powered factories around Denny since the start of industrialization. The Denovan Printworks, where the McAuslans found work, was actually in the adjacent village of Denovan. Most of the employees lived in Denny, which had almost five thousand inhabitants, whereas Denovan had just over a hundred. The printworks, though large, enjoyed a bucolic setting near the river. Above it on a wooded knoll stood the handsome Gothic parish church. Although sources give varying numbers—employment fluctuated according to market demand—Denovan

---

[1] Sources for Denny include Lewis, *Topographical Dictionary of Scotland*, 1:278–79; Dempster, "Parish of Denny," 8:115–38; and Watson, "Parish of Dunipace," 8:379–89.

[2] William McKechnie to Peter McAuslan, November 10, 1848 (#1 McAuslan Papers); Peter McAuslan to Agnes McAuslan Allan, March 1, 1884 (#33 McAuslan Papers), 5.

appears to have reached its peak of about fifteen hundred employees when the McAuslans arrived.[3]

While the McAuslans were settling into new routines in Denny, Peter's sister Agnes was making plans for her wedding. Through the McAuslans' friendship with the Robert Allan family, Agnes fell in love with John Allan, who had become a hand-block printer. Following Church of Scotland tradition, the couple posted their intentions twice in the Auld Kirk, Kirkintilloch, in August 1847. Then, in the Denny Parish church, their names were proclaimed to the congregation before they were married there on August 27, 1847. After the wedding festivities, they set off for Barrhead, a town near Paisley where John had found a new position.[4]

Six months after the wedding, Peter's grandmother Agnes Baird Adamson and his two young uncles, Sandy and Dougal Adamson, were suddenly preparing to emigrate to America under the auspices of the Mormons. After Joseph Smith's death, the church leaders under President Brigham Young had suspended the emigration of groups from the British Isles while the Mormons were vacating their headquarters in Nauvoo, Illinois, amid continuing persecution. This evacuation was the first step toward finding a permanent home where mobs would not follow them. On February 1, 1848, four years after Smith's martyrdom, the British converts finally read in their bimonthly newspaper, the *Millennial Star*: "The channel of Saints' emigration to the land of Zion, is now opened. The long-wished for time of gathering has come. Good tidings from Mount Zion! The resting place of Israel, for the last days, has been discovered. Beautiful for situation, and the ultimate joy of the whole earth is the stake of Zion established in the mountains."[5]

The Mormons first settled this "Zion" in 1847 in the valley of the Great Salt Lake in what was then part of Mexico. The United States acquired it at the end of the Mexican-American War, just six months after the first pioneer company arrived. The Mormons, who had hoped to escape the United States and have peace in which to build their own society, once more belonged to that nation. They were in a remote region, undesired except by the American Indians for whom it was home. The valley nes-

[3] Jarvis, *Corsets in Stripeside*, 24; Watson, "Parish of Dunipace," 8:383–85; *Stirling Journal and Advertiser*, February 16, 1844, 4.

[4] OPR, Kirkintilloch, Dunbartonshire 498/4 Marriages, August 15 and 22, 1847; OPR, Denny, Stirlingshire 476/1 Marriages, August 14, 1847; Allan, "John Allan," 2–3.

[5] Orson Spencer, "Emigration!" *Millennial Star* 10 (February 1, 1848): 40.

Wedding picture of Agnes McAuslan and John Allan, August 27, 1847.
From a daguerreotype. *Courtesy of Ada Redd Rigby, Blanding, Utah.*

tled at the foot of the snow-covered Wasatch Range, part of the Rocky
Mountains. The melting snow provided a water source in spring and early
summer, and the Mormons quickly realized that the fertile land needed
only to be irrigated to be productive. To this valley the church leaders
now encouraged all Mormons to gather as quickly as possible to build the
Kingdom of God in preparation for the Second Coming of Christ.

For many British Mormons, the call to gather not only fulfilled their
religious dreams but also fit their economic situation. Orson Spencer,
the president of the British Mission and editor of the *Millennial Star*,
continued in his article, "Now rejoice, and lift up your heads, O ye pure
in heart, and let the labouring and heavy laden, that have been bowed

down under the weight of accumulated oppressions, in every nation, prepare themselves to come to their inheritance in the land of promise. The
day of release dawns, and the notes of millennial jubilee reverberate from
the mountain heights of Zion."

This article was followed by another filled with details of emigration.[6]
Spencer's excitement was palpable. He emphasized the urgency of gathering and the mounting indications that the day of judgment was near:
"Go to whatever country you will, the signs of the times are truly ominous. The outrages, crimes, and shocking disasters . . . are preparing men
out of all nations to welcome the intelligence, that *Zion* . . . is established. . . . No favourable opportunity [to emigrate] should be lost, lest
in the commotion and revolution of governments, or the event of war,
this present channel of emigration should be obstructed." Samuel W.
Richards, president of the church in Scotland, was in Liverpool preparing to return to America with his brother Franklin D. Richards, counselor to the British Mission president, Orson Spencer. But when they
learned that emigration could commence again, Samuel returned to Scotland to organize those ready to leave.[7]

Peter's Adamson grandmother and uncles had saved in anticipation
of this signal. They were among the seventy Scots who signed up to be
on the first ship sailing to New Orleans. Although other Saints from
Great Britain had gone before them, they were the first party that would
travel straight through to the Great Salt Lake Valley. In the rush to get
ready—organizing clothing, bedding, cookware, and tools to take with
them—they needed to dispose of other possessions. One emigrant in the
same group wrote that he sold his things at half price so as to dispose of
them quickly.[8] Grandmother Adamson likely gave some things to her
children who were not going.

On February 12, 1848—less than two weeks after the formal announcement in the *Millennial Star*—the Adamsons, with many others, left Glasgow on the coastal steamer *Admiral* and headed for Liverpool, where they
would board the sailing ship *Carnatic*. Most likely the McAuslans went
to the Broomielaw Dock in Glasgow to see the family off, mingling with
others who were seeing their relatives and friends perhaps for the last time.

---

[6] Orson Spencer, editorial, *Millennial Star* 10 (February 1, 1848): 41–42.

[7] Ibid., 43, emphasis in original; Buchanan, "From the Missouri to the Clyde: Samuel W. Richards
in Scotland, 1846–1848," 35.

[8] Carruth, Autobiography and Journal, 15.

The Adamsons' view of the significance of their journey as part of God's plan can be gathered from the formal grandeur of the first sentences of Sandy Adamson's journal: "I, Alexander Adamson, journeying to the Camp of Israel in the far west of America. That being baptized for the work of God and the testimony of Jesus, and I and Mother and Bishop Dougal commanded by God to gather with them and left Baillieston Toll [Road], Barney [Barony] Parish, our national land Scotland." "Camp of Israel" was the name given to the main body of the Saints waiting on both sides of the Missouri River at Council Bluffs, Iowa, and Winter Quarters, the not-yet-organized Nebraska Territory, for the start of their trek to the Salt Lake Valley.[9]

Though sad to see the Adamsons leave, the McAuslans must also have been moved by their dedication, their faith, and especially their excited anticipation at going to Zion. Their departure appears to have prompted Peter to begin seriously considering Mormonism for himself. The editor of the *Millennial Star* noted the testimony given by those who left: "From the first day that they begin to sell their furniture and goods, the voice of emigration preaches loudly, and the attention of multitudes is attracted to the onward progress of the great work of God. Thus the Saints are preaching by flight like unto Lot."[10]

Orson Spencer stressed urgency because political upheavals threatened to close the chance to emigrate. Unrest was simmering across Europe. In February, Karl Marx published his *Communist Manifesto* and the Revolution of 1848 began in France. The French king, Louis Philippe, fled Paris as the people raised barricades in the streets and demanded electoral reform, a democratic republic, and benefits for the working classes. On the Continent that spring, revolution spread to Germany, Austria, Italy, and Hungary. The people demanded liberal constitutions and reforms for the working classes. In four days in June ten thousand people were killed or wounded in Paris, and their blood ran in the streets. The French Assembly finally drafted a new constitution and established the Second French Republic. Peter McAuslan described 1848 as "that ever memorable year of revolutions and tumbling down of thrones." The

---

[9] Anderson, "Extracts from the Journal of Alexander Adamson," 3. Baillieston is actually in Old Monkland Parish, which borders Barony Parish; both are in Lanarkshire. The term "bishop" was without meaning among the British Mormons; in Utah today, a bishop is head of a local ward and thus generally equivalent to a Catholic parish priest or a Protestant minister.

[10] Orson Spencer, "Beloved Saints," *Millennial Star* 10 (March 1, 1848): 74.

working classes felt that they were witnessing a historic time, when old institutions that had impeded liberty and justice would be swept away and a new era would remedy social problems.[11]

Although Great Britain escaped the revolutionary tumult spreading across continental Europe, it was not free of trouble. Members of the working classes, watching unemployment and its attendant hunger spread, grew increasingly apprehensive. Encouraged by Chartist outcries against the general misery, laborers finally rioted on March 6, 1848, in Glasgow. A mob went on the rampage, plundered shops, wrecked whatever was in their way, and shouted for bread and justice. In April the Chartists organized a gathering of some ten thousand in Edinburgh, while in London they tried to present their petition for parliamentary reform. But the reform effort failed, and the movement petered out.[12]

This period of political turmoil, of despair and hope, coincided with dramatic growth in Mormon conversions. Many viewed the "signs of the times," which were regularly noted in the *Millennial Star*, as evidence that the new faith was the answer to their longing. But substantial growth for the British Mormons did not begin until there appeared a John the Baptist to warn the people and a St. Paul to spread the word. The Mormon leaders in Utah had sent talented missionaries to fill those roles. Their John the Baptist was Orson Pratt, one of the twelve apostles of the faith. He was president of the British Mission for just under two and a half years, from August 1848 to January 1851. In that time the number of Mormon baptisms in the whole of Great Britain nearly tripled. In 1847, before Pratt arrived, there were 2,918 baptisms; in 1848, after he had been there only six months, 6,520 people were baptized. In 1849, baptisms rose to 8,620, and the number was 8,017 in 1850. For 1852, a year after Pratt's departure, the figure dropped to 3,400, considerably less than half the number of baptisms during his peak success. To take just the Glasgow Conference, in 1849 under Pratt's leadership an average of 65 persons were baptized each month. But in 1852, after he left, the average dropped to 26 a month.[13]

Orson Pratt's success can be attributed to his oratory skills and especially to the power of his pen. He wrote a series of pamphlets, first

---

[11] McAuslan to McAuslan Allan, March 1, 1884 (#33 McAuslan Papers), 5; [Naisbitt], "Leaves" (June 10, 1878): 357.

[12] Oakley, *Our Illustrious Forbears*, 91; Knox, *Industrial Nation*, 73.

[13] Evans, *Century of "Mormonism,"* 244. The figures come from *Report of the Glasgow Quarterly Conference . . . 1st January, 1850*, 2; and from conference reports summarized in the *Millennial Star* 11 (April 15, 1849): 122; 11 (September 15, 1849): 287; 14 (July 10, 1852): 318; 15 (January 29, 1853): 78.

published individually in the *Millennial Star*, then reprinted by the tens of thousands, and finally bound together in a book in 1851. His writings were cogent and convincing, leading many former skeptics to convert. Historian Edward W. Tullidge, who joined the church in this period, recalled that the British "almost worshipped" Pratt and considered him their "theological father." Along with his pamphlets, Pratt set up a "vast missionary machinery" with, Tullidge estimated, five thousand elders to proselytize across Great Britain.[14]

Scottish convert T. B. H. Stenhouse wrote that Pratt's influence "spread like a consuming fire among the Saints": "The excitement was contagious, . . . the elders were powerful, the Saints were zealous, the public listened, the spirit ran from heart to heart, and miracles were common."[15] Furthering Orson Pratt's influence was the Mormons' new St. Paul, Eli B. Kelsey, the president of the Glasgow Conference. Besides being a vigorous speaker, Kelsey ordered Pratt's pamphlets by the thousands and devised systems to circulate them among nonmembers and members. Kelsey wrote to Orson Pratt: "The work of the Lord is rolling on rapidly in this conference. Many scores are obeying the Gospel; indeed some branches have doubled their members within the last two months. The circulation of the printed word is doing good." Kelsey became a legend among the missionaries: "He was like a tempest sweeping over the . . . countryside—converts, miracles, and stories of his preaching power following in his wake."[16]

Peter McAuslan was one of the recipients of this drive to spread the word. An avid reader—his wife later wrote that he "never gets tired reading"—he would have feasted on discussions with missionaries or other church members. When he died, one American editorial described him as "a man of more than ordinary intelligence, a great reader and a writer of much ability. . . . While he was not aggressive, he was frequently more than a match for his opponents in an argument."[17]

Discussion and debate characterized Mormon missionary endeavors in Great Britain. In Scotland, meetings were set up to challenge ministers of the churches of all denominations and sects, including the Irvingites,

---

[14] Edward W. Tullidge, *History of Salt Lake City and Its Founders*, as quoted in Breck England, *Life and Thought of Orson Pratt*, 155–56.

[15] Stenhouse, *The Rocky Mountain Saints*, 10.

[16] Eli B. Kelsey to Orson Pratt, *Millennial Star* 11 (February 15, 1849): 62; Walker, *Wayward Saints*, 129.

[17] Agnes McAuslin McAuslan to Elizabeth McAuslin Maxwell, May 18, 1886 (McAuslan Papers), 2; *Sutter County Farmer*, December 25, 1908, 6.

Campbellites, Baptists, Methodists, Swedenborgians, and Sabbatarians. William Gibson, then president of the Edinburgh Conference, took enormous delight in besting his opponents, and according to his own account, he never lost a debate.[18]

The Mormon missionaries knew their Bible well; their arguments relied on their skill at calling up particular verses and limiting discussion to a literal interpretation of them. As Gibson put it, if the Bible is not plain, "what use is it to the poor?" The clergy of the Church of Scotland, the related Free Church, and other denominations, however, had university educations and understood the Bible in terms of historical and cultural setting, metaphor, allegory, and the context of the passage. They found it nearly impossible to argue from a literal standpoint and so would turn to challenging the missionaries on sensational subjects: they reiterated rumors of polygamy, called for proofs of healing miracles, or brought up the charge that the Book of Mormon story had been plagiarized from a manuscript by Solomon Spaulding. On at least one occasion, a minister became so frustrated that he threw the Book of Mormon on the floor and stomped on it.[19]

Gibson proudly noted that in comparison with those who knew Greek, Hebrew, and Latin, he was "an unlearned man." This contrast between the educated clergy and the working-class Mormons only further confirmed for those listening that an unbridgeable gulf existed between "them and us," between capital and labor, between rich and poor. They saw that not only were their basic needs ignored but their opinions were disparaged as well. Not surprisingly, they longed to escape the old unjust order and find a new righteous one.[20] The Mormon kingdom in the West fit that desire.

---

[18] Gibson, Journal, 1:23, 28–29, 38, 63, 75, 77–78, 81, 83, 86, 89. Gibson's "journal" was actually written later than the events he described; for example, on page 61 in an entry for 1845, he recounts an incident about his emigration in 1851.

[19] Ibid., 1:38; Gibson, Journal #150, 114.

[20] Gibson, Journal, 1:38. A contemporary review of Mormonism saw its appeal in similar terms: "We may attribute the welcome which Mormonism has met from our working classes to the prevalence of discontent among the poor against the rich. The repinings of labour against capital, which have covered England [and Scotland] with strikes and Europe with barricades, are at once sanctioned and consoled by the missionaries of the 'Saints.' They invite their hearers to fly from oppression to that happy land where the poor are lords of the soil, where no cruel mill-owners can trample on the 'rights of labour,' where social inequalities are unknown, and where all the citizens are united by the bonds of a universal brotherhood and a common faith"; Conybeare, *Mormonism*, 379. Also see Harrison, "Popular History," 14.

Peter's niece described the McAuslans' experience with the missionaries:

> Mormon missionaries were making their way through Scotland at this time. Coming from America which was synonamous [*sic*] with freedom and liberty and whose foundation had been laid on justice and equality for all, Grandfather [Peter McAuslan, Sr.] invited them to his home. They described a Zion which they were building in Utah, where men and women should be free and whose leaders were founding a future empire devoted to the building up of an intelligent and spiritual people. [21]

The new land of America, the missionaries said, would witness the redemption of the faithful and the Second Coming of Christ. It appeared logical and in accordance with the Bible. One convert of the period told of his first encounter with a Mormon missionary: "The great difference that I observed in his preaching, to that of the other sects' preaching was, that I *could understand it*; I saw it ran beautifully coincident with the Scriptures."[22]

The immediate catalyst for Peter's conversion appears to have been directly related to the arrival of Orson Pratt, who had been called to become president of the British Mission. At Pratt's first general conference, held in Manchester, England, in August 1848, he spoke at length and with fervor about Zion: Who were the people of Zion? What were the good tidings that Zion brought? Why was Zion commanded to "get up into the high mountain"? His discourse, covering five printed pages, appeared in the September 1 issue of the *Millennial Star*, just a month before Peter was baptized. It invoked the biblical verses of Micah 4:1–4:

> But in the last days it shall come to pass, that the mountain of the house of the Lord shall be established in the top of the mountains, and it shall be exalted above the hills; and people shall flow unto it. And many nations shall come, and say, Come, and let us go up to the mountain of the Lord, and to the house of the God of Jacob; and he will teach us of his ways, and we will walk in his paths: for the law shall go forth of Zion, and the word of the Lord from Jerusalem. And he shall judge among many people, and rebuke strong nations afar off; and they shall beat their swords into plowshares, and their spears into pruning hooks; nation shall not lift up a sword against nation, neither shall they learn war any more. But they shall sit

---

[21] Aird, "Family History," 8.
[22] Rowan, "Concise Historical Account," 15, emphasis his.

every man under his vine and under his fig tree; and none shall make them afraid; for the mouth of the Lord of hosts hath spoken it.

Peter's account of his own motivation for conversion, written years later, referenced the same Bible verses:

> The idea of a redeemed World took a strong hold on my mind, for did not God's prophets declare that the time would come when man would beat there Swords into Ploughshirs and there Speers into proomhooks [pruning hooks] and study war no more? In that day there would be nothing to hurt or defile in all the Holy mountain of the Lord. The knowledge of the Lord would cover the Earth as water cover[s] the channel of the great deep, that every man would have the pleasure of setting under his own vine and fig tree, none dareing to make him afraid.[23]

In his August address, after quoting the verses from Micah, Pratt then added the connection to the Zion of the Latter-day Saints: "Without new revelation Zion would not know the precise time to 'get up into the high mountain,'—they would not know the precise mountain where God would have his house to be built." Pratt continued,

> It is to accomplish this great, this marvelous, this wonderful work, that Zion in the *last days* is commanded to "*get up into the high mountain.*" Thousands of her noble enterprising sons have already traversed the widely-extended plains of North America, and have ascended the great central range of mountains that form, as it were, the back-bone of that continent; and among its deep, retired, and lonely recesses they have "*sought out*" a resting place for the children of Zion.[24]

One can imagine Peter's emotions building as his mind struggled to understand. He had seen the signs of the coming millennium: the poverty and misery of the working classes, the contrast between how laborers and capitalists lived, the revolutions fermenting across Europe, the dislocations of the Industrial Revolution that forced families to move from place to place in search of work, the threat to his and his family's livelihood as fashion and technology changed ever more quickly, the fractured Church of Scotland, and the various competing religious claims. Surely this new faith signified the arrival of a new age. His grandmother

---

[23] McAuslan, miscellaneous note [ca. 1907] (#56 McAuslan Papers).
[24] "Conference Minutes, General Conference," *Millennial Star* 10 (September 1, 1848): 264, emphasis in original.

and uncles had already embraced the bright vision of a refuge of hope and justice in America, the first step in a transformed world.

Pratt's lucid exposition must have been the culminating piece that made it all fit together, convincing Peter that God had indeed sent new prophets to earth, first Joseph Smith and now Brigham Young. Peter's last doubts disappeared as he surrendered himself to God and whatever new life God would have him live. A sense of relief and calm must have flooded him as he now looked toward Zion, a place of peace instead of oppression, where God's wisdom would flow down on his people and where a perfected world would begin.

Although Falkirk, where the Mormons had established a branch of the church, was only five miles away, Peter traveled fifteen miles to Baillieston, a town east of Glasgow, where his mother's sister, Aunt Agnes Adamson Anderson, and her husband, Archibald, lived and had been baptized the year before. Here Peter requested baptism. On October 3, 1848, he was immersed by James Jardine, a coal miner and the same elder who had baptized his aunt and uncle. Two weeks later, on October 17, Peter returned to Baillieston to be confirmed by Jardine. The record shows that Peter's membership in the church was moved from Baillieston to the Falkirk Branch the same month.[25]

The *Millennial Star*'s depiction of the new life of a member of the Latter-day Saints would have applied to Peter:

> He being now in Christ a new creature, old things have passed away, and all that is before him appears new. His course of conduct now so changed and exemplary, [he] preaches to his family, kindred, and friends, with a persuasion tenfold more powerful than Cambridge eloquence, until as in numerous instances which have come under our observation, the whole family, one after another, are induced to render obedience to the faith, and walk together as the heirs of the grace of life.[26]

And so it happened in Peter's family. Shortly before his parents' conversion, however, Peter had a vision. The possibility of having visions had been preached from the start as one of the evidences of the truth of the Mormon church. One convert wrote, "We were taught to believe in, and contend for, the Supernatural gifts of the Spirit." Orson Pratt had

---

25 Record of Members, Tollcross Branch, 8 (Baillieston was then part of the Tollcross Branch); Record of Members, Falkirk Branch, 6–7.
26 "General Conference," *Millennial Star* 12 (November 15, 1850): 348.

explained such manifestations in the same conference talk that influenced Peter so greatly: "The Lord could not raise up a people called Zion, without restoring to the earth the gospel as predicted by John in his prophecy. That *gospel*, when restored, must produce the same blessings among the children of Zion as were enjoyed in ancient times, namely, visions, dreams, new revelations, prophecies, healings, and, in fine, all the miraculous gifts promised to believers."[27] Peter had prayed for such a blessing.

Peter's vision occurred in the early hours of November 6, 1848, about three weeks after he was confirmed and when his parents were on a Sunday visit to the Andersons in Baillieston. He wrote that he had gone to bed on a Sunday evening after his usual prayers but had awakened at about three or four o'clock in the morning. "I felt imbued with a hevenly cireen [serene] calm and benign feeling, a feeling that I had never experienced in my life before." Peter then described what occurred under this influence:

> A vision was presented to me, my eyes being shut, of a group of specters to the number of about 7. Thire appearance looked as if they might be about 3 feet in hight. They were enveloped from head to foot in vales of crape so that I could not distinguish any of their features. These specters came floting over me (in distance it looked about 3 or 4 feet) one by one and passed away as I was involuntarly repeating the following words: I am going to die, I am going to die, I am going to die. Three times did I repeat that sentence, and all the specters were gone. When a sweet angalic voice said, Thou shalt see one of those by Friday night and it shall be made known unto thee why thou hast been permited to live and your head shall be turned. Then I felt as if the tips of the fingers of a hand had tiped [tapped] me on the left side of the neck three times and that peculiar feeling that I was inveloped [in] left me and I was in my normal condition again.[28]

Friday night came, and Peter doubted that he would see anything else, believing that the words of the angelic voice must have some allegorical, not literal, meaning. But in his sleep, he had another vision:

> To my surprise and astonishment I dream't that I was flying through the air towards Falkirk. I was about a mile on the way when one of those specters came right up in front of me, tooke as it were possion [possession] of me and shook me from head to foot. It made me tremble like as

[27] Rowan, "Concise Historical Account," 16; "Conference Minutes," *Millennial Star* 10 (September 1, 1848): 263, emphasis in original.
[28] McAuslan, undated note (#61 McAuslan Papers).

if every nerve in my body was shook as from an elictric battry. There was no mistake of the presence that took hold of me. I saw it plain and distinct. Its likeness was in perfect accord with those I saw on Sunday evening, the size and crape invelope were the same to all appearance. It was threating and menassing in spirit, and uttered the following never to be forgotten words: You Big Bugger that you are, would you do what your Mother bede you[?] And its power was gone and I was wide awake thinking on the strange occurance.[29]

Peter soon interpreted this vision to mean that God had answered his prayers and sent an angel on the Sunday night to confirm him in the truth of the Mormon church. It gave him "faith to testify to its being the work of God, which I did for severle years afterwards with great confidence." As for the specter in the second vision, he believed it was "a Spirit of Satan the advesary of souls who was permited to have power over me for a momment so that I should by expearence know the power of God or good and the power of the Divile or evil."[30]

His parents returned from Baillieston on the Sunday night of his first vision. Archibald Anderson, then an elder in the church, had sent word back by them to Peter that he should go to Falkirk and bring an elder to Denny to have his parents baptized, "as they wished to join the church also." Peter had been attending meetings regularly at Falkirk on Sundays, his day off from work. Right at that time, Rev. A. Duncanson, a minister of a Congregational church in Falkirk, was holding a series of lectures against Mormonism. The president of the Edinburgh Conference, William Gibson, came once a week to refute what Duncanson said, based on the notes that the branch president, David O. Calder, took at the lectures. According to his own assessment, Gibson outwitted Duncanson in these debates, and the latter quickly lost his popularity and was seldom heard of afterward. During one of these visits, on November 11, 1848, Gibson traveled the five miles from Falkirk to Denny to baptize Peter's mother, father, brothers William and Frank, and sister Ann in the River Carron.[31] Peter's blessings had multiplied: first the visions to confirm him in the faith, and then his family's conversion. Now he and his family could walk together in God's grace.

---

[29] Ibid.
[30] Ibid.
[31] Ibid.; Gibson, Journal, 1:86; Record of Members, Falkirk Branch; Falkirk Council Archives, *Guide to Archives—Churches*, 43.

Sketch of Orson Pratt drawn by Peter McAuslan, March 1849.
Pencil on paper; original size 7 by 10.5 inches.
Courtesy of Donna Miller Forguson, Live Oak, California.

5

Among the Saints

WHEN PETER WAS OFF WORK, HE SPENT HIS TIME ATTENDING meetings, reading Mormon literature, and savoring the fellowship of the Saints. A fellow convert described the days after baptism: "Our bosoms were full of the Holy Ghost, and our duties were delightful to us. We held a prayer meeting nearly every night in some of the houses belonging to the Saints in the form of a family prayer meeting."[1]

Cholera reappeared in 1848 to dampen their joy. It surfaced in Edinburgh in October, the same month Peter was baptized, and spread to Glasgow in November. The course of the disease was fast and ugly. Much feared, it struck without warning and was characterized by violent and uncontrollable diarrhea and vomiting, excruciating pain and muscle spasms, and dehydration that left the person with a shrunken, bluish appearance, all within a matter of hours.[2]

In February 1849, cholera reached the building next to Peter's, and his roommate, Robert Salmon, became deathly afraid. Robert and his wife, Mary, were longtime friends of the McAuslans from Kirkintilloch. Robert was rooming with Peter most likely because he had found work at Denovan Printworks but had not moved his wife and seven children. In those days of high unemployment and falling wages, many were forced to live far from home, seeing their families only on Sundays.[3]

---

[1] Rowan, "Concise Historical Account," 16.
[2] MacLaren, "Bourgeois Ideology," 39–40; Flinn et al., *Scottish Population History*, 374.
[3] Peter McAuslan to Agnes McAuslan Allan, March 1, 1884 (#33 McAuslan Papers), 5 of transcription; 1841 Scotland Census, Kirkintilloch, Dunbartonshire, Enumeration District 12 (498), 16; Gibson, Journal, 1:78.

Peter had discussed Mormonism with Robert and hoped he would ask for baptism. "He gave it some serious thought," wrote Peter, "and felt as if he would like to obay if he could but have faith in its truth." One night after they had retired, a vision came to Robert. In Peter's words:

> Three men stood before him. The first was a glorious looking personage the light radeateing from his person all around. A portion of the light shone upon the side of the head of the second person which he knew to be like me. The third person was like himself. [As] he was standing gaszening at the other two, an impressionable voice said to him, This is the way, walk ye in it. The interpretation of the vision came to his mind like a flash of lighting. The first person represented Christ. He held the power and authority of the priesthood. A portion of that authority and priesthood had been bestoed upon me (I had then been ordained to the office of a priest of the Aaronic division of priesthood) which bestoes authority to preach the gospel and babptise for the remession of sins.[4]

This vision gave Robert the assurance he was looking for. On March 3, 1849, Peter baptized Robert and Mary Salmon in Denny, and they were confirmed on March 11 in Falkirk. Peter concluded his account by stating, "After he obaid the gospel he was intirely releaved from all fear, and in [its place] came faith and confidence." Peter baptized others in Denny as well: three of his sisters, two other women, and another couple.[5]

Besides the Salmons' baptism, March 1849 brought a new excitement. Orson Pratt came to both the Edinburgh and Glasgow quarterly conferences. Peter attended one and perhaps both. The Edinburgh conference was on March 18 and 19, followed by Glasgow on March 24 and 25. Thousands came to hear Pratt in Edinburgh, where the local members had rented rooms large enough to hold three thousand. After he spoke, the audience clamored for a discussion, but Pratt said he had not come to debate. When they shouted more insistently, Pratt left the room, followed by their cheers. In Glasgow he spoke to members on March 25, and after the conference, on March 26 and 28, he spoke to thousands in the City Hall. There a number of ministers confronted him, asking why he did not cure the sick and blind and give speech to the dumb. Pratt responded that such signs were for those who believed and were bap-

---

[4] McAuslan to McAuslan Allan (#33 McAuslan Papers), 5.
[5] Record of Members, Falkirk Branch, 6-9; McAuslan to McAuslan Allan (#33 McAuslan Papers), 5.

Orson Pratt.
Engraving by Frederick Piercy,
1849, used as the frontispiece in
Pratt's *A Series of Pamphlets*.
*Courtesy of Jared Pratt Family
Association.*

tized. On the second night when Pratt spoke on the Kingdom of God,
no one interrupted him.[6]

At one or more of these meetings, Peter made a sketch of Pratt.
Although he did not label the pencil drawing, there is little doubt as to
the identity of the subject when the drawing is compared with an engraving made of Pratt the same year by Frederick Piercy. The underlying
morphology—the high forehead, the similar hairline, the spacing of the
eyes and their intentness, the long nose, the rounded chin, the jawline,
the shape of the head, and even its tilt all appear to match closely. The
scroll and pen in his hands are in keeping with Pratt's prolific writing.

In late 1849, the owner of Denovan Printworks started introducing

---

[6] MacMaster, Diaries, 22–24; *Report of the Glasgow Quarterly Conference . . . March 24 and 25, 1849,*
7–8; Glasgow Conference, March 26, 1849, Manuscript History of the British Mission; Richardson, Diaries, 7–8.

cylinder printing machines in a drive to remain competitive with the growing American industry for the West Indian market in shawls and bandannas. Advances in cylinder presses now made it possible to replace hand-block printing, the most expensive part in production. Peter had chosen pattern drawing over hand-block printing, hoping to keep his skills in demand even with the advent of new machinery. But from the owner's standpoint, designing was also expensive, and costs could be cut by copying older or foreign designs or filling the space with patterns with little consideration for the item being produced. Thus pattern designers too began to lose their jobs.[7]

These changes forced Peter to leave Denny in August 1850. His brother William, now eighteen and still an apprentice pattern drawer, followed a couple of weeks later, and the rest of the family in early October and November.[8] Peter first moved to Glasgow, where he spent about five weeks. There he met Agnes McAuslin, who, with a similar last name, may have been a distant relative. Agnes, then twenty, was a power-loom weaver in a factory in Bridgeton, on the east edge of Glasgow near Glasgow Green, the great park where many labor rallies assembled and parades began. Bridgeton had become one of the most polluted towns in the area. Peter and Agnes probably started courting in the late summer or early fall of 1850. He had marriage on his mind, for he was now twenty-six. In his luggage when he left Scotland were at least seven books, two of which were on marriage. Peter expressed his view on marriage in an undated letter, saying that if we wish to eliminate hell on earth, we must learn to pick good mates; then "rightly born" children will follow.[9]

Agnes was the oldest daughter of a stonemason. She lived with her parents, William and Jane McAuslin, her sister, Elizabeth, and three younger brothers, John, James, and William, in a two- or three-story tenement with at least two other families. Agnes and her mother had converted to Mormonism in January 1847, followed by her sister in March. The next January, her brother John was baptized and then, in February

---

[7] The copyright law protected designs for only nine months. Jarvis, *Corsets in Stripeside*, 25; Turnbull, *History of the Calico Printing Industry*, 101–105, 115, 134, 143; Robinson, *History of Printed Textiles*, 30.

[8] Record of Members, Falkirk Branch, 6–7.

[9] The two books were Fowler, *Marriage*, and Culverwell, *Marriage Contract*. Peter McAuslan to the "Editor," n.d. (#62 McAuslan Papers).

1848, her father and brother James. The youngest brother does not appear to have joined the church.[10]

Peter's time in Glasgow was short. By late September 1850 he had moved eight miles southeast to Barrhead, about three miles from Paisley. Family members and friends were already there: his sister Agnes and her husband, John Allan; his brother William, who had come straight from Denny; and Robert Salmon with his wife, Mary, and now eight children, who had come the preceding May. Their encouragement and the fact that one of the former managers of Bellfield Printworks in Kirkintilloch now owned a plant in Barrhead persuaded Peter to look there for work. In October and November his parents and younger sisters and brothers arrived. They all moved into a tenement called Craig's Land in the Grahamston district of Barrhead, not far from the railway station.[11]

The McAuslans found jobs in their old manager's plant, the Fereneze Printworks. It specialized in high-quality calico shawls and bandannas, and cylinder machines had not yet replaced the artisans. By 1851 nearly the whole family was employed there: the elder Peter as a block printer, the younger Peter as a pattern drawer, William as an apprentice, Jane and Ann in the warehouse, Frank as an apprentice block printer, and Christina and Janet as tearers. Mother Betsy was at home caring for the family, and David, then eight, was at school.[12] Located just three miles from Paisley, Fereneze printed many of its shawls in a Paisley pattern. Peter's artistic skill appears to have reached a new height here, as shown by one of the drawings he brought to America.

When not at work, Peter kept company with the Mormons in Barrhead. The records show that in March 1851 he baptized two of Robert Salmon's children and a man named Robert McBurnie. But the serenity of the Scottish Mormons suddenly broke. In the January 1851 quarterly conference in Glasgow, two members, Elder David Drummond and Thomas Barr, spoke out against Joseph Clements, the American elder who had been president of the conference for the previous year.

[10] 1851 Scotland Census, Barony, Lanarkshire, Enumeration District 23 (622), 9; Record of Members, Glasgow Branch, several listings, including 40–41, 92–93, 217–18.

[11] Record of Members, Glasgow Branch, 263, 303; Record of Members, Barrhead Branch, 43–45; 1851 Scotland Census, Neilston, Renfrewshire (included Barrhead), Enumeration District 14 (572), 14, 39–40; Cameron, "Calico Printing in Campsie," 51.

[12] McWhirter, *Mine Ain Grey Toon*, 41. Another source on Barrhead for this period is R. Murray, *Annals of Barrhead*. 1851 Scotland Census, Neilston, Enumeration District 14 (572), 14–15.

Peter McAuslan's calico drawing in a Paisley pattern, circa 1851. The design was repeated around the edges of a printed shawl. Pencil on tan paper, now very brittle; original size 16 by 13.25 inches. *Courtesy of Donna Miller Forguson, Live Oak, California.*

Clements, thirty-three, was an American born in New Jersey who, with his wife, had converted to Mormonism in 1841. They had moved to Nauvoo, but then had gone to St. Louis in 1847 in preparation for emigrating to Utah. In 1848, however, before they could set off, Clements was called to go on a mission to Great Britain.[13]

The Glasgow men were objecting to the way Clements handled the funds for the conference. Clements responded, "Our enemies talk about money speculations, but had money been the object I had in view, I would have stayed at home. . . . Still I am not without ambition, neither do I mean to labour for nought." Barr asked the conference to petition Orson Pratt for a new president. Clements lashed out, calling the two men hypocrites and accusing them of "colleaging [*sic*] with apostates." Accusations flew back and forth, but in the end, in 1850 and the first half of 1851, the period of Clements's presidency, well over a hundred members of the Glasgow Conference were cut off for opposing him.[14]

Clements left the Glasgow Conference abruptly in late July or early August 1851. Franklin D. Richards, then president of the British Mission, called a meeting of the church leaders to discuss Clements's leaving his post without an official release. Edward W. Tullidge, a British convert five years younger than Peter and baptized ten days before he was, wrote: "A trial of the case was held in the Church under the direction of the general authorities at Liverpool, the result of which was that those disaffected were given the privilege of re-baptism. . . . About a hundred were thus restored to fellowship."[15] Nineteenth-century Mormons were frequently rebaptized for repentance and reaffirmation of their faith, but in this case, those who had been excommunicated were rejoining the church.

---

[13] Record of Members, Paisley Branch, March 29, 1851; *Report of the Glasgow Quarterly Conference . . . on 1st January, 1851*, 3–4; "Appointments," *Millennial Star* 11 (October 1, 1849): 294; C. H. Nielson, *Salt Lake City 14th Ward Album Quilt*, 194.

[14] *Report of the Glasgow Quarterly Conference . . . on 1st January, 1851*, 3–5; "List of Members Cut Off in the Glasgow Branch," Record of Members, Glasgow Branch. The minutes book of the Glasgow Conference for the period March 1850 to the end of 1851 was "badly mutilated by having leaves cut out"; note appended to the entry for September 2, 1850, Glasgow Conference, Manuscript History.

[15] F. D. Richards, Journal, August 15, 1851; Tullidge, *Tullidge's Histories*, 332. Joseph Clements returned to the United States in September 1851 with a sixteen-year-old Glasgow girl, Margaret Donaldson, and his first wife divorced him soon after he arrived back. When he married Margaret is not known, but in 1853 she had a daughter born in Indiana. Joseph and Margaret emigrated to Utah in 1855, and there had seven more children. C. H. Nielson, *Salt Lake City 14th Ward Album Quilt*, 194–95; Ancestry.com; John Hindley Co., Mormon Pioneer Overland Travel.

Both Franklin D. Richards and his brother Samuel W. Richards traveled to Glasgow to attend the quarterly conference on January 1, 1852. Robert L. Campbell, a Scot, had just been named pastor of the church in Scotland. He opened the meeting by stating, "I desire to feel like a clean sheet of paper, unruffled and placid, for the Spirit of God to write on my heart. . . . It vexes my heart when a President of a Branch gets slack, and loses the spirit. . . . Men that take liberties with the funds of a Church will find a curse come upon them." Franklin Richards followed, saying, "You have had your feelings abused . . . and many have been cut off, but you have turned them home, being too many." Agnes McAuslin's sister, Elizabeth, and brother John were among those cut off and rebaptized. Peter learned from their distress and the general turmoil that even American elders had failings and that God's church on earth was not yet perfected.[16]

By July 1851, Peter and his brother William had moved to Kilmarnock, a manufacturing town about sixteen miles south of Barrhead and considerably larger, with a population of more than twenty-one thousand. Most likely the brothers were looking for work once again, for there was a widespread strike in calico printing that year. Probably Kilmarnock, which employed about twelve hundred people in printing shawls in at least eight printworks, had escaped it. It was there on July 21 that Peter was ordained an elder by Clements, just before the latter suddenly left Scotland. The local records show that Peter then went on to baptize at least three women in Kilmarnock.[17] His faith in Mormonism does not appear to have been diminished by the Clements affair.

In midsummer 1851 the religion gained new attention. Charles Mackay, a noted journalist, poet, historian, and songwriter, published a book titled *The Mormons: or Latter-day Saints; A Contemporary History.* Quickly becoming popular among the middle and upper classes, it was reviewed by leading journals and soon prompted the clergy to admonish their flocks against the new faith. The book eventually went through at least

---

[16] *Report of the Glasgow Conference . . . 1st January, 1852,* 4–8; "Record of Re-baptisms," Record of Members, Glasgow Branch, 176, 177. By the end of 1852, David Drummond, again in good standing, contributed the substantial amount of £22 to the church, much of it to help John Lyon, then president of the Glasgow Conference, to emigrate with his family. Lyon recorded his gratitude in his notebook. See also Lyon, *John Lyon,* 166.

[17] McKay, *History of Kilmarnock,* 210, 286; Johnston, *History of the Working Classes,* 311; Lewis, *Topographical Dictionary of Scotland,* 1:42; Record of Members, Kilmarnock Branch.

five British editions under varying titles. Mackay's book combined his own descriptions with items previously published and with both pro- and anti-Mormon statements. It brought many new converts to the faith, but it caused others to question, resulting in their excommunication. Franklin D. Richards, president of the British Mission, wrote to Brigham Young, "The result of this publicity . . . [is] on the one hand, an addition to the church by baptism of 8066 souls in 1852 [*sic*; should be 1851], and also in the excommunications of 3046 from the British church."[18]

Persecution of the Saints had become regular fare, and in meetings some anti-Mormons would slip in to whistle, clap, stamp, crow, bray, hoot, or in other ways make noise, to put out the gaslights, to break the seats, and even to pull down the chandeliers. Outside, some yelled and shouted and on occasion threw stones. But this harassment was no different from that meted out to Primitive Methodists, Bible Christians, teetotalers, and Millerites and in almost all cases occurred in small towns, not cities. The Saints were taught that such persecution was a sign of the true faith and must be endured. The day would come, they believed, when God would avenge them.[19]

Such troubles mostly pulled the faithful together and gave a new fervency to their beliefs, but Mackay's book, anti-Mormon lectures by the clergy, and persecution persuaded the weakhearted to back out. Some members had understood little of their new religion when they were baptized during the surge of conversions under Orson Pratt; when they learned more, they left. Franklin Richards noted that the conference presidents were "mortified" to discover that the number of excommunications approached the number of baptisms. Among those "pruned" was Peter's aunt Agnes Adamson Anderson, though no reason was given.[20]

In spite of this series of distressing events, Peter and the rest of the McAuslans remained firm in their conviction and hope of going to Zion.

---

[18] Franklin D. Richards to Brigham Young, February 24, 1852, in Journal History, February 24, 1852, 12. See also Arrington, "Charles Mackay," 32–34.

[19] Gibson, Journal, 1:18, 23, 93; Ririe, [Autobiography], 9:345; *Report of the Glasgow Quarterly Conference . . . June 24, 1849*, 6; Thorp, "Sectarian Violence," 138; George D. Watt, "Address to the Saints in Scotland," *Millennial Star* 8 (August 1, 1846): 20.

[20] Richards to Young, Journal History, February 24, 1852, 12–13; Agnes Adamson Anderson was cut off on June 13, 1852; Record of Members, Baillieston Branch, 363–64. In 1852 in the Glasgow Conference there were 312 baptisms and 281 excommunications; see the half-year statistical reports in the *Millennial Star* 14 (July 10, 1852): 318, and 15 (January 29, 1853): 78.

Their faith brought many occasions of joy. One was a "soirée" when Robert Campbell, the newly appointed president of the Glasgow Conference, and the American elder Appleton Harmon visited Kilmarnock in the fall of 1851 while Peter and his brother William were living there. "We had a veriety of amusements such as songs speaches dialogues recitatives and refreshments which made the affair quite cheerful and lively to a late hour," wrote Harmon.[21] The McAuslan brothers must have enjoyed this fellowship.

The family increasingly thought about "gathering" to the Promised Land. In conferences and in the *Millennial Star*, the Saints were continually urged to flee and go to Zion "where we shall be enabled to learn how to subdue all evil powers . . . by the intelligence poured upon us from heaven."[22] Mackay's popular book included a romanticized engraving of Salt Lake City that probably fed the McAuslans' expectations. Some idea of how Peter viewed this Promised Land is reflected in the lines he penned from the Mormon hymn "O Ye Mountains High" in the back of his copy of the Book of Mormon: "O ye mountains high, / Where the clear blue sky, / Arches over the vales of the free."

In October 1852, Peter and his brother William moved back to Barrhead, probably because the strike was over and work once more available. By this time, calico printing was considerably past its peak, and a number of the largest printworks in Scotland had gone out of business, leaving only small, specialized firms. These aimed at the upper end of the market by increasing the novelty in color and design of their products. This high-end market segment was not so fiercely competitive and enabled the small printworks to continue for a few more years. But by 1860 almost all handblock printing had disappeared in the face of cylinder machines and changes in fashion. All through the 1850s the artisans from the formerly thriving printworks streamed out of Scotland to Lancashire, England, where work still existed. Those who remained in Scotland suffered not only unemployment but also a sharp loss of status for themselves and their families.[23]

The McAuslans did not head for Lancashire. Instead, the economic conditions increased their desire to gather to Utah and led them to make

---

[21] Harmon, Autobiography and Diary, 215.

[22] *Quarterly Report of the Edinburgh Conference . . . September 5, 1852*, 6.

[23] Record of Members, Kilmarnock Branch, 45; Turnbull, *History of the Calico Printing Industry*, 82, 93, 111, 116; Storey, *Thames and Hudson Manual*, 45; Slaven, *Development of the West of Scotland*, 107; and Treble, "Occupied Male Labour Force," 191.

"The Great Salt Lake City."
The romanticized engraving added to the
expectations of "Zion" held by many British converts.
From Charles Mackay, The Mormons: or Latter-day Saints, *235.*

serious plans to emigrate. Only Betsy would not go, for she was still working as a domestic servant in Kirkintilloch and was now engaged to William Cunningham, an active member of the Free Church who opposed Mormonism. Peter, his sister Agnes, and John Allan all hoped to go with the family, and on December 10, 1852, they paid a deposit and had their names entered in the register in Liverpool to sail on the ship *International*. But their names were crossed off in the books before the ship sailed at the end of February 1853. John Allan alluded to the reason in a letter sent to his father-in-law, Peter McAuslan, Sr., in Utah. The elder Peter had asked them to work and save for another year, probably because his own finances were stretched.[24] Peter perhaps was just as glad, for his relationship with Agnes McAuslin in Bridgeton was developing.

Depressed by the declining economy and longing to emigrate, the Saints in Great Britain were suddenly shaken by the announcement of polygamy in the January 1, 1853, *Millennial Star*. Although rumors had flown for years and polygamy had been practiced in secret in both Nauvoo and Utah by the church leaders, the converts in Europe thought such stories were lies promulgated by the clergy and anti-Mormons. T. B. H. Stenhouse, a Scottish convert just three weeks younger than Peter, later wrote that this revelation "fell like a thunderbolt upon the Saints, and fearfully shattered the mission." He added, "The British elders, who in their ignorance had been denying polygamy, and stigmatizing their opponents as calumniators, up to the very day of its publication, were confounded and paralyzed."[25]

The missionaries from America had consistently and vehemently denied polygamy, even when some of them, such as Parley P. Pratt, had more than one wife. Edward Martin, a thirty-four-year-old missionary and president of the Glasgow Conference, explained at a conference why Joseph Smith's revelation had not been shared when it was first given: "It was because it was not for the people in these lands; it was only for them in Zion, who had proved themselves before the Lord, and were counted worthy of these blessings." Later in the same talk, he reiterated that polygamy was not preached before to the world because "these things

[24] Register of the ship *International*; John Allan to Peter McAuslan, Sr., August 24, 1854 (#8 McAuslan Papers), 1.

[25] Stenhouse, *Rocky Mountain Saints*, 201.

are for the saints, and *only* for those of them who are *tried* and *proven*, and are pure in heart."[26]

The announcement in the *Star* of Joseph Smith's revelation regarding polygamy was carefully introduced by Samuel W. Richards, then president of the British Mission and editor of the *Star*. He began in the January 1 issue with a four-page address about the new year. "The full catalogue of mighty events that may transpire . . . before another circle of the seasons has rolled around, is not for us to describe," he wrote. Not until the fourth page did he enlarge: "Things which are now mysteries to them [the Saints] will bye and bye become perfectly plain, and in their turn be comprehended, whilst other mysteries remain to be solved and made plain."[27]

This enigmatic introduction was followed by Joseph Smith's revelation. In the first paragraph, God tells Joseph, "Prepare thy heart to receive and obey the instructions which I am about to give unto you, for all those who have this law revealed unto them, must obey the same; for behold! I reveal unto you a new and an everlasting covenant; and if ye abide not that covenant, then are ye damned." Smith's revelation likewise ran four pages. Not until the end of the second does God recount the promise he made to Abraham, that his seed would be "as innumerable as the stars." On the third page, God declares that the promise he gave to Abraham is for Joseph Smith also, that Abraham taking Hagar as a wife in addition to Sarah was not adultery because God had commanded it. The revelation said that the priesthood is included in this law, that if wives are given to them, they do not commit adultery, "for

---

[26] Polygamy had been denied in the *Millennial Star* several times; see Parley P. Pratt, "Editorial Remarks," 3 (August 1, 1842): 74; "Fragment of an Address, by P. P. Pratt," 6 (July 1, 1845): 22–23 (Pratt had five living wives at this time); and Thomas Smith (an English convert who had emigrated in 1841 and lived in Nauvoo, but then returned on a mission), "Who Is the Liar?" 12 (January 15, 1850) 29–30. *Report of the Glasgow Conference . . . 3d July, 1853*, 7–8 (emphasis in original). Edward Martin was born in Preston, Lancashire, England, in 1818. An early convert, he sailed on the ship *Sheffield* for the United States with Brigham Young, John Taylor, and other leaders in 1841. In Nauvoo he was a painter for the temple. In 1846 he joined the Mormon Battalion in the Mexican-American War, and in August 1847 he came to Utah from California over the Sierra Nevada. Not yet married, he was called on a mission to Great Britain in 1852. Sonne, *Ships, Saints, and Mariners*, 17; William Clayton's Journal, Journal History, December 31, 1844, 15; Levi W. Hancock/Jefferson Hunt/James Pace/Andrew Lytle Company, Mormon Pioneer Overland Travel; "Eighth General Epistle," *Millennial Star* 15 (February 19, 1853): 115.

[27] Samuel W. Richards, "Address on the Opening of the New Year," *Millennial Star* 15 (January 1, 1853): 1.

they are given unto him to multiply and replenish the earth, according to my commandment."[28]

One British convert wrote, "The minds of many of the Saints were filled with gloom; many honest-hearted, God-fearing souls were crushed, their hopes were blasted, and many withdrew in despair." Likewise distressed, the McAuslans must have trusted that in Zion, where God's intelligence would pour down upon them, they would come to understand. From what they had learned, it was only for the leaders in Utah and for the select few who were counted worthy. Peter later wrote that he believed that once he got to Utah, he "would have the pleasure of seeing and hearing a Prophet, Seer, and Revelator of the Lord"; surely such a prophet would make all things clear.[29]

Peter's parents had set their faces toward Zion. They had saved for years and had already sent in the £100 for the family to emigrate the next month.[30] Thus, with new determination and only shadowy misgivings, the elder Peter and Betsy finished disposing of the household effects they could not take with them. With their children they traveled by train from Barrhead to Glasgow and there boarded a steamer on February 19, 1853, for the overnight trip to Liverpool, from where their ship would sail. There were ten of them: the elder Peter and Mother Betsy, both aged fifty-two; Jane, twenty-four; William, twenty; Ann, eighteen; Frank, sixteen; Christina, fourteen; Janet, twelve; David, ten; and William's fiancée from Kilmarnock, Mary Muir, seventeen. The three siblings not going—Peter, Agnes with John Allan, and Betsy in Kirkintilloch—would have gone to see them off at Broomielaw Dock in Glasgow, as five years earlier they had bid farewell to their grandmother and uncles. Peter and the Allans must have wondered how long it would be before they would be reunited. But for Betsy it was the final, poignant break with her family. She could entertain little hope of seeing them again.

---

[28] "Revelation, Given to Joseph Smith, Nauvoo, July 12, 1843," *Millennial Star* 15 (January 1, 1853): 5–8. God's covenant with Abraham is from Genesis 15. This revelation is now Doctrine and Covenants (D&C) 132.

[29] Derry, *Autobiography*, 11; Peter McAuslan to Robert Salmon, December 1860 (#14 McAuslan Papers), 1.

[30] The McAuslans were part of the £10 company, a plan that brought an emigrant from Liverpool to Utah for £10. See Aird, "Bound for Zion," 300–25.

6

Farewell to Scotland

ON FEBRUARY 19, 1853, ABOUT ONE HUNDRED ADULTS WITH THEIR children left Glasgow, Peter's parents and siblings among them. "When at 8 oclock evening, the boat began to clear the key [quay], the brethrine all in good spirits & rejoicing in the privledge of going to a Land blist by god as a refuge in the day of judgement, yet there joy was mingled with sorrow in Leaving the Land that gave them birth, as also there frinds, & Parents that they loved," wrote Andrew Ferguson, a Scottish coal miner. He had come to see friends off who were leaving on the steam packet for Liverpool, where they would board the sailing ship *International* for New Orleans.[1]

Ferguson described the mood of those left behind: "The hart of the saint is to obey this grate command of god (gather) so off they went Leaving meny of the saints on shore who had thronged to take the party [parting] hand, with glad harts, yet sorrow that they were not so highly Privledged but antisapating the day will soon come wh[en] such will be there position." Peter, his sister Agnes, and John Allan in bidding the family good-bye must have shared these mixed feelings and hoped they would all be reunited within a year or two at the most.[2]

Peter and his sweetheart, Agnes McAuslin, continued to live in their separate homes, she in Bridgeton in Glasgow and he six miles away in Barrhead near Paisley. With trains running frequently between the two, Peter must have regularly visited her during the rest of 1853. One can imagine them talking about the urgency of emigrating and how they wished

---

[1] Ferguson, Diaries and Autobiography, 57–58.
[2] Ibid., 58.

Broomielaw Quay, Glasgow, circa 1853.
Moored next to the ticket office are the river and coastal steam packets.
In the background, on the south side of the Clyde, are oceangoing sailing ships.
Courtesy of Culture and Sport Glasgow (Museums).

to marry and go to Zion together the next year. In the meantime they worked at their individual jobs, putting aside as much money as possible.

The deposit Peter had made to go on the ship *International* with his family had been transferred to his account for the 1854 emigration. Edward Martin, the president of the Glasgow Conference, wrote that on January 30, 1854, he went to Barrhead to "transact business" with Peter and his brother-in-law John Allan. This business most likely concerned John and Agnes Allan's withdrawal from that year's emigration so they could work and save for another year, and the transfer of their deposit to a future sailing. Two weeks later on February 16, 17, and 18, Martin sent notices giving the time of the emigrants' departure. Peter, Agnes McAuslin, and her brother John McAuslin, a stone mason who was to travel with them, received the notices that they were to sail on the ship *John M. Wood* in about ten days. The letters ordered them to be in Liverpool by February 25. A Scot who emigrated later expressed the excitement Peter and Agnes must have felt: "The letter came . . . telling us passages for all our family had been secured . . . & [to] come to Liverpool inside of 3 days. . . . [It] caused great rejoiceing. Brother Sam ran around the house shouting Boys that is the best letter ever came to our house[!]"[3]

On February 24, Peter said good-bye to his sister Agnes and John Allan in Barrhead and, with a sense of obeying God's command, climbed aboard the evening train for Glasgow. He spent the night in Cowcaddens in north-central Glasgow with his sister and brother-in-law Betsy and William Cunningham. The next morning, he bade them a final farewell and went the mile and a half to Broomielaw Quay, where he found his fiancée, Agnes, and her nineteen-year-old brother John McAuslin; and no doubt their family was present to see them off. Here they met Robert Campbell, the pastor of the Scottish conferences.[4] He was a thirty-one-year-old Scot who had converted to Mormonism in 1842 and emigrated to the United States and Nauvoo in 1845, only to flee with the Saints to Winter Quarters the next year. He had traveled overland to Salt Lake City in 1848 in the same company as Peter's Adamson grandmother and uncles. In 1850 Campbell had been called on a mission to Scotland and was now returning with plans to go straight through to Salt Lake City.

Campbell was leading a group of at least forty-nine Saints from Glasgow. Edward Martin came to the Broomielaw Quay to see them off on the steam packet *Commodore* for the twenty-two-hour trip to Liverpool. Peter wrote that they made their "fairwell" at 11:00 A.M. The morning was fine, but with a rather "keen" wind blowing from the north.[5] Emotion

---

[3] The deposit transfer is noted after the names of John and Agnes Allan on the register of the ship *John M. Wood*. Martin, Journal, February 16–18, 1854; Lindsay, Autobiography, 272.

[4] McAuslan, trip notebook (#5 McAuslan Papers), 1. Measuring four by six inches, the notebook consists of eleven pages; the ink is faded and partly illegible. Pages have been cut out; they were most likely notes that Peter sent to Agnes and John Allan, giving advice for their trip.

[5] "Emigrated to Zion on the 25th Day of Feby. 1854," Record of Members, Glasgow Branch, 269. Not on that list but also accompanying Campbell were members from other branches; among these were Peter McAuslan, Peter Sinclair, and Thomas Todd, his wife, and their two sons. Sinclair, Journal, February 25, 1854; Todd, Autobiography, 4. Martin, Journal, February 25, 1854. The hours for the trip are given by Richardson, Diaries, 18. Questions of authenticity have arisen about Peter Sinclair's journal of 1856–62, which was acquired in 1981 by the LDS Church Archives from Mark Hofmann, a criminal forger and counterfeiter. There are no concerns about the earlier 1853–54 journal used here, which was loaned by a Sinclair relative to the Family History Library in Salt Lake City. The library filmed it in 1950 and gave a copy to the LDS Church Archives. The original 1853–54 diary was returned to the family.

must have filled their hearts as the steamer pulled away from the quay and they strained to see the last of their waving relatives and friends. Agnes especially must have had conflicting feelings of joy at the thought of getting married and going to Zion and sadness at leaving her family. Her brother John was traveling with them, and Elizabeth would come to Utah two years later, but she would never see the others again.

When the steamer reached Greenock where the River Clyde opens into the Firth of Clyde, they were greeted once more by Edward Martin. He had come by train to escort some Saints who had missed the boat in Glasgow. Peter wrote that they enjoyed the trip down the river and into the Firth until they reached more open water near Ailsa Craig, a rocky island ten miles off the southern Scottish coast near Girvan. There Peter and Agnes began to feel seasick. They walked the deck to keep it at bay.[6]

Peter described staying on deck all night: "About as beautiful a night as we could expec[t] at this season of the year, the sky being clear and the stars shining most splendidly." What were Peter's thoughts as the starlight gave him his last glimpse of the hills of southeastern Scotland from the deck of the steamer taking them away forever? Perhaps he had none, for his notes are filled only with practicalities and advice for his sister Agnes and John Allan who were planning to come the next year— for example, "It is best to keep your chests all in one place." Nevertheless, one can reasonably speculate that despite all the hardships, he felt nostalgia at leaving the land of his birth, while at the same time he gloried in the prospect of a new life with his bride and birth family in God's holy Zion. There, he hoped, they would find people of "one heart and one mind," and they would walk in God's paths.[7]

As the cold night wore on, however, Peter stopped thinking of anything but the present: "I never wearied as much for the [gentle?] rays of the mourning sun as I did that night. Sickness was very common throughout the steamboat during the night, the passengers [tucked?] themselves away into the warmest places they could find, rolling themselves up in plaids, bed covers, &c." Morning finally came with its renewed warmth. Peter continued, "Then we got our faces washed and we looked as [well?] as we could. We were happy to come in sight of land and have a bite of bread and [cup?] of coffy which we bought of the steward of the steamboat."[8]

---

[6] Martin, Journal, February 25, 1854; McAuslan, trip notes (#5 McAuslan Papers), 1–2.

[7] McAuslan, trip notes (#5 McAuslan Papers), 2, 4, 11; 2 Nephi 1:21.

[8] McAuslan, trip notes (#5 McAuslan Papers), 2–3.

The *Commodore* steamed into Liverpool's Clarence Dock, reserved for the steam packets because they were a fire hazard to the wooden sailing ships. Once the boat moored, an officer came on board to search for liquor. Peter wrote,

> Some refused to have there boxes searched but had to submit. Those who had it got it taken from them & I was anxious to have ours down that we might have them roped up again, and when he saw our willingness to assist him, after he had lightly searched one of ours, he passed the other chests by mearly asking if we had any spirits in them. We had not a drop & [illegible] but invited him to search them. This was sufficient; he did not. I understand that you can take one bottle with a glass full out of it for private use, but not more.[9]

Edward Martin was waiting on the dock to greet them. He had come to Liverpool by the faster and more expensive train after seeing the Saints off in Scotland. He helped them pile the boxes and chests on the dock and set up a rotating guard over them. Peter and John McAuslin had the first watch. By the time they were relieved, they were tired and hungry and so went to a nearby eating house, where they had "a good supper." Martin, having arrived in Liverpool hours before the steam packet, had arranged for lodgings for the group. One of their Glasgow companions gave Peter and John the address of a lodging house, but it was full. The landlord took them to another where there were two beds in a room, with three to a bed. The women were similarly lodged. The cost for two to a bed was sixpence each; for three to a bed, fivepence. As Liverpool was notorious for thieves, guards attended each lodging house and made extra money by brushing shoes and boots. Some lodging houses had dining rooms, but where Peter, Agnes, and John stayed, they were permitted to use the kitchen to cook their own meals, saving them some expense. They stayed there two nights.[10]

Those sailing on the *John M. Wood* whose diaries have survived mentioned going to Bramley-Moore Dock to see the square-rigger a day or so before being allowed to move on board. It was a three-masted, two-deck sailing ship with a square stern and had been built the year before in Maine. Frederick Andrew, a convert from Stockport, forty miles from

---

[9] Ibid., 3–4.

[10] The train from Glasgow to Liverpool took ten hours, and the steam packet, twenty-two hours. Martin, Journal, February 25, 1854; McAuslan, trip notes (#5 McAuslan Papers), 3–6.

Liverpool, wrote, "I found it one of the finest vessels that I had seen. It is about 60 or 70 yards long and about 48 feet broad and 7 feet 8 inches between decks in the steerage."[11]

As the major emigrant port for Great Britain, Liverpool was notorious for its dangers to the naive. Even former mayor of Liverpool and chairman of the docks John Bramley-Moore, for whom the dock where the *John M. Wood* lay was named, warned, "The frauds and impositions now practiced on the emigrant, from the moment he arrives in Liverpool to the time of his embarkation, are perfectly incredible. . . . There is scarcely an emigrant who arrives who is not plundered of his money— plundered at every stage and every step."[12] But the Mormon organization served its members well, for the British Mission office chartered entire ships, directed the emigrants to honest boardinghouses, and made the arrangements for tickets and for getting passengers onto the ship as quickly as possible to save the expense of lodging houses.

Peter wrote that the party's chests and boxes were taken in a large wagon from the Clarence Dock, where the steam packet had moored, to the Bramley-Moore Dock, about four docks to the north. Peter then described what followed: "A very efficient watch was organized and has been kept up ever since. All the time we lay in dock there was nesity [necessity] for a deck watch being kept up as our chests were all lying between decks, and [the ship was] taking in cargo all the time we lay in dock. Without a watch there had been every opportunity for our chests being plundered."[13]

Liverpool was somewhat bigger than Glasgow but lacked the latter's stone buildings. "Liverpool is a town extreme in its comercial relations with other nations and of course the trafic in the streets along the docks with wagons and horses is very great," Peter observed. "The horses here are strong, large and beautifull to luke [look] upon. Some of the streets are built of very good buildings but buildings in general are built of brick. There are a great many store houses."[14]

On Tuesday, February 28, before their luggage was taken to the ship, Peter said they received their final instructions and counsel from Edward

---

[11] Sonne, *Ships, Saints, and Mariners*, 121–22; Andrew, Diary, February 24, 1854.

[12] John Bramley-Moore to the Select Committee Inquiring into the Operation of the Passenger Acts, House of Commons, 1851, vol. 19, and reprinted as "Caution to Emigrants," *Millennial Star* 15 (April 2, 1853): 222.

[13] McAuslan, trip notes (#5 McAuslan Papers), 6.

[14] Ibid., 10–11.

Edward Martin, president of the Glasgow Conference, who married Peter and Agnes. Photograph taken in 1855. *Courtesy of the Church Archives, the Church of Jesus Christ of Latter-day Saints.*

Martin. The emigrants were allowed to board the *John M. Wood* that day even though the ship was not ready to sail. They had expected to depart that evening or the next day, but instead were delayed for several days. On March 1, Peter and Agnes went ashore and were married in the British Mission office by Edward Martin. Peter was thirty years old, and Agnes twenty-four. Their decision may have been influenced by the sleeping arrangements on board. Married couples and their young children slept in the more stable midsection of the ship, with single men and single women at either end. Perhaps the couple were able to get a better bunk by marrying prior to departure than they could hope for if they had married midway on the ocean.[15] Once more it is surprising that Peter recorded no more than the barest facts of their marriage. As in the case of not describing his feelings upon leaving Scotland, the explanation is most likely that his notes were intended for his sister Agnes and John Allan. They would have known about his wedding plans before he left, so perhaps all that was needed was confirmation that it had taken place.

---

[15] Ibid., 7, 10. Martin's journal does not mention marrying them.

Marriage certificate of Peter McAuslan and Agnes McAuslin.
Courtesy of Donna Miller Forguson, Live Oak, California.

The shipping companies were to supply their ships with food for the voyage according to a series of Passenger Acts, but the laws were seldom enforced. The amount of food was to cover seventy days and included bread or biscuit, flour, oatmeal, rice, sugar, tea, salt, and water. The LDS British Mission office added pork, molasses, butter, cheese, and vinegar. Emigrants, however, were advised to buy more flour and sugar and other items such as potatoes, ham, dried salt fish, onions, pickled onions, preserves, cayenne pepper, baking powder, mustard, baking soda, lime juice, plums, and currants. Peter, Agnes, and John bought more than fifty pounds of potatoes as well as onions, turnips, and oatmeal. The potatoes and onions kept well the whole voyage, and the turnips for three or four weeks. "They have been of great service to us," Peter noted.[16]

The allotment of provisions for the first week was handed out on March 1, the day they expected to sail. Peter was not impressed: "[The] biskets

---

[16] Coleman, *Going to America,* 287–94; S. W. Richards, "Emigration," *Millennial Star* 14 (November 27, 1852): 633; Piercy, *Route from Liverpool,* 55–56; McAuslan, trip notes (#5 McAuslan Papers), 11.

are of that corse hard quality which is common at sea [i.e., hardtack]. Oatmeal is not to be compared with the meal . . . considered good in Scotland. There are a great many seeds in it." Although round, the oats did not swell with boiling and had an unpleasant taste. Peter, Agnes, and John made porridge with oats they had bought and oatcakes with the ship's meal. "We can eat the cakes made of it very well because we are oblidged to do it or else we would have to fast some times," Peter wrote. If those oats were typical, he thought it no surprise that the English preferred flour. "I could very well be an Englishman myself!" he exclaimed.[17]

Without making a distinction between what the ship supplied and what the mission office added, Peter continued, "The flour is good of the 2nd quality, the rice is of the cheapest kind. Pork is of the coursest quality but does very well in the absence of better." He then gave a recipe for making the salt pork palatable: "Steeped all night and washed well in salt water, then boiled in salt water and washed in fresh, then roasted in the oven. It does not bad for Makey [Mackay?] rice soup along with two or three potatoes and onions."[18]

His complaints about the food continued: "The suger is of the very worst quality that my eyes ever beheld or my tonge ever tasted. The darkest coloured I ever saw and full of sand. The tea is bad yet we take it that the bad taste of the water might be destroyed." The butter was tolerable, as was the cheese, though "some of it might do well enough to feed the pigs with." He went on: "Molasses I do not think that I ever got worse. It is what we call treacle. It is unpleasant to the smell as well as the taste being sourish. The vinegar is also bad, but has to do for the want of better. It was brown coloured and bad to have, is also weake, the clear kind is far the best." In addition, Peter felt cheated on the allotment: "The flour is measured. I have seen it weighed. Four persons ought to receive 4 lbs., but only receive 3¼ lbs. Whos fault this is I do not know. We feel the want of this more then anything else. We take no flour with us, but if I was coming again I would take flour above everything else."[19]

Peter's assessment of the food's quality and amount was echoed in testimonies given to Parliament. In May 1854, two months after the *John*

---

[17] Ibid., 7–10.
[18] Ibid., 8.
[19] Ibid., 8–10. Shortchanging provisions happened on other ships; see Coleman, *Going to America*, 104.

M. Wood sailed, the House of Commons organized a Select Committee on Emigrant Ships to look into whether the Passenger Acts needed improvement. A Dr. William O'Doherty had made nine or ten transatlantic voyages; when asked if the food stipulated by the Passenger Acts was adequate, he responded, "I do not think it is; I know it is not what you would give your servants." He had never seen potatoes given out, and the biscuits were not fit to eat. William Philipps, a London shipowner and ship broker whose vessels took fifteen thousand emigrants to America each year, testified that the diet "is sufficient to stave off starvation, but it is not enough to live upon." A third said that the "sensible" emigrant brought extra rations with him. In a similar inquiry in 1851, one passenger said he had seen another at the rail watching oatmeal float away that he had thrown overboard because it was so bad.[20]

The ship was carrying cargo to New Orleans, and the loading went on for twelve days, causing a postponement in sailing. Although ships were often delayed in getting under way, it was usually because of poor weather. In this case, the delay was most likely caused by the interruption of shipping related to the Crimean War. Just a few days before Peter and Agnes arrived in Liverpool, the first British troops had sailed for Turkey. Ships were being requisitioned for the war, and the remaining commercial vessels were left to carry more than the normal amount of cargo.

The loading continued at night, as Peter described after they moved on board: "Lights had to be all out by 9 oclock P.M. between decks. Some nights however they were all night taken in cargo and dureing all the time they were doing so they continued to curse and swear at a most fearfull extent, swearing by Jesus Christ, by God Allmighty, by the Holy Ghost, and by every name that the wicked hearts could devize. This continued all the time that our cargo was being taken in." Another emigrant on the *John M. Wood* wrote of "men working night and day, loading her with railway slips [rails] and other things." On March 7 the ship pulled out, but to the passengers' disappointment, it moved only to another part of the dock because the tide was too low. More cargo was taken on. On March 9, the ship nearly left again, but an inspection revealed the lack of a "hospital," probably a simple sick bay. Finally, on March 10, after

---

[20] Coleman, *Going to America*, 113–14.

the emigrants passed a perfunctory health inspection, the ship was cleared for sailing. But once again it was delayed to take on more cargo.[21]

In a special supplement the *Illustrated London News* chronicled the emigration from Liverpool for America. Describing the anticipation onboard, the reporter wrote, "The scenes that occur between decks on the day before the sailing of a packet, and during the time that a ship may be unavoidably detained in dock, are not generally of a character to impress the spectator with the idea of any great or overwhelming grief on the part of the emigrants at leaving the old country. On the contrary, all is bustle, excitement, and merriment."[22]

The waiting and false starts finally came to an end on March 12. Peter wrote, "We should sail out of port on Sabbeth the 12th of March about 10 o'clock A.M. It was as splendedd a day as we could desire. We injoyed the sail down the mersys [Mersey River] very much." It took the steam tugboat a couple of hours to tow the ship from the dock, down the few miles of the Mersey River, and into the Irish Sea, where it left them.[23] The sails—the wings that would carry the passengers to the Promised Land—were set. The emigrants were on their way!

---

[21] McAuslan, trip notes (#5 McAuslan Papers), 6; Andrew, Diary, March 3–7, 1854; MacMaster, Diaries, 333–34; S. W. Richards, Journals, March 9–10, 1854; S. W. Richards, "Emigration Report," *Millennial Star* 16 (May 13, 1854): 297.

[22] *Illustrated London News*, June 6, 1850, 21.

[23] McAuslan, trip notes (#5 McAuslan Papers), 11; MacMaster, Diaries, 334.

Emigrant ship leaving Liverpool, with the Perch Rock Fort and
Lighthouse at the mouth of the Mersey River in the background.
From Frederick Piercy, *Route from Liverpool to Great Salt Lake Valley.*
Courtesy of the Church Archives, the Church of Jesus Christ of Latter-day Saints.

7

Sails Set for New Orleans

THE PASSENGERS' JOY UPON THEIR DEPARTURE WAS SHORT-LIVED. The wind died, the sails fell slack, and they were not underway. Getting to Zion was not going to be so easy. At four that afternoon, no breeze stirred. The emigrants continued to lash their boxes and everything else that was loose, to be ready for the wind their leaders assured them would come. As if in confirmation, the wind began to rise before nightfall, and by midnight it had become so strong that the captain had to reef sails and tack about. By that time he had ordered all passengers below deck and the hatches closed. Water tins not fastened down "went rattling to the tempest tune," and men, women, and children alike, along with pots and pans and bags of potatoes, were "knocked about as [if] they were drunk." Peter wrote, "Agnes and me began to be sick. We both went to bed, and as night came on, it began to be . . . stormey and continued also all night."[1]

The wild seas prompted the captain, Richard R. C. Hartley, an experienced master, to signal for a pilot. The pilot arrived and stayed with the ship for the next five days as it was tossed north by the Isle of Man, then back within sight of Liverpool, then south near the coast of Wales, and then north again toward Liverpool. Every diary or reminiscence described the misery of the emigrants confined below decks without fresh air or light. Thomas Todd wrote, "Hell for four days." John Sutton remembered, "No tongue could describe the scene between those decks. . . . Such an experience I shall never forget while on earth." Only one emigrant,

---

[1] MacMaster, Diaries, 334; Sutton, Autobiography, 4; McAuslan, trip notes (#5 McAuslan Papers), 11. The quotations before the last sentence are from MacMaster. McAuslan's trip notes end abruptly the next day.

Thomas Poulter, who had been a steward in the Royal Navy, said he was not bothered by the pitching ship. "Sea sickness in all its horrid forms came over the Saints," he wrote. "I at this time made myself very useful."[2]

On the fifth day, March 16, the storm began to abate, and the ship came in sight of Ireland. When it neared Cork, a boat came to take the ship's pilot ashore. But shortly afterward a headwind rose, making most of the passengers sick again. Finally, when the ship cleared the Irish coast, it found a fair wind. The captain had the forward studding sails (or stuns'ls)—extra sails rigged at the side of the square sails—raised to increase the ship's speed, but "squally winds" broke the yard of one. The next day a replacement was put up, but its boom soon broke.[3]

The company of Saints on the *John M. Wood* had been organized by the British Mission president, Samuel Richards, before they left Liverpool, but during the days of the storm, structure and discipline collapsed. Once the majority found their sea legs, order was reestablished. Richards had appointed Robert L. Campbell, pastor of the Scottish conferences with whom Peter, Agnes, and John had traveled from Glasgow, as president of the ship's company. Alexander F. MacDonald, another Scot, and Jabez Woodard, an Englishman who had been a missionary in Italy, were made his counselors.[4]

Fifty-nine of the 393 passengers on board were Swiss and Italians; the rest were evenly divided between English and Scots. Before seeing them off, Richards had also divided the ship's company into ten wards, or branches, each having approximately forty people, and appointed a president over each. In spite of the equal breakdown of nationality between the Scots and the English, six of the branch presidents were Scots, three were English, and one was Swiss. Among these, Peter McAuslan was appointed president of the third branch. The leaders were charged with seeing that order and cleanliness were enforced within their wards and with holding prayer meetings at 5:30 in the morning and 8:00 at night. Each ward was assigned specific times to use the galley, thus staggering the meals.[5]

[2] Sonne, *Ships, Saints, and Mariners*, 122; MacMaster, Diaries, 334–35; Rampton, Diary, 31–2; Andrew, Diary, March 14, 1854; Todd, Autobiography, 4; Sutton, Autobiography, 4; Poulter, "Life," 44:137.

[3] MacMaster, Diaries, 225, 336; Andrew, Diary, March 17–19, 1854.

[4] S. W. Richards, Journals, March 5, 1854.

[5] The terms "ward" and "branch" were interchangeable on the ship, although they refer to different LDS organizations today. Register of the ship *John M. Wood*; Sinclair, Journal, March 4, 1854.

In good weather the passengers lived up on deck and life was pleasant, but when the weather was poor and they were forced to stay below, patience was tested by their confined quarters. To create some sense of privacy and a place to dress, the emigrants strung up material as curtains around their berths. The berths, one above the other, were each six feet long and three feet wide to accommodate two people. With nails and cord, the emigrants lashed to the walls and bunks their tins for water (dispensed daily), boxes containing provisions (issued on Thursdays), cooking and eating utensils, and clothes.[6]

Days were spent preparing meals, washing up, airing bedding on deck on good days (it was impossible to wash it), and staying out of the way of the ship's crew as they raised or reefed sails, repaired frayed ropes, and performed the myriad tasks of sailing a ship. Some of the adults set up a school for the children, lessons in English for the Swiss and Italian Saints, and classes in French or Italian for interested English speakers. The Liverpool Mission office had delivered good-quality canvas to the ship to be made into wagon covers and tents for the overland journey. The cutting and sewing were divided among the wards. On Sundays, Campbell and the branch presidents held church services and meetings and, in the evening, a sacrament (communion) meeting in each branch. Thomas Poulter, the former navy steward, found life on the Mormon-run ship significantly better than on other ships on which he had sailed: "I might say it was a heaven afloat. The fear of God was in our midst. We were happy for the spirit of love and peace was in our midst."[7]

On March 19, when the ship cleared the Irish coast, the temperature was still very cold. Three days later a bright sun warmed the air, and the passengers came up on deck to sing and play music. Captain Hartley once more ordered the stuns'ls raised, and the ship skimmed forward. But joy quickly disappeared for Thomas Todd of Kilmarnock, Scotland, and his wife Margaret when their fifteen-month-old son died of whooping cough. This was the first death on the ship, and at noon on March 23 his small body was sewn in canvas and committed to the sea. Three days later a little girl died of "inflammation of the lungs." The week

---

[6] Mackay, *Mormons*, 253; Piercy, *Route from Liverpool*, 55–57; Sinclair, Journal, March 30, 1854.

[7] Piercy, *Route from Liverpool*, 50–51; MacMaster, Diaries, 337, 338; Sinclair, Journal, March 24, 1854; Poulter, "Life," 137.

before she had seemed fine.[8] Peter noted that "our Captain has kept the most northeruly [*sic*] route for the sake of the health of the passengers." As the wind came up in the late afternoon on March 25, the company caught sight of the island of Barra in the Outer Hebrides, the last land they would see until they reached the Bahamas.[9]

A few days turned sunny enough for the passengers to sew tents and wagon covers on deck, but on March 30, hurricane-like winds arose and many were seasick once more. William MacMaster, a Scot and branch president, wrote, "In the evening they [the crew] were afraid of the main yard coming down. It blew so hard and about 11 oclock at night it rained very heavy and the wind changed and in the puting [*sic*] about of the shipe, she shipped some heavy seas and the rain and sea came down the main hatch . . . so that many were afraid and I rose and put on my cloth[e]s."[10]

On April 2 a third child died. The first adult died a day later, a woman who had been ill for some time with consumption (i.e., tuberculosis).[11] In spite of these deaths, several diarists remarked on the beauty of the sea. Frederick Andrew wrote,

> It is awfully grand tonight to watch the sun go down in the West and cast its golden rays between the clouds and to see the mighty waters all in motion and sometimes rise up like a mountain and cast up its spray so that it falls again like showers of rain. Also the clouds hang in the air with various shades and the moon about 2 or 3 days old above our heads shines bright and the stars all around us glitter like silvery dots in the firmament so that the scenery altogether is beautiful.[12]

The more succinct MacMaster wrote, "It is beautiful to look on the wonders of the Mighty God on the great deep."[13]

By now the company, with their diverse backgrounds, had become a Mormon village. Besides obeying the counsel of their leaders, they were learning communal living and denying self in the interests of the collective good. And they shared joy. The twenty-fourth anniversary of the

---

[8] The father of the little girl, Henry Stoffell from Manchester, England, was a deserter from the army; quite possibly he preferred going to America over the Crimea. MacMaster, Diaries, 336; Andrew, Diary, March 22 and 27, 1854; Todd, Autobiography, 4–5; "Arrival of the 'John M. Wood,'" *Millennial Star* 16 (June 10, 1854): 366.

[9] McAuslan, Trip notebook, 10; Andrew, Diary, March 24–27, 1854; MacMaster, Diaries, 337–38.

[10] MacMaster, Diaries, 338–39.

[11] "Arrival of the 'John M. Wood,'" 366; MacMaster, Diaries, 339; Andrew, Diary, April 2–3, 1854.

[12] Andrew, Diary, April 2–3, 1854.

[13] MacMaster, Diaries, 339.

"Mormon hymn-singing on board of emigrant ship."
From Charles Mackay, *The Mormons: or Latter-day Saints*, 253.

founding of the church was celebrated on April 6 with fasting, prayer, and addresses by Robert Campbell and the branch presidents. "We had a good time of it," wrote MacMaster. This day was also the first hot one they had experienced. The ship was at a standstill, with "not a breath to move the water, and it was as smooth as glass," according to Andrew. Finally around midnight the wind came up again and caught the sails.[14]

Two days later, a baby boy died from "water on the head [brain]," or hydrocephalus. Thus, less than a month into the voyage, four young children had died. Such numbers were not unusual and, except for the case of hydrocephalus, were probably related to the children's not having yet developed immunity to infections and diseases.[15]

---

[14] May, "Rites of Passage," 39–40; MacMaster, Diaries, 340; Andrew, Diary, April 6, 1854.
[15] "Arrival of the 'John M. Wood,'" 366–67.

When rain showers came, the emigrants rushed on deck to catch the rain in buckets and tins. This water not only supplemented their daily rations but also gave them something with which to wash. As the ship sailed south and the temperature rose, especially between decks, people suffered from heat rashes. Water for bathing was increasingly treasured. On some evenings a hose was fitted up as a saltwater shower for bathing on deck. Peter Sinclair described the process: "Sisters first, a tent rig[g]ed at the baithhouse [*sic*] door for undressing & dressing."[16]

As the heat increased, those who were sick were brought up on deck, where the air was cooler and fresh. One evening, Jabez Woodard gave a lecture on his missionary travels in Italy and Malta, and on another, Alexander MacDonald spoke of his travels in the Highlands of Scotland. April 12 was hot and windless, but nevertheless MacMaster's ward met and shared a good spirit, some even speaking in tongues while others interpreted. On that day an English couple were married, the first wedding onboard.[17]

The days in general continued monotonously, with the emigrants looking at the same broad expanse of water and sky and the same spars, tackle, and sails, with only the height of the waves or formations of clouds to add variety. The tedium continued as they neared the western Atlantic. The wind died, the ship was becalmed for several days, and the sun reflected hotly off the smooth sea. But on the second day of this weather, the cry of "Fire!" came from the galley. Emigrants harbored a great dread of fire, especially because of the well-known burning of the ship *Ocean Monarch* five years before, when only half the company had been rescued by nearby ships.[18]

The fire on the *John M. Wood* was started by the hot stovepipe in the galley, which extended through the dried-out timbers of the cookhouse roof. As it was noon and most were on deck eating their dinners, people dropped their tin plates and rushed to fill buckets with seawater to douse the flames. The second mate came with a hose and soon put out the fire. Sinclair wrote, "We lost our dinner as [did] many more for the wattar was sent in the galley . . . carrying all before it." The excitement was soon over and a "quiet gratitude went up from many hearts," wrote one emigrant.[19]

---

[16] MacMaster, Diaries, 340–41; Andrew, Diary, April 8, 10–12, 1854; Sinclair, Journal, April 15, 1854.

[17] MacMaster, Diaries, 341, 344; "Arrival of the 'John M. Wood,'" 367.

[18] Andrew, Diary, April 13, 1854; Naisbitt, "Recollections," 230. The *Ocean Monarch*, built in the United States in 1847, burned in August 1848. Articles about the tragedy were widely published, including in the *Millennial Star* (September 1, 1848) even though no passengers were Mormons.

[19] Sinclair, Journal, April 13, 1854; Naisbitt, "Recollections," 230.

On April 19, Hannah Poulter, the wife of the former navy steward, gave birth to twins, a boy and a girl. Her husband wrote, "As good luck would have it the hospital was empty. . . . My prayer was answered in the mid-wife. A fine broad Scotch woman came and offered her services showing me papers that she had served in the hospitals. At six o'clock in the morning we were all on our knees when Hannah was confined with twins." The midwife, Isabella Barr, and her two sons had come from Glasgow in the same group as Peter and Agnes.[20]

Other ships had been in evidence for several days, but now, suddenly, the passengers aboard the *John M. Wood* saw their first indication of land. In the evening on April 19 they could see the lighthouse on the southern end of the island of Great Abaco in the Bahamas. During the night the ship sailed into Providence Channel through the center of the Bahaman chain. The next day they saw eight ships and in the evening passed Little Isaac Island. Sailing south in the Straits of Florida they spotted the lighthouse on Gun Cay, south of Bimini. Frederick Andrew noted, "The route being strange to the captain and mates, I understand we was near running ashore. They tried the depth of the water and found we had only 8½ yards deep."[21]

Thomas Poulter said the joy was so great at the safe delivery of the twins and the health of his wife that some of their branch decided to hold a grand tea to celebrate. Poulter invited the captain and mates: "The first mate proposed the toasts. The boy to be called John Montgomery Wood Poulter and the girl to be christened Hanna Montgomery Wood Poulter." The children were thus named in honor of the ship.[22]

Poulter continued his description of the merriment: "The band played for we had a fine band dressed in green and gold trimmings. This was the first and last of the band." Frederick Andrew also described the occasion: "The 4th and 5th branches has got up a tea party today and . . . had a first rate do of it. One of the best they ever attended. They had pies and pudding, bakes and tarts of various sorts, boiled and roasted pork, tea and butter cakes, ham and other varieties and after the feast they

---

[20] Poulter, "Life," 137.

[21] Andrew, Diary, April 19–21; Sinclair, Journal, April 19–20, 1854; MacMaster, Diaries, 343. The transcription of Andrew's diary calls the Little Isaac rocks the "little Gaac" rocks. MacMaster called the Gun Cay lighthouse the "Gunlock" lighthouse.

[22] John M. Wood had been a state representative in Maine, where the ship was built. The children were actually blessed, a ceremony conducted by priesthood holders in a sacrament meeting to name and bless newborns. Poulter, "Life," 137; Sinclair, Journal, April 21, 1854.

enjoyed themselves with songs reciting &c." The etcetera included a skit about Joseph Smith and the Devil. This must have been based on Parley P. Pratt's witty short story, "A Dialogue between Joseph Smith and the Devil," in which Satan discusses with Smith how Mormonism is disrupting Christianity and thereby interfering with his power on earth. The tea included about eighty people—two wards or branches—the maximum number who could be seated at one time. Peter and Agnes were among the celebrants, as Sinclair wrote that the presidents and their wives from the third, fourth, and fifth branches were included.[23]

That night the passengers saw two lights quite close together to the south, which were probably lighthouses on Cuba. The next day, they saw land again too, also probably Cuba. The day after the great tea party, the Saints held their usual Sunday meeting on deck. "Our presidents gave us some very good council pertaining to going into New Orleans and how we should conduct ourselves when we go on shore for our own safety," noted Andrew. That evening when the fourth and fifth branches held a sacrament meeting, two men spoke in tongues, one an "Indian tongue," according to Sinclair.[24]

The sights multiplied: the islands of the Dry Tortugas, seventy miles west of the Florida Keys; schools of porpoises playing alongside the ship; flying fish landing on the deck; and birds alighting in the rigging. On April 27 brown streaks appeared in the water, indicating silt from the Mississippi River. Weeds and logs floated by, even though no land could be seen. These signs prompted conversations about "Columbus and his sailors seeing something of the same kind when they come near to the land."[25]

The captain hoisted a flag requesting a pilot, and one soon arrived to guide the ship to the sandbar at the mouth of the river. Formed by sediments carried down the Mississippi River that are deposited as it meets the Gulf, the bar is complex, with shallow seas and currents that shift with the tide. The emigrants quickly acknowledged the need for a pilot when they spotted a shipwreck: "We could just see the top of the vessel and its 3 masts standing straight up," wrote Andrew. That night they anchored near the bar.[26]

23 Poulter, "Life," 137; Andrew, Diary, April 22, 1854; Sinclair, Journal, April 21, 1854; Rampton, Diary, 35. Pratt's "Dialogue" was first published in the *New York Herald*, January 1, 1844.

24 Sinclair, Journal, April 22–23, 1854; Andrew, Diary, April 22–23, 1854; MacMaster, Diaries, 343–44.

25 Sinclair, Journal, April 23, 1854; Andrew, Diary, April 25–26, 1854; Moyle, Reminiscences, 8–9.

26 MacMaster, Diaries, 344–45; Naisbitt, "Recollections," 231; Andrew, Diary, April 27, 1854.

During the night a woman died of dysentery. Early the next morning as the ship was anchored at the bar, the Saints sang a hymn, and MacMaster, the president of her branch on board, said a prayer before her body was lowered into the sea. That morning, April 28, fourteen or fifteen sailing ships and four or five steamships, all at anchor, crowded the waters. Even though the wind was blowing hard, two steam tugboats arrived during the morning. With one on each side, they dragged the *John M. Wood* across the muddy bar and then towed it the three miles to Balize, where the ship dropped anchor in the afternoon. Balize, a desolate-looking village built on pilings to keep the houses from sinking into the reeds and mud, was home for the tugboat pilots. The weather then turned cold and windy, forcing the emigrants to don more clothing.[27]

For the next two days, the ship rode at anchor, waiting for a steamboat to take it to New Orleans. At last, on May 1 a steamer arrived. Rather than towing the *John M. Wood* upriver, the steamboat lashed it to one side and a second ship to the other. Mile by mile the three vessels slowly moved up the Mississippi. It was a hundred miles to New Orleans, and each bend brought fresh scenes: first a lighthouse north of Balize, then "green bushey trees with white and yellow blooms, . . . also plantations of sugar, green meadows, orange trees, and others of great variety," wrote Andrew. Then came Fort Jackson, built in 1842, and Fort Philip, built in 1792. Five miles beyond the forts stood a quarantine station; here the steamboat stopped and doctors came aboard. The passengers had to walk two by two past the doctors. Once they had passed inspection, the ships started upriver again.[28]

The immigrants marveled at finally being in America. MacMaster wrote:

> It cheered the hearts of the saints to look on the Land of Joseph where God in the last days sends forth his [sacraments?] to the nations of the Earth that all may know that God lives, and my heart in this dase [days] rejoice[s] to look on it also and to know that the blood of prophets and saints dose stain this land in the last days, for this God will visit it in his due time.[29]

Henry Naisbitt echoed his sentiments:

> To catch sight of that land long hidden from observation now supposed to be consecrated to liberty, and looked to as the "choice land" upon which

---

[27] Andrew, Diary, April 27–28, 1854; MacMaster, Diaries, 345; "Arrival of the 'John M. Wood,'" 367; Sinclair, Journal, April 28, 1854.

[28] Sinclair, Journal, April 28–May 2, 1854; Andrew, Diary, April 29–May 1, 1854; Davies, Diary, 9.

[29] MacMaster, Diaries, 345.

Zion shall be established in "the last days" was to have peculiar feelings awakened, these were heightened too by the trip up the "Father of Waters," with its semi-tropical borders, the land of the sugar-cane and the cotton grove, with the congenial fruits, foliage, birds, butterflies, and insects of an almost fairy land.[30]

As they neared New Orleans, they were greeted with additional sights of the area. "Trees veiled in moss, sugar plantations, and cotton fields stretched as far as the eye could reach, the whitewashed quarters of the slaves, the rambling unarchitectural dwellings of the planters, the great steamboats laden with cotton and crowded with passengers from the lower to the hurricane deck, with strains of music, and colored help, in the main, continually arrested our attention," wrote Naisbitt. It was May 2, and at two o'clock in the afternoon the ship finally made fast at the levee in New Orleans.[31]

The emigrants had arrived. The voyage had taken fifty-one days, three shorter than average.[32] Two adults and four children had died, one couple had married, and twins had been born. The passengers had survived a five-day storm, the scare of a fire, and perhaps a potential running aground. A fellow Scot described the community they had become:

> We were strangers to each other when we met in Liverpool, but we soon got acquainted, being all children of the Kingdom of God. . . . I fully realize that the Banner of Zion was waving over us. . . . We were familiar enough to worship the same God, and be obedient to the brethren that brother Samuel Richards placed over us. Order was established, and all went on well. Consequently, love and unity were manifested and made sure in our midst.[33]

Peter, Agnes, and John had taken their first strides into Zion. Now, along with their fellow passengers, they were eager to rush down the gangplank, escape the ship's confines, step on terra firma, and find something more palatable to eat than the dull fare of the past seven weeks. They wanted to finally feel American soil beneath their feet and then to explore this exotic "Frenchified" city.[34]

---

[30] Naisbitt, "Leaves" (July 1, 1878): 404.

[31] Naisbitt, "Recollections," 231.

[32] Sonne, *Saints on the Seas*, 73, 150.

[33] Robert G. Taylor to Thomas G. Taylor, October 28, 1854, *Millennial Star* 17 (March 17, 1855): 172–73. See also May, "Rites of Passage," for his study of the Mormon emigrants who "entered Zion" when they boarded the ship.

[34] "Frenchified" comes from Naisbitt in "Leaves," 404. The French first settled the city in 1717.

8

The Destroyer Rides upon the Waters

ALTHOUGH THE IMMIGRANTS WERE EAGER TO LEAVE THE SHIP, they were not allowed to just yet. Peter, Agnes, John, and the others had to be content for the moment to view New Orleans from the ship's railing. Sailing ships crowded the waterfront, their masts a forest, and farther along, rows of ornate white steamboats with black smokestacks packed the shore. The levee protecting the low-lying city sloped gradually toward the river to form a wide esplanade for the busy wharf: vessels were being loaded or unloaded, mule-drawn drays hauled merchandise, and mountainous stacks of baled cotton attested to New Orleans' being the largest cotton market in the world.[1]

After the captain of the *John M. Wood* handed over the ship's manifest to a U.S. Customs official, "Captain" James Brown, the Mormon agent in New Orleans, arrived. Brown was responsible for receiving the immigrants and speedily arranging for their transport upriver. He had already booked passage for them on the *Josiah Lawrence* the next day. Brown ordered the immigrants to set guards at the hatches to prevent thieves from coming aboard and stealing their possessions. He warned those going ashore to be moderate in what they ate after their bland diet of the past two months. And he cautioned them to watch out for swindlers who might first offer "ardent spirits."[2]

---

[1] Peter and Agnes left no writings about their trip up the rivers and overland to Utah. The following account is thus drawn from the diaries of two fellow Scots, William MacMaster and Peter Sinclair, and of an Englishman, Frederick Andrew, all of whom had sailed with the McAuslan couple on the *John M. Wood*. These journals are supplemented by reminiscences, as well as notices and letters printed in the *Millennial Star* and the *Deseret News*.

[2] James Brown, fifty-two, had been a captain in the Mormon Battalion. Piercy, *Route from Liverpool*, 71; Sinclair, Journal, May 2, 1854.

View of New Orleans from the Lower Cotton Press, 1852.
Lithograph by D. W. Moody, after J. W. Hill and B. F. Smith, Jr.,
delineators. *Courtesy of the Historic New Orleans Collection.*

Although the day was hot and the air filled with dust and glare, most
of the immigrants eagerly set off for the French Quarter to mail letters,
buy food and newspapers, and see the city. In their heavy, drab clothing
they looked like dull cowbirds venturing among the city's goldfinches
and tanagers, for they were quickly surrounded by color and an exuber-
ance they had never before seen: coral-colored stucco buildings with lacy
cast-iron railings, men in summer whites, African American women in
vivid dresses, roses and azaleas of every shade, and an astonishing variety of fruits and vegetables in the market.[3]

But for most British Mormons, slavery cast a pall over the city. The
British had outlawed slavery twenty years earlier, and even then the slave
trade had not been on their shores. The emigrants were horrified by what
they saw. New Orleans was the major slave market of the South, and
slaves were auctioned daily in the rotundas of the city's big St. Charles

---

[3] Wharton, *Queen of the South*, 25; Buice, "When the Saints Came Marching In," 235; Piercy, *Route from Liverpool*, 159.

Hotel and St. Louis Hotel. Until they were on the auction block, slaves were kept in "jails" or "yards" to be viewed by prospective buyers. "There was something repulsive in the idea of slavery, something solemn in seeing these well, yet gaudily dressed descendants of Ham, subjected to general inspection as 'twere a horse," wrote one of the immigrants.[4]

The next morning, Frederick Andrew wrote, "All was hurry and bustle with the passengers hauling out their boxes and getting them ready for inspection. . . . We was very busy all day opening our boxes for [U.S. Customs] inspection and then packing them up again and getting them into the steamer to go to St. Louis." By five o'clock in the evening, the *John M. Wood* passengers were on board the steamboat *Josiah Lawrence*. James Brown, the Mormon agent, was traveling with them, for he did not feel well and wanted to escape the sickly climate of New Orleans. With the ring of the captain's big bell echoed by the jangle of smaller signal bells, then a show of black smoke and a piercing whistle, the steamboat backed away from the levee.[5]

The *Josiah Lawrence* was no floating palace with fancy ornamentation and elegant chandeliers in the saloon. A side-wheeler built in 1848, it was bigger than average and primarily meant for freight. The average life of a steamboat from wear, not accidents, was four to five years, and thus at six years, the *Josiah Lawrence* was well past its prime. William MacMaster, not usually given to criticism, called it a "roten tub" and complained, "Every steamer on the river went a head of her."[6]

As a cabin cost four to six times deck passage, which few of the Mormons could afford, most traveled on the main deck with the furnace, boilers, and engines, stacks of fuel wood, the partitioned-off kitchen for preparing cabin-class meals, whatever cargo the boat was carrying, and the immigrants' luggage. The six hundred deck passengers—Mormon and non-Mormon—were not allowed on the upper decks. There was no lavatory, so buckets were used. There was one long stove for the deck immigrants, but with so many, there was little chance to use it. To sleep, this human cargo had to bed down aft among the crates, barrels, and

---

[4] Reinders, *End of an Era*, 25, 27, 151; Naisbitt, "Leaves," 404.

[5] Andrew, Diary, May 2, 1854; "Arrival of the 'John M. Wood'," 367; Orson Pratt to Brigham Young, June 29, 1854, LDS Church Archives.

[6] Sonne, *Ships, Saints, and Mariners*, 124; Hunter, *Steamboats*, 74, 100–101, 101n124; MacMaster, Diaries, 345–46.

bags of goods the boat was carrying north. They slept in their clothes, for there was no privacy in which to change. A Mormon passenger the year before described these boats as "floating hells."[7]

The officers of the Mormon company had cabins, and this arrangement of leaders living in comfort while the poor were relegated to the equivalent of a pen below them upset Thomas Poulter:

> But alas, alas! How soon the spirit of love and happiness was to depart. . . . All that could not afford to hire a cabin had to go below and do the best we could, like so many cattle. While the officers of the Saints, Captain Brown, and the rich of our company had first class cabins and ate and drank at the mess tables of the best of the land, the poor below had to take care of themselves in the best way that they could. . . . We had no prayer, we had no singing. The rich Saints with their Elders would come down to see us. Yes to see us, confined like so many cattle in hot stinking quarters.[8]

Without prayers, singing, or the sacrament (communion), the cohesion the Saints had enjoyed on the ship vanished.

Because the *John M. Wood* had made a relatively short trip, the provisions left over from the ship were transferred to the steamboat for distribution. Many bought extra food in New Orleans and obtained more when the boat stopped in towns and cities along the way. But because cooking was so difficult, deck passengers usually ate picnic items such as sausage, dried herrings, and crackers and cheese; and they drank the river water.[9]

Only the view gave relief from the squalor of the main deck. William MacMaster wrote that "the scenery of the Missipie is very gran and a very crooked river to[o]." The river was so crooked, in fact, that when the boat was on a southward bend of a river loop, the sun appeared to rise in the west. Another in their company wrote enthusiastically, "It was a new world to me, the trees and foliage, and all the scenery was so different from anything that I had seen before, that I was delighted with it." Frederick Andrew was equally pleased: "On each side it is beautifully deco-

---

[7] The deck fare for the *Josiah Lawrence* from New Orleans to St. Louis was $3.50 per person. Job Smith, returning from a mission to England and going upriver the week before the McAuslans, paid $13 for a cabin. "Arrival of the 'John M. Wood'," 366; Smith, Diary and Autobiography, 199; Hunter, *Steamboats*, 421–26; Piercy, *Route from Liverpool*, 74, 76; William Eddington to T. B. H. Stenhouse, October 31, 1854, *Millennial Star* 17 (February 17, 1855): 106. The number of passengers comes from Sinclair, Journal, May 14, 1854.

[8] Poulter, "Life," 44:137–38.

[9] Hunter, *Steamboats*, 419, 425; Piercy, *Route from Liverpool*, 56, 76; "Arrival of the 'John M. Wood,'" 366.

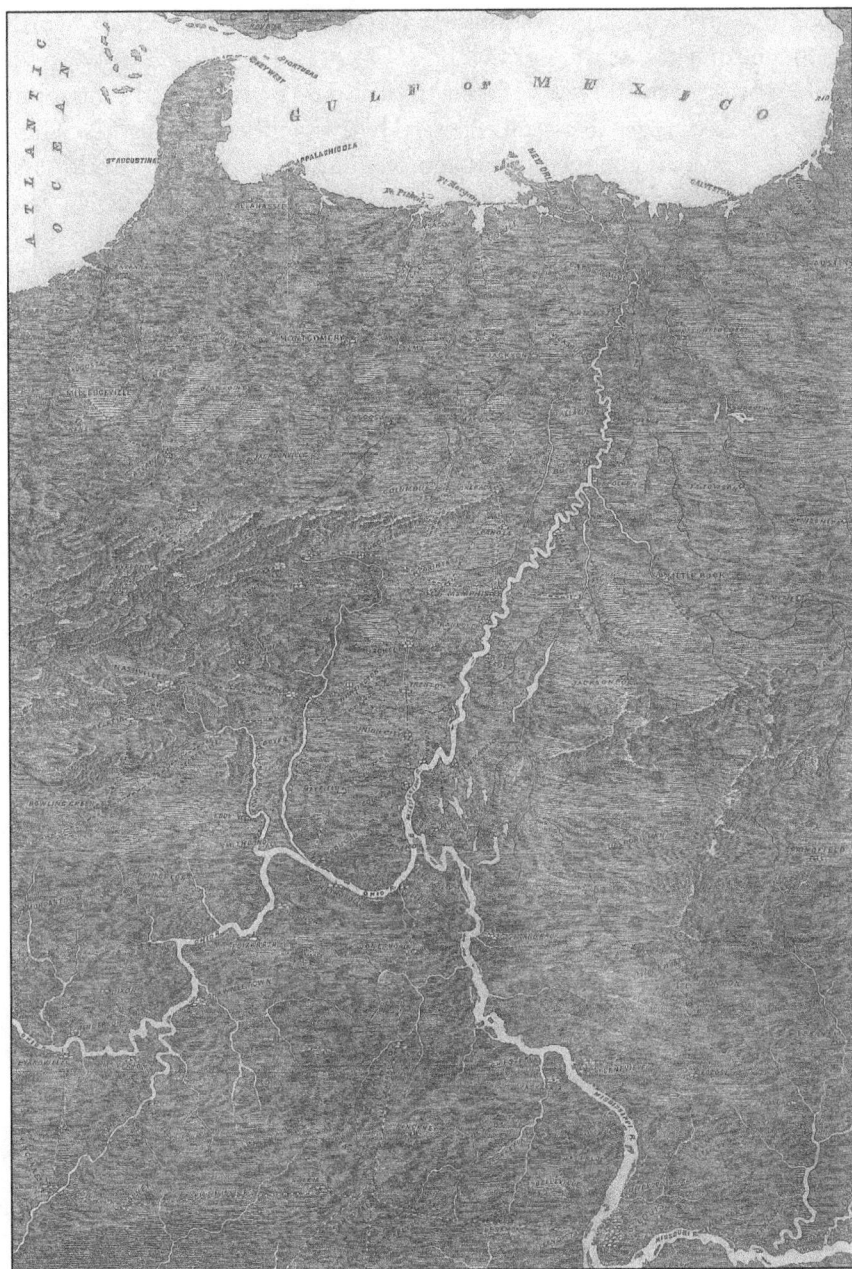

Bird's-eye view of the Mississippi River and adjacent country from
St. Louis to the Gulf of Mexico. *From* Harper's Weekly, *July 6, 1861, 421.*

rated with green trees, plantations etc. It is delightful to behold. It is worth all the journey to see the sight."[10]

The passage from New Orleans to St. Louis averaged eight days, but the *Josiah Lawrence* took twelve, passed by every other boat, as MacMaster said. The boat chugged its way upriver day and night. On two nights, however, it was forced to stop because the fog was so thick. Sinclair said that early on May 7, the boat ran into a bank on account of the thick mist and "carried a considerable quantity of earth off on our bow." Steamboats typically stopped twice a day to take on wood, but the *Josiah Lawrence* burned about forty cords daily, requiring three or four stops a day at the frequent woodyards along the banks.[11]

On May 9, the sixth day of the trip, cholera appeared. A twelve-year-old boy not belonging to the Saints died, followed by one of their own, a three-year-old girl. A few hours later the crew buried both children in the soft banks of the river. There was time for only a quick prayer before the parents had to leave the little bodies in an unmarked spot along the river.[12]

Although cases of cholera had occurred in the early 1850s, 1854 saw an epidemic. Not as widespread as the pandemic of 1848–1849, it spread primarily along the rivers, carried by steamboats. If river towns learned that a boat was infected, they frequently would not allow it to land. Captains, in an effort to hide the disease, would land on deserted stretches in the middle of the night to quickly and quietly bury the dead. With their shallow drafts, steamboats could nose into a bank at any point.[13]

The passengers on the *Josiah Lawrence* had expected to land at Memphis about midnight the day the children died, and many had stayed up to see it, but in sheeting rain, thunder, and lightning, the boat ran aground on a sandbar. At dawn it was still stuck fast. The crew worked all morning, and finally to everyone's joy they were able to shove the steamer back into deeper water. Then, shortly before noon, a young boy died. When the boat finally docked at Memphis, many went ashore to see the city and buy food. An hour and a half after leaving Memphis, the captain brought the boat to the shore to bury the latest cholera victim.[14]

---

[10] MacMaster, Diaries, 345–46; Moyle, Reminiscences, 9; Andrew, Diary, May 4, 1854.

[11] Rampton, Diary, 36; Andrew, Diary, May 4 and 10, 1854; Sinclair, Journal, May 6, 1854.

[12] Andrew, Diary, May 9, 1854; MacMaster, Diaries, 346; Sinclair, Journal, May 7–9, 1854; "List of deaths."

[13] F. D. Richards, "The Cholera," *Millennial Star* 16 (September 9, 1854): 567; Hunter, *Steamboats*, 430–35.

[14] Andrew, Diary, May 9 and 10; MacMaster, Diaries, 346; "List of deaths"; Sinclair, Journal, May 9–10.

The violent and uncontrollable diarrhea and vomiting that characterized cholera must only have increased the misery on the crowded and filthy main deck. The Saints began to talk about "the Destroyer." William W. Phelps, an early church member, had had a daylight vision in August 1831 on the Missouri River in which he "saw the destroyer riding in power upon the face of the waters." Joseph Smith's subsequent revelation had stated: "No flesh shall be safe upon the waters. And it shall be said in days to come that none is able to go up to the land of Zion upon the water, but he that is upright in heart."[15]

The emigrating Saints now recalled that in April 1852 a party of Mormons had traveled up the Missouri River on a steamboat named the *Saluda*. Without warning, its boilers exploded, killing about twenty-eight of the eighty Mormons on board. The converts in Great Britain were aware of Joseph Smith's revelation, but they were told that if they kept God's commandments, particularly the command to gather to Zion, they could, "in the full assurance of the Holy Ghost claim the protection of heaven."[16] How, then, to understand the *Saluda* disaster and those now dying from cholera?

News of the *Saluda* explosion had reached the British members via the May 29, 1852, issue of the *Millennial Star*. The editor, Samuel W. Richards, after describing the tragedy, had warned those who planned to emigrate that obedience to the laws of God must be carried out promptly and with "unyielding faith." The next issue of the *Millennial Star*, by then a weekly, carried news of a fresh disaster: a mine accident in Wales that killed nineteen Mormons.[17] Although this latest disaster had not occurred on the great American rivers, Samuel Richards again had considered the cause:

> The destroyer is abroad in the earth, and going about as a roaring lion, seeking whom he may devour. . . . Therefore, dear brethren and sisters, as the powers of darkness appear to be rousing up to afflict and to destroy, we feel to exhort you to be very faithful, prayerful, watchful, and diligent, and to give careful heed to the counsel and instruction of those whom God in His infinite goodness has been pleased to place over you.[18]

---

[15] D&C 61: Introduction, 5–19.
[16] Hartley, "'Don't Go Aboard the *Saluda!*'"; S. W. Richards, "Address to the Saints," *Millennial Star* 14 (July 24, 1852): 338.
[17] Samuel W. Richards, editorials, *Millennial Star* 14 (May 29, 1852): 217–18, and 14 (June 5, 1852): 232–33.
[18] Samuel W. Richards, editorial, *Millennial Star* 14 (June 5, 1852): 233.

Obedience to the laws of God and to the counsel of those called to lead the emigrants, plus unyielding faith, had to be their path.

Peter left no writings on his thoughts about these explanations, and presumably he trusted the church leaders' deeper understanding of the faith. However, by 1854 people in general had begun to understand that cleanliness, drainage of sewers, ventilation, and pure water would save lives, even though the cholera bacteria, transmitted through water contaminated with fecal matter, was not yet known. But for the Mormon immigrants now witnessing death, Joseph Smith's revelation was explicit and vivid. The only escape was great and unwavering faith.[19]

Following the death of the young boy near Memphis, William Mac-Master wrote, "Death rides on this river or as the Lord said to Joseph, they will require great faith to go to Zion on the waters in the last days." Three days later MacMaster said that the church leaders began to meet in prayer so that "the Lord might save his people while on this river from the power of the destroyer." In the morning and again at night they prayed on the top deck.[20] None of the diarists mentioned leaders coming down to anoint the sick.

The deaths of Saints continued. On May 11 a ten-month-old Swiss girl died. That night when the leaders were praying on the upper deck, a twenty-one-year-old woman succumbed. Sinclair said that some of the "rough strangers" on the boat attended the burial and "appeared to be much touched" and that "their . . . swearing . . . was laid aside and quickness with thoughtfulness reigned."[21]

In the midst of this pall of death, Thomas Poulter, anxious to get to Zion, asked one of the Scottish sisters to make a flag that he could fly from his tent when they crossed the plains. This she did:

> It was a fine flag, the red, white and blue and no stars but a beehive in the middle. While she made this flag it drew around us quite a crowd. This sister that made my flag was fair to look upon. A singer, a voice like a bird. "Sister, I love to sing the songs, the songs of Zion. Will you sing?" "I will,"

[19] Rosenberg, *Cholera Years*, 148–50.

[20] MacMaster, Diaries, 346–47. Others also wrote of the Destroyer: W. Empey to S. W. Richards, June 16, 1854, *Millennial Star* 16 (July 29, 1854): 477; Erastus Snow to F. D. Richards, September 12, 1854, *Millennial Star* 16 (October 28, 1854): 685; Sinclair, Journal, May 13, 1854; and Hodgert, *Journal*, 30–31 (May 9, 1854).

[21] "List of deaths"; Andrew, Diary, May 11, 1854; MacMaster, Diaries, 346; Sinclair, Journal, May 11 and 12, 1854.

she said, "Brother Poulter, if you will help me." My! she sang like an angel. The poor Saints gathered around us and when it came to the choruses they sang with power.[22]

Poulter remarked that her singing brought the non-Mormons onboard to listen to her as well: "They stood like statues struck with wonder at the echo of the Scotch sister's lovely voice. Poor she was, but the spirit of the Gods were upon her and what dith they say? 'Madam if you please sing us another song!' 'Yes, sir,' was her response. Again went up her lofty strains. It filled the steamer, it floated in the air, spirits of the just were around us."[23]

During the night of May 12 the boat ran into a snag that came up through the guard boards of the bow. Early the next morning, Isabella Barr from Glasgow, the midwife who had delivered the twins, died from cholera. Peter and Agnes must have mourned her, for she had traveled with them since Glasgow. Sinclair, also one of their companions from Scotland, prayed, "O Lord stay the hand of the destroyer from among thy Saints for Christ's sake, that unitedly they may thank & prais[e] the[e]." According to MacMaster, she had been "very useful when she was well among the sick when on the sea and on this river." The morning turned wet, and a thunder and lightning storm swept down the river. A squall cracked and bent the steamboat's funnel.[24]

About one o'clock on the morning of May 14, the crew quietly buried Isabella on a deserted bank under the light of the moon. The steamer now was not far from St. Louis, and the quarantine station was just a few miles below on Quarantine Island. Before reaching it, the captain took the boat to the shore and sent off about forty young men to walk the last five miles to St. Louis. He had overloaded the *Josiah Lawrence* and now feared he would be fined and the steamboat detained at the island. But when the walking group reached St. Louis, they discovered that the company had been detained at Quarantine Island after all and they were not allowed to go there.[25]

The island, a sandbar covered with small willows, lay in the Mississippi River four miles below St. Louis. An old steamboat, the *Hannibal*,

---

[22] Poulter, "Life," 138.

[23] Ibid.

[24] "List of deaths"; Sinclair, Journal, May 13, 1854; MacMaster, Diaries, 347.

[25] Sinclair, Journal, May 14, 1854; Andrew, Diary, May 14, 1854; Naisbitt, "Recollections," 231; Naisbitt, "Leaves," 404.

had been moved there to serve as shelter and a hospital. The diarists described it as an "old hulk" and complained that it was dirty. The *Josiah Lawrence* unloaded the passengers and their luggage and departed. Quarantine Island affected the immigrants, for the diaries and reminiscences dwell on their days there.[26]

The doctor on the island warned the newly arrived not to go behind the old steamboat because that was where those who had died of smallpox and cholera were buried. This frightened some of the Saints. They believed that the porous, sandy soil gave off a miasma from the dead, spreading the disease to the well. Five had died in the last four days on the river; eight more died in the next four days on the island.[27] Peter and Agnes must have begun to wonder about the assurances made by the leaders in Scotland of God's protection to those gathering to Zion.

Henry Naisbitt, part of the group walking to St. Louis, offered to help take supplies to the island where his wife and her parents were in quarantine. When he arrived, he found his wife "fast sinking under this uncompromising foe." Then he too became ill. "For a time it seemed ominous," he wrote. Then he recalled that he had had a dream or vision in which he was involved in "activity in the Temple ordinance," so he quickly retired to a willow thicket to pray. His prayer was answered by a voice that said very distinctly, "With long life will I satisfy thee, and show thee my salvation." Naisbitt ended with, "The response was quick and the realization sure, for the grim monster loosed his hold." Cholera left them both, and they were able to go to St. Louis with the rest. Finally, on May 18, their fourth day on the island, the Saints were given permission to leave. In the evening two tugboats sent by the Mormon agent in St. Louis came for them. They had to leave behind one of the group from Glasgow, a young man who was not expected to live.[28]

The Mormon emigration agent in St. Louis, William A. Empey, transferred some of the Saints that same evening to the side-wheeler *Sam Cloon*. Built in 1851, it was an improvement over the *Josiah Lawrence*.

[26] Moyle, Reminiscences, 10; Poulter, "Life," 138; MacMaster, Diaries, 347–48; Andrew, Diary, May 15, 1854; Sinclair, Journal, May 15–18, 1854.

[27] Poulter, "Life," 138; Naisbitt, "Leaves," 404; Naisbitt, "Recollections," 231; "List of deaths"; MacMaster, Diaries, 348; Andrew, Diary, May 16–18.

[28] The one left behind was Herbert Calton, a twenty-four-year-old described by Andrew as a "stout lively young man." He had been in Peter and Agnes's group since Glasgow and had been a cook on the *John M. Wood*. Naisbitt, "Recollections," 231–32; Naisbitt, "Leaves," 404; Andrew, Diary, May 17–18, 1854; Sinclair, Journal, May 18, 1854.

Others, including Peter, Agnes, and John were to leave the next day on the steamboat *Australia*, built just the year before.[29] The emigrants bought food and newspapers, mailed letters, and obtained a few personal supplies for the overland trek. Smaller than New Orleans, St. Louis was nevertheless growing fast and was a major inland port for agricultural and manufactured goods. In this peak period of river travel before the Civil War, St. Louis was at a strategic point close to where the Missouri, Ohio, and Illinois rivers empty into the Mississippi. In addition, it was the major supply center for emigrants headed west.

Peter Sinclair wrote that the Mormons in St. Louis met in a music or concert hall and that the next morning some of the immigrants went there to hear Orson Pratt preach. Pratt had arrived a couple of weeks before from Washington, D.C., where he had been publishing a newspaper called the *Seer*. It was the first time that Sinclair had heard Pratt speak: "Oh! How my soul rejoiced to hear an inspired apostle clear up what man had disputed about for ages." Peter and Agnes, although they had heard Pratt in Scotland, must have been equally pleased to see him again. They attended the afternoon sessions as well, including partaking "of the Sacrament for the first time on American soil." Sinclair concluded: "Both meetgs. a real treat. I felt to rejoice & praise the Lord."[30]

Latter-day Saints had been arriving in St. Louis since mid-March. The first group were Scandinavians, mostly Danish. They had been hard hit by cholera; eighteen had died coming up the Mississippi, and another seven in the first three days in St. Louis. Mormon agent Empey had arrived in early February from a mission in England, where he had presided over the Preston Conference. At age forty-six, he was experienced in pioneering skills and leadership. As an agent, he worked with Horace S. Eldredge, who had been sent from Salt Lake City a year and a half before to preside over the St. Louis Conference. Eldredge, not quite forty years old, was six feet tall and handsome, with "sharp gray eyes." The many-faceted responsibilities of the two men included buying oxen and cows and driving them to camp, often over long distances; ordering wagons in Cincinnati and St. Louis, which were then sent by steamboat to the out-

---

[29] At least one family, the MacDonalds, took still another steamboat, the *Honduras*, which had been built in 1852. Receipts for transportation; Lloyd, *Steamboat Directory*, 280–82; Andrew, Diary, May 18, 1854; MacDonald, Autobiography, 15; Sinclair, Journal, May 18, 1854.

[30] Sinclair, Journal, May 19, 1854.

fitting camp near Kansas City, Missouri; and buying ox yokes, tent poles, chains, axes, Dutch ovens, and ropes, as well as provisions for the three-month trek.[31]

Besides Empey and Eldredge, by mid-May the St. Louis Conference office staff included Orson Pratt and James Brown, who had assisted the immigrants in New Orleans. Others arrived to help out and lead companies to Salt Lake City, including Job Smith, who was returning from a mission in England, and Daniel Garn (often spelled Carn), who had been president of the German Mission.[32]

Because Eldredge was sick, Empey was left to care for the incoming groups, especially the Scandinavians, and to arrange for the burial of those who died. On April 10 he wrote, "This day I visited the sick & to behold those that were dying with the collery. It was awful to behold. To hear the prayers that they might be taken out of their misery etc." Ten days later he wrote that one woman who died left "a fine child," and he had to find someone to take it. "Oh the awful scene to behold to see the children or to see a husband mourning for his affectionate wife & see a woman lamenting for her husband," he wrote. "It would cause the stoutest man to drop a tear. God be merciful to us & save us from the grasp of the distruction." As soon as he could, he sent them by steamboat to Westport Landing at Kansas City, Missouri, where a camping place for the companies had been arranged. In a letter reporting on the immigration to Samuel W. Richards in Liverpool, Empey reiterated what so many of the Saints talked of: "Truly the word of the Lord, through the Prophet Joseph, is receiving a more extensive fulfillment. The Destroyer rideth upon the waters, and the day is at hand when none shall go up to Zion except the pure in heart."[33]

Cholera had not yet loosened its grip on the passengers from the *John M. Wood*. In the evening of May 19, Peter, Agnes, and John left St. Louis with the others on the steamboat *Australia* and were soon going up the Missouri River. A few hours later, one of their Scottish companions died, leaving behind a wife and two small children. The captain waited until

---

[31] "St. Louis," *Millennial Star* 16 (April 22, 1854): 249; "Departure," *Millennial Star* 16 (January 21, 1854): 42; Eldredge, Journal, entries for February 7 to April 11, 1854; "Highly Important from Utah," April 9, 1858, *New York Times* (May 24, 1858): 1.

[32] Orson Pratt to Brigham Young, June 29 1854, LDS Church Archives.

[33] Eldredge, Journal, April 1, 1854; Empey, Diary, 115, 117; "The Camp at Kansas," *Millennial Star* 16 (July 29, 1854): 469.

the middle of the night to bury him on a deserted bank. Two days later the youngest child of the same family died and was buried before dawn. One of the Saints wrote that the deaths "rendered it a sad and weary journey."[34]

The Missouri River had many more hazards than the Mississippi. One local newspaper bragged that the river was "the muddiest, the deepest, the shallowest, the bar-iest, the snaggiest, the sandiest, the catfishiest, the swiftest, the steamboatiest, and the uncertainest river in all the world." Now, in the spring, the river was "swollen and turbid," which made night travel extremely hazardous, but the *Australia* proceeded anyway.[35]

The steamboat was carrying a load of wagons for the Saints; the wagon boxes were hauled up to an upper deck, where the Mormon immigrants were allowed to make their beds. Although exposed to the weather, they were more comfortable than on the main deck. They passed a number of small towns, stopping at none. On May 24 in the afternoon they arrived at Westport Landing, where Kansas City was located. One of their group wrote that there were only a "few straggling houses by the river" and one or two stores. The Saints went about half a mile upriver to make their first camp.[36]

---

[34] "List of deaths"; MacMaster, Diaries, 349; Derry, *Autobiography*, 18.

[35] The newspaper is quoted in Van Ravensway, "Character and History of the Mississippi," 17; Hunter, *Steamboats*, 259; Naisbitt, "Leaves," 434.

[36] MacMaster, Diaries, 349; Moyle, Reminiscences, 11.

Yoking a wild bull.
Pencil drawing by William Henry Jackson.
Courtesy of the National Park Service.

9

Going Home to Zion

THE McAUSLANS SET TO WORK RAISING THEIR TENTS TO CAMP for the first time. But the cholera they so fervently hoped had been left behind on the riverboats struck their group again. Three days after arriving, a fourteen-year-old boy and a man who had a wife and three young children died. The families of both had been companions of Peter and Agnes since Glasgow. Sorrow and fear thus mingled with excitement in the camp.[1]

Sunday, May 28, brought a thunderstorm that forced the Saints into their tents to partake of the sacrament. During the night, the rain flooded several tents, so the next day most moved to higher ground about a mile south of Kansas City, where the main body of the Saints was camping on "McGee's" land. A Swiss member, who had also come on the *John M. Wood*, wrote, "The fixing of tents under the trees in the wood, the building of a campfire, the baking of our bread in baking kettles, the washing of our clothes and the tending of our baby boy just learning to walk were sometimes trying. . . . But, though some of the work was hard and many were the privations that we were beginning to feel, we still felt happy."[2]

They were to camp on McGee's land for the next five weeks. The emigration that year needed close to four hundred wagons, and many had not yet arrived. Peter Sinclair, a Scot who had traveled with Peter and Agnes from Glasgow, noted, "Some companies stoped for want of waggons. No inteligence in camp why this long delay doing nothing. Saints generally

---

[1] MacMaster, Diaries, 350.

[2] The main Mormon camp was on land owned by Milton McGee, a Kansas City promoter. MacMaster, Diaries, 350; MacDonald, Autobiography, 15–16; Graehl, "Story," 57.

desirous of geting away and is astonished at so long delay." Peter and Agnes must have been likewise surprised and puzzled. Confusion reigned in the campground, which by now included about two thousand people. In spite of the hundreds of white tents arranged neatly in long rows, little else showed order. One Saint described seeing "the commotion, the irregular living and disorder," and retreated to the forest where he had set up camp. The unity they had experienced on the ship had been broken on the steamboat and now seemed buried under a lack of organization.[3]

When William Empey, the agent in St. Louis and now at the main camp, was temporarily called away, he left William MacMaster in charge. Peter Sinclair was pleased: "I, loving order, and as there apeared to be no proper organisation existing was glad to hear such inteligance, hoping that proper order would prevail." He applied to MacMaster for a wagon and was promised one, but when the next load came, others quickly claimed them. Two days later, he lost out again. The next day, he complained to the leaders, but still none was available. He wrote in his diary, "O! Let it not be known among the gentiles that people suffers among the Saints by obey[ing] councel and upholding the Authorities. . . . O! Lord, help thy officers to act wisely that they may retain thy spirit and the confidence of thy Saints."[4]

Cholera continued its deadly work among those who had come on the *John M. Wood.* The day after the McAuslans moved to McGee's land, a Scottish woman died, and in the next three days three others succumbed. On May 30 Agnes celebrated her twenty-fifth birthday, and a few weeks later she discovered she was pregnant. The days were hot, and a succession of thunderstorms swept over the camp, leaving everything soaked. On most evenings they could see lightning flash along the horizon. By the first week in June, some wagon trains were formed and moved a few miles southwest, just beyond the town of Westport on the edge of the frontier. The departures were staggered so as not to impede each other's progress on the plains.[5]

In Salt Lake City the *Deseret News,* which usually published details of each year's overland companies, ran short of paper and so printed only

---

[3] W. Empey to S. W. Richards, June 16, 1854, *Millennial Star* 16 (July 29, 1854): 477; Sinclair, Journal, June 20 and July 4, 1854; Hoth, Diary, June 16, 1854.

[4] Sinclair, Journal, June 21–24, 1854.

[5] "List of deaths"; MacMaster, Diaries, 350–52; Sinclair, Journal, July 18, 1854; Hoth, Diary, June 16, 1854. The town of Westport, as distinct from Westport Landing, was about four miles south of Kansas City.

spotty information about the 1854 immigration. Even without rosters, one can conclude with a high degree of confidence that Peter, Agnes, and John traveled in the Daniel Garn company. Of the forty-seven known Scots with whom they traveled from Glasgow, thirty-nine were still alive. Of these, twenty are known to have traveled with a particular company: thirteen with the Garn Company, four with Robert Campbell's company (three of them his family), and three with William Empey in the last company. Peter Sinclair, forced to wait for a wagon, was one of those in the last company. When the Garn Company left, Sinclair wrote, "Most all the John M. Woods passengers is off." Although irked at the disorganization that prevented his own departure, he wrote, "Nevertheless I rejoice greatly in going home to Zion."[6]

Finally the McAuslans' great day for starting came. It took both July 1 and 2 to get the entire group under way. The Garn Company consisted of 447 people and about forty wagons. Besides Garn, there were three captains of tens: William MacMaster, who kept a diary; Thomas Todd, another Scot, who left a reminiscence; and a Brother Lamb. Todd wrote that each wagon of ten people had two yoke of oxen and two cows. Daniel Garn, their leader, was a Pennsylvanian who had been a bishop and a policeman in Nauvoo. He had traveled to Utah in 1848 in the Brigham Young Company as a captain of fifty and thus was an experienced hand. Now fifty-one years old, he had just returned from a mission to Germany, where he had been arrested for preaching the Gospel. Also in the Garn Company were the Scots Alexander F. MacDonald and his wife, Elizabeth, who were traveling with his father and her mother and sister. Elizabeth, reflecting Peter and Agnes's feelings as well, wrote, "On starting, I felt exceedingly thankful to the Lord for His goodness to us as a family, for I realized that we had been preserved upon the sea and upon the rivers in the midst of disease and death."[7]

---

[6] Peter McAuslan wrote that they arrived in Salt Lake City about the end of September in 1854. On September 30 the Garn Company started through Emigration Canyon just before reaching the city. Records show that Peter and Agnes were already in Salt Lake City when the Campbell and Empey companies arrived between October 28 and 31. Journal History, 1854 Supplement, 1; Mormon Pioneer Overland Travel; Sinclair, Journal, June 15 and 24, July 4, 1854; Peter McAuslan to Margaret McAuslan Day, April 14, 1905 (#55 McAuslan Papers); Record of Members, Nineteenth Ward, October 23, 1854, 99.

[7] As noted in the last chapter, McAuslan left no writings of the overland trek. Two fellow Scots, however, did: Peter Sinclair, a detailed account of the outfitting camp; and William MacMaster, a diary of the Garn Company. In addition, several in the Garn Company wrote reminiscences. Mormon Pioneer Overland Travel, Daniel Garn Company (1854); MacMaster, Diaries, 353; Todd, Autobiography, 5; MacDonald, Autobiography, 16.

Nearly all British immigrants recorded the circus that ensued as the urban men tried to make the oxen move. Most of the animals were unbroken, and the teams were not used to working together. One of the McAuslans' companions wrote,

> Captain [Garn] was a waching us and . . . tould us to tak the whip an use it and say whoah duke gee brandy and so on. Now the fun commenced. Then we went after them prety lively and when the cattle went gee too much we would run to the off side and yelling at them woah and bunting them with the stock of the whip. Then they would go ha to much and we was a puffing and sweeting. . . . This was a great experience and a tuff one.[8]

Elizabeth MacDonald remarked, "The length of the road was nothing to the width! . . . The oxen were not at all particular to keep the road; for in the first of our experience with them, they several times ran away and upset the wagon." On that first exhausting day, they traveled two miles.[9]

Between Kansas City, Missouri, and Fort Kearny, Nebraska Territory, the immigrants were traveling in what had just been made Kansas Territory.[10] The land was pastoral, with rolling hills and serpentine lines of oaks and walnut trees marking the course of each stream. In spite of the pleasant country and being away from the crowded outfitting camp, deaths continued. In the McAuslans' company a young man died on July 5, followed by MacMaster's one-year-old son on July 12. MacMaster buried him on the top of a hill near St. Mary's Mission and noted, "He died on his way to Zion in the last days so he rests in peace with his Lord."[11]

The Saints' route took them across a succession of rivers and streams: the Kansas River (by "Smith's" ferry); Cross Creek (by toll bridge); again the Kansas River at St. Mary's Mission (by toll bridge); the Red or Little Vermilion Creek and Rock Creek (both by fording); and the most difficult of the trip so far, the Black or Big Vermilion River (by fording). Then they forded the Big Blue River, which was only three feet deep.[12]

---

[8] Davies, Diary, 13–14.

[9] MacDonald, Autobiography, 17; MacMaster, Diaries, 353–54.

[10] A little over a month before the McAuslans left Kansas City to start west, Congress passed the Kansas-Nebraska Act on May 30, 1854. Besides establishing the two territories, the act gave popular sovereignty to the territories to decide whether they would allow slavery or not. The act became a hotly debated sectional issue over slavery, and in Kansas the debate became violent.

[11] St. Mary's Mission was a Belgian Jesuit Catholic mission to the Potawatomi Indians established in 1848. MacMaster, Diaries, 354.

[12] Receipts for Smith's ferry and toll bridges at Cross Creek and St. Mary's Mission; MacMaster, Diaries, 355.

Shortly before reaching the Little Blue River, which they would follow for several days, the cattle stampeded. One immigrant wrote, "The
teems started out on the run and they tangled up fast to-gether. It was
a wonder that no one was kild and nothing brock." A few days later, the
same man said, "We had another stamped[e]. This was in the night while
they was in the corrall. The captain was afraid of Indeans that night. We
made the corrall with wagons every evening. The cattle that night bunted
the wagons pretty lively and the captain shouted to the gard to let them
go and they went out on the run. Next morning after breakfast we got
them together, some 15 miles away." Typically the animals grazed near
the camp, watched by guards. The wagon corrals were used in the morning for sorting and yoking the oxen. When Indians were a threat, however, the animals would be corralled at night after grazing in the evening.[13]

The Little Blue River was a delight. One emigrant described it as beautiful, with wild grapes and plums and deer along it, and it had everything
the overland traveler needed: water, feed for the animals, and wood for
cooking fires. He regretted having to leave it. By now more acclimated to
life on the trail, the immigrants began to appreciate the scenery and enjoy
themselves in spite of the heat, dust, work, and daily trials. In the evenings
they sat on oxen yokes around campfires and sang hymns, and when the
bugle called, they assembled for prayer. Sinclair, traveling in the last train,
wrote, "My soul rejoices as we march Zionward and views the land which
the Lord has blest for the gathering of his Saints," and later he stated that
he felt "refreshed to hear the Saints sing praises to their King."[14]

Soon they crossed into Nebraska Territory and left the tallgrass prairie
and streams that drain into the Kansas portion of the Missouri River.
About three days after leaving the Little Blue, they began the gradual
descent into the wide, flat valley of the North Platte River. Here began
the shortgrass prairies, or Great Plains. The immigrants could see the
miles-wide river stretching endlessly to the horizon. There were no trees,
not even willows along the banks, and the water was shallow and yellow
with suspended sand.

For three days they followed the road along the Platte until July 29
when they passed Fort Kearny, camping about six miles beyond it. Some
stopped at the fort to repair their wagons or buy additional supplies.

---

[13] Davies, Diary, 15; Sinclair, Journal, July 23, 26, and 28, 1854.
[14] Sutherland, Journal, August 15–18, 1854; Sinclair, Journal, July 17 and August 20–21, 1854.

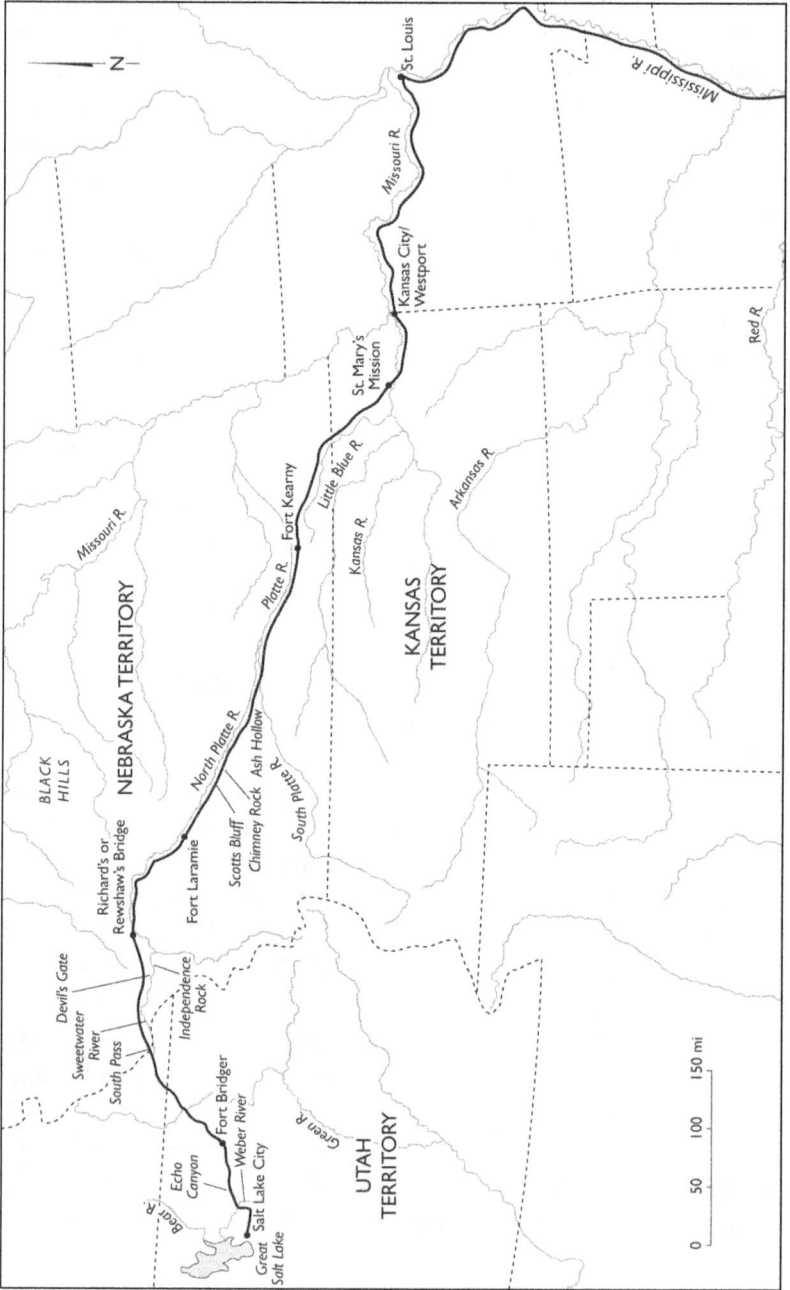

The McAuslans' route from Westport Landing at Kansas City to Salt Lake City.
Map by Bill Nelson.

Although insignificant in appearance, the fort had a vital role in protecting immigrants and functioning as a munitions depot between Forts Leavenworth and Laramie. A few Saints abandoned the journey at Fort Kearny. One member of the Garn Company wrote that three from his wagon stayed behind there. A member of another company said that two families parted with them there as well, adding that one had made "a shipwreck of the faith." Fort Kearny was the last practical place to drop out.[15]

Because of their starting point, the 1854 Saints traveled on the south side of the Platte River. This was in contrast to most Mormon trains; beginning from farther up the Missouri River at Winter Quarters or Council Bluffs, they went along the north bank. With the tree-lined creeks behind them and open prairies ahead, the immigrants had to rely on bison droppings for fuel. The "buffalo chips" meant buffalo, or more correctly, bison had passed that way, and all along the Platte River Valley until the fork of the South Platte, the companies saw vast herds. One in the McAuslans' group wrote, "The buffalos on the plains in them days was by tens of thousands. The boys wounded a young bull and he came a snorting and cross the road between the wagons but they down him and feched one quarter to camp." That was the group's first taste of bison.[16]

On August 5, just before the South Platte River joins the North Platte, MacMaster mentioned that they had passed the "church" train captained by Orson Pratt and Horace Eldredge, a wagon train carrying merchandise ordered by Brigham Young. MacMaster also wrote that the church train's cattle had stampeded that morning and some of the group's men were out hunting for them. Later in the same entry he noted that the Garn Company met Erastus Snow and Ezra T. Benson, both church apostles, coming from Salt Lake City. With them were Orson Spencer, Ira Eldredge (Horace's older brother), and several others headed east on missions. Benson and Ira Eldredge had been sent by Brigham Young specifically to help the church train. As these Mormon leaders traveled east, they met the emigrant companies one after the other. Diarists in the various companies reported feeling overcome with joy to meet them.[17]

---

[15] MacMaster, Diaries, 355; Sutherland, Journal, August 20–22, 1854; Davies, Diary, 14; Mitchell, Journal, July 27, 1854.

[16] Davies, Diary, 15.

[17] MacMaster, Diaries, 355–56; Brigham Young to Franklin D. Richards, August 2, 1854, *Millennial Star* 16 (October 28, 1854): 684. For the immigrants' reactions to meeting the Salt Lake leaders, see Mitchell, Journal, August 4, 1854 (Brown Co.); MacMaster, Diaries, August 5, 1854 (Garn Co.); Sutherland, Journal, August 14, 1854 (Campbell Co.); Sinclair, Journal, August 15, 1854 (Empey Co.).

Thomas Poulter, the father of the twins born on the ship, however, remembered that Benson warned them that "we should not find Salt Lake a heaven but all kinds of fish and said he, 'Some of the biggest rogues in all the world. Now brethren look out for sharpers.'"[18]

The church train had suffered a lack of animals right from the start. It needed at least a dozen more yoke of lead oxen to move all the wagons at once. Two men had gone back to Kansas City to buy more, and in their absence the company had struggled along by moving as many wagons forward as possible and then taking the oxen back to bring up the remaining ones, making them cover the same ground three times. Now, with still two hundred miles to go before they reached even the halfway mark of Fort Laramie, their troubles had multiplied when their stock stampeded.[19]

For four days, men searched for the animals, but 120 were never recovered. The loss left the wagon train paralyzed. The company yoked up cows and any other loose stock to limp forward a few miles each day. Here the Mormon immigration system illustrated its strength. Strung out along the trail for two to three hundred miles, the companies were linked by their sense of community, and one group could call on another for at least some assistance. In this case the companies responded liberally, for it was one of the Twelve Apostles asking. Ezra T. Benson with Horace Eldredge hurried ahead in a light carriage, requesting oxen from the six emigration companies in front of them, the closest of which was the Garn Company.[20]

The response to their plea was immediate. MacMaster wrote that the Garn Company sent thirty-five yoke of oxen and twenty men to help. Other companies likewise responded, even one that was short of teams and had yoked up every cow and lame ox. When Benson and Horace Eldredge passed the Garn Company again on their return trip, Garn gave them an additional twenty yoke of oxen. The total of 110 oxen thus given by Garn's company must have been nearly all the loose stock they had.[21]

Soon afterward the McAuslans and the others in the Garn Company

---

[18] Poulter, "Life," 141 (Field Co.). That the immigrants might find "sharpers" or "rogues" in Salt Lake City was completely unexpected. Yet among the complaints voiced by some who lost their faith and left Utah in the late 1850s was that they had been swindled. See Aird, "'You Nasty Apostates, Clear Out,'" 161–62.

[19] Orson Pratt, Ezra T. Benson, Horace S. Eldredge, Ira Eldredge, and Frederick Kesler to Brigham Young, August 8, 1854, *Deseret News*, August 31, 1854, 2.

[20] Erastus Snow to F. D. Richards, September 12, 1854, *Millennial Star* 16 (October 28, 1854): 685–86; Pratt et al. to Young, August 8, 1854.

[21] MacMaster, Diaries, 356–57; Larsen, journal excerpts, August 12, 1854; James Brown to Brigham Young, August 12, 1854, Brigham Young, Office Files; Mitchell, Journal, August 2 and 12, 1854.

crossed the South Platte River and almost immediately climbed Windlass Hill above Ash Hollow. From the top they had an expansive view. Although the climb up was not difficult, the descent was precipitous, perhaps the most dangerous stretch of the journey. They let some wagons down with ropes, and others by locking the rear wheels. At the bottom they found Ash Hollow to be "most gorgeous."[22]

Forty miles beyond Ash Hollow, the Garn Company stopped to repair wagons and reorganize stock. With far fewer animals and those remaining already weakened—several died during the four days there—they needed to lighten the loads. Using a spring scale, Garn weighed what each wagon was carrying. MacMaster noted that "many of the people had more then they should have and they had to burn many good things." While they were camped there, Orson Pratt—relieved as leader of the church train—arrived with Samuel W. Richards, the just-released president of the British Mission. Richards had left Liverpool on July 8 on a fast steamship, arrived in Boston twelve days later, then gone by train to St. Louis and finally by steamboat to Weston, Missouri. Traveling in a light carriage, he had caught up with the church train and, now with Pratt, was hurrying home to Utah, making sixty miles a day and expecting to be in Salt Lake City by August 26. Their brief visit must have made the Saints acutely aware of the slowness of travel by wagon and oxen.[23]

After four layover days, the Garn Company started again, passing Courthouse and Jailhouse rocks. Large eroded monoliths about four miles to the south, they were the first of a series of sedimentary outcrops, scenic wonders of the West. Fifteen miles farther on was Chimney Rock, the most celebrated landmark, and from there one could see Scotts Bluff, the next in the series. Between the South Platte River and Scotts Bluff, three more in the Garn Company died; no cause was recorded.[24]

The Garn Company was now in Indian Territory. Three years before, the federal government had made a treaty (the Fort Laramie, or Horse Creek, Treaty) with the tribes of the Great Plains. It provided for an annual payment of goods in exchange for allowing emigrants to pass through their lands unmolested. As the Mormon companies approached

[22] MacMaster, Diaries, 356; Davies, Diary, 14; Sutherland, Journal, September 3, 1854.

[23] MacMaster, Diaries, 357; "Departure of Elder S. W. Richards," *Millennial Star* 16 (July 22, 1854): 457; "Elder Samuel W. Richards," *Millennial Star* 16 (September 16, 1854): 585; "Arrivals, Immigration, &c.," *Deseret News*, August 31, 1854, 3; Snow to Richards, September 12, 1854, 686.

[24] MacMaster, Diaries, 356, 358.

Fort Laramie in late July and early August, more than four thousand Indians, particularly the Western, or Teton, Sioux, were gathered there awaiting their annual distribution. The commissioner of Indian Affairs, however, had been delayed. Most overland emigrants, especially those going to California and Oregon, had long since passed Fort Laramie, but the Mormon companies had started late. On August 17, when Olsen's Scandinavian company was about eight miles east of Fort Laramie and traveling past the Indian camps, a lame cow lagged behind and wandered into a circle of two to three hundred lodges belonging to the Brulé Sioux. One of the Mormon men started after her but became frightened by all the Indians and turned around. A Sioux shot the cow and invited his friends to join in the feast, for they were hungry and tired of waiting. According to a journal keeper in the Scandinavian company, "They shot one of our cows which was lame and we let them have the meat."[25]

The Olsen Company reported their loss to the commander at Fort Laramie and moved on. Although a Sioux chief came to the fort to offer compensation, it was refused. Believing the Indians would not resist a show of force, the commanding officer allowed John L. Grattan, a brash young officer, to go to the Indian village to bring in the offender who had shot the cow. Thus on August 19, two days after the cow had been killed, Grattan set out with twenty-nine volunteers, two cannons, and a drunk interpreter. A melee ensued, and after it was over, Grattan, all twenty-nine soldiers, the interpreter, and the Sioux chief lay dead.[26]

Fearing soldiers would come from the fort, the Indian women immediately struck camp and began to move north across the Platte. The Sioux men, however, were angry and threatened to wipe out all the whites at the nearby trading posts and at Fort Laramie. For the next three days, Indians looted the trading posts. Thoroughly frightened, the traders fled to Fort Laramie.

The fort was in grave danger. Altogether the Indian warriors numbered a thousand to fifteen hundred. The fort, completely undermanned, had fewer then fifty men, all infantry. The commanding officer moved his men into old Fort John, the original fort, which could be defended more easily; sent a man to ride to Fort Kearny for reinforcements; and

---

[25] McChristian, *Fort Laramie*, chapter 3; Larsen, journal excerpts, August 17, 1854. McChristian puts the incident of the lame cow on August 18, but Larsen, who kept a diary, has it on August 17.

[26] Accounts of the Grattan massacre and its role in starting the Sioux Wars include McCann, "Grattan Massacre"; Paul, *Blue Water Creek*; and Hedren, *Fort Laramie*.

asked one of the traders to bury Grattan and the dead soldiers. After the Indians left the valley, the traders buried Grattan and his men in a shallow grave, mounding the earth over them.

On August 21, two days after the massacre, the Garn Company was about eleven miles east of the site. MacMaster wrote, "We came to a house alone 19 mil[e]s from the Fort and we was there informed that the indans and the solders at the fort had a fight. . . . We ware ordered to load our guns and make ready for an attack from the indans." They went one more mile and then camped. "In the evening," MacMaster continued, "to [two] men on horse back came to our camp on their way to Fort Levenworth for help. It would take them eleven days or nine. We placed armed men round the camp and cattle all night."[27]

The next morning, now three days after the massacre, MacMaster said they moved forward three miles, placing them about seven miles from the massacre site. There they camped "putting our wagons in a car-all and our tents inside of it as we were afraid that the indans was storming the fort." Given that tents were always set up outside the wagon corral, their decision to set them up inside reveals the degree of their fear.[28]

Daniel Garn, the company's leader, thought he should consult with Apostle Ezra T. Benson and Ira Eldredge, now in charge of the church train, which was close behind them. The next day the two companies moved forward together. Although the number of wagons and people in the church train is not definitely known, one reminiscence placed it at forty wagons. The two companies thus had about eighty wagons and some five hundred people, a strength that the Sioux might hesitate to attack.[29] Nevertheless, one can imagine the immigrants wrapping their faith tightly around them like a thick cloak and hurrying forward as they prayed for God's protection.

In a cloud of dust, they traveled hard. In passing the massacre site, Elizabeth MacDonald of the Garn Company wrote: "We passed where an Indian encampment had been broken up by a company of U.S. troops. . . . We saw signs of the fatal contest; it had been so recent that some of the fires of the camp were still burning." Altogether they traveled twenty

[27] MacMaster, Diaries, 358.

[28] Ibid.; Sinclair, Journal, July 26, 1854.

[29] MacMaster, Diaries, 358–59; E. T. Benson to Brigham Young and Council, September 20, 1854, *Deseret News*, September 28, 1854, 3. The number of forty wagons for the church train is from John Bagley, "Reminiscences," 53.

miles, much more than the average thirteen a day, and camped five miles beyond Fort Laramie.[30]

As they pushed their oxen forward, others joined them. According to one account, "The trappers also was coming towards us for dear life. We all crossed the [Laramie] river [at the fort] all right. We had a larg camp that night. We thought we would haft to fight but the Indians had their reveng." Ezra T. Benson also reported, "The whole country is quite in an excitement, the traders fleeing in all directions, and expecting a general war." Although war did not follow immediately, the Grattan massacre, as it became known, was the catalyst for the merciless punitive expeditions of General William S. Harney. Not until 1890 and the massacre at Wounded Knee Creek in South Dakota did the wars against the Sioux finally end.[31]

From Fort Laramie, they started the next leg of the trek, to South Pass through the crest of the Rocky Mountains, 275 miles away. It would take them three weeks. Having bid farewell to the easy part of the Platte River road, their way became rough and strewn with boulders as it climbed the Black Hills and descended through steep ravines. Small pines and junipers dotted the hills and gave them a black appearance. Sagebrush began to appear, along with yellow-flowering rabbit brush, cheerful black-eyed Susans, and prickly pear cactus. As fear of an Indian attack subsided, one in the Garn Company wrote, "We [his company and the church train] camped together for a few nights then we sapperated. I beloved that the Lord over ruled it [the danger] for our good." Large, unwieldy groups slowed progress and made it difficult to find forage for the animals.[32]

In the days that followed, the Garn Company encountered thunder, hail, and rainstorms.[33] Diary entries became short, merely noting miles traveled, camp locations, and deaths. The longing for Zion was still with the immigrants, but the sense of community lessened daily as they increasingly fixed their thoughts only on the tasks that would keep their wagons moving forward.

Finally they met the North Platte River again and crossed it near present-day Casper. A toll bridge built by the French-Canadian trader John

---

[30] MacDonald, Autobiography, 17–18; MacMaster, Diaries, 359.

[31] The trappers were the former beaver trappers who by this period had become traders. Davies, Diary, 16; Benson to Young and Council, September 20, 1854; Paul, *Blue Water Creek.*

[32] The Black Hills are now considered part of the Laramie Mountains. Davis, Diary, 16.

[33] MacMaster, Diaries, 360.

Baptiste Richard had been completed the year before near the second Mormon ferry site, but the companies all forded the river. They could not afford the toll, and the river was low enough at that time of year.[34]

By now, all the companies were running short of food and had to ration the little they had. Agnes must have particularly felt the reduced portions, for she was four and a half months pregnant. One company leader, after assessing what flour they had, called for a day of fast, an enormous hardship when all were exerting themselves physically.

In Salt Lake City, meanwhile, Brigham Young was asking the bishops to send aid to the immigrants. The editor of the *Deseret News* wrote that "a speedy and liberal turn out" was essential, "for we are all one temporally as well as spiritually, literally as well as figuratively, or we are not what we profess to be."[35]

The Garn Company reached the Sweetwater River in early September. The immigrants had not seen buffalo chips since near Fort Laramie and had used the wood of juniper and cottonwood trees, but now, near the Sweetwater, they had to rely on sagebrush for fuel. It threw out great heat but also burned quickly.[36]

Independence Rock, looking like a beached whale and covered with names of emigrants, and Devil's Gate a few miles farther on were well-known landmarks, curiosities "worthy of a travelers notice," wrote one Mormon. Near Independence Rock they found two trading posts, where some residents kept herds of stock to sell and, at a greatly reduced price, would also buy exhausted and weak animals. The Garn Company pushed on and camped a few miles from Devil's Gate. The Sweetwater River flows through this four-hundred-foot-high perpendicular rock, split in two as if by lightning. Only thirty feet wide at the base of the slit, the passage was too narrow for the immigrants to follow the river through it, and the trail thus wound south a few miles.[37]

Elizabeth MacDonald wrote that "day after day we continued our dreary journey over rivers and plains." They still had almost 100 miles to go before

---

[34] Those unfamiliar with the French pronunciation of "Richard" called it "Reshaw's" Bridge. Mac-Master, Diaries, 360; Sutherland, Journal, September 15 and 28, 1854.

[35] For a more complete analysis of the food shortages, see Aird, "Bound for Zion," 308–12, 316–21. Larsen, journal excerpts, September 2, 1854; "Arrivals, Immigration, &c.," *Deseret News*, August 31, 1854, 3.

[36] MacMaster, Diaries, 361.

[37] Sutherland, Journal, September 29, 1854; Hoth, Diary, September 27, 1854; MacMaster, Diaries, 361.

reaching South Pass, and from there, 230 miles to the Salt Lake Valley. It took them eight weary days to finally reach South Pass on September 13. Just before the company topped the pass, MacMaster wrote that "three wagons from the valley came up and camped with us . . . and a meeting of some friends took [place between] mother and son, brothers and sisters." Joy mingled with the realization that they were on the homeward stretch.[38]

Without towering mountains or fearful cliffs, South Pass is deceptive. At 7,550 feet in elevation, the pass is a gently sloped saddle about thirty miles wide and dotted with sagebrush. Although the passage was insignificant, its meaning was not: on the far side all streams flowed to the Great Basin or the Pacific Ocean. The Garn Company descended to Pacific Springs on the western slope to rest for a few hours before moving a little farther to camp. Water was plentiful, feed good for the animals, and sagebrush abundant for fires. The next day, just before the company came to the Big Sandy River, they met John Taylor, another of the Twelve Apostles. He was headed east to New York to preside over the church in the eastern states. Peter Sinclair noted that Taylor was with others also going on missions; they had eleven wagons with mule teams, and some were riding mules. Sinclair commented that the Taylor party halted their train for only a few minutes, so the immigrants hardly saw or spoke to them.[39]

On September 17, after the Garn Company had forded the Green River, another contingent arrived from the Salt Lake Valley, looking for family members and bringing food. Among them was Peter's thirty-two-year-old uncle, Sandy Adamson.[40] Peter's uncles and grandmother had come to Utah in 1848, and it had been six years since they had seen each other. It must have been a joyful reunion, and now Peter, Agnes, and John could travel with Sandy in his wagon the rest of the way to Salt Lake City. Most likely they left the Garn Company at this point, perhaps with others who had come from Salt Lake. With fresh animals and without the drag of a large company, they could move faster. But it also marked the end of their place in the overland community.

In the next few days, they crossed and recrossed Ham's Fork and then Black's Fork and passed Fort Bridger, where some mountain men were

---

[38] MacDonald, Autobiography, 17–18; MacMaster, Diaries, 361–62.
[39] MacMaster, Diaries, 362; Sinclair, Journal, September 21, 1854.
[40] MacMaster, Diaries, 362.

living.[41] Traveling again through thunder, lightning, and rain, they forded the Bear River to go over the divide into the Weber River drainage, passed Cache Cave, and finally descended into Echo Canyon. Here they found a canyon with steep hills on the south side and high perpendicular red cliffs on the north. Parts of the cliffs had been eroded into fantastic shapes, which made a remarkable parade for European eyes: Castle Rock, Winged Rock, Kettle Rocks, Hanging Rock, Jack in the Pulpit Rock, Tumble Down Rocks, Temple Rock, Steamboat Rocks, Monument Rock, Pulpit Rock, Conglomerate Peaks, and Witch Rocks. A shot, the bellow of an ox, or a shout produced an eerie echo.

The little party forded the Weber River and turned south up a side canyon to "Pratt's Pass" (Main Canyon, or Little East Canyon). At the top of the ridge, they could suddenly see the many mountains that still lay between them and Salt Lake City, a discouraging sight. After camping near Dixie Hollow and probably the next night near the base of Big Mountain, they had a long, hard haul up the mountain, with an extremely steep descent on the other side, made more hazardous by the stumps of trees that had been cut to make the road. From the top of Big Mountain, they had their first tantalizing view of the southern end of Salt Lake Valley. Their next climb was over Little Mountain; after the descent, they likely camped near the start of Emigration Canyon. The canyon was steep and they had to cross the creek several times, but now at the end of September, the upper slopes would have been dabbed with the bright reds and pinks of scrub oak. At the mouth of Emigration Canyon, they had to skirt a high hill. Then suddenly their long-wished-for valley spread out before them.

"This was indeed a haven of rest after a tiresome journey," wrote Elizabeth MacDonald. Another emigrant that year was quite overcome: "Tears trickled down my face with joy; my feelings on that occasion were so wrought upon, that all the riches of Europe, I am sure, could not have given me more pleasure. The city in the distance appeared to me as a

---

[41] The year before, in late August 1853, Brigham Young, acting in his role of ex officio superintendent of Indian Affairs, had sent a posse to raid Fort Bridger. Young had heard that mountaineer and trader Jim Bridger was selling ammunition and alcohol to the Indians. Already having lost much of their land to Mormon settlers, the Indians were feeling hostile. The posse found alcohol but no ammunition. Bridger escaped just before they arrived and in the fall of 1854 was living with his family on a farm south of Westport, Missouri. Alter, *Jim Bridger*, 248–59.

holy place. I felt well, the Spirit of the Most High was with me, and all my fatigue and sufferings were entirely forgotten."[42]

Starting up again after that first arresting view, the emigrants traveled along the "bench," the former shoreline of ancient Lake Bonneville. Elizabeth MacDonald wrote that many friends and relatives came to greet the company as they emerged from the canyon. Peter, Agnes, and John, traveling with Sandy Adamson, probably arrived a day or two before the main company. The *Deseret News* reported that the Garn Company arrived on October 1, but Peter later wrote that they had arrived at the end of September. Worn with fatigue, dirty, and tattered in spite of their efforts to look presentable, they found the road on the bench edged with sunflowers nodding toward the afternoon sun. The day was warm. Before long, the road led down the steep hill and into the city. Their route took them on Emigration Road (now 300 South), then north on State or Main Street, past Temple Square, and northwest again to the McAuslans' house in the Nineteenth Ward. Peter probably stopped first to see his grandmother, Agnes Baird Adamson. He had not seen her in six years, and he wanted to introduce his new wife. She lived with her sons Sandy and Dougal in a house one block south of that belonging to Peter's parents.[43]

They had left Scotland seven months earlier, sailed the ocean, steamed up rivers, and walked 1,190 miles overland.[44] They believed that God had preserved them from cholera and warring Indians. And now they were expecting their first child. It had been a wearisome journey, but at long last they could say, "We are home!"

---

[42] MacDonald, Autobiography, 18; Robert G. Taylor to Thomas G. Taylor, October 28, 1858, *Millennial Star* 17 (March 17, 1855): 173.

[43] MacDonald, Autobiography, 18; "Immigration, Oct. 3," *Deseret News*, October 5, 1854, 2; McAuslan to McAuslan Day (#55 McAuslan Papers).

[44] The mileage comes from Sutherland, Journal, last page.

10

The Promised Land

IN SPITE OF EXHAUSTION FROM THE TRIP, PETER, AGNES, AND John were elated at arriving in Zion. Now, at the end of September 1854, they were finally reunited with family and friends; they could rest from the daily, tiresome chores of the journey; and here they would find the peace and godliness that had been promised. To crown their joy, they were soon to see and hear their prophet, revelator, and seer, Brigham Young. The semiannual church conference took place in the Tabernacle five days after their arrival. Along with the majority of the people of Salt Lake City and surrounding settlements, they attended the three days of addresses by church leaders and singing by the choir. On the opening day, President Young spoke, charging all whose emigration had been supported by the Perpetual Emigrating Fund, the church's loan program, to repay what they owed as speedily as possible so that other poor Saints could emigrate. He talked of the working-class Saints still in Great Britain who longed to leave but could barely afford an evening meal. It was a subject always close to Peter's heart.[1]

Orson Pratt was among those who spoke the second day. After again exhorting people to pay off their debt to the PEF, he began to apologize for any unsound doctrine he might have once taught. "So far as I have ever preached abroad in the world, and published, one thing is certain, I have not published anything but what I verily believed to be true, . . . and I have generally endeavored to show the people from the written word of God, as well as reason, wherein it was true." He continued, "I may have erred in some principles; I do not profess to be wise, or to have

---

[1] Brigham Young, October 6, 1854, *Journal of Discourses*, 2:49–53.

more understanding than many others. I am not called with the same calling as those who preside over all the Church."[2]

Pratt was reacting to a reprimand President Young had given him two weeks earlier in a prayer meeting of the highest leaders of the church. Young had objected to Pratt's writings that God is omniscient, rather than that God is eternally progressing in knowledge. Additionally, Pratt had taught that Adam had been literally created out of the dust of the earth. This was in contrast to Young's Adam-God doctrine, which asserted that Adam had come from another world, bringing one of his wives, Eve, with him, and that Adam was the same as God and the father of Jesus Christ.[3]

On the final evening, with the largest crowd of the conference in attendance, President Young spoke again, expounding once more on the doctrine that Adam was God. Without mentioning his name, Young referred to Pratt's publications on preexistence and made clear they were in error: "So many among us are preaching, lecturing, contemplating upon, and conversing about things away beyond our reach. . . . Consequently, when you hear philosophers argue the point how the first god came, how intelligence came, how worlds came, and how angels came, they are talking about that which is beyond their conception. . . . It manifests their folly."[4]

This was not the "one heart, one mind" that Peter had expected in Zion. Instead here was discord among the highest levels of the church hierarchy. In addition, the writings of the man who had so influenced Peter's own conversion were being questioned by the head of the church. Arriving with expectations about the elevated life he would find among the Saints, this was only the first test of Peter's faith. In the months to come, a series of natural disasters, personal losses, and the church's reaction to them would challenge his love of the religion that had brought him from Scotland. He would come to doubt whether President Young was any more inspired than many other men and also to question the doctrines that Young and the other authorities were soon to teach.[5]

---

[2] Orson Pratt, October 7, 1854, *Journal of Discourses*, 2:58–59.

[3] Bergera, *Conflict in the Quorum*, 113–14. Brigham Young first expounded the Adam-God doctrine at the semiannual general conference on April 9, 1852. See Collier, *Teachings of President Young*, 343–74. The Adam-God doctrine is no longer taught by the LDS Church. Regarding this period, George A. Hicks, whom Peter was to meet in a couple of years, wrote, "If he [President Young] said Adam was the God of this world, the people believed it or pretended to believe it. In all matters he was the sun of our system." Hicks, "History of George Armstrong Hicks," 24.

[4] Bergera, *Conflict in the Quorum*, 115–16; Collier, *Teachings of President Young*, 343, 345.

[5] "One heart, one mind" comes from the Mormon Book of Moses 7:18. Peter described his experiences in Utah in a letter written a year after he left; they will be detailed in later chapters.

The original Salt Lake Tabernacle, built in 1852, where Peter and Agnes first
heard Brigham Young speak. From *Harper's Weekly*, September 18, 1858.
Used by permission, Utah State Historical Society, all rights reserved.

October 15 brought the first frost and signaled winter's imminent
approach. Peter's father had bought a lot in the Nineteenth Ward a month
after the main part of the family arrived in 1853. Sometime later he bought
the adjacent lot in anticipation of Peter and Agnes's arrival, and a new
house perhaps was waiting for them. Assuming the house of Peter's parents was typical for Salt Lake City in this period—made of adobe, with
two or three rooms—it was crowded with his parents and five of his siblings: Ann, twenty; Frank, eighteen; Christina, sixteen; Janet, fourteen;
and David, almost twelve. Peter's sister Jane, whose husband, William
Evans, had left for the California gold fields the previous spring, may also
have been living with them, along with her baby, Eliza.[6]

In all Salt Lake City records, Peter is listed as a laborer. Certainly in
this raw country there was no demand for calico patterns. What kind of

---

[6] "Transfers of City Lots," 12, 398. The description of pioneer houses is from Lingren, "Autobiography," 1:240. William, the second-oldest son of the elder Peter and Betsy, and his wife, Mary Muir,
had traveled to Utah also, but in 1854–55 they were living in Tooele, to the west of Salt Lake City.

work he obtained is not known, but the labor tithing records (each man had to contribute one day in ten to the church's public works) show that in March 1855 he worked as a mason laborer on the temple foundations.[7]

The mail arrived on December 1 and included two letters for the McAuslans, one for Peter's father and one for himself. The first was from John Allan, who had married Peter's older sister, Agnes. He reported that they had waited before emigrating, as the elder Peter had asked them to, but they were no better off, for work was scarce. There had been a great many plant closings among the printworks, including five around Paisley and one in Kilmarnock. "I think that it is a good thing that Peter went away and think he would have been idle mostly all summer," Allan wrote. In spite of not being able to save more, the Allans hoped to emigrate the next spring. The second letter was to Peter from Robert Salmon, whom he had baptized in Denny, Scotland. Now living in Barrhead, where Peter had also lived, he wrote that their branch of the church was not baptizing many new members. He also noted, "Trade is very flat at presant and I have little prospects of getting to see you and all the Saints in Utah, for some time yet, although I have a great desire to be with the Saints in there gathering Place."[8]

On Christmas Day eighteen to twenty U.S. soldiers and some young Mormon men engaged in a fray not far from the McAuslan homes. Alonzo H. Raleigh, then counselor to the bishop of the Nineteenth Ward, wrote, "There was quite a row took place in the streets today betweene the Soldiers of Uncle Sam & som of our Boys." Colonel Edward J. Steptoe and his command of 175 officers and soldiers were wintering in Salt Lake City, and on Christmas a city merchant had treated some of the soldiers to alcohol. Apostle George A. Smith wrote, "Mr. Perry, a merchant of this city, presented the soldiers with so much of the 'good critter,' that they kicked up a fight among themselves in their quarters on [Enoch] Reese's premises [on South Temple Street], a party rushed to the street, and managed to get up a row with some young men. The officer of the day did his best to quiet the row, which however was not done until a good many heads got badly bruised, and the city authorities arrived." Steptoe had orders to take stock and troops to California, but a second order had come as he and his men left Fort Leavenworth:

---

[7] Trustee-in-Trust, "Tithing hands," Raleigh's Time Book B, 12.
[8] John Allan to Peter McAuslan, Sr., August 24, 1854 (#8 McAuslan Papers), 1–4; Robert Salmon to Peter McAuslan, Jr., August 24, 1854 (#9 McAuslan Papers), 3–4.

he was to stop off in Utah and punish the Indians responsible for the 1853 murder of Captain John W. Gunnison and his railroad survey party. Although Steptoe's troops brought needed currency, they were a constant irritant to the Mormons until they left again in April 1855.[9]

The winter of 1854–55 proved extremely mild. In early February many started sowing grain and transplanting fruit trees. Peter began farming for the first time under the tutelage of his father, who had already been through one growing season in Utah. Peter had learned to handle oxen and cattle during the long and strenuous journey to Salt Lake City, but he had never before planted what his family would depend on for the next year. His father too was still learning, for an agricultural life was vastly different and an abrupt change from the urban factory existence they had known in Scotland. What to plant, when to plant, how to go about it, how to irrigate, and how to keep weeds down were skills they must quickly learn.[10] In addition, they needed to gain knowledge about the care of pigs and chickens or other farmyard animals, when and how to slaughter them, and how to prepare the meat. Peter must have enjoyed being free of the fetid atmosphere and long hours of the textile plants, but to transition swiftly to this new life must have caused anxiety.

Agnes and Peter's first child, Peter Alexander McAuslan, was born on February 3, 1855, and on March 15 he was blessed.[11] By the end of March, men were fencing new areas to farm and sowing more wheat. Cattle were moved up onto the benches and across the Jordan River, where the grass was already up. The mild weather also allowed some non-Mormon entrepreneurs who had wintered in the Salt Lake Valley to start for California in late March and early April with large herds of cattle intended for the market there. Some Mormons went with them.

---

[9] George A. Smith to Joseph F. Smith, December 27, 1854, Journal History, December 27, 1854; Raleigh, Journal, 91; George A. Smith to Franklin D. Richards, December 28, 1854, *Millennial Star* 17 (April 21, 1855): 253;. MacKinnon, "Sex, Subalterns, and Steptoe," 227–35.

[10] Englishman Thomas A. Poulter, who had traveled with Peter and Agnes on the ship *John M. Wood*, recounted his troubles in learning to farm in Bountiful, Utah: "In a short time I found the weeds getting ahead of me. But the Bishop kept saying, 'Cheer up, Brother, don't lose courage. Keep on trying.'" When Poulter found his American-born neighbor's garden had no weeds, he asked him how to keep them down. Poulter wrote that "with a laugh and a sneer," his neighbor replied, "Well, you see Brother, you English folk have to learn a good deal." Poulter finally discovered the solution: "One morning it rained. The next morning I was up early and I saw this dear Brother and his only son with two rakes working as if for life, raking up the ground all around the crops and in the rows of corn. . . . I had learned the trick." Poulter, "Life," 143–44.

[11] Mormons are not baptized before eight years old, when they are considered accountable. Babies are blessed during a sacrament meeting a month or two after birth. Record of Members, Nineteenth Ward, 10.

"A few of our brethren are leaving for California, having got the California fever," wrote George A. Smith. Among them was Agnes's brother John McAuslin. He was now twenty years old and restless. His leaving "without counsel" meant that he was also abandoning his Mormon faith, and those who left for the gold fields were often excommunicated.[12]

April 6 saw the opening of the twenty-fifth annual conference of the church. Colonel Steptoe, fearing trouble between the soldiers and the people coming for the conference, moved his men forty-five miles southwest to Rush Valley, where the army stock grazed.[13] The *Deseret News* reported that at the conference "President Brigham Young said that twenty-five years ago to-day, the Prophet Joseph Smith organized this Church with six members; reviewed the rise, building up, and marvellous increase of the Church; and gave much useful instruction." The bishop of the Nineteenth Ward presented the statistics: 579 residents, 8 of whom were "teachers." Peter McAuslan, Sr., had been ordained a teacher in January 1854, and his son Peter is recorded as one in May 1856. Teachers in this period were mature men, the most capable available. They were officers of the ward who functioned as the "legs and feet" of the bishop, checking on the spiritual as well as temporal well-being of each family in the ward and acting as peace officers to mediate disputes. They helped collect tithing, for in addition to contributing one day out of ten in labor, each head of household yearly tithed 10 percent of his increase in stock, crops raised, or items made, such as butter or cheese. Teachers were also to be the "watchmen to guard against all manner of iniquity," such as drunkenness or failure to attend meetings.[14]

When Colonel Steptoe and his men left for California in late April, a number of Mormon women who wished to leave Utah went with them.

---

[12] The membership records of the Nineteenth Ward show that on March 25, May 10, and May 19, 1855, people were excommunicated for leaving for California "without counsel"; Record of Members, Nineteenth Ward, 46. George A. Smith to Franklin D. Richards, February 7, March 29, and September 30, 1855, *Millennial Star* 17 (April 28, June 23, and December 15, 1855): 269, 396–97, and 799.

[13] The trouble was also related to Lieutenant Sylvester Mowry, who had taken a fancy to Mary Ann Young, the wife of Brigham Young's son, Joseph A. Young. As Joseph was on a mission, Mowry applied his considerable charm with some success, causing great excitement among the Mormons and resulting in Colonel Steptoe's ordering Mowry to stay in the Rush Valley camp and not return to Salt Lake City. Mowry to Bicknall, April 27, 1855; Rufus Ingalls to Thomas S. Jesup, August 25, 1855, *Report of the Secretary of War, 1855*, 158.

[14] "Minutes," *Deseret News*, April 11, 1855, 4; Bishop's Records, Nineteenth Ward; Record of Members, Nineteenth Ward, 51, 61; Hartley, "Ordained and Acting Teachers," 377, 383. Teachers as "legs and feet" comes from Hartley, "Ordained and Acting Teachers," 392. The "watchmen" quotation comes from Edward Hunter, then presiding bishop, as quoted in Hartley, "From Men to Boys," 96. See also D&C 20:53–55.

Conversation about the women's faithlessness died down as worries rose about the warm, dry weather and the need to irrigate their crops. Then on April 25 the *Deseret News* ominously announced: "The Grasshoppers—are coming out very numerous, threatening to destroy all vegetation as fast as it appears. Exercise your faith, brethren, that the Lord may bless your crops, rebuke the destroyer, and bring your labors and exertions to a successful issue."[15]

The grasshoppers were actually Rocky Mountain locusts, *Melanoplus spretus*, a species now extinct. In an outbreak cycle, prevailing winds carried them from the Rocky Mountains, and they settled wherever they found good food, especially farm crops. As they swept into the American heartland, they left fields denuded and thousands of eggs behind to hatch the next year. When the nymphs emerged the next spring, they aggregated in bands, and when they developed wings, they began to swarm, rising in immense clouds, glittering as the sun caught the flash of their wings. Noon would turn to dusk. In a seemingly arbitrary way, a swarm would alight on a field or orchard, bending young trees nearly double under their weight. People compared the noise of their chewing and the rush of their wings through the air to the crackling and rasping of a prairie fire.[16]

The periodic locust outbreaks were triggered by drought, which suppressed the fungal diseases that could kill the insects. Wheat was a favorite crop, whereas peas and beans were not, and corn, being sturdy, generally survived. This was a "living fire" in sound and action, for a single swarm "metabolically burned 4,000 pounds of vegetation an hour." When such a conflagration finally ended, the stench of the putrefying bodies was overpowering. The rotting insects contaminated surface water and even wells.[17]

The specter of total crop failure and famine was terrifying to the Saints. The biblical plagues of Exodus had come to Utah. God had sent locusts to Egypt because Pharaoh refused to humble himself before the Lord. But why, then, was God afflicting the Saints, his own people? President Young said it was punishment for their laxness, sinfulness, and not husbanding the grain they had raised in 1854: "People must be chastened. . . . All that we have received as chastisement is from the hand of the Lord . . . [and]

---

[15] Heber C. Kimball to William Kimball, May 20, 1855, Journal History, May 29, 1855, 3–4. Although this letter appeared in the *Millennial Star* 17 (August 18, 1855): 519, the part about the women leaving had been excised. MacKinnon, "Sex, Subalterns, and Steptoe," 237–40; "The Weather," *Deseret News*, April 25, 1855, 5; George A. Smith to Franklin D. Richards, April 27, 1855, *Millennial Star* 17 (August 11, 1855): 507; "The Grasshoppers," *Deseret News*, April 25, 1855, 5.

[16] The best account of the Rocky Mountain locust is Lockwood, *Locust*, 9, 21–30.

[17] Ibid., 3, 22, 55, 251.

is but a small portion of what we will receive, if we do not take care of the things the Lord bestows upon us."[18]

The locust invasion of 1855 was the worst Utah was ever to experience. The first, second, and even third sowings of crops were mostly destroyed. Even peach trees loaded with fruit were completely stripped of every leaf and peach, leaving the bare pits hanging by their stems.[19] John Fell Squires, nine years old at the time and living in the Twentieth Ward, later recalled the invasion:

> It was all a fellow could do to face them when they began to [a]light. . . . They never closed their . . . jaws until every thing of a green nature was devouerd [*sic*] right down to window blinds and green paint. . . . It would not take them long to eat up a fellow's pantaloons when the color suited them. . . . They left the whole surrounding country brown and leafless and ourselves looking blue. Just think one thousand miles from market, *too* late in the season to plant another crop, little or no food in the country, so that famine stared us in the face.[20]

On July 9 the eastern mail arrived and brought a letter for Peter from a friend in Scotland. One of his sentences seemed to mock their situation: "I hope that you now find yourself easy . . . and that your Mother and Father are now finding the land of promise also a land of performance." Reports of locusts diminished in the following weeks, and people expressed hope that the insects were gone for good. But they were disappointed, for in early September the *Deseret News* once more reported the descent of "a few thousand million grasshoppers" and made a harsh prediction: "The last prospect for bread . . . is therefore suddenly snapped asunder."[21]

As the summer wore on, letters and the newspaper began to comment less on the locust devastation and more on the drought. With little snow in the mountains the previous winter and only light rains since, water for irrigation had become a critical problem. The few plants that had

---

[18] Brigham Young, October 8, 1855, *Journal of Discourses*, 3:116–17. In May 1848, crickets had invaded Utah and begun consuming the crops of the pioneers. A month later, California gulls, spring and summer residents of the Great Salt Lake, swooped in to feed on them, saving part of the crop. Over time, this incident became the "miracle of the seagulls." For 1855, however, only one mention of gulls has been found, and it was when the locusts first appeared: George A. Smith to Franklin D. Richards, April 27, 1855, *Millennial Star* 17 (August 11, 1855): 507.

[19] Heber C. Kimball to William Kimball, May 29, 1855, *Millennial Star* 17 (August 18, 1855): 519; "Still They Come!" *Deseret News*, June 27, 1855, 5; Carter, "Fish and the Famine," 97.

[20] Squires, Autobiography, 6, emphasis his.

[21] William McKechnie to Peter McAuslan, April 1, 1855 (#11 McAuslan Papers), 2–3; Brigham Young to Franklin D. Richards, July 30, 1855, *Millennial Star* 17 (October 20, 1855): 667; *Deseret News*, September 5, 1855, 5.

survived the locusts were wilting. Alonzo Raleigh, counselor to the bishop of the Nineteenth Ward and in June commissioned as justice of the peace for Salt Lake City, noted cases of water stealing in his journal: Between July 16 and 21, he arrested two men and fined another two for "takeing the watter unlawfully."[22]

The drought and locusts meant that there was no grass to cut for hay, and the normal rangelands on the benches, over the Jordan River, and on Antelope Island were bare. The leaders were thus forced to drive about two thousand church stock and a thousand of their personal animals northeast to Cache Valley in late July. Work on the temple foundations was halted, for the twenty ox teams employed to haul rock from Red Butte Canyon for the foundations had no feed and were also sent to Cache Valley.[23]

In Salt Lake City, President Young "wished the people not to fret their gizzards about the failure of crops or any thing else. The Lord would take care of his people, and if they did their duty we would yet have a good Crop." Believing that the first duty was building the Kingdom of God, Young continued to push the church building program at a brisk pace. The Endowment House, used for secret religious rites, was finished on April 10 and dedicated on May 5, 1855. A wall had been built around Temple Block, and the laying of the coping stone was progressing well. And the digging of the Big Cottonwood Canal had started. It was to carry water from Big Cottonwood Canyon to Parley's Canyon and eventually to the center of the city. Its function was primarily to barge enormous granite blocks for building the temple and secondarily to bring needed irrigation water into town, as City Creek was inadequate. The kingdom was being built. But the work depended on tithing, and the crop failure meant that less than usual was coming in. In September, President Young preached about gathering the poor from Great Britain but then turned to castigate those who were behind in their tithing: "I want to have you understand fully that I intend to put the screws upon you, and . . . if you do not pay up now and help us, we will levy on your property and take every farthing you have on the earth." Brigham Young was determined to build Zion.[24]

---

[22] Raleigh, Journal, 108, 111.

[23] Young to Richards, July 30, 1855, 667; Raleigh, Journal, 113.

[24] S. W. Richards, Diary, 239; Brigham Young, Heber C. Kimball, Jedediah M. Grant, "Twelfth General Epistle," ca. April 10, 1855, *Millennial Star* 17 (August 11, 1855): 498, 502; Brigham Young, Heber C. Kimball, Jedediah M. Grant, "Thirteenth General Epistle," October 29, 1855, *Millennial Star* 18 (January 26, 1855): 50; Brigham Young, September 16, 1855, *Journal of Discourses*, 3:6. The reduction in tithing is given in Bitton and Wilcox, "Pestiferous Ironclads," 345–46.

The stricken settlers could at least look forward to once more seeing family and friends who were expected in the fall immigration. On October 24, 1855, a PEF company arrived, led by Milo Andrus. Among the members was Archibald Anderson, husband of Peter's aunt Agnes Adamson Anderson (she and three of their children would not arrive until the next year). Five days later, on October 29, 1855, to Peter's delight, John and Agnes Allan arrived with the Charles A. Harper PEF Company. The Allans moved in with Peter and Agnes for the winter. The immediate McAuslan family was together again except for Betsy, the daughter who had decided to stay in Scotland.[25]

Frost came in October and destroyed much of the late corn and wheat. "It is good there is something to try the Saints, or the sieve would not have its cleaning effect as it now does," wrote George A. Smith, referring to those whose faith was overwhelmed by the succession of natural disasters and who wished to leave. But that would not be possible until the next spring, when the grass had grown enough to support their animals. In November, Peter worked as a mason laborer at the Public Works, and he and his father also fulfilled their labor tithing by working on the Big Cottonwood Canal.[26]

The first snows began in November, but each quickly melted. By December 19 the *Deseret News* reported snow several feet deep in the canyons of the Wasatch Range and declared, "If another mail from the east should be brought through during the winter, it will be more than we expect." December 21 and 22 brought a storm of hurricane-like wind and snow, which damaged many sheds and fences. Three days later Peter and Agnes celebrated Christmas with his family and the Adamsons. But for the rest of December and January, one snowstorm followed another, with temperatures as low as twelve degrees below freezing. Once more the Saints were isolated in their mountain fastness. Although the weather was harsh, the snow gave assurance that they would not suffer through another drought the next summer.[27]

Tithing records show that Peter's father gained a cow, two pigs, and four chickens over the course of 1855. They also record that he raised corn,

---

[25] Journal History, October 24, 1855, 1; "Immigration List," *Deseret News*, September 12, 1855, 6.

[26] George A. Smith to Franklin D. Richards, October 31, 1855, *Millennial Star* 18 (January 26, 1856): 62; Trustee-in-Trust, Raleigh's Time Book A, November 1855.

[27] "Weather," *Deseret News*, November 14, 1855, 5; "To Our Readers," *Deseret News*, December 19, 1855, 4; "The Weather," *Deseret News*, December 26, 1855, 5; Robert L. Campbell to Franklin D. Richards, January 7, 1856, *Millennial Star* 18 (May 24, 1856): 332.

potatoes, and beets, the latter a vegetable that in most places was hard hit by locusts. His wheat crop had failed, nor did he raise hay, onions, carrots, or parsnips, all items that would be listed on his next year's tithing. Until the family's supplies ran short, their diet for the coming year would thus consist of corn, cornbread, potatoes, some beets, milk, and eggs. They probably did not have enough, however, to sustain the large McAuslan family until the early harvest in midsummer. Peter, Agnes with a nursing baby, and the Allans living with them would have shared the same diet.[28]

Even before the start of the new year, fuel became scarce. The *Deseret News* reported that many families, having failed to cut wood in the canyons before the snow became too deep, were suffering. Some had enough for only a week's cooking and heating. By January 17, snow in the city was two to three feet deep. By the end of the month, cattle were dying. The locusts had cropped the range grasses, and the deep snows made it impossible for the animals to reach what little survived.[29]

Only Jedediah Grant, first counselor to Brigham Young, saw the severe winter, coming on top of the crop failure, as a blessing: it meant that the Saints had to depend on God. Grant commented that the lack of food "keeps the corrupt at bay, for they [the army or federal appointees] know that they would have to starve, or import their rations, should they come to injure us in the Territory of Utah." On the same day, Brigham Young preached on being prepared for future times of scarcity, suggesting a program that has become integral to Mormon beliefs: "I do not apprehend the least danger of starving, for until we eat up the last mule, from the tip of the ear to the end of the fly whipper, I am not afraid of starving to death. . . . [But] we never ought to be without three, or five years provisions on hand."[30]

The hard year of 1855 had ended. It was not at all what Peter had expected to find in the "Promised Land." And the new year, with its prospect of famine, seemed to offer only further hardships. Nevertheless, his family were all together, and Peter and Agnes took great delight in Peter Alexander, their ten-month-old baby.

---

[28] Bishop's Records, Nineteenth Ward, October 30, 1855; Local Unit Financial Records, Nineteenth Ward, December 31, 1855. The paucity of beets is from George A. Smith to the editor of the *Mormon*, June 20, 1855, *Millennial Star* 17 (October 6, 1855): 366.

[29] "Hard Times," *Deseret News*, January 16, 1856, 5; Journal History, January 17, 1856, 1; "Cold and Snow," *Deseret News*, January 30, 1856, 5.

[30] Jedediah M. Grant, January 27, 1856, *Journal of Discourses*, 3:201; Brigham Young, January 27, 1856, *Journal of Discourses*, 3:196.

II

Famine, Loss, and Reformation

IN DECEMBER 1855 THE UTAH TERRITORIAL LEGISLATURE PASSED a bill authorizing a census and an election of delegates from every county to a constitutional convention. The purpose was to draw up a constitution and a memorial to the U.S. Congress requesting that Utah be admitted to the Union as a state. The Mormons had sent similar memorials to Congress in 1852, 1853, and 1854, but their applications had been ignored. Brigham Young decided they must now take the initiative in forming a constitutional convention. His great desire was to be free of "that odious, tyrannical, and absurd system of colonial government" that gave the president and the Senate jurisdiction over territories. If Utah became a state, the Mormons would have much more control over their own affairs, including not only the ability to elect their own officials but also—in this period of the Kansas-Nebraska Act and its support for popular sovereignty—the right to practice polygamy without interference. Independence was essential. After Young made several more attempts to distance Utah from the federal government, Peter McAuslan wrote, "They had full faith that the Lord would fight there Battles and sustain them as an independent Kingdom to the dismay and overthrow of all there enemies."[1]

The census took place in January and February 1856 and was intentionally padded to meet the population requirements for statehood. For example, the listing for the McAuslans showed a Susan in the family, the Adamsons acquired a nonexistent John, and Agnes and John Allan were listed with four children, though they had none. The census also

---

[1] "Affairs at the Capital," *Deseret News*, January 2, 1856, 5; Arrington, *Brigham Young*, 237-38; Bigler, *Forgotten Kingdom*, 101, 121; Brigham Young, "Governor's Message," *Deseret News*, December 19, 1855, 4; Peter McAuslan to Robert Salmon, December 1860 (#14 McAuslan Papers), 4.

showed the Nineteenth Ward as having 2,113 inhabitants, whereas the bishop had reported 614 residents at the fall conference four months before. The census figures were obviously exaggerated, but Young was determined to have his way.[2]

Besides the census, January and February 1856 brought deep snow and death to cattle by the hundreds. Heber C. Kimball wrote that at least half of the estimated twenty-five hundred head that had been taken to Cache Valley had died. Cattle and horses were dying in the city as well; only those kept in barns and fed hay had a chance to survive. Eventually President Young estimated that two-thirds of the stock had died. It was a severe blow to the Mormon kingdom, for cattle drives to California had been a primary source of cash.[3]

Along with the continual storms came wintry blasts from the Tabernacle pulpit, holding the people responsible for the natural disasters that had come upon them. Only repentance and renewed commitment would end God's chastisement. Orson Pratt said on February 10, "One calamity after another, one punishment after another. . . . Will it not learn us a lesson? . . . O Lord, let thy chastening hand be upon this people, until they learn to obey those good and wholesome counsels that are poured out from this stand by those who preside over us." His words must have given cold comfort to the likes of William Knox, who lived in the Sixteenth Ward with his wife and three children and had been employed at the Public Works until they shut down. Just before Pratt's sermon, Knox, a ward teacher, wrote, "I have ascertained the amount of provisions that is in my destrect. If it were devided it would not serve the people one month. Besides, we are one thousand miles from aney other Country and, with that, Bound in by Snow. . . . Out of fire wood. Very cold."[4]

---

[2] 1856 Utah Census, 498–500; Dilts, "Historical Background," iii. The petition for statehood was delayed until 1858. The newly formed Republican Party demanded an end to the "twin relics of barbarism—polygamy and slavery" in the territories, and John Taylor and George A. Smith, the delegates sent to present the Utah memorial, quickly saw the futility of their mission. Lyman, *Political Deliverance*, 8–9.

[3] Brigham Young, in saying that two-thirds of the cattle had died, meant the church's stock and his personal stock, not all the animals in the territory. The worst losses were in Cache Valley. Heber C. Kimball to William Kimball, February 29, 1856, *Millennial Star* 18 (June 21, 1856): 396–97; Brigham Young to Charles C. Rich, April 3, 1856, Brigham Young, Letterpress Copybook Transcriptions, 649, 652; Arrington, *Great Basin Kingdom*, 125–36.

[4] Orson Pratt, February 10, 1856, *Journal of Discourses*, 3:297; William Knox, Journal, February 8, 1856, as quoted in Carter, "Fish and the Famine," 108. The Public Works had closed because there was not enough food in the Tithing Office to give to the workers for their pay; they were told to go raise their own grain, even though it would be late March before seeding could begin. Heber C. Kimball to William Kimball, February 29, 1856, 396; *Deseret News*, March 26, 1856, 8.

Every diary and letter from winter to late June 1856 testifies to famine. People dug for roots—primarily thistle and sego lily—and some begged in the streets. The church leaders rationed their families. Both Brigham Young and Heber C. Kimball allowed the members of their large families only half a pound of bread a day so as to give what they saved to the poor. At the end of February, Kimball wrote that several wards had less than two weeks' worth of food left. "Dollars and cents do not count now, in these times, for they are the tightest that I have ever seen in the Territory of Utah."[5]

In early March 1856, President Young began a course to which Peter took great exception. In the Tabernacle, Young once more chastised members about their spiritual state: "I will tell you what this people need, with regard to preaching; you need, figuratively, to have it rain pitchforks, tines downwards, from this pulpit, Sunday after Sunday. Instead of the smooth, beautiful, sweet, still, silk-velvet-lipped preaching, you should have sermons like peals of thunder, and perhaps we then can get the scales from our eyes." In the same sermon, Young demonstrated what he meant: "Do you not know that Jesus told the truth when he said, 'They that are not for us are against us'? . . . The time is coming when justice will be laid to the line and righteousness to the plummet; when we shall take the old broad sword and ask, 'Are you for God?' and if you are not heartily on the Lord's side, you will be hewn down." The same day, President Young's counselor Jedediah Grant took up the cry with fervor: "I not only wish but pray, in the name of Israel's God, that the time was come in which to unsheath the sword, like Moroni of old, and to cleanse the inside of the platter, and we would not wait for the decisions of grand or traverse juries, but we would walk into you and completely use up every curse[d person] who will not do right."[6]

President Young increased the stridency of his preaching two weeks later. "There is not a man or woman, who violates the covenants made

---

[5] Raleigh, Journal, 133; Brigham Young to George Q. Cannon, April 3, 1856, Brigham Young, Letterpress Copybook Transcriptions, 653; Heber C. Kimball to William Kimball, February 29, 1856, 396.

[6] Brigham Young, March 2, 1856, *Journal of Discourses*, 3:222, 225–26; J. M. Grant, March 2, 1856, *Journal of Discourses*, 3:236. For an alternate view of Brigham Young's preaching style and its impact, see Ronald W. Walker, "Raining Pitchforks." Walker acknowledges the crudities and episodically brutal language of Young's preaching, especially during the Reformation, but views this style benignly rather than focusing on the atmosphere of violence and intimidation that it spawned. For a discussion of the impact of such provocative language on the tone of Utah society when it came from a supreme leader, see MacKinnon, *At Sword's Point, Part 1,* chapter 12.

Brigham Young, circa 1855.
Engraving by Augustin Francois Lemaitr
From Jules Rémy and Julius Brenchley,
Voyage au Pays des Mormons, frontispiece.
*Used by permission, Utah State Historical
Society, all rights reserved.*

with their God, that will not be required to pay the debt," he asserted. "The blood of Christ will never wipe that out, your own blood must atone for it; and the judgments of the Almighty will come, sooner or later, and every man and woman will have to atone for breaking their covenants."[7] The teachings on blood atonement were just beginning.

Brigham Young's outbursts did not come from nothing. He had fumed for some time that the Saints were not living their faith. The previous October he had appointed "home missionaries" to go throughout the territory and reform the members. In January 1856, Robert Campbell, the Scot who had led Peter and Agnes and the party from Glasgow to Utah, described in a letter how the program was working and why it was necessary: "The [Home] Missionaries . . . have found in many localities a great necessity for such a mission, in consequence of the Saints getting lukewarm, and setting their hearts on horses, cattle, farms, and property, more than on building up the kingdom."[8]

---

[7] Brigham Young, March 16, 1856, *Journal of Discourses*, 3:247. Blood atonement is not now a doctrine of the LDS Church.

[8] Brigham Young, October 8, 1855, *Journal of Discourses*, 3:116; Robert L. Campbell to Franklin D. Richards, January 7, 1856, *Millennial Star* 18 (May 24, 1856): 332.

But now, in the midst of famine, President Young decided that everyone needed a thorough shaking. The underlying belief was that natural disasters were punishments from God for sinfulness. In his sermon on March 16, the president, although sympathetic to those who had no other recourse than begging, denounced those who profited from the generosity of others: "I say to those who send their children to beg from house to house, and who are lugging home a dozen loads a-day—stop that." He admonished the local leaders, "Bishops, appoint assistants to visit every house in your Wards, and instruct them to take the liberty of lifting up the chest lids, and of looking under the floors and under the beds, for I tell you that some will hide their provisions and lie to you, and tell you that they have nothing."[9]

A more fundamental motivation, however, rested behind the leaders' violent preaching. The Mormons believed that the millennium, when Christ would return to earth, was imminent and the church must "prepare as a bride to receive her bridegroom." Only by the strictest adherence to the law of God—individually and collectively—would they be found righteous enough. They were God's chosen people, the new Israel, and God would judge them with severity. Ten years earlier Young had made similar threatening statements about blood atonement when the "Camp of Israel," the pioneer company that left Nauvoo, were temporarily settled in Cutler's Park in what is today part of Omaha. Referring to the immoral behavior of some of the young men, President Young said to the Twelve Apostles and the High Council on September 12, 1846, "If we allow men to come here and set up their own plans, three years will not roll around before we will have cutting of throats here." Slitting the throat from ear to ear was the method and sign of blood atonement. In November and December 1846, Young had continued to preach about killing people who did not abide by the Law of God.[10]

President Young had preached obedience to God's "celestial" law ever since Nauvoo: while the people slogged through the mud of Iowa, during the deaths and disease in Winter Quarters, and through the rigors

---

[9] Brigham Young, March 16, 1856, *Journal of Discourses*, 3:260.

[10] Brigham Young and Heber C. Kimball, "Fourteenth General Epistle," December 10, 1856, *Millennial Star* 19 (April 18, 1857): 253. God's law included a sentence of death to apostates, adulterers, blasphemers, murderers, and thieves; see, e.g., Exodus 22:19 and Leviticus 20:10 and 24:16–17. I am grateful to Ronald O. Barney for pointing out these verses and the events of this earlier period; see his *Mormon Vanguard Brigade*, 79n74, 81n82, 90, 90n110.

and uncertainties of the trek west to the Rocky Mountains. "My people must be tried in all things, that they may be prepared to receive the glory I have for them," Young wrote in Winter Quarters in his only statement that was elevated to the rank of revelation. All along their journey from Nauvoo, President Young blamed their sufferings on disobedience to God and said that only by unity and complete obedience to God's law, as expounded by the church leaders, could they succeed in reaching a new home. Fear linked hands with faith as the people sought God's guidance to lead them to the right place.[11]

President Young's current threats to those who broke God's law did not stop thieves from stealing fifty-nine pounds of flour from Golightly's Bakery on April 13, 1956. The bakery was broken into again on May 11, and a hundred pounds taken. The same night, burglars stole a thousand pounds from Heber C. Kimball's flour mill. Obviously these amounts were not simply the result of one family's desperation but were carried out by some who saw a chance to profit from people's willingness to buy flour at any price.[12]

In spite of his harsh sermons, Brigham Young was concerned for his people. He talked of sending some fourteen wagons to Oregon and Washington territories to bring back dried salmon to help tide the Saints over until harvest. Almost all building in the city was stopped when the workers were directed to till the earth and raise crops. By late May the weather had turned warm and spring rains came weekly. The prospects for a good harvest rose, and many spoke of "a good time coming." In June, wild greens and early vegetables helped fill out the diet of roots.[13]

But as hopes rose, streams fell. Showers became less frequent and the creeks became a trickle. In June, President Young issued new calls to finish the Big Cottonwood Canal so as to bring water to the city, and at least twenty-four men from the Nineteenth Ward volunteered to work on it.[14] On June 23 and again on July 16 and 17 the temperature at night

---

[11] Bennett, "'My Idea Is to Go Right Through,'" 55–70; D&C 136:31.

[12] General Church Minutes, April 13 and May 11, 1856, as quoted in Carter, "Fish and the Famine," 113.

[13] W. Woodruff to O. Pratt, May 28, 1856, *Millennial Star* 18 (August 9, 1856): 507; Heber C. Kimball to William Kimball, April 13, 1856, *Millennial Star* 18 (July 26, 1856): 477; Wilford Woodruff to John Taylor, May 29, 1856, Journal History, May 29, 1856, 2–3; Cornaby, *Autobiography and Poems*, 42.

[14] Brigham Young, June 8, 1856, *Journal of Discourses*, 3:328–29; Record of Members, Nineteenth Ward, 62; Raleigh, Journal, 138–39. The Big Cottonwood Canal was ultimately abandoned. The porous gravel of the prehistoric Lake Bonneville deposits through which it was dug would not hold water. Brigham Young reported its failure in the Tabernacle on March 2, 1862, *Journal of Discourses*, 9:239.

plunged so low that frost damaged the crops. The Tithing Office handed out its last stores of flour on July 2 and thereafter primarily issued fish caught in Utah Lake. The dreaded locusts arrived again, but this time only in Cache and Box Elder counties, north of Salt Lake City. Caterpillars and worms became the new scourge across the territory. Nevertheless, in late June the barley harvest commenced, with wheat following in July. Although the lack of water stunted the wheat, almost miraculously the heads filled out. The crop in the Salt Lake Valley was small relative to that in Utah County and farther south, but finally, by the end of July, everyone could declare that the famine was over.[15]

In the midst of this rejoicing, Peter and Agnes suffered a tragic loss when their son, Peter Alexander, died on August 15, 1856, at the age of nineteen months. The sexton records give the cause as "flux and teething," but more likely it was dysentery brought on by being weaned and thus exposed to contaminated water against which he had no resistance. His cheerful prattle was silenced; a great void opened in their lives.[16]

While Peter and Agnes were grieving, President Young continued his rhetorical building of the Kingdom of God. On August 31, two weeks after little Peter's death, he held forth in the Bowery: "As the Lord lives, we are bound to become a sovereign State in the Union, or an independent nation by ourselves, and let them drive us from this place if they can; they cannot do it." He continued that within twenty-six years—in contrast to the persecution of the past twenty-six years since the church's founding—"the Elders of this Church will be as much thought of as the kings on their thrones." This would come about with the arrival of the millennium, when "Jesus Christ will be the President, and we are his officers."[17]

President Young's sermons on the coming reign of Christ and the need for the people to be purified built to a crescendo during the fall. On Sep-

---

[15] Wilford Woodruff to the Editor of the *Mormon*, July 31, 1856, Journal History, July 31, 1856, 3; Carter, "Fish and the Famine," 123; "Prospects," *Deseret News*, July 2, 1856, 5; W. Woodruff to the Editor of the *Western Standard*, July 3, 1856, *Millennial Star* 18 (September 27, 1856): 618; W. Woodruff to Orson Pratt, July 31, 1856, *Millennial Star* 18 (October 11, 1856): 651–52.

[16] A single young child's soft leather shoe was found among Peter McAuslan's papers; it appears to be a carefully preserved keepsake of Peter Alexander. Peter McAuslan to Agnes McAuslan Allan, 1898 (#49 McAuslan Papers); Sexton's Internment Records, Salt Lake City Cemetery, page 31-A, no. 754; Frederick Buckner, M.D., to the author, February 8, 2002.

[17] Brigham Young, August 31, 1856, *Journal of Discourses*, 4:40–41. Twenty-six years later, however—in 1882—President Young had been dead for five years, the anti-polygamy Edmunds Act was passed, and the church leaders were driven to living "on the underground" as federal authorities pursued them for "unlawful co-habitation."

tember 14, Apostle Wilford Woodruff wrote in his journal that "Prest. Young arose and delivered unto the Saints, one of the strongest addresses that was ever delivered to this Church and kingdom. . . . The Latter day Saints . . . were most strictly and strongly, chastized [*sic*] and rebuked by Prest. Young. . . . He spoke by the power of God and the demonstration of the Holy Ghost, and his voice was like the thunderings of Mount Sinai."[18]

The following Sunday, September 21, brought more preaching. As in March, President Young again recommended blood atonement:

> There are sins that men commit for which they cannot receive forgiveness in this world, or in that which is to come, and if they had their eyes open to see their true condition, they would be perfectly willing to have their blood spilt upon the ground, that the smoke thereof might ascend to heaven as an offering for their sins; and the smoking incense would atone for their sins. . . . I know, when you hear my brethren telling about cutting people off from the earth, that you consider it is strong doctrine; but it is to save them, not to destroy them.[19]

Jedediah Grant, Young's second counselor, called for this ultimate sacrifice: "We have those amongst us that are full of all manner of abominations, those who need to have their blood shed, for water will not do, their sins are of too deep a dye." The period of purification that followed those sermons became known as the Reformation. Although no formal rituals for blood atonement occurred, it was a time of intense emotion, and for Peter and many others it aroused alarm and revulsion. The Reformation preaching was to continue through the rest of 1856 and into the new year. Home missionaries, Brigham Young's counselors, or one of the Twelve carried the call for repentance to every nook of the kingdom.[20]

Into this highly charged atmosphere arrived the companies of new immigrants. Because those in Utah were struggling just to survive, they had not been able to repay their Perpetual Emigrating Fund loans. In an effort to bring more poor members from Europe anyway, President

---

[18] Woodruff, Journal, September 14, 1856, 26:639–40.

[19] Brigham Young, September 21, 1856, *Journal of Discourses*, 4:53; Jedediah M. Grant, September 21, 1856, *Journal of Discourses*, 4:49.

[20] Although some historians see the radical preaching phase of the Reformation as winding down after the death of Jedediah Grant on December 1, 1856, it continued with just as much vehemence into 1857, especially in the outlying settlements; Peterson, "Mormon Reformation" (PhD diss.), 52–53. Peterson's "Mormon Reformation" and his "Mormon Reformation of 1856–1857" are the finest studies of the Reformation to date.

Young had devised a plan to have the immigrants pull handcarts, thereby saving the cost of ox teams and wagons. The first experiment with this type of emigration, during the summer of 1856, included about eighteen hundred souls and aroused intense interest among the faithful. When the first two handcart companies arrived together on September 26, a great celebration ensued. Wilford Woodruff wrote, "Presidents Young and Kimball, and many citizens, with a detachment of the [Nauvoo Legion] Lancers, and the brass bands, went out to meet and escort them into the City." He continued, "Our hearts swelled until we were speechless with joy. . . . As I gazed upon the scene, meditating upon the future result, it looked to me like the first hoisting of the floodgates of deliverance to the oppressed millions."[21]

The joy was double for the McAuslans, for among the dust-covered newcomers in Daniel McArthur's company were Agnes's sister, Elizabeth McAuslin Maxwell, and her husband, Arthur. In addition, Peter's aunt Agnes Adamson Anderson arrived with three sons to once more join her husband, Archibald, who had come the year before. Peter's wife, Agnes, in particular must have been overcome with emotion, still grieving over her lost son but ecstatic to be reunited with her sister, the only member of her birth family now in Utah.[22]

On October 2 the third handcart company arrived. It further confirmed the practicality of bringing the poor to Utah in an inexpensive and simple way. Two days later, Franklin D. Richards, the British Mission president returning to Salt Lake City with eleven missionaries, arrived in speedy carriages drawn by horses and mules. He brought news that the last two handcart companies had been passed in early September, still along the North Platte River. Although way behind, they were in good spirits and averaging fourteen to sixteen miles a day. President Young was not pleased. He wrote to Orson Pratt in Liverpool, "We had no idea there were any more companies upon the Plains." He had presumed that the leaders in charge of the emigration would not send on any who had arrived from Great Britain too far into the season. "But so it is, and now too late to remedy." On Sunday, October 5, President Young called for mule and horse teams, tons of flour, extra teamsters,

---

[21] Wilford Woodruff to Orson Pratt, September 30, 1856, *Millennial Star* 18 (December 13, 1856): 794–95.

[22] The sisters were close and corresponded for years after Agnes left Utah. Hafen and Hafen, *Handcarts to Zion*, 282, 284.

vegetables, bedding, and clothing of all types to be taken to the last two companies. The rescuers were to abandon the handcarts and bring the people in with the wagons and teams. Young refused to start the fall conference until all was arranged.[23]

Even as the rescuers were setting out, the Reformation continued. The home missionaries and church leaders demanded confessions, often in public, and then rebaptisms, sometimes of an entire ward at a time. In the Nineteenth Ward, meetings were held almost every night. On October 30, President Young described the Reformation in a letter: "Let the sinner be afraid, and the hypocrite fear, and tremble, and let the fire of the Almighty consume the wicked and ungodly, that their place may be no more known upon the earth." The remorseful and frightened Saints responded. Franklin Richards wrote, "Misdeeds are not only publicly denounced, but the doers and their deeds are named before the public congregations. The arrows of the Almighty are with the *Presidency*. . . . Already the power of the Holy Ghost has, in some instances, been so great upon them, that they have had to refrain from speaking for the people have shrunk before them, because of the power of their words." Englishwoman Hannah Tapfield King had a more jaundiced view: "The people shrunk, shivered, wept, [and] groaned like whipped children. They were told to get up in meeting and confess their sins. They did so 'till it was sickening, and brought disease."[24]

On November 3, President Young introduced a catechism to be used in questioning the members. They were to be asked if they had murdered, committed adultery, betrayed a brother, borne false witness, been drunk, stolen, lied, or contracted debts with no prospect of repaying. The list continued: Had they worked faithfully for their wages? Had they coveted what belonged to another? Had they used the Lord's name in vain? Had the men presided in their families as servants of God? Had they paid their tithing? As the catechism was implemented, other questions were added: Had they bathed regularly? Had they used irrigation

---

[23] R. D. Richards and Daniel Spencer, "Journey from Florence to G. S. L. City," *Deseret News*, October 22, 1856, 2; Brigham Young to Orson Pratt, October 30, 1856, *Millennial Star* 19 (February 14, 1857): 99; S. W. Richards to George Turnball, October 7, 1856, *Millennial Star* 19 (January 17, 1857): 41–42.

[24] Ibid., 42; Record of Members, Nineteenth Ward, 71–72, 102–103; Young to Orson Pratt, October 30, 1856, 98; F. D. Richards to Orson Pratt, Ezra T. Benson, and James A. Little, November 1, 1856, *Millennial Star* 19 (February 14, 1857): 109, emphasis his; King, Journals, 142. King became a plural wife of Brigham Young in 1872 even though she was still married to Thomas O. King.

water belonging to another? Had they cut hay when they had no right to it? Had they spoken against any principle in the Bible or Mormon scriptures or revelation given to a prophet of the church? According to Hannah King, the bishop and at least two teachers questioned family members separately in each house. She continued, "I do believe many in those times were frightened into praying and confessing sins they never committed. It was a fearful time for all."[25]

Charles Derry, an Englishman who had come on the *John M. Wood* with Peter and Agnes, was repelled by the Reformation. In a retrospective account, he described questions that did not appear on the official list: "Another object of the 'reformation' seemed to be to discover who were the doubters as to his [Brigham Young's] claim to Divine calling as Prophet and President of the church of Christ. This object was manifest when we saw the anxiety of the inquisitors to know in what light we regarded President Young. Woe betide the man who dared to express a doubt as to the divinity of his calling. . . . He was a marked man." Derry told of women being called to special meetings to be queried about their attitudes toward polygamy. It was a crime against celestial law to prevent their husbands from taking more wives, they were told, and it was their duty to seek out new wives for their husbands. Derry ended his description of the Reformation with this statement: "Polygamy, blood atonement, and their oppressing system of tithing, together with the necessity of honoring the 'file leaders' . . . as the Lord's anointed, were the burden of their teaching."[26]

On November 8, a number of members in the Nineteenth Ward were cut off from the church. The next day, the sacrament (communion) was removed from the Saints in toto until all had repented and made restitution for their sins, for "if they partook when they were not right, they were eating and drinking damnation to their own souls." With this gesture, President Young dramatically told the Saints that they were symbolically excluded from Christ's atonement and thus, in essence, excommunicated.[27]

---

[25] Peterson, "Mormon Reformation," 29; E. E. Campbell, *Establishing Zion*, 191–92; King, Journals, 143.

[26] Derry left the Mormons in 1859 to go east. He joined the Reorganized Church of Jesus Christ of Latter Day Saints (now Community of Christ) and eventually became one of its apostles. His account was first published in 1908. Derry, *Autobiography*, 40–42.

[27] Record of Members, Nineteenth Ward, 46, 105, 109; Heber C. Kimball, November 9, 1856, *Journal of Discourses*, 4:80–83; Church Historian's Office, History of the Church, November 9, 1856, 26:963–64; Brigham Young to E. T. Benson, January 26, 1857, Brigham Young, Letterpress Copybook Transcriptions, 319.

By this time it was apparent that the two late handcart companies were in trouble with the onset of winter storms on the High Plains. On November 2, George D. Grant, who was in charge of the relief effort, sent back a report to President Young: "Between five and six hundred men, women and children, worn down by drawing hand carts through snow and mud; fainting by the way side; falling, chilled by the cold; children crying, their limbs stiffened by cold, their feet bleeding and some of them bare to snow and frost. The sight is almost too much for the stoutest of us." He added that only about a third of them were still able to walk. On November 9, 1856, the rescue parties brought the next-to-last handcart company under James G. Willie into the city in wagons. Sixty-seven out of five hundred had died. The bishops from the different wards placed the immigrants into homes, and Bishop Raleigh took a number into the Nineteenth Ward. Many were suffering from frostbite.[28]

On November 30 the last handcart company, led by Edward Martin, the elder who had married Peter and Agnes in Liverpool, arrived with the help of the rescuers. Probate judge Elias Smith wrote that the rescue party consisted of 104 wagons, 351 mules and horses, and 32 oxen. It was Sunday, and in the Tabernacle President Young preached, "As soon as this meeting is dismissed I want the brethren and sisters to repair to their homes, where their Bishops will call on them to take in some of this company; the Bishops will distribute them as the people can receive them." He noted that the immigrants needed careful nursing: "Some you will find with their feet frozen to their ankles; some are frozen to their knees and some have their hands frosted." About a quarter of the Martin Company had perished from exposure and starvation. Raleigh reported that he took seventeen into the ward and "had them washed, warmed, fed & made as comfortable as their condition would admit of. They are frozen, more or less."[29]

The litany of disasters—locusts, drought, severe winters, famine, and now the handcart company tragedy—undoubtedly challenged Peter's belief in the special providence of God over the Saints. Some saw the afflictions as tests, but others came to see the explanations by the church authorities as a deception. George A. Hicks, with whom Peter was soon

---

[28] George D. Grant to Brigham Young, November 2, 1856, "The Companies Yet on the Plains," *Deseret News*, November 19, 1856, 5; Raleigh, Journal, 149.

[29] Thomas, *Elias Smith's Journal*, 1: November 30, 1856; Brigham Young, "Remarks by President Brigham Young, Tabernacle, Nov. 30, 1856," *Deseret News*, December 10, 1856, 8; Raleigh, Journal, 151.

The handcart emigrants in a storm.
From T. B. H. Stenhouse, The Rocky Mountain Saints, *310.*

to become acquainted, wrote, "The deaths and sufferings of the Saints in those [handcart] companies has been the means of completely revolutionizing my mind. At that time I believed that the Universe was governed by the will of a Supreme being and that He kept the whole human family under his eye as it were and meted out to all according to their needs, as a good father would do for his children." But in spite of all the supplications the handcart Saints had made to God, "there was no God to help them." Hicks concluded, "I do not believe that 'God' will ever have a better opportunity to help poor suffering humanity than then. The truth is the Universe is governed by laws immutable and unchangeable."[30]

On November 12, Peter's grandmother Agnes Baird Adamson died of dysentery. She was seventy-four years old. In 1848 at age sixty-seven she and her sons Sandy and Dougal had walked from Winter Quarters on the Missouri River to Utah. Although her death was not unexpected, the family mourned the loss of their matriarch.[31]

---

[30] Hicks, "History of George Armstrong Hicks," 31. I am grateful to Will Bagley for a photocopy of this journal.

[31] State of Utah Death Certificate, Registrar's No. 734; Sexton's Internment Records, Salt Lake City Cemetery, Salt Lake City, page 30-A, no. 733.

And still the Reformation continued. On November 26, John Young, the eldest brother of President Young, spoke to the Nineteenth Ward and read the catechism so that they could prepare to be questioned individually and "weighed in the balances."[32] Peter wrote about this meeting:

> When the Celestial law is fully put in force there shall no one leave the Mormon church and go over to the enemy. The enemy here alluded to is the world or all who do not believe in Mormonism—"all who are not for us are against us" and of course enemies. How do they mean to accomplish this? The Angel of the Lord shall destroy them. . . . Who did I hear preach these doctrins? John Young, Head Patriarch, and many other dignatrys of the church.[33]

On December 1, 1856, the day after the last handcart company arrived, Brigham Young's counselor Jedediah Grant died from "lung fever," a combination of typhoid and pneumonia brought on by exhaustion from Reformation preaching and from standing for long periods in cold water to rebaptize the contrite. He was forty years old. In Liverpool, Orson Pratt wrote a tribute in the *Millennial Star*: "His voice was like a thunder-bolt, and his words like the vivid lightning to the hypocrite and transgressor. The words of burning truth flowed from his lips, piercing, penetrating, searching the inmost recesses of the heart. His unceasing labours . . . will never be forgotten in time nor eternity."[34]

December 3 brought the most terrifying talk that Peter had heard. The meeting was held in the Nineteenth Ward for the male members only. Raleigh described in his journal what he had preached: "I declared my intentions to carry out the law of God, to the verry letter in Sanctifying Israel & cleanzing the inside of the Platter by wiping out inniquity from our midst."[35] Peter wrote of the meeting:

> I heard the Bishop of the 19 Ward declare that if the Celestial Law was put in force, they the people of the Lord would be cutting one another's throats. We were also taught—that our minds might be prepared for coming events—to beware of Sympathy, as that feeling would destroy a great

---

[32] Raleigh, Journal, 151; Record of Members, Nineteenth Ward, 116.

[33] Peter McAuslan to Robert Salmon, December 1860 (#14 McAuslan Papers), 2–3. John Smith, the oldest son of Hyrum Smith, was the presiding church patriarch, but on October 8, 1853, John Young had been sustained as a local patriarch.

[34] Orson Pratt, "Death of President Jedediah M. Grant," *Millennial Star* 19 (March 21, 1857): 185.

[35] Record of Members, Nineteenth Ward, 117; Raleigh, Journal, 151–52.

many in this Church. How that to beware of sympathy? Because when that time comes and is at hand you may see the dead Bodys of your Fathers, your Brothers, or your nearest, dearest relatives and friends lying upon the Streets, and if you should pass by, say not a word to anybody, nither ask the cause, just conduct yourself as if nothing had happened. All is right, it was done by athority.[36]

Shortly after this priesthood meeting, Peter took the family's animals south to find winter feed.[37] His twenty-year-old brother, Frank, most likely went with him to help with the stock and to build a house where Agnes, now pregnant again, could join him once the worst of winter was over. Peter probably felt relieved to have these tasks in front of him rather than only fearful thoughts about the Reformation preaching and where it might lead.

---

[36] McAuslan to Salmon, 3. George A. Hicks, who lived in Spanish Fork, described John Young's visit on September 27–29, 1856, in a similar way. See epilogue, 286n13.

[37] Family lore says that the bishop took the family's barn, which was more substantial than most, to house some of the handcart immigrants. The family objected, fearing their animals would die. The bishop replied that the barn belonged to God. This, the story says, was the reason for taking the animals south in December. Although the story is plausible, I have not been able to verify it. E. M. Aird, "Family History," 12.

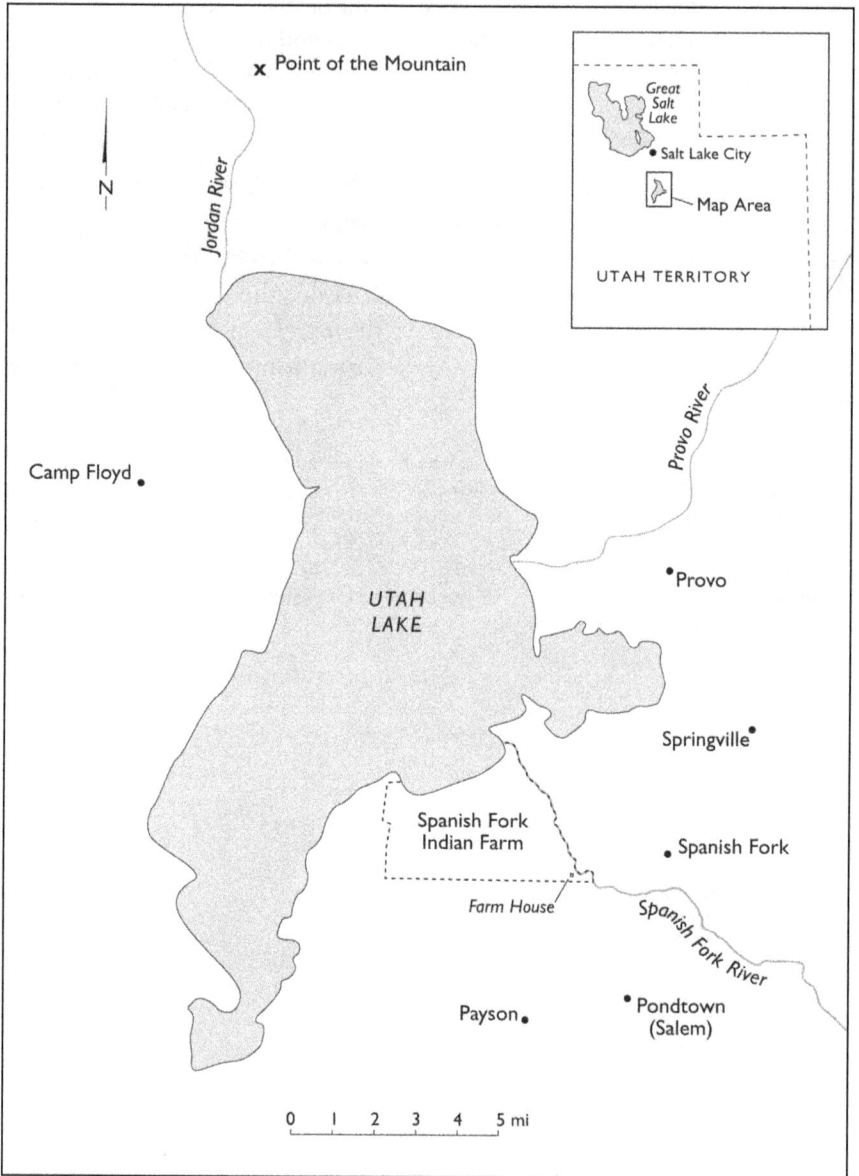

x Point of the Mountain

Jordan River

N

Great
Salt
Lake

• Salt Lake City

Map Area

UTAH TERRITORY

Provo River

Camp Floyd •

• Provo

UTAH
LAKE

Springville •

Spanish Fork
Indian Farm

• Spanish Fork

Farm House

Spanish Fork River

• Pondtown
(Salem)

Payson •

0   1   2   3   4   5 mi

Utah County.
Map by Bill Nelson.

12

Murder for Apostasy

SNOW THREATENED AS PETER AND FRANK SLOWLY TRAVELED south with their wagon, oxen, and stock. December 12 and 13, 1856, brought the heaviest snowstorm to hit the Salt Lake and Utah valleys since the Mormons had arrived. It took the two brothers several days to reach Spanish Fork, a town in southern Utah County on a river of the same name. The settlement had the warmest winter temperatures in the area, and the animals had a good chance of surviving the winter without shelter. Livestock here had not died off as they had in the northern counties the previous winter.[1]

First settled in 1851, Spanish Fork grew in 1856 when President Young advised those living in nearby low-lying Palmyra to move to the newer town. Spanish Fork was twelve miles south of Provo and sixty miles south of Salt Lake City. Higher than Palmyra, it suffered less from having saleratus, a salt of carbonic acid, seep into the soil, rendering it unproductive. Besides the milder climate, the town offered arable land and plenty of water. English immigrant Hannah Cornaby, who had moved there with her husband less than two months before Peter and Frank arrived, later wrote, "Spanish Fork . . . consisted principally of large wheat stacks, temporary dwellings, and houses in course of erection. The huge wheat stacks had a great attraction for us, who had so recently passed through a famine."[2] The sight of bountiful grain must have delighted Peter and Frank as well.

Near the town lay the Spanish Fork Indian Farm, a reservation where

---

[1] Jensen, Manuscript History and Historical Reports, Spanish Fork; Janetski, "Ute of Utah Lake," 26; George A. Smith to Franklin D. Richards, March 1, 1856, *Millennial Star* 18 (June 14, 1856): 379.
[2] Cornaby, *Autobiography and Poems*, 43–44.

U.S. Indian agent Dr. Garland Hurt was attempting to teach the native Utes how to farm, now that their former hunting-and-gathering grounds in Utah Valley had been claimed by Mormon settlers. Many non-Indians had been hired to build a large two-story farmhouse and office, construct a dam and dig an irrigation canal, and clear the land of thick brush so that it could be plowed. The number of white employees varied, depending on the current project, but sources give it as fifty to possibly as many as a hundred men. Their wages put needed money into circulation. Besides the milder weather, the possibility of employment may well have attracted Peter to Spanish Fork.[3]

The first task for Peter and Frank was to build a shelter for the winter. In this period in Spanish Fork, dugouts were common. Often built into hillsides, here they were typically excavated in the flats. The structure consisted of a room-size rectangle dug four or five feet deep with sides built up about three feet above ground. At one end it had a doorway with steps leading down, and at the other a stone fireplace. A ridgepole ran the length; against it smaller poles were closely laid, and then willows, straw, and dirt finished the roof. A quilt or piece of canvas served for a door. Altogether it formed an inexpensive and warm abode that could be fairly quickly built. Others in the town were also working on dugouts to help house a number of the last handcart immigrants who had recently been brought to Spanish Fork.[4]

In Salt Lake City on December 10, 1856, less than a week after Jedediah Grant's funeral, Brigham Young and his remaining counselor, Heber C. Kimball, issued the Fourteenth General Epistle. Although not specifically mentioning the doctrine of blood atonement, they warned members that they were "left without excuse before the Lord, to reap the reward of their iniquity, . . . to feel the wrath, the withering, bitter anguish which the justice of a justly incensed and offended Creator will pour out upon them." One might have expected the Reformation fervor to have

---

[3] From 1855 to 1857 the Indian Farm accounts show that a third of expenditures, not including the salaries of Hurt or the farm manager, went for resident white labor, and another third for daily white labor. The Utes mostly herded cattle and helped with the harvesting. Beeton, "Teach Them to Till the Soil," 306. No list of those who worked on the farm has come to light. Garland Hurt to Brigham Young, June 30, 1856, "Utah Superintendency," *Report of the Secretary of the Interior, November 29, 1856*, 782–83; Beck, "History," 4; Butler, "Autobiography," 428.

[4] Evans, "Thomas D. Evans," 14:284–85; [Tullidge], "History of Spanish Fork," 143; Warner, *History of Spanish Fork*, 83.

abated now that the fiery and severe Grant was dead, but there was no immediate indication of it. This epistle quickly reached Spanish Fork, where Peter and Frank could read it.[5]

The winter of 1856–57 proved to be the worst the Saints had experienced since coming to Utah, because of the depth of snow on the ground. At the end of January, President Young wrote that the average was two feet: "excellent sleighing, but bad for cattle." In letter after letter that January he highlighted the plight of the livestock and remarked that in the future the Saints "must prepare feed for them, as they do in the Eastern States." He sent men south with the church cattle to find pasturage. Once again the Saints were isolated with no mail reaching them from the East for several months and even the mail from southern California late because of the deep snow.[6]

On January 4, 1857, Daniel H. Wells was appointed President Young's new second counselor to replace Jedediah Grant. Wells was also commander of the Nauvoo Legion, the Utah territorial militia. Although dedicated and ready to defend Zion at a moment's notice, he was considerably more diplomatic and forbearing than Jedediah Grant had been. Twelve days after his appointment, Young wrote a letter offering mercy to a member who had asked how he might be restored to the church: "I seek not to condemn you, and desire of you to live as the righteous do, and in this time of mercy, that you may not be excluded." Although Young showed moments of such mercy, he did not relax his ban on dances or theatrical presentations and still withheld the sacrament.[7]

Two letters President Young wrote in early February 1857 show another side of him—his desire to control what went on in the territory and his suspicion of "Gentiles," or non-Mormons. The first letter was to Aaron Johnson, bishop of Springville, less than six miles from Spanish Fork, and the second to "Bishops and Presidents South." The letters were prompted by the Christmas Day release from the penitentiary in Salt

---

[5] Brigham Young and Heber C. Kimball, "Fourteenth General Epistle," December 10, 1856, *Millennial Star* 19 (April 18, 1857): 252–53.

[6] Brigham Young to Orson Pratt, January 31, 1857, *Millennial Star* 19 (May 30, 1857): 348; Brigham Young to Bishops South, January 22; and to Amasa Lyman and Charles C. Rich, January 5, 1857, both in Brigham Young, Letterpress Copybook Transcriptions, 305–306, 263.

[7] Brigham Young to John Bair, January 16; and to E. T. Benson, January 26, 1857, Brigham Young, Letterpress Copybook Transcriptions, 290, 319; Brigham Young to Orson Pratt, January 31, 1857, *Millennial Star* 19 (May 30, 1857): 349.

Lake City of two drifters, John G. Ambrose and Thomas Betts, who had been imprisoned for larceny. With more moderate weather in February, they were setting out for California by the southern route. Young feared that the men would steal church-owned horses that he had sent south for winter grazing.[8]

But his letters warning the leaders to watch the two men's activities went much further. After outlining his suspicions about the released prisoners, he wrote: "If any such thing as we have suggested should occur we shall regret to hear a favorable report; we do not expect there would be any prosecutions for false imprisonment or tale bearers left for witnesses. . . . Bro Johnson, you know about these things, have a few men that can be trusted on hand, and make no noise about it and keep this letter safe. We write for your eye alone and to men that can be trusted." The second letter was similarly worded but added another directive: "Be on the look out now, & have a few trusty men ready in case of need to pursue, retake & punish."[9]

In a case of mistaken identity, four other travelers to California were ambushed on the night of February 17 as they camped along the Santa Clara River in southern Utah. The men scrambled out of the firelight, except for one who had been shot in the face. In spite of finding more than fifty bullet holes in their bedding the next morning, they all survived. It appears that the attackers believed they were pursing, retaking, and punishing the former prisoners according to Young's wishes; but the intended targets of the assault passed through the area unmolested two days later.[10]

President Young's letters had a further, more deadly effect and show that the Reformation had not dissipated. Aaron Johnson, bishop of Springville, to whom the first letter had been addressed, called a series of council meetings. At the first one, held shortly after he received the letter, he spoke of people going away, that they might steal horses, and that he had instructions that they needed to be watched.[11] Before a second

---

[8] Brigham Young to Aaron Johnson, February 3; and to Bishops and Presidents South, February 6, 1857, Brigham Young, Letterpress Copybook Transcriptions, 352, 387.

[9] Ibid.

[10] Ardis Parshall has pieced together the puzzle of what happened to the released prisoners; Parshall, "'Pursue, Retake and Punish,'" 64–86.

[11] J. M. Stewart to the Editor, July 4, 1859, *Valley Tan*, August 24, 1859, 2; "Confession of Abraham Durfee," April 1, 1859, *Valley Tan*, April 19, 1859, 4; Affidavit of Joseph Bartholomew," March 29, 1859, *Valley Tan*, April 19, 1859, 1.

meeting, Brigham Young's discourse in the Tabernacle in Salt Lake City on February 8 was published in the *Deseret News*, which shortly afterward reached Utah County. In this sermon, Young again preached blood atonement and then added, "But now I say, in the name of the Lord, that if this people will sin no more, but faithfully live their religion, their sins will be forgiven them without taking life." Yet in the next paragraph, he asked that if a person knows they have broken the celestial law and knows that the only way to atone is to have his own blood shed, "Is there a man or woman in this house but what would say, 'shed my blood that I may be saved and exalted with the Gods?'" Young then went a step further:

> Will you love your brothers or sisters likewise, when they have committed a sin that cannot be atoned for without the sheding of their blood? Will you love that man or woman well enough to shed their blood? That is what Jesus Christ meant. . . . This is loving our neighbour as ourselves; if he needs help, help him; and if he wants salvation and it is necessary to spill his blood on the earth in order that he may be saved, spill it.[12]

Within days of this issue of the *Deseret News* reaching Springville, Bishop Aaron Johnson called a second council meeting. In this one, instead of singling out the released prisoners, he called attention to William R. Parrish, a longtime church member. In Nauvoo after Joseph Smith's death in 1844, controversy had arisen over who should succeed him. Parrish sided with the Twelve Apostles, declaring he would support them even if it led him to hell. Now a Springville resident, Parrish had become disillusioned and was planning to go to California by the southern route with his two oldest sons. When times were safer, he planned to return to get his wife and four younger sons.[13]

At this second meeting the bishop called two men, Gardiner G. "Duff" Potter and Abraham Durfee, to find out when the Parrishes were planning to leave. According to one participant, Bishop Johnson said, "Some of us would yet 'see the red stuff run.' He said he had a letter, and the remark was made by some one that 'dead men tell no tales.'" Bishop Johnson's counselor, John M. Stewart, another witness to this meeting, said that Potter asked for the privilege of killing Parrish wherever he could find "the damned curse." The bishop had replied, "Shed no blood

---

[12] Brigham Young, February 8, 1857, *Journal of Discourses*, 4:219; "Discourse," *Deseret News*, February 18, 1857, 4–5.
[13] For Parrish's siding with the Twelve, see Stenhouse, *Rocky Mountain Saints*, 462.

in Springville." Stewart understood that "blood would probably be shed, not *in* Springville, but *out* of it." Following the bishop's orders, Potter and Durfee found Parrish and told him that they too wished to leave Utah. They soon gained his confidence. A third council meeting was called by the bishop, after which events moved quickly. On March 15, 1857, outside the city gates, William Parrish was killed by knife wounds after a hard struggle, and one of his sons was shot dead. Duff Potter was also killed, having been mistaken for the young Parrish son.[14]

John M. Stewart, as justice of the peace, was called upon to hold an inquest. Wilber J. Earl, a city alderman, former justice of the peace, and participant in all three council meetings leading up to the murders, dictated the selection of jurors to him. With the bodies lying before him, Stewart, now fully afraid, obeyed. The farcical inquest reached a verdict that "they came to their deaths by the hands of an assassin, or assassins, to the jury unknown." Stewart, by territorial law, was required to report the proceedings to the county court, but Bishop Johnson told him not to comply.[15] The Parrish-Potter murders were never investigated by church authorities.[16] Aaron Johnson continued as bishop and remained in President Young's favor.[17]

Was this loving your neighbors to gain eternal salvation for them? Or was it a broader application of the letter about the released prisoners? Did Aaron Johnson—reportedly "a quiet, inoffensive man"—take President Young's sentence, "Bro Johnson, you know about these things," as license to cleanse Zion of its impurities? Perhaps Johnson viewed himself in a

---

[14] "Affidavit of Joseph Bartholomew"; "Confession of Abraham Durfee"; Stewart to the Editor, July 4, 1859, emphasis his. For a detailed account of the Parrish-Potter murders, see Aird, "'You Nasty Apostates, Clear Out,'" 173–91. The testimonies, affidavits, and Durfee's confession for the Parrish-Potter murders can also be found in Cradlebaugh, *Utah and the Mormons*, 43–61.

[15] Stewart to the Editor, July 4, 1859. "Coroner's Inquest," copied by Hosea Stout in March 1859, from the "Justice's Docket for Springville Presinct," Hosea Stout Papers, Letters and Miscellaneous, Utah State Historical Society. See Brooks, *On the Mormon Frontier*, 691n50.

[16] In 1871 in a civil court, Aaron Johnson was indicted, arrested, and released on $10,000 bail for the murder of the Parrishes. The April 1872 Supreme Court decision, *Clinton v. Englebrecht* (U.S. 80:434), resulted in the release of 130 indicted men, including Johnson, because the Court ruled that the federal jury selection procedure was improper. Johnson, *Aaron Johnson*, 585–86; "Criminal Cases in District Courts of Utah," *Letter from the Attorney General*, 11; Firmage and Mangrum, *Zion in the Courts*, 145–46.

[17] An example of President Young's continuing good regard for Johnson is his warm invitation to join the celebration of Pioneer Day in Big Cottonwood Canyon; Brigham Young to Aaron Johnson, July 7, 1857, Brigham Young, Letterpress Copybook Transcriptions, 706.

cosmic role, that as a member of God's elect he was called to wipe out those belonging to the Antichrist.[18]

For some, the killings confirmed their worst fears and were the catalyst for deciding to quit Utah as soon as the snow in the mountains permitted.[19] Two weeks after the murders, U.S. surveyor David H. Burr wrote to his superior in Washington, D.C., saying that the slaying of the Parrishes had finally convinced him that his own life was truly in danger:

> Brigham Young has declared openly that the surveyors shall not be suffered to trespass on *their* lands as they did the last season. . . . I have been cursed and denounced in their public meetings; and the most diabolical threats made against me. . . . The same threats have been made against disaffected Mormons. We were inclined to think them idle menaces, until a few days since, when three men were killed at Springville, sixty miles from this place, for making the attempt [to leave the territory].[20]

On April 15, 1857, when the mountain road became passable, Burr and assorted other federal officials, gentiles, and disillusioned Mormons started fleeing eastward. Lawyer Hosea Stout wrote, "The fire of the reformation is burning many out who flee from the Territory afraid of their lives," and another lawyer, Elias Smith, recorded, "Apostates are yet leaving, some of them with Handcarts, and not a few of them are off, before their nearest neighbors know they are thinking of going or that they are tired of Mormonism."[21] But Peter did not go yet.

Nevertheless, the murder of the Parrishes became a major reason for Peter McAuslan's loss of faith. A year after leaving Utah, he answered a letter from Robert Salmon, his old friend in Scotland whom he had baptized. Salmon and other friends there had written, asking him why he had abandoned Mormonism. Peter answered with reluctance, for, he said, "it is not attall according to my feelings to write on this subject."

---

[18] The description of Johnson as inoffensive comes from Stenhouse, *Rocky Mountain Saints*, 462. Cook, *Aaron Johnson Correspondence*, viii–ix. Paul H. Peterson pointed out that the excesses of the Reformation were more common in outlying areas, such as Utah County, where such leaders as Wilford Woodruff were not present to moderate the intemperate statements preached in the Tabernacle. Peterson, "Mormon Reformation," 51–52.

[19] A John Davies wrote to his brother that the Parrish murders were the reason for his own departure; "The Mormons," *New York Times*, September 28, 1857, 2.

[20] David H. Burr to Thomas A. Hendricks, March 28, 1857, "The Utah Expedition," 35th Cong., 1st sess., 119–20.

[21] Brooks, *On the Mormon Frontier*, 625; Thomas, *Elias Smith's Journal*, 1: April 17, 1857.

In another part he explained that he believed each person should judge for themselves and not be influenced by his or anyone else's experience. Nevertheless, he stated his reasons, which now give a rare insight into this period by someone who still felt "very charityable towards them [Mormons] as a people."[22]

The letter is given in full in the epilogue, but Peter's reasons can be summarized as follows: (1) He came to the conclusion that Brigham Young was no more inspired than many other men. (2) He felt that the insistence on obeying those in authority, whether right or wrong, would result in failing to use one's God-given ability to reason, which would mean the end of intellectual and moral development. (3) He found that Mormons held doctrines that, when acted upon, "are destructive of the rights of there fellow man." For example, the leaders taught that when God's celestial law was fully put in force, everyone must obey, and those who did not would be slain. He also heard it preached that if a person found the dead bodies of those dear to him or her, he or she must say nothing, for they had been killed by authority. (4) He wrote that those who renounced the faith, such as the Parrishes, and were courageous enough to speak out would be done away with "faster than a murderer or an adulterer"; he then described the murders in some detail. (5) The Parrish murders, he wrote, were a result of the "reformation excitement" when it was expected that the celestial laws were going to be put in force right away. (6) He reiterated that the Mormons had already declared their independence from the United States and that God would fight their battles and sustain them as an independent kingdom to the dismay of their enemies. (7) And finally, he wrote that they had been taught that the enemies within— those who had lost their faith or disobeyed counsel—were more to be feared than nonmembers and should be killed. In Heber C. Kimball's words, it was "cleansing the inside of the Platter first."[23]

Peter, though shocked by the Parrish murders, was still a believer. Although the murders became one of the main reasons for his loss of faith, he did not experience a sudden apostasy. Instead, his alarm at the killing of people who had simply lost their faith and wanted to leave marked a milestone in his path of disillusionment. It could not have been easy for him to turn away from the faith to which he had given his all and that had

---

[22] Peter McAuslan to Robert Salmon, December 1860 (#14 McAuslan Papers).

[23] Ibid.

brought him from his homeland to Utah, where he had such hopes for receiving the wisdom that would flow down from God. The Reformation and its effects, however, were eating away at his faith, and eventually he would reach the point where he could no longer remain a Mormon.

The fear of being considered an enemy within is illustrated in an 1859 letter from John M. Stewart, who was the bishop's counselor and justice of the peace in Springville at the time of the Parrish murders but had since moved to southern California. Stewart explained why he had not argued when one of Aaron Johnson's men told him whom to select for the inquest jury:

> I am perfectly aware that that portion of the community who have no knowledge of the under-currents and wire-workings of Mormonism will consider me a "poor concern," for suffering myself to be swayed in my official duties by ecclesiastical dignitaries; for suffering myself . . . to be governed by the Bishop. But I perfectly understood that to act without counsel, or to disobey counsel, was to transgress; and if I had never understood it before I could not help but understand it then, by the example of the three dead bodies right before my eyes, that "The way of the transgressor is (was) hard."[24]

The Reformation had other effects as well. Although not often mentioned in the Tabernacle, home missionaries, bishops, and ward teachers began to push plural marriage as a sign of one's commitment to God's laws, teaching that it was the only way to inherit the highest levels of heaven. By December 1856, President Young was receiving an increasing number of requests to take plural wives. In the Nineteenth Ward in Salt Lake City, where Peter's parents and unmarried siblings still lived, their neighbor Nelson Wheeler Whipple observed, "Among other teachings and instructions the plurality of wives was strongly urged and a great number of the men took more wives. Some two, three, four and as high as eight." President Young even wanted the *Millennial Star* to point out to unmarried female converts in Great Britain that "the sisters who have crossed the plains this season in the Hand Cart coy's. [companies] are almost all married off."[25]

---

[24] Stewart to the Editor, 2.
[25] Peterson, "Mormon Reformation," 31; Brigham Young, Letterpress Copybook Transcriptions, January 16–30, 1857; Whipple, Autobiography, 56; Brigham Young to E. T. Benson, January 26, 1857, Brigham Young, Letterpress Copybook Transcriptions, 319.

The Reformation momentum increased as spring came on. Wilford Woodruff wrote that "all are trying to get wives until there is hardly a girl 14 years old in Utah, but what is married, or just going to be." Peter's family was not immune to this emotional and spiritual frenzy. His youngest sister, Janet, age seventeen, was married on March 19, 1857, as a plural wife to John Allan, the husband of Peter's older sister, Agnes.[26]

Peter, however, resisted the pressure to take another wife. Although this doctrine was not a reason for his leaving the faith, Peter did comment on polygamy in his letter to Robert Salmon the year after leaving Utah: "There was generall teaching to all to go ahead and get more wifes as they could to receive a Celestiall Salvation with it. . . . You must see at once that a man after he has got two or three wives and they have children by him, natural affection, even if he should lose faith in Mormonism, binds him to his children, and as the saying amongst them is, 'if he should appostatize[,] his property won't.'" Peter even suspected a further motive: the church leaders were "anxious to get them into it, before the expected fight with *Uncle Sam* [in the Utah War], for if a man will fight for anything it will be for his wives and children."[27]

After the Parrish murders, President Young may have realized that some matters were spiraling beyond his control. Whether that was the case or not, two weeks later, in early April, the Reformation began to wind down. One indication was a letter Young wrote to the bishop of Beaver in southern Utah: "I do not wish to know the names nor the errors of them who are called saints: Let it suffice that they confess and forsake their sins, & live nearer to the Lord than they have hitherto done." He also wrote to the bishop of Parowan, telling him to assure the members that all their sins were forgiven, "save it be the sin against the Holy Ghost."[28] But Peter did not know of these letters.

In March and April the Saints were rebaptized.[29] After four months of being denied the sacrament in their meetings, the people felt blessed

---

[26] Wilford Woodruff to George A. Smith, Journal History, April 1, 1857, 2; Allan, "John Allan," 3; Temple Records Index Bureau.

[27] McAuslan to Salmon, 4.

[28] Brigham Young to Philo T. Farnsworth, April 4, 1857; and to Tarleton Lewis, April 9, 1857, Brigham Young, Letterpress Copybook Transcriptions, 540, 544. The sin against the Holy Ghost refers to those who, having received the Holy Ghost after baptism and the laying on of hands, turn away and deny it, thus in essence denying the faith.

[29] The Spanish Fork Record of Members is spotty before May 1858. Thus the date of Peter McAuslan's rebaptism is not known, but along with the others, it must have been in March or April 1857.

to see it restored among them in early April and took it as a sign that once more they were in good standing in the eyes of the leadership.[30] With rebaptism, the sacrament, and the cleansing of the territory by the departure of many government officials, gentiles, and apostates, the Reformation in effect ended. The fanatical ideas and sentiments preached and exhorted during the previous year, however, could not be so easily turned off.

Although President Young's harsh rhetoric regarding the Saints finally let up, it did not when it came to federal appointees. The church leaders were against the U.S. surveyors because they suspected that the surveyors' motive was to push the Mormons off the land they had settled and laid claim to. They were against federal judges because they believed that the laws passed by the all-Mormon Territorial Legislature and upheld in the all-Mormon territorial probate courts were part of God's kingdom and thus of a higher order than federal laws and courts. They were against U.S. Indian agents for fear that the latter would turn the Native people against them. The previous December Young had written to John M. Bernhisel, the Utah delegate to Congress, saying that both Garland Hurt and surveyor David H. Burr were "corrupt as hell, and we know it, and they would cut our throats, and destroy this people if they had the power." He wrote to George A. Smith that all federal appointees were "consummate know nothing scamps," and that "we have seriously resolved to send them back as fast as they come let the consequences be what they may."[31]

In Spanish Fork, resident George A. Hicks wrote,

It was in the winter of 1856 & 7 that we first heard that there was hostile preparations being made by the government of the United States against the people of Utah and that an army was all ready to march in the Spring for Utah. We as a people were not frightened by the news, we put our trust in God and believed we were His people and He was able to take care of

---

[30] King, Journals, 129. Mormons recognize only one sacrament; most Protestants celebrate two (baptism and communion), and Catholics seven (baptism, confirmation, communion, penance or reconciliation, healing of the sick, matrimony, and holy orders).

[31] Congress had failed to establish preemption and homesteading in the 1850 territorial Organic Act, and thus Mormons could not secure title to the land until a federal land office opened in Utah in 1869. For sentiments about Mormon laws being higher than federal ones, see Brooks, *On the Mormon Frontier*, February 13, 1857, 622 and 622n85. Brigham Young to J. M. Bernhisel, December 10, 1856; and to George A. Smith, January 3, 1857, Brigham Young, Letterpress Copybook Transcriptions, 231–32, 259.

His Saints. However, we made preparations by organizing a "standing army" and drilling them for service.[32]

Except for some calls to put down the Mormons and polygamy during the 1856 election, the church leaders had no reason to think newly inaugurated President Buchanan was planning aggressive action against them. Young, in fact, wrote to Thomas L. Kane in January 1857 that "we are satisfied with the appointment of Buchanan as future President, we believe he will be friend to the good, that Fillmore was our friend, but Buchanan will not be a whit behind."[33]

Nevertheless, on January 14, 1857, the Territorial Legislature passed an act to reorganize Utah's militia, the Nauvoo Legion. The commander, Daniel H. Wells, began to effect the change on April 11 by creating military districts. Spanish Fork was in the fifth, which was named the Peteetneet District after a friendly Indian chief. It covered Utah County south of Provo and was organized under the supervision of Aaron Johnson of Springville. Peter was mustered into the legion on April 20 in Spanish Fork as part of the Fourth Platoon, Company F, Third Battalion, First Regiment of Infantry. He was a sergeant reporting to Lieutenant George A. Hicks. A June 15 record of their service lists Peter as having one pound of rifle powder, a quarter pound of lead, and one powder horn, but no firearm. Like all Nauvoo Legion units, the Fourth Platoon was poorly equipped, and the ten men between them had only three muskets, two rifles, two pounds of powder, and a quarter pound of lead. Hicks wrote, "We believed it was our duty to do all we were able to do and God would do the rest and we were full of faith that the set time had come to favor Zion." By the end of June, Brigham Young was reiterating this sentiment in a letter: "The day is nigh at hand when the Lord will mete out a reward to the wicked according to their deserts, when the day of strife comes he will fight our Battles and cleanse this goodly land from its polution [*sic*]."[34]

32 Hicks, "History of George Armstrong Hicks," 29. Hicks wrote his autobiography in 1878 and as a result made an error in time: the "standing army" concept arose not in the winter of 1856–57 but a year later.

33 Brigham Young to Thomas L. Kane, January 31, 1857, Brigham Young, Letterpress Copybook Transcriptions, 356.

34 "Militia of Utah," *Deseret News*, April 1, 1857, 4; Church Historian's Office, History of the Church, April 11, 1857, 27:147–48; Utah County Military District, Utah Territorial Muster Rolls, rolls for April 20, June 15, and July 15, 1857; Hicks, "History of George Armstrong Hicks," 29; Brigham Young to George Taylor & Others, June 29, 1857, Brigham Young, Letterpress Copybook Transcriptions, 679. A discussion of the lack of arms in the Nauvoo Legion is in Furniss, *Mormon Conflict*, 133–35.

That spring also saw the organization of new Quorums of Seventy. Brigham Young's older brother Joseph was the president of the Seventies Council in Salt Lake City, and in May he traveled with several others through Utah, Juab, and Sanpete counties "on a special mission to preach the gospel, set in order the Seventies and organize several new quorums." A quorum consisted of seventy members of the Melchizedek priesthood, seven of whom were presidents, which reported to the Seventies Council in Salt Lake City. It was based on biblical precedents, particularly Luke 10:1, in which Christ sent out seventy followers "into every city and place" as missionaries. There was no limit to the number of such quorums, and on that trip Joseph Young formed eight new ones, one of which was the Fiftieth Quorum of Seventy in Spanish Fork. Peter at that time was a Melchizedek priest and belonged to an Elders Quorum, but now he was nominated to this higher organization. According to Joseph Young, to become a member of the Seventies Quorum, one needed a recommendation from the president of his Elders Quorum and also from the bishop of his ward, "giving evidence of their fellowship, faith, integrity and good moral character."[35]

Robert Campbell, with whom Peter and Agnes traveled from Glasgow, was now clerk of the Seventies Council in Salt Lake City. He wrote to Dennis Dorrity, the newly appointed president of the Fiftieth Quorum, instructing him to call a meeting at least every two weeks, in order to "examine their spirits and standing and see that they are magnifying their holy calling . . . and carrying out the principles of the reformation by 'getting the Holy Ghost & keeping it.'" Thus, although today the duty of a seventy is missionary service and proselytizing, the purpose in 1857 appears to have been applied more locally and to have emphasized carrying forward the work of the Reformation.[36]

---

[35] Mormonism has two priesthoods: the Aaronic, or lesser priesthood, now for boys but in the nineteenth century for men; and the Melchizedek, or higher priesthood; see Hartley, "From Men to Boys." "Visit of Prests. Joseph Young and A. P. Rockwood to Utah, Juab and San Pete Counties," *Deseret News*, May 27, 1857, 8; Hamilton, Journals, May 3, 1857; Record of Fiftieth Quorum of Seventies, 49; "To the Presidents and members of the Quorums of Seventies," *Deseret News*, January 28, 1857, 8.

[36] Robert Campbell to Dennis Dorrity, December 16, 1857, Record of Fiftieth Quorum of Seventies, 496; "Visit of Prests. Joseph Young," 8. Stenhouse commented that often the roles of the High Priests' Quorum—"to preside over the Saints wherever they are located in a collective body"—and the Seventies Quorum were interchangeable in this period; Stenhouse, *Rocky Mountain Saints*, 560.

That Peter was still a member in good standing in this period is shown by his being ordained a seventy—the thirty-fourth of seventy members—on June 7, 1857. Six weeks later on July 19, he and three others were called as teachers for the Seventies Quorum. Their duties paralleled those of a teacher for a ward—to visit quorum members, inquire into their spiritual and temporal welfare, and be guardians against any manner of iniquity.[37]

On June 15 the militia in Spanish Fork was mustered in the public square to elect a brigadier general for the Peteetneet District and for an inspection of arms and ammunition. The men elected Aaron Johnson, who was already in command. With militia drills, planting and tending crops of buckwheat, squash, and potatoes, and perhaps building an adobe house, Peter's days were full, and in the evenings he attended both ward and Seventies meetings. On Sundays he and Agnes attended sacrament meetings. On July 3, Agnes delivered a baby girl, whom they named Jane Kennedy McAuslan after Agnes's mother. Although there would always be an empty place in their hearts left by the death of Peter Alexander, they again felt blessed.[38]

Brigham Young was feeling pleased as well and credited the Reformation for the improved times. At the end of June he wrote to the Liverpool office, "Everything is flourishing with this people, because of their renewed diligence and faithfulness. Our city looks as though it had taken an emetic, and vomited forth apostates, officials, and in fact all the filth which was weighing us down. The prospects were never better for a bountiful harvest, than at present. There is now more grain, and food is cheaper than has ever been the case previously at this season of the year." The feelings of prosperity were widespread. One resident in Spanish Fork described the mood: "The people generally went to work with the determination to make their homes and their surroundings pleasant and agreeable and . . . peace seemed to have taken up her abode with the people again."[39]

Peace was short-lived. Word that Parley Pratt, brother of Orson Pratt and a beloved apostle, missionary, and theologian, had been murdered

---

[37] Record of Fiftieth Quorum of Seventies, 4–5, 300.

[38] Aaron Johnson to John L. Butler, June 13, 1857, in Cook, *Aaron Johnson Correspondence*, 28–29; Peter McAuslan to Agnes McAuslan Allan, 1898 (#49 McAuslan Papers). Peter's crops come from his tithing records; Local Unit Financial Records, Spanish Fork, 102.

[39] Brigham Young to Orson Pratt and Ezra T. Benson, June 30, 1857, *Millennial Star* 19 (August 29, 1857): 556; Brockbank, *Autobiography*, 24.

in Arkansas by the husband of a woman whom Parley had taken as a plural wife brought an outcry of grief and recalled the murders of Joseph and Hyrum Smith. On July 21, 1857, Charles L. Walker, a Salt Lake City resident, expressed the feeling among the Saints: "O ye fools your time is short when God shall avenge the blood of the Prophets."[40]

This anger against those who persecuted them reached new heights when even worse news reached them: the U.S. Army was marching to Utah to put down the "Mormon rebellion." Word had come on July 24 when the church leaders and more than two thousand invited members were celebrating Pioneer Day in Big Cottonwood Canyon in the Wasatch Mountains just southeast of Salt Lake City, where it was cool and refreshing. Although President Young already knew about the approaching army, the announcement there had a dramatic impact on those in attendance. What he probably did not know and what was particularly chilling was the news that General William S. "Squaw Killer" Harney was to command the expedition. In Spanish Fork, a resident wrote, "The news of the contemplated invasion soon spread thro the Territory and threw a damper over the spirits of the people. Not that they had lost faith but that they might have to suffer afflictions and sorrow in an increased degree." The happy summer of peace and plenty was over.[41]

---

[40] Larson and Larson, *Diary of Charles Lowell Walker*, 1:5.

[41] Brockbank, *Autobiography*, 25. A summary of when church leaders first knew that the army was coming is given in Cooley, *Diary of Brigham Young*, 49n52.

13
Troubles and Terror

THE REASONS BEHIND THE NEWLY INAUGURATED PRESIDENT James Buchanan's decision to send troops to Utah were many. An immediate cause was two memorials with resolutions sent to the president by the Utah Territorial Legislature in early 1857. The signers asked that men of their own choosing be named to federal positions in Utah. The first memorial contained provocative language nullifying federal law when it conflicted with territorial law and denigrating appointees chosen in Washington, D.C., as "false hearted men," "base and corrupt," and an "insult to humanity." It declared that the Mormons would resist any attempts by government officials to overrule territorial laws and insisted they would send away any who tried. The second memorial proposed such appointees as the notorious murderer William A. Hickman as an alternate for U.S. district attorney and Aaron Johnson, the perpetrator of the Parrish murders, for judge.[1]

Another factor in Buchanan's decision was the letters and reports over a six-year period written by federal officials who had fled Utah, fearing for their lives. These documents described how the Mormons lacked respect for federal authority, made treasonous statements, hindered the officials' ability to carry out their duties, threatened their lives and those of disaffected Mormons, treated the decisions of federal courts as invalid when they conflicted with those of the territorial probate courts, and attempted to gain the loyalty of the Indians by making a distinction

---

[1] "Memorial and Resolutions to the President of the United States, Concerning Certain Officers of the Territory of Utah" and "Memorial to the President of the United States," January 6, 1857, in MacKinnon, *At Sword's Point, Part 1,* 67–73.

between (the good) Mormons and (the bad) "Americans."[2] Also underlying Buchanan's decision was national outrage at the practice of
polygamy and the Republican Party platform in the recent presidential
election that linked polygamy with slavery as "twin relics of barbarism."
The expedition's exact purpose is muddled, but at a minimum it was to
install and protect the new federal officials, including a governor to replace
Brigham Young.[3] Buchanan was convinced that the Mormon people
would never accept anyone else in a role held by Young. By late July 1857,
Indian agent Garland Hurt was the only federal appointee left in Utah.
Still intent on carrying out his duties, he stayed on the Spanish Fork
Indian Farm.

On August 2, 1857, President Young preached that "God designs to
cut the thread between us and the world." The same day and the next,
he wrote to the bishops of southern Utah, exhorting them to save their
grain, sell none to "our enemies," note those who disobeyed this order,
use all available wool to make clothing, save ammunition, keep firearms
in order, and "prepare yourselves in all things . . . for that which may
hereafter come to pass." In another letter he told the Saints at Fort Bridger
to buy all the guns and ammunition from emigrants that they could, and
then admonished them to "fix your guns for shooting but lay low." To
those in Florence, Nebraska Territory, he wrote, "The Lord is hasten-
ing his work, and . . . the 'Redemption of Zion draweth nigh.'" By August
5 he was calling for the Saints in San Bernardino in California and Carson Valley (in today's Nevada) and the missionaries in the eastern states
and abroad to hurry home. On August 8 he wrote to Horace S. Eldredge
in St. Louis, "You may query will the soldiers be really permitted to enter
Salt Lake Valley? *No! they will not!!!*"[4]

Meanwhile in Spanish Fork the meetings of the Seventies Quorum
were taking place regularly. On August 2 one of the presidents, H. B.

---

[2] Many of the letters and reports of federal officials are in "Utah Expedition." The events that led to
Buchanan's decision to send an army to Utah are detailed in MacKinnon, "And the War Came."
[3] For more on the confusion surrounding the decision to send an expedition to Utah, what size it
should be, and its precise purpose, see MacKinnon, *At Sword's Point, Part 1*, chapter 5.
[4] Brigham Young, August 2, 1857, *Journal of Discourses*, 5:99; Brigham Young to Bishop Bronson,
August 2; to Philo T. Farnsworth, August 3; to Lewis Robinson, August 4; to William Felshaw,
August 4; to Samuel W. Richards and George Snider, August 5; and to H. S. Eldredge, August
8, 1857 (emphasis his), Brigham Young, Letterpress Copybook Transcriptions, 732, 739, 757–58,
759–60, 781–84, 771.

M. Jolley, "said that the Spirit of God was not so strongly manifested in them as it was last winter." He continued that, for himself, he "could submit to no authority in this world, but the priesthood, and that if he should be told by the priesthood over him to do something, which he thought was wrong, he would do it rather than cherish a rebellious spirit—that the priesthood was our only source for Salvation." In the meeting on August 30, obedience was emphasized again, this time specifically applied to preparing for the coming army, "for the cause we were engaged in was a just one." President Dennis Dorrity then "councilled the brethren to live their religion, without which no one would be able to stand the test awaiting them."[5]

Less than six miles away in Springville, the atmosphere of terror had not ended with the Parrish murders. Zephaniah J. Warren, a longtime Mormon who had lived in Nauvoo, had arrived back in Springville from a trip to California just after the murders. Like Peter, he was deeply disturbed: "Seeing the place and the appearance of blood, I became somewhat excited and spoke very reproachfully of the leading men of Springville; however, I tried to reconcile my mind enough to stay until I could dispose of my property, and get away with my family. I did not say much to anybody, unless I was interrogated." More than five months later, on the night of August 31, 1857, he was in bed with a cold when a knock came at his door. Two policemen were there and said that Wilber J. Earl wanted to speak to him outside and insisted that he go with them. In the street were six other well-armed men. They told him to be still and go with them to the city gate. When he refused, Earl grabbed him and with a knife to his throat said, "If you speak another loud word . . . I will cut your throat on the spot." The men then dragged him through the city gate, but when they heard someone coming, they threw Warren into a ditch. When all was quiet, Earl returned, seized him by the throat again, and said, "You damned old American, you will never write or talk any more about people that have been murdered." The men then conferred across the street and finally returned to tell Warren that they had decided to let him live a few days if he would swear not to tell what they had done that night. Earl added, "We have declared war against the whole world, and at any time we can put you aside very easy."

---

[5] Record of Fiftieth Quorum of Seventies, August 2 and 30.

Although it is unlikely that Peter knew of this episode, it captures the environment of fear experienced by dissenters or those who spoke out.[6]

On September 2, 1857, two days after Warren's fearful experience, Peter participated in a trial held by the Spanish Fork Seventies Quorum involving two of its members: James Laird, a thirty-three-year-old Scot who had come to Utah with his wife and three young children in the Willie Handcart Company the year before, and William Berry, twenty years old from Tennessee and a younger brother of John W. Berry, first counselor to Bishop John L. Butler. The nature of this trial is not known, but others in Spanish Fork in this period involved debt or land disputes.[7] Dennis Dorrity, president of the Seventies Quorum, presided. Peter described what took place:

> The case was Berry vs. Laird to be tried before a quorum of "Seventies." . . . After the evidence we were asked for our opinions on the case. The president in his remarks had allready indicated his conclusions. I had also formed an opinion but my opinion was not in unison with the presiding Officer's. I learned afterwards that I was not allone in my opinion but I was the only one who dared to give his opinion and did do so. And for giving an opinion in conflict with the Authority over me in the Church, I was then and there suspended from the Church.[8]

Peter was not actually suspended from the church, only from the Seventies Quorum, for eleven days later, on September 13, the quorum minutes read:

> A trial was held in the second ward school house Sep 2. Br. Laird against Br. Berry. . . . Br. Laird acknowledged his fault in respect to some things

---

[6] Affidavit of Zephaniah J. Warren, March 26, 1859, *Valley Tan*, April 19, 1859, 2. Although the *Valley Tan* was anti-Mormon in its editorials, its reporting of the March–April 1859 court and statements taken by Judge John Cradlebaugh are reliable. Joseph Bartholomew also told of more than one occasion when he was taken up into the mountains by several men implicated in the Parrish murders who, he believed, intended to kill him, but he managed to escape. Affidavit of Joseph Bartholomew, *Valley Tan*, April 19, 1859, 1, 4. Earl was also implicated in the murder of Henry Forbes in January 1858 (see chapter 14).

[7] Minutes from the trial have either been lost or are restricted. William S. Berry was killed on August 10, 1884, while on a mission to Tennessee, along with his companion, John H. Gibbs. William Berry's brother and counselor to the bishop, John W. Berry, was on a mission at the time of the trial. Sources for other trial subjects come from Hamilton, Journals, January 17, 1859; Hicks, "History of George Armstrong Hicks," 29; and Journal History, April 24, 1858, 1–2.

[8] Peter McAuslan to Agnes McAuslan Allan, March 1, 1887 (#33 McAuslan Papers), 6–7 of transcription. A similar description is found in Peter McAuslan to Agnes McAuslan Allan, March 1, 1887 (#34 McAuslan Papers), 12–13 of transcription. These were drafts of the letter he actually sent his sister.

which took place during the trial, and asked forgiveness of the Quorum. Prest. Dorrity said that he thought he was sincere, and moved that he be again received into the Quorum, seconded, and carried unanimously. Br. McAuslin said that he had done wrong in stating his feelings in the manner he did and in respect to Prest. Dorrity &c. Pres. Dorrity made a few remarks, and moved that he be again received into the Quorum, seconded, and carried unanimously.[9]

In his apology, Peter sounds sincerely contrite, but in a letter he wrote to his sister more than twenty-five years later, it appears that this trial still rankled and had marked a crisis in his belief: "From that day to this, I have never felt like becoming a Slave to any Religion. If the expression is permissible, I prefer to be a freeman in hell, rather than a Slave in a Mormon heaven." In another draft he wrote,

That proved to be . . . [an] eye opener. I'de rather be a dog and bay at the moon then give up my right to do my own thinking and become a Slave to such base Authority. That transaction brought forceabley to my mind the words of Shakesphere, 'Man proud man drest in a little brief authority plays such fantastic tricks before high heaven as make the angels weep.' I do not know neither do I say that Bro. . . . [Dorrity] went beyond his Authority, but I would rather say that [he] desplayed a Spirit of zeal to bring all [in] subjection to Authority and bring about that condition so much desired by the highest Authority in the Church.[10]

Peter continued to his sister, "As both you and me have heard it proclaimed not only once but hundreds of times, in fact it was the Alpha and Omega in all the Speaches of the highest in Authority 'to have no

---

[9] Record of Fiftieth Quorum of Seventies, September 13, 1857. Who took which side in the trial is not known, but it appears by Laird's apology that McAuslan sided with him—an Irishman who had lived in Scotland, married a Scottish woman, and had many Scottish friends—and that Dorrity sided with William Berry, who besides being the brother of the bishop's counselor, was also the brother of a future plural wife, Martha Elizabeth Berry, whom Dorrity married in early 1859 after she left John D. Lee. For James Laird (1825–84), see Mortimer, *How Beautiful Upon the Mountains*, 408–409; and http://members.aol.com/rdwinmill/James_and_Mary_Laird.htm. For William S. Berry (1838–84), born in Tennessee, see "The Late Elder W. S. Berry," *Deseret News*, August 27, 1884, 3.

[10] McAuslan to McAuslan Allan (#33 and #34 McAuslan Papers), 7 and 13 of transcriptions. George D. Watt, the first Mormon convert in Great Britain, president of the Scottish conferences in 1846–47, and the transcriber of most of President Young's sermons in the 1850s and 1860s, became disillusioned in part because of the lack of personal freedom under Young. Watt blamed his defection on his "mixture of English and Scottish blood," which could not be driven, but would respond to sympathy and kindness." Papanikolas, *Peoples of Utah*, 91. "I'd rather be a dog" comes from Shakespeare's *Julius Caesar*, Act 4. "Man, proud man" comes from *Measure for Measure*, Act 2.

mind of your own, do as you are told asking no questions.' Brother Heber's sermon on [the] Potter and the Clay." Peter's reference to the potter and clay is from Isaiah 64:8: "But now, O Lord, thou art our father; we are the clay, and thou our potter; and we all are the work of thy hand." Heber C. Kimball often preached on this text.[11]

Although many years had passed, his memory of this trial remained vivid. Peter continued, "As Hebber used to say, the voice of Brigham is the Voice of God to me. So the voice of your Bishop is the voice of God to you. And as J. Grant used to say, if those set over you in the Church tell you to kill your brother, do it and ask no questions." He also wrote,

> To be obedient to the priesthood or in other words do as you are told by those set over you, asking no questions, was one of the prominent features of a Mormon's education, and a man who has learned that lesson well, he is prepared to commit murder or commit any other act in the catelouge of crimes. Reason sets not upon that man's throne. It has abdicated; he had become a Serfe, a Slave to another. "If I a Slave by natures law designed, why was an independent wish ere planted in my mind[?]" This principle of Priestly authority has ever been and ever will be a curse to the people.[12]

Peter, always ready to discuss his beliefs at length and argue his position, sounds uncharacteristically meek and remorseful in his apology as recorded in the Seventies Quorum minutes. The atmosphere of the times—fear of being labeled an "apostate" with its derogatory connotation of being a traitor, perhaps even fear of being killed—made him decide to conform until a more propitious time. The trial became the turning point for Peter. As he explained to his sister,

> I do not wish you to think that I have any personal grudge against Bro. Doughterty [Dorrity] or any one else in the Mormon Faith. I believe that Mormons as a class will rank for honesty and morality as high as any other class amongst the religious systems of to day. If not higher. I have reason to thank the above mentioned Brother for giveing me a practical illustration of what a true faithful saint in the Mormon Church consists of: That

---

11 McAuslan to McAuslan Allan (#33 McAuslan Papers), 7. Examples of Heber C. Kimball's preaching on the potter and the clay can be found in the *Journal of Discourses* for February 25, 1855; September 21, 1856; October 5, 1856; April 19, 1857; August 2, 1857; and September 27, 1857.

12 McAuslan to McAuslan Allan (#33 and #34 McAuslan Papers), 6 and 12 of transcriptions. The last quotation McAuslan gives is from Robert Burns's poem "Man Was Made to Mourn": "If I'm design'd yon lordling's slave, / By Nature's law design'd—, / Why was an independent wish, / E'er planted in my mind?"

is, to have no mind of your own, but to be as willing to be moulded as the clay is, in the hand of the Potter. Practical Mormonism means, on the part of the subjects, Blind obedience, unquestioning submission to authority.[13]

While Peter's personal crisis was taking place, a much larger event was unfolding in southern Utah: the Mountain Meadows massacre. A party of emigrants from Arkansas with plans to go into cattle ranching in California was traveling through Utah on the southern route with a large herd of stock at just the wrong moment. Six weeks earlier the Saints had learned that President Buchanan was sending an army under the command of General Harney to install a new governor. Since the end of July, Brigham Young and his leaders had been warning the people of a possible coming conflict, ordering them not to sell a single kernel of grain or anything else to outsiders, and admonishing them to prepare their firearms and ammunition. The Arkansas emigrants, led by John T. Baker and Alexander Fancher, finally reached Mountain Meadows, about thirty-five miles southwest of Cedar City, on September 5 and camped to rest and graze their animals before starting across the desert to southern California. Southern Paiute Indians—incited by the Mormon leaders who had promised them the emigrants' cattle—and at least one Mormon, John D. Lee, who was dressed and painted like an Indian, attacked the wagon train before daybreak the next morning. Several of the emigrants were killed. The rest quickly circled the wagons into a defensive corral, pushed dirt under them so arrows or bullets could not penetrate below, and began firing back with their accurate muzzle-loading Kentucky rifles, killing or wounding some of the attackers. After the initial assault, there were two more concerted attacks in the morning and evening of the next day in which the Indians together with some fifty or sixty Mormons participated. After that there was desultory sniping for two more days. The Arkansas company held their own, although as the days passed, their water and ammunition ran low. By September 10 some Indians were angry, saying it was much more difficult than the Mormons had told them it would be, they had lost too many of their men, and Mormon "magic" for healing their wounded had not worked; they left, driving off some of the cattle. But at the same time other Indians joined the attack on the emigrants.

---

[13] McAuslan to McAuslan Allan (#34 McAuslan Papers), 13 of transcription.

The Mormons were now in a predicament: Too few Indians remained to effectively continue the fight, and they worried that the resentful Paiutes might turn on them just when they were preparing to face the U.S. Army. If the Mormons let the emigrants go, they would report the devastating attack in San Bernardino, including their suspicion that white men were involved, and perhaps the federal government would send a second army from that direction. The men most responsible for the decision that followed were Isaac Haight, mayor and stake president of Cedar City as well as a major in the Nauvoo Legion, and John D. Lee, also a major in the Nauvoo Legion and a religiously adopted son of Brigham Young. In a fateful series of military and religious meetings, these men and their colleagues devised a plan to eliminate the entire wagon train and blame it on the Paiutes. In essence, they hoped to cover up one crime with another. Starting at midnight on September 9 and continuing into the early hours of the next day, Haight convinced William H. Dame, the commander of the Nauvoo Legion's ninth military district in southern Utah and stake president in Parowan, of the need to involve the militia.

Thus on September 11, 1857, John D. Lee and another man approached the Arkansas wagon corral with a white flag. They promised the emigrants safe passage with a Mormon escort to Cedar City if they would give up their arms and leave their wagons so that the Indians would not attack them on the way. The emigrants must have been desperate to accept such terms. Mormons from the local ranks of the Nauvoo Legion brought up two wagons. They loaded the first with the Arkansas firearms and then put the young children and the wounded emigrants in both. After the wagons were driven out, the women and older children came on foot, and then the men in single file, with a member of the militia walking beside each emigrant. After they had proceeded about a mile toward Cedar City, Major John Higbee of the Nauvoo Legion called "Halt!" At this signal each Mormon turned and shot the Arkansas emigrant at his side. The Paiutes, rushing out from behind rocks and shrubbery, joined the Mormon men in slaughtering and bludgeoning the children and women. In a few moments 120 defenseless men, women, and children were dead. Only 17 children who were considered too young to remember were spared.[14]

---

[14] The best accounts of the Mountain Meadows massacre are Brooks, *Mountain Meadow Massacre*; Bagley, *Blood of the Prophets*; and Walker, Turley, and Leonard, *Tragedy at Mountain Meadows*.

Certainly what Peter wrote later—"if those set over you in the Church tell you to kill your brother, do it and ask no questions"—played a part in why the men under the leaders participated in the massacre. That kind of obedience to religious leaders, added to obedience to military superiors— with the roles often confused—and combined with suspicion and hatred of outsiders, fear that the coming army would instigate a new round of persecutions, and the rabid preaching of the Reformation made a recipe for atrocity.[15] In this incident, as in the Parrish-Potter murders, the overlapping religious, civil, and military roles, from Brigham Young on down, resulted in few if any checks on fanaticism. But the crime at Mountain Meadows was compounded further: the butchery was followed by systematic looting. Being a well-off company with a large herd of stock and, from all evidence, having a substantial amount of cash as well as wagons, clothing, and all the gear necessary for travel, the dead emigrants had left plenty of booty. The leaders involved took most of the stock and wagons, while many personal effects ended up in the Cedar City Tithing House.[16]

Instead of the massacre being blamed on the Indians, news of Mormon involvement spread quickly. U.S. Indian agent Garland Hurt had a series of visitors to the Spanish Fork Indian Farm, the first while the initial attack on the Arkansas emigrants was taking place. On September 10, George Hancock, a merchant in nearby Payson, told Hurt that the emigrants were in trouble with the Paiutes. On the day of the massacre itself, a Ute Indian returned from the south, where he had been collecting pine nuts; while there he had heard the news from a band of Paiutes. On September 14, three days later, another Ute arrived after traveling all night to confirm the news, adding that Mormons were behind the Paiute attack. Word began to spread among the white employees at the farm that all the emigrants had been killed, and the report was confirmed by still other visitors to the farm, with the Indians insisting that it was the Mormons, not the Indians, who had done the killing. Hurt, in his role as U.S. Indian agent, decided to investigate. On September 17 he sent a trusted young Indian named Pete, who was fluent in English, to travel

---

[15] McAuslan to McAuslan Allan (#34 Peter McAuslan Papers), 12 of transcription. Another participant with more than one role was Philip Klingensmith, bishop of Cedar City and a private in the Nauvoo Legion.

[16] Juanita Brooks suggests that the gold carried by the emigrants later may have been given for temple building; Brooks, *John D. Lee*, 372–76.

south by a back way to see what he could learn. Pete returned six days later to report that he had met some Paiutes who said they had participated in the massacre, but that "the Mormons persuaded them into it." John D. Lee, they said, had come to their village and told them the Americans were "bad people" who would kill an Indian any chance they had, and thus goaded them on with the promise that "if they were not strong enough to whip them, the Mormons would help."[17]

Peter soon learned of the massacre, perhaps from an employee on the farm or from Hurt himself. He said later that he learned "from a good authority that the Mormons and not the Indians were responsible for that terrible crime."[18] One can imagine the turmoil in Peter's mind. During the eleven days between the Seventies trial and his apology to President Dorrity, the massacre in southern Utah had taken place, and news was quickly filtering north to the nearby Indian Farm. These early reports, coming on top of his heightened emotion about the trial, probably influenced Peter's decision to humbly apologize to Dorrity.

Indian agent Hurt, in the meantime, was facing his own crisis. As the only non-Mormon federal official left in the territory, he quickly realized the precariousness of his position. His way out had become abruptly blocked by Governor Young, who imposed martial law on September 15 in a proclamation that read in part: "No persons shall be allowed to pass or repass into or through or from this Territory without a permit from the proper officer." The "proper officer" was Young himself. Bishop John L. Butler of Spanish Fork wrote regarding that martial law, "This put Gentiles in a sweet [sweat]. They did not know what to do." Although Hurt had initially enjoyed an amicable relationship with Young, who was the superintendent of Indian Affairs, it had long since soured. Hurt came to believe that the Mormons who were sent on missions to the Indians taught the Natives to distinguish between the "good" Mormons and the "bad" Americans. Hurt had reported to the secretary of the interior that such a program, whether accidental or intentional, could lead the Indians to side with the Mormons in a conflict with the federal government.[19]

---

[17] Garland Hurt to Jacob Forney, December 4, 1857, "Utah Expedition," 202–203.

[18] Guinn, *History of the State of California*, 660.

[19] "Proclamation by the Governor," in Roberts, *Comprehensive History of the Church*, 4:274; Butler, "Autobiography," 429; Morgan, "Administration of Indian Affairs in Utah," 383–409: Garland Hurt to George W. Manypenny, May 2, 1855, "Utah Superintendency," 593–94.

Now Hurt was suddenly aware that 120 non-Mormon cattle ranchers and their families had been massacred on the southern road. Although the army was on its way to Utah, it had started late, and it was becoming increasingly apparent to Hurt that they would not reach the Salt Lake Valley before winter storms stopped them. That meant he would have no contact with the army or government officials for at least six months. Isolated, afraid, and with only the Indians as friends, Hurt had to decide what to do. The Utes, fearing for his safety, encouraged him to let them escort him over the mountains without a pass from Governor Young to the safety of the army.

The local Mormon leaders for their part were becoming increasingly suspicious of Hurt. He was a U.S. agent and had gained the affection and loyalty of the Utes, who might turn on the Mormons in a conflict. In Spanish Fork, George A. Hicks suspected that the real reason the Mormons were afraid to let Hurt leave was that he would report to the army the generally poor condition of the Nauvoo Legion and would also act as a guide to them. The bishop of Payson wrote to Aaron Johnson in Springville that he thought Hurt might try to make his escape when the Mormon leaders were at the semiannual church conference in early October. Johnson, however, had already received news from John L. Butler, the bishop of Spanish Fork, that Hurt was planning to go sooner than that and, with the help of the Indians, get over the mountains to Fort Laramie.[20]

On September 26 and 27 a flurry of messages and orders flew by express horseback riders between Brigadier General Aaron Johnson in Springville and Brigham Young and General Daniel H. Wells in Salt Lake City, and then between Johnson and the Nauvoo Legion officers in Springville, Spanish Fork, and Payson. Young instructed Johnson to take possession of the property at the Indian Farm and to "convey" Hurt to Salt Lake City, while at the same time preventing a collision with the Indians. These orders and confusing reports about Hurt led Johnson to rush to Salt Lake City to confer directly with President Young about how to handle the situation. Johnson left on September 26 and did not return until nearly midnight the next day.[21]

---

[20] Hicks, "History of George Armstrong Hicks," 32; Chas. B. Hancock to Aaron Johnson, September 26, 1857; and Aaron Johnson to Daniel H. Wells, October [no day or year], in Cook, *Aaron Johnson Correspondence*, 65–68. Butler obtained the news of Hurt's planned departure through Dick James, an Indian interpreter.

[21] Letters, orders, and reports, September 26–28, 1857, in Cook, *Aaron Johnson Correspondence*, 59–89.

While Johnson was gone, word continued to leak from the farm that Hurt was about to escape. The local militia officers decided on September 27 that they could not wait for Johnson's return but had to take Hurt prisoner that day. As they started toward the Indian Farm with their troops, the Utes, highly alarmed, rushed to Hurt in the farmhouse, crying, "Friend! friend! the Mormons will kill you!" They insisted that Hurt leave and quickly saddled his horse. The Indian interpreter then arrived with a note from Bishop John L. Butler in which he said that news of Hurt's impending departure was known, that it was in violation of martial law, and that they "were resolved to enforce the law at all hazards." Hurt, now fearing the Indians were right and he would be killed, set out with three Indian youths, riding rapidly west instead of east, as expected. They managed to elude their pursuers and hide for the day, returning at night to the now-deserted farm to gather up papers, clothes, and food, and then slipped past a guard to escape up Spanish Fork Canyon and into the mountains.[22]

The Seventies Quorum meeting that day was cancelled. The minutes read, "No meeting: The Brethren being called upon to intercept the flight of Garland Hurt, Indian agent, from the country." Peter's commanding officer in the Nauvoo Legion, George A. Hicks, later gave a perspective from the troops. He wrote that their units were called to the public square and from there marched toward the Indian Farm. They were poorly equipped: "While we were crossing the Spanish Fork River bottom a halt was called and the brethren *were told to arm themselves with clubs.* Those who had no guns did so and there were not a few." About halfway there, they were met by the militia from other settlements until they were about 400 strong. While the military leaders conferred, some 250 Indians came between them and the farmhouse. Hicks reported, "They uttered yells of defiance and daring us to come on, yelling and whooping in the most terrific manner." Suddenly another militia officer galloped up at full speed to where they waited and reported that Hurt had already escaped. "Our bird had flown. . . . I am glad we did not get him for more than likely he would have been killed if we had," Hicks acknowledged. "There is no doubt but the Indians were sent to keep us back while their Dr. made good his escape."[23]

---

[22] Garland Hurt to A. S. Johnston, October 24, 1857, "Utah Expedition," 205–208.
[23] Record of Fiftieth Quorum of Seventies, September 27, 1857; Hicks, "History of George Armstrong Hicks," 32, emphasis his.

Indian agent Garland Hurt's escape from
the Spanish Fork Indian Farm, September 27, 1857.
The two men on the left are thought to be Colonel
Charles B. Hancock and his brother George W. Hancock
of Payson. Painting by C. C. A. Christensen. *Used by permission, Utah State Historical Society, all rights reserved.*

The militia, including Peter with his river-bottom club, was ordered home again. Surely relieved that Hurt got away, Peter must have become increasingly concerned as his doubts about Mormonism grew. To whom could he turn, now that the last federal official had fled the territory?

At the end of September 1857, General Wells of the Nauvoo Legion ordered 1,250 men from different military districts to Echo Canyon in the Wasatch Mountains to barricade the narrow passage against the approach of the U.S. Army. Hicks described his hope of being chosen to go:

I remember when a company started for Echo Canyon . . . that many were forbidden the privilege of going for some must stay at home. I for one, though very anxious to go out, was not permitted to go because others were in better circumstances to fit themselves out. . . . As the company started away, we all gave three cheers for God and liberty. We were at that time a God trusting people and all our leaders . . . taught us to believe that we could keep the whole world out of these mountains.[24]

Peter, not having a firearm, also was not selected. A few days later another group from Utah County was chosen to go to Salt Lake City with provisions for thirty days in order to be ready, wrote President Young, "to march to any point required at a moments notice." Altogether about 600 militia camped on Union Square and another 500 were stationed at other points around Salt Lake City.[25]

While defenses were being thrown up in Echo Canyon and troops stationed in Salt Lake City, other men were sent to harass the army and its supply wagons. On October 5, near the Green River, Major Lot Smith and a small company of militia surprised and burned two unguarded government trains carrying bacon and other provisions—enough to feed the army for two months. Some days later they made off with more than a thousand head of army cattle.

As fear increased that the army might actually come into the valley before winter, the tenor of preaching by the church leaders rose. On October 8, President Young assured the Saints, "I expect that we are fully able to defend ourselves, and that our enemies will not be able to come within a hundred miles of us. I know that ten men, such as I could name and select, could stop them. . . . I count five such men equal to twenty-five thousand, and believe that two of them could put ten thousand to flight." Peter recalled these statements a year after he left: "As they had allready declaired there independence from the United States, they had full faith that the lord would fight there Battles and sustain them as an independent Kingdom to the dismay and overthrow of all there enemies, even the Prophet himself declaring that with Ten men of the right stripe he could defie all the armies of the U.S."[26]

On October 25, Orson Hyde, one of the Twelve Apostles, declared, "The ungodly must be consumed by the devouring fire. . . . 'He that is not

---

[24] Ibid., 29.

[25] Brigham Young to Andrew Cunningham, October 9, 1857, Brigham Young, Letterpress Copybook Transcriptions, 903.

[26] Brigham Young, October 18, 1857, *Journal of Discourses*, 5:339–40. D&C 133:58 reads: "To prepare the weak for those things which are coming on the earth, and for the Lord's errand in the day when the weak shall confound the wise, and the little one become a strong nation, and two shall put their tens of thousands to flight." McAuslan to Salmon (#14 McAuslan Papers), 4.

for us is against us.' . . . Let the wrath of God be upon . . . all that wish evil to Zion." And on November 8, Heber C. Kimball once again preached obedience: "If you are told by your leader to do a thing, do it. None of your business whether it is right or wrong. . . . God designs we should be pure men, holding the oracles of God in holy and pure vessels; but when it is necessary that blood should be shed, we should be as ready to do that as to eat an apple." He went on to say they would kill members who failed to be faithful: "We shall clean the platter of all such scoundrels; and if men and women will not live their religion, . . . we will 'lay judgment to the line and righteousness to the plummet,' and we will let you know that the earth can swallow you up . . . and as brother Taylor says, you may dig your graves, and we will slay you, and you may crawl into them."[27]

In November, the preaching of Orson Hyde and Heber C. Kimball had its effect. Six men from California—known as the Aiken party, for the names of two brothers in it—arrived in the Mormon settlements on October 31, expecting to find the army already there. Whether they came, as seems likely, to set up a gambling operation to profit from the 2,400 soldiers or just to see what Salt Lake City was like and, hoping to profit by supplying animals to the army, planned then to continue east is not known. From Carson Valley on the east side of the Sierra Nevada, the Californians had caught up with a company of Mormon colonizers whom President Young had called back to defend the Wasatch Front settlements from the U.S. Army. The Aiken party's reason for joining the returning members was to obtain safety from the Indians as they crossed the Great Basin, but in the end it may have cost them their lives. One of the Mormons rode ahead to alert a Nauvoo Legion officer at the first Mormon settlement at Box Elder (now Brigham City) about the men traveling with them, and when the company arrived shortly thereafter, the Californians were taken prisoner and accused of being army spies.

Tricked out of their weapons but still in possession of what was estimated to be between $6,000 and $25,000 and good horses, the prisoners were taken under guard to Salt Lake City. Finally, on November 20, four of the six were escorted south, presumably to return to California by the southern route. Four Mormons went with them, including the notorious killer Porter Rockwell. On November 25, about twenty-five

---

[27] Orson Hyde, October 25, 1857, *Journal of Discourses*, 5:355–56; Heber C. Kimball, November 8, 1857, *Journal of Discourses*, 6:30, 32, 34–35.

miles south of Nephi at the crossing of the Sevier River, the Aiken party men were attacked by a combined force of those escorting them and four others sent ahead from Nephi by the bishop as reinforcements. Two of the Californians were killed, and the other two, badly wounded, struggled back to Nephi, where their wounds were tended to. Then, on November 28, the two were driven north in a buggy to return to Salt Lake City. But at Willow Creek, about twenty-five miles south of Spanish Fork, they were shot to death. About the same time, one of the two Aiken party men still in Salt Lake City was taken north to near Bountiful and there killed by William A. Hickman, another infamous assassin. The fate of the sixth man is unknown.

Besides being suspected as government spies, the Aiken party men were wealthy. The substantial sums of money stolen from them were most likely used by the Mormon leaders in preparations to fight the army. As in the Parrish murders and the Mountain Meadows massacre, Governor Young failed to conduct an investigation or punish those involved.[28]

The U.S. Army had not arrived in Salt Lake City, as the Aiken party had expected, because the troops were trapped in the mountains by a blizzard in early November. Barely in time, the recently appointed commander, Colonel Albert Sidney Johnston, reached the army and immediately collected the scattered troops to move them toward Fort Bridger. More than three thousand of their stock had already died in the heavy snow and cold. The army reached Fort Bridger a month and a half after Nauvoo Legion soldiers had burned it to the ground. Realizing his men could not make it to the Salt Lake Valley, Colonel Johnston established a winter camp near Fort Bridger, which he named Camp Scott in honor of Winfield Scott, the army's general in chief.

One hundred and sixty miles away in Spanish Fork, the Seventies Quorum continued to meet every few days in November. President Dennis Dorrity and the clerk for the quorum had been among those called to build the defenses in Echo Canyon. In their absence, another of the seven presidents presided, and Peter acted as clerk. The meetings were

---

[28] The only thorough account of the Aiken murders is Bigler, "Aiken Party Executions," 457–76. See also an affidavit taken in 1859 in Cradlebaugh, *Utah and the Mormons,* 64–65. For a discussion of violence in Utah in this period, much of which resulted from the untempered sermons preached by church leaders, see MacKinnon, "'Lonely Bones.'"

primarily about the quorum teachers: to hear their reports, including that given by Peter, to add to their number, and "to ascertain if there were any improper feelings existing in any of the Council or teachers, that were calculated to prevent them from enjoying the spirit of their Callings—[and] if there were, to get straightened up before going forth to teach the Quorum."[29]

Also in November in Fillmore, about ninety miles south of Spanish Fork and thirty south of where two of the Aiken party were soon to be murdered at the Sevier River, N. B. Baldwin, a member of the Seventies Quorum there, was experiencing less benign meetings. He wrote that "the spirit of bloodthirstiness was the prevailing topic" and that members "were permitted to abuse and threaten the lives of myself and some others for merely expressing our views in a meeting of seventies."[30] Baldwin captured much of the atmosphere of terror and fear that prevailed in Utah and was especially strong in the settlements south of Salt Lake City in 1857. Peter—at least temporarily—suppressed his own fears and doubts. The times were too dangerous.

---

[29] Record of Fiftieth Quorum of Seventies, November 23 and 25, 1857.

[30] N. B. Baldwin to Brigham Young, November 15, 1857, LDS Church Archives, as quoted in Peterson, "Mormon Reformation," 51.

14

A Year of Disruption

DURING THE WINTER AND EARLY SPRING OF 1857–58, CHURCH
leaders preached defiance to their enemies, while the U.S. Army remained
snowbound in winter quarters at Fort Bridger in the mountains east of
Salt Lake City. On January 16, 1858, about two thousand of the faithful
gathered in the Tabernacle for a reading of a memorial written by the
Territorial Legislature to President Buchanan and the two houses of
Congress.

Strongly worded, the memorial protested that the memorial they had
sent the previous year requesting men of their own choosing to be
appointed to federal territorial positions had never been acknowledged,
instead being treated only with "silent contempt." It charged that the federal appointees now about to descend on Utah had been found among
"the reckless, the drunken, the unprincipled, the dissolute, the houseless
and penniless" who had "depraved and corrupt tastes." It asked the government to "stay the suicidal hand of crawling sycophants and corrupt
rulers." It also complained that the president had not informed them as
to why he was sending an army, which was now on their border. It asked
if "the horrid scenes of Missouri and Illinois" were to be repeated by the
national government, and if the army was being sent to protect the rights
of the citizens, adding, "That is needless, because those rights have never
been in the least infringed upon in Utah." Among the signers were John
D. Lee and Isaac Haight, the two men most implicated in the Mountain
Meadows massacre four months earlier.[1]

---

[1] "Memorial" [written January 6, 1858], *Deseret News*, January 13, 1858, 4–5.

After the reading, President Young spoke once more of the wrongs the Saints had borne in Ohio, Missouri, and Illinois, and he declared that the intent of the army was to "destroy the Everlasting Priesthood from the face of the Earth." Young recalled how Joseph and Hyrum Smith had given themselves up to the authorities. He declared vehemently to the congregation that he "would never give himself up to the Damnd Scoundrells and said that he carried a long Bowie knife and swore by the eternal Gods that if they came to take him he would send them to Hell across Lots"— that is, kill them and send them on a shortcut to hell. He stated that the earlier persecutions of the Saints had been local, but now they had been raised to a national level, and if the army "persisted in trying to take the lives of him and his Bretheren by the help of God and his Bretheren that he would make Millions of them Bite the Dust to which the congregation shouted Amen which rent the air as it went up to Heaven."[2]

The Territorial Legislature's memorial was supplemented with addresses and resolutions written by committees selected during that January 16 meeting. They expressed the people's satisfaction with Brigham Young as governor and their contempt for federal policies. The package was sent to Washington, D.C., and presented to Congress by John M. Bernhisel, the Utah delegate. These documents made Congress and President Buchanan believe that Utah was mad with rebellion. Further confirming their view was Governor Young's declaration of martial law, the Nauvoo Legion's burning of government property, the defenses in Echo Canyon, and the incendiary sermons during the fall. The Mormons, from their perspective, could only see the army as eager to destroy their religion and bring a new round of persecutions, which they had sought to escape by moving west.[3]

Although Peter McAuslan did not record his thoughts for 1858, one can follow the probable tracks of his increasing disillusionment in the events of that year. One such circumstance was another murder in nearby Springville, the same town where the Parrishes had been killed ten months earlier.

Henry Forbes, a non-Mormon from Illinois, where he was said to have a wife and young children, was heading home from California. He

---

[2] Larson and Larson, *Diary of Charles Lowell Walker*, 1:14.

[3] "Memorial," 4–5. William P. MacKinnon noted that this memorial resulted in a federal grand jury at Camp Scott returning an indictment of treason against all the signers, i.e., the entire Utah Territorial Legislature; see MacKinnon, "And the War Came," 28n15. See also Firmage and Mangrum, *Zion in the Courts*, 245.

arrived in Utah with revolvers and a good horse and with plans to go on to Fort Bridger. Governor Young's martial law prevented him from leaving Utah, however, and thus he was temporarily boarding with Parshall Terry in Springville. Some time after his arrival, his horse and revolvers were stolen; Terry claimed Indians had taken them. Then, on the evening of January 24, 1858, Forbes was taken out along the road to Provo by at least two men and shot dead.[4]

No inquest was held. After the murder, Parshall Terry was seen riding Forbes's horse and wearing his pistols. Two Springville residents, Joseph Bartholomew and Abraham Durfee, had been asked to participate in the killing but had declined. Each pointed fingers at Wilber J. Earl and Sanford Fuller. Both suggested the murder was planned: Bartholomew testified that Fuller had said "there was such a thing in contemplation," and Durfee that Earl had told him "it was orders to kill Forbes."[5]

As in the Mountain Meadows massacre and the Parrish-Potter murders, the men involved held multiple positions: Wilber J. Earl was a private in an infantry company of the Nauvoo Legion, a city alderman and former justice of the peace, and a member of the bishop's council (at least at the time of the Parrish murders). Sanford Fuller was a private in a cavalry company and appears to have been a city policeman as well as a ward teacher. Was Forbes murdered because he might report to the army on the poor resources of the Mormons? Was it purging themselves of impurities in their midst? Was it related to Wilber J. Earl's threat made the previous August to Zephaniah Warren because of his consternation over the Parrish murders ("We have declared war against the whole world, and at any time we can put you aside very easy")? A suggestion of a military motive comes from a letter that Brigadier General Aaron Johnson wrote the previous November to a Nauvoo Legion colonel in Springville. Johnson ordered the colonel to collect clothes for the men building defenses in Echo Canyon, adding that if he did not receive enough donations, he should help himself, "for now is the time it is needed by our brethren." Parshall Terry appeared to be helping himself to revolvers and a horse, as the brethren needed them as well. Peter later wrote that Mor-

---

[4] "Charge," *Deseret News*, March 16, 1859, 1; "Discharge of the Grand Jury," *Valley Tan*, April 5, 1859, 2; "Court Doings at Provo," *Deseret News*, April 6, 1859, 2; "Murder of —— Forbes," *Valley Tan*, April 19, 1859, 2.

[5] Earl, Fuller, Bartholomew, and Durfee had each played a part in the Parrish murders ten months earlier. "Affidavit of Joseph Bartholomew" and "Affidavit of Abraham Durfee," both in *Valley Tan*, April 19, 1859, 4 and 2.

mons were taught unconditional obedience and "that it is right to Murder, Steal and commit Arson, when God gives command." Once again
life had been mercilessly taken, and no one was charged with the murder. But Henry Forbes was dead. A year later, a letter still awaited him
at the post office in Camp Floyd, never to be claimed.[6]

This crime is not mentioned in the Spanish Fork Seventies Quorum
minutes even though it was committed just a few miles away. Nevertheless, word of it no doubt spread as quickly as news of the earlier murders
had. Although Peter did not refer to it directly, it must have confirmed
for him that outsiders and nonconformists were not safe.

The full import of the killing was probably overwhelmed by mounting anxiety at the approach of the army. For one meeting of the Seventies Quorum, Peter had again been appointed to replace the clerk, who
was moving to Salt Lake City. The minutes of the subsequent meetings
portray a period of gloom: "Some of the Brethern then spoke of the darkness that they felt & it seamed as if they could not get rid of it." One
member "spoke of America comming against us and of England back-
ing them up." At a meeting on February 1, one of the leaders talked of
"a test that was comming on the Saints." President Dorrity ended that
meeting with his desire that the members stop swearing, sustain (uphold)
the authorities, and "stopt horse reacing on [the] Sabbath."[7]

On February 10, 1858, the *Deseret News* printed President Buchanan's
annual message, given the preceding December 8. "The people of Utah,"
it read, "almost exclusively, belong to this church, and believing with a
fanatical spirit that he [Young] is Governor of the Territory by divine
appointment, they obey his commands as if they were direct revelations
from Heaven. . . . Governor Young has, by proclamation, declared his
determination to maintain his power by force, and has already committed acts of hostility against the United States. Unless he should retrace
his steps, the Territory of Utah will be in a state of open rebellion. . . .
This is the first rebellion which has existed in our Territories; and humanity itself requires that we should put it down in such a manner that it
shall be the last. . . . We ought to go there with such an imposing force

---

[6] Utah County Military District, 1850–66, Utah Territorial Militia Muster Rolls; Aaron Johnson to
John S. Fullmer, November 10, 1857, in Cook, *Aaron Johnson Correspondence*, 108; Peter McAuslan to Agnes McAuslan Allan, March 1, 1884 (#34 McAuslan Papers), 12 of transcription; "List
of Letters," *Valley Tan*, February 1, 1859, 4.

[7] Record of Fiftieth Quorum of Seventies, January 11, 18, and February 1, 1858. For the unruly behavior of youth, see Bitton, "Zion's Rowdies."

as to convince these deluded people that resistance would be vain, and thus spare the effusion of blood."[8]

Two days after the paper appeared in Salt Lake City, Peter's fellow Scot Henry Hamilton in Spanish Fork reported on it at length in his diary: "He [Buchanan] says that . . . there remains no Government but the despotism of Brigham Young. . . . He also spoke of . . . raising 4 additional regiments to send on to Utah so as to bring the Mormons to it right there and then so as to stop the efusion of blood." Four days after the president's message was published, Apostle John Taylor preached at the Sunday meeting in the Tabernacle. Charles L. Walker reported on what he said: "We were like Jesus in the days of Herod who sought the life of Christ because he was afraid of him becoming the King of the Jews. So in like maner President Buchanan is trying to take the lives and liberties of us as a People and to destroy us from the face of the Eearth [*sic*] and said that President Buchanan should be a type [of] Herod; to which the congregation shouted Amen."[9]

Words and emotions continued to mount day by day until a clash with the army appeared inevitable. The government's efforts the previous September had done little to lower the temperature. At that time Quartermaster Captain Stewart Van Vliet had come to Salt Lake City to obtain contracts for supplies for the army, determine where the troops might set up camp and graze their animals, and assess the mood of the church leaders. Van Vliet—a diplomat who had known the Mormons when they were at Winter Quarters on the banks of the Missouri River before their exodus to Utah a decade earlier—was the right man for the delicate mission. He was politely received by President Young and the other leaders but was assured that the army would not be allowed into Salt Lake Valley. When Van Vliet said that President Buchanan would then send in an even larger force to overwhelm them, Young declared they should not find them, as the Saints would have left, leaving only a scorched earth behind.

Brigham Young's assertion to Captain Van Vliet was not just a threat or bluff. The previous April, Young had taken 141 people, including all the top church leaders in the territory except for one apostle, Wilford Woodruff, on a month-long journey to the northernmost Mormon settlement, at Fort Limhi on the Salmon River. North of Fort Hall in present-day Idaho, it had been established as a mission to the Bannock and

[8] "President's Message," *Deseret News*, February 10, 1858, 3, 7.
[9] Hamilton, Journals, February 12, 1858; Larson and Larson, *Diary of Charles Lowell Walker*, 1:20.

Shoshone Indians. Young was interested in finding a refuge for the Saints, and when he returned, he told Wilford Woodruff that only Mormons "would want the cold North country."[10]

Now ten months later, in February 1858, a series of events began to solidify Young's plans. Although he appeared to favor the idea of moving his people north, he did not neglect other possibilities. On February 23 he wrote to all the bishops in the southern settlements that he wanted them to select "some old men and boys" (i.e., not Nauvoo Legion members) to go to the region of White Mountain—a vague term in Indian stories referring to the desert regions west of the southern Mormon settlements—"and find places where we can raise grain and hide up our families and stock in case of necessity." When they found a suitable place or places, they were to plant seeds so as to have a crop that year.[11]

Two days after Young sent this letter, Thomas L. Kane, a friend of the Saints and a humanitarian from Philadelphia who had first met the Mormons in 1846, arrived in Salt Lake City. Because snow had closed the overland route, he had sailed at the beginning of January 1858 from New York City to Panama, then traveled by train across the isthmus, and then again by ship to Los Angeles. From there he went on horseback to Salt Lake City, arriving exhausted and sick on February 25. Nevertheless, determined to do what he could to end the conflict between the Mormons and the federal government, he met with President Young and other church leaders several times. Young, though friendly, was willing only to be "dictated by the Spirit day by day."[12] After fruitless meetings, Kane left on March 8 to travel to the army's winter camp.

On the same day that Kane arrived in Salt Lake City, but far to the north, two hundred Bannock and Shoshone warriors attacked at the grazing grounds at Fort Limhi. They killed two Mormons who tried to protect the herd, wounded five others, and drove off several hundred cattle and horses. Two riders from the fort managed to slip away and, riding hard, brought the news to Young in eight days. President Young quickly organized a rescue party for the northern settlers. As the Nauvoo Legion soldiers started out, Young realized that a northern retreat for the Saints had vanished.

Rumors swiftly reached Young that the army had incited the Indians

---

[10] Bigler, *Forgotten Kingdom*, 137–38, 142–45; Bigler, *Fort Limhi*, 135–60.

[11] There were also rumors of moves to Canada, Mexico, and elsewhere. "White Mountain" is sometimes given as a plural "White Mountains." Stott, *Search for Sanctuary*, 49.

[12] Roberts, *Comprehensive History of the Church*, 4:346, 348–49; Ririe, [Autobiography], 9:365.

to attack. If that was true and the Indians throughout the region were siding with the army, the Mormons were in a perilous position indeed. On March 9, Young quickly sent a message after Kane, who had started for the army's Camp Scott the day before. Young offered provisions to Colonel Albert Sidney Johnston for the troops, but Johnston refused to accept anything from the man he had come to fight. However, Alfred Cumming, the newly appointed governor for the territory who was wintering with the army, interpreted the offer as an olive branch.[13]

President Young now seriously turned his attention to finding a retreat in the Southwest for his people. A month after sending out the "old men and boys," Young broached his White Mountain plan in a sermon in the Tabernacle. On March 21, 1858, he turned the usual Sunday meeting into a special conference that, in an effort to keep it secret, was not published in the *Deseret News*; instead a quickly printed circular was sent out confidentially to all the bishops.

What Young presented at that meeting was a reversal of the defiance of the previous fall: "We have been preparing to use up our enemies by fighting them, and if we take that course and shed the blood of our enemies, we will see the time . . . when we will have to flee from our homes and leave the spoil to them. . . . If we open the ball upon them by slaying the United States soldiery, just so sure they would be fired with anger to lavishly . . . compass our destruction." He then introduced the new exodus: "There is a desert region in this Territory larger than any of the Eastern States, that no white man knows anything about. . . . It is a desert country with long distances from water to water, with wide sandy and alkali places entirely destitute of vegetation and miry when wet. . . . Probably there is room in that region for 500,000 persons to live scattered about where there is good grass and water. I am going there." He then described what he planned to do as soon as the snow melted: "I am going to start part of my family. I am going to a place that I can say to our enemies, 'whither I go you cannot come.' "[14]

President Young then declared that they would leave Salt Lake City as the Russians had left Sebastopol in the Crimean War: After the British had laid siege to that city for over a year in 1854–55, the Russians, realizing the futility of further resistance, burned the city and left the ruins to the victor. Young would do the same: "I am for letting them [the army] come

---

[13] Bigler, *Forgotten Kingdom*, 184–88; Hafen and Hafen, *Utah Expedition*, 263–89.
[14] As quoted in Stott, *Search for Sanctuary*, 56–58.

and take 'Sebastopol.'" Later in the meeting, Young suggested that those who had not lost their homes in Missouri or Illinois be the "pioneers" to the White Mountain refuge. That evening in the Nineteenth Ward, Bishop Alonzo Raleigh called Peter's brother William. William McAuslan was one of thirty men with families called from the Nineteenth Ward to be part of the "Western desert 1st Company." William packed five hundred pounds of flour to take with him, his wife, Mary, and their two small children.[15]

On March 21, the same day as his Sebastopol talk, President Young sent an express rider to George W. Bean, the leader of the White Mountain expedition, which was then about a hundred miles south of Provo. His message urged speed in finding a suitable place for the Saints. To ensure success quickly, Young called for a second expedition to set off from near Cedar City in southern Utah.[16] Although President Young could not keep secret a vast movement of people, he hoped to keep their destination confidential.

With the Sebastopol circular, Young included a letter to Aaron Johnson in Springville: "We shall need many teams for the present movement, and we expect you to assist us as much as you can." He added that the Saints in the Salt Lake and northern settlements would stop planting any crops and thus urged Johnson to have people in his area plant more than usual. Aaron Johnson's reply to President Young told of the surprise and confusion such a sudden change of policy gave the local people: "The Brethren & Sisters here, will do all they can to go, stay, or help others as they shall be counseled. . . . It was a little of a stumper to some at first thinking it was a tolerable short corner, but as soon as they advanced a few steps farther, so as to see around the corner, they could see it was clear." To move mentally and physically from a fully armed, belligerent state to a noncombative, acquiescent one ready to move elsewhere required an abrupt shift in perspective.[17]

---

[15] William and Mary had come to Utah with Peter McAuslan, Sr., and Betsy in 1853. Soon after arriving, they joined those called to strengthen the settlement at Tooele, but by 1856 they were back in Salt Lake City. Stott, *Search for Sanctuary*, 58–60; Bishop's Records, Nineteenth Ward.

[16] Young's belief in a sanctuary that could support half a million people appears to have been based on faulty information obtained some years earlier from mountain man Elijah Barney Ward and from an 1848 map of explorer John C. Fremont, who claimed there was an east-west mountain range at the southern rim of the Great Basin. Fremont's fifth expedition crossed the Great Basin almost exactly where the mountain range was supposed to be, but he did not revise his earlier reports. Stott, *Search for Sanctuary*, 5–17, 67–68, 85–87, 106–13.

[17] Brigham Young to Aaron Johnson, March 24, 1858, and Aaron Johnson to Brigham Young, March 26, 1858, both in Cook, *Aaron Johnson Correspondence*, 121–22.

In the Spanish Fork Seventies Quorum, "a circular was then read from the first Presidencie on the moveing South of the Saints to the deserts and mountains, and on the burning of our houses &c. if necessary." One member then rose to air a subject more pressing to him. He "give his fealings upon horse raceing. he did not felloship it." Dennis Dorrity, president of the quorum, returned the discussion to the circular and "spoke of us holding ourselves as good musical instruments in the hands of a skilfull musation [and] exhorted the Brethern to be obedient to Council." Dorrity, in closing the meeting, returned to the immediate: He "spoke of horse raceing on Sabbath he wished it to be done away with."[18]

As the pioneer families prepared to leave Salt Lake City, military readiness continued. On March 31, infantry companies set out for Echo Canyon, and on April 1 in Springville, Aaron Johnson issued orders to hold company musters for the inspection of arms and ammunition and to see that "everything is held in readiness for a sudden movement in any direction."[19]

Brigham Young had launched a year of disruption. The temple foundations were covered with dirt to protect them. The church books, the *Deseret News* press, and the grain in the tithing house were packed and moved to Provo and Fillmore. President Young and the other church leaders started south with their large families on April 1 to make a temporary home in Provo, but the men returned for the Sunday meeting on April 4 and the annual conference on April 6. On Sunday President Young spoke in the Tabernacle in a manner reminiscent of that of the previous fall and winter. As recorded by Charles L. Walker,

> Bro Brigham made Some good remarks on our Situation as a People, the blessings we enjoyed, the Persecutions the Church had been subgect to since its organiziation the treatment of the unitid States towards us, their Cursed meaness their Disposition to Destroy us from the face of the Earth, their wickedness corruption and abomination of what they call and say is Christanity and civilizeation. Said he felt righteously mad enough to go right out to the camp of our enemies and slay them, said he would have to hold back and let the wicked Slay the wicked[. S]howed that if we spilt their blood their [there] was an atonement[. If] we let them kill themselves they would go to Hell and stay there.[20]

---

[18] Record of Fiftieth Quorum of Seventies, March 28, 1858.

[19] Church Historian's Office, *History of Brigham Young*, 221; Aaron Johnson to John S. Fullmer, April 1, 1858, in Cook, *Aaron Johnson Correspondence*, 125.

[20] Larson and Larson, *Diary of Charles Lowell Walker*, 1:27–28.

At the church conference two days later, Young abruptly changed the White Mountain plan and ordered all the people in Salt Lake, Davis, and Tooele counties to move to Utah County. Thus no longer was it just the pioneer families who were going, but the entire population of those counties. And no longer were they headed for a desert refuge—still to be located—but only as far as Provo and the surrounding settlements. Before leaving, people were to board up their windows and doors and scatter straw and kindling around their houses so that at the first sign of the army's taking possession, the men on guard could set fire to them. Many families lacked wagons and draft animals, but Young ordered those in Utah County with means to come north and help the poorer Saints move.[21]

Not everyone was pleased with President Young's evacuation policy. A Salt Lake merchant who was in the city in early April reported, "The mass of the people, however, are not favorable to this movement, although they are preparing to participate in it, and are earnestly wishing that the army may enter the Valley before they start."[22] William Carruth, a Scottish friend of Agnes and John Allan, wrote,

> I must here acknowledge that it was somewhat of a trial to me to leave my home and go I knew not where, perhaps into a desert country with a small family destitute of the comforts of life. Thes were the feelings of a great number of the people, but on reflection I would say the God that lead the children of Isrial out of the land of Egypt is the God of this people and he will protect and deliver us.[23]

President Young's change in policy—from his assurances that the Lord would fight their battles and that not one soldier would be permitted to enter the valley, to the wholesale disruptive move south—indicated a reassessment of their situation. After Captain Van Vliet told him that the government would send massive forces to overpower them unless they allowed the army in, Young had to acknowledge that the Lord's protection of them was likely to be deferred and that the army would come—not only the troops that had wintered at Fort Bridger but possibly reinforcements as well. The attack on Fort Limhi raised the specter that the Indians throughout the region would not rise to defend them, and thus they were surrounded by danger. Past persecutions and a belief

[21] Church Historian's Office, *History of Brigham Young*, 223; Ririe, [Autobiography], 9:365.

[22] "Highly Important from Utah," *New York Times*, May 24, 1858, 1.

[23] Carruth, Autobiography and Journal, 31.

that the soldiers would pillage and rape if allowed among the Saints left Young with only one option: to leave, as they had so often before. Young also came to realize that such a retreat would serve him well in the eastern newspapers and result in sympathy for their plight. Perhaps too, moving would reinforce the Saints' own identity as a persecuted people. By now the population was approximately half foreign, primarily from Great Britain and Scandinavia. Few of these immigrants had suffered through the events in Ohio, Missouri, or Illinois. Now they too could experience being driven from their homes and learn what it was to be a Saint. And finally, a cynical analysis would include the possibility that President Young wanted the people farther away and thus less likely to try to escape to the army. His declaration of martial law already prevented movement, especially with guards stationed at every canyon mouth, but moving south would further dampen temptation.[24]

Although the fleeing Saints had enough food to take with them, clothing was a different matter. One woman wrote her parents in New Jersey,

> Our clothing is nearly all worn out, and it is not possible to buy any more here. . . . I think sometimes that if you could see me, you might enjoy a hearty laugh at my expense, but fortunately for me, I have now no mirror, and therefore my own appearance does not annoy me much. I still have in my possession an article for daily wear, which once bore the appellation of "a dress," but so transformed is it that it would be difficult for a casual observer to decide which was the original dress piece. My husband also wears a coat of many colors. As for buying shoes and stockings, they are quite out of the question.[25]

John Fell Squires, just twelve years old, commented, "We resembled a panorama of crazy quilts on dress parade, but we were all in the fashion of the time."[26]

The Move South, as it came to be called, brought some four hundred families to Spanish Fork, including all of Peter's family except one sister who went to Provo with her husband. The newcomers probably doubled the population. Spanish Fork resident Hannah Cornaby wrote that

---

[24] Furniss, *Mormon Conflict*, 184. That the population was half foreign comes from Burton, *City of the Saints*, 326. That Brigham Young wanted those who had not been through the earlier sufferings to be the pioneers to the White Mountain refuge suggests wanting to solidify the people's identify.

[25] "G. R." to her parents in New Jersey, May 1858, "Mormon Fanaticism," *New York Times*, June 24, 1858, 1.

[26] Squires, *Autobiography*, 13.

the move "made our little town quite lively. Several families encamped upon our lot, constructing temporary shelter for themselves." Bishop John L. Butler wrote, "They covered the bottom and made dug outs under the side of the benches. And the cattel rainged on the benches and they ate all the feed off so that our own cattle fared verry slim that fall. The folks came to me to give them places to build, and I had so much to do that I did not know hardly which to begin at first. I did not have time to eat meals I was so busy."[27]

While the Saints from Salt Lake City and north were struggling to move south, the peacemaker Thomas L. Kane returned to Salt Lake City after a month with the army, where he had tried to find a way to avert a clash. With him came Alfred Cumming, the new governor appointed by President Buchanan. He was an enormously heavy man from Georgia who had most recently been superintendent of Indian Affairs for the upper Missouri River, with his base in St. Louis. Kane and Cumming, with a Mormon escort, entered Salt Lake City on April 12. President Young and other church leaders came north from Provo to meet them the next day. On Sunday, April 25, Young, having acquiesced to the new situation, introduced Governor Cumming to those still in Salt Lake City who had gathered in the Tabernacle. "The people then showed in a very unmistabeable manerer [*sic*] that they did not want him to be their governor nor have any thing to do with him," recorded Charles L. Walker. Nevertheless Cumming promised the Saints he would do nothing against their will and offered protection to any who wanted to leave.[28]

In Utah County the Move South brought disorder and misery. On April 17 and 18, the weather turned cold and wet, and some snow fell. The raggedly clad people on the road had little shelter—just their wagon and a cover if they had one—as they struggled forward through the mud. Those who had already arrived shivered wherever they were: in tents, wickiups of cane and rushes, or dugouts. Most had to cook outside on stoves they had brought or over campfires. After the weather improved, the immigrants started farming little garden plots, for they had no idea how long they might have to stay.[29]

---

[27] Crow, "History of the Life of Stephen Markham," 7. Don Carlos Johnson (*Brief History of Springville*, 50) wrote that the Move South doubled the population of Springville. Cornaby, *Autobiography and Poems*, 49; Butler, "Autobiography," 432.

[28] Larson and Larson, *Diary of Charles Lowell Walker*, 1:30.

[29] Ibid., 1:29, entries for April 17 and 18, 1858; Hamilton, Journals, April 18; Johnson, *Brief History of Springville*, 50.

15

The Army Cometh

IN APRIL 1858, WHILE PEOPLE WERE MOVING SOUTH INTO UTAH County, the sense of fear and terror continued in Springville. John M. Stewart, Bishop Aaron Johnson's counselor and justice of the peace who had been forced to accept a dictated jury for the inquest of the Parrish-Potter murders, increasingly felt that his life was in danger. He had voiced his objections to the murders and as a result had "incurred the enmity of the more fanatical." Having been threatened, and afraid that he might be killed, he left suddenly on April 21 at night to try to get to the army's protection at Camp Scott. He did not tell his family of his intentions. Setting out up a canyon in the mountains, he became confused in the dark and stormy weather and made little progress. The next night, April 22, he was captured by Nauvoo Legion guards in Provo Canyon, and lacking the requisite pass under martial law, he was brought to Provo. President Young, back from Salt Lake City, interviewed him there, telling him he was endangering his life, for if he got to the army, they would hang him as a spy, but it was more likely that he would perish on the way from the inclement weather. Cold and shaken, Stewart was escorted back to Springville, where Aaron Johnson and a few friends met him. At Johnson's house "a long talk was held and Stewart's safety being pledged, he returned to his home."[1]

Two days later in Payson, about six miles southwest of Spanish Fork, a different kind of terror took place. A family from Salt Lake City—a

---

[1] D. C. Johnson, *Brief History of Springville, Utah*, 48, 49; Church Historian's Office, History of the Church, April 23, 1858, 28:429–30. Stewart and his family left for San Bernardino soon after the army arrived; Johnson, *Brief History of Springville*, 41.

mother, two sons by her first marriage, and a daughter by her second—arrived as part of the Move South. They were Hannah Gailey Jones Hatch; Henry Jones, in his early twenties; John Jones, Jr., about sixteen; and Ellen Hannah Hatch, five years old. Hannah had married Jacob Hatch around 1847 near Kanesville (Council Bluffs), Iowa., and they had emigrated to Salt Lake City in 1850. Five years later, after Jacob had physically threatened her, Hannah had divorced him. In late February 1858, Hannah's son Henry was attacked in Salt Lake City. Hosea Stout recorded the event in his journal: "This evening several persons disguised as Indians entered Henry Jones' house and dragged him out of bed with a whore and castrated him by a square & close amputation." Henry survived this mutilation and in early April moved south with his mother and siblings to Payson, where they built a dugout. Although Stout wrote that Henry had been caught with a whore, rumor had it that he was having an incestuous relationship with his mother.[2]

Less than a month after settling in Payson, Henry Jones and his mother were killed. According to a man who boarded in Bishop Charles Hancock's house in Payson, the bishop held council meetings in his upper room for three weeks before the murders. One of the men attending was the bishop's brother George W. Hancock. The night of the murders, April 24, 1858, the same men, now armed, gathered at the bishop's house and then left in a group, saying they were going to guard the horse corral because they had learned that Henry Jones was planning to steal horses. About nine or ten o'clock that night, the group of men, firing their guns, approached the Jones dugout. Henry and John managed to scramble up the chimney and run. The men charged into the dugout, and Hannah, pleading for the lives of her sons, was shot dead by one of them. A neighbor came and took little Ellen to her father's house, for he had also moved to Payson. In the meantime, Henry ran three miles to the fort in Pondtown (now Salem) with the men in pursuit. But he was caught, led back on the road toward Payson, and shot. In the early morning, someone carried his body back to Payson, placed it next to that

---

[2] Some family data come from Ancestry.com. F. W. Young, "A Record of the Early Settlement of Payson"; Sons of Utah Pioneers, Utah Pioneer Card Index; *Complaint of Hannah Hatch vs. Jacob Hatch*, August 14, 1855, and *Petition for Divorce, Hannah Hatch vs. Jacob Hatch*, August 15, 1855, Probate Court, Salt Lake Co.; Brooks, *On the Mormon Frontier*, 2:653.

of his dead mother, and knocked out the supports so that the whole dugout fell and buried them.[3]

Henry had indeed planned to steal a horse to escape, for he told one man, "There was a very bad feeling against them [his family] and he wanted to get away to meet the troops. He afterwards intended to come back with the troops to get his mother and sister; . . . [he] said that they had castrated him and he was afraid they would take his life." After the murders, the man who boarded at the bishop's house reported on what Bishop Hancock had said in their Sunday meeting from the stand: "As to the killing of Jones and his mother, he cared nothing about it, and it would have been done in daylight if circumstances would have permitted it." The boarder added, "150 or 200 persons [were] present. He gave no reasons for killing them." And no inquest was held.[4]

Although these murders took place a few miles from Spanish Fork, Peter did not specifically mention them or the earlier murder of Henry Forbes in his writings. His interest was in the Parrishes, for they were killed simply for losing their faith. These new murders, however, must have further confirmed for him what he later wrote in a letter: "With all their [the Mormons'] honesty, they have often been led to do wrong, even to the taking of the lives of their fellows. This I know by my experience in Utah. Two prominent instances of such you will remember of when I mearly mention the names of the places at which they occurred, *Springville* and *Mountain Meadows*."[5]

George A. Hicks, to whom Peter reported in the Nauvoo Legion,

---

[3] "Affidavit of Nathaniel Case," *Valley Tan*, April 19, 1859, 2; "Hancock Murder Case," *Deseret News*, February 14, 1891, 26; "Looks Bad for Hancock," *Salt Lake Tribune*, March 21, 1890, 7; "Affidavit of Thomas Hollingshead," *Valley Tan*, April 19, 1859, 2. Affidavits for the Jones murders are also in Cradlebaugh, *Utah and the Mormons*, 61–64.

[4] "Looks Bad for Hancock," 7; "Affidavit of Nathaniel Case," 2. A grand jury held in Nephi in August 1859 indicted George W. Hancock as the principal and seven others as accessories in the murder of Henry Jones, but the deputy attorney general reported to Attorney General Alexander Wilson, "None of these parties are in custody, and I suppose there is little likelihood of the arrest of any of them." Alexander Wilson to J. S. Black, November 15, 1859, *Message of the President of the United States*, 36th Cong., 1st sess., 31–32. Thirty-one years later, on November 4, 1889, George W. Hancock was arrested and charged with the murder. Although he was found guilty and sentenced to ten years in the penitentiary, the case was appealed. The Utah Supreme Court ruled that procedural errors necessitated a new trial. It was never held. See articles in the *Deseret News* for November 16, 1889; May 3, 1890; and February 14, 1891.

[5] Peter McAuslan to unknown person (probably his nephew Arthur Maxwell, Jr.), ca. 1886 (#61 McAuslan Papers), emphasis his.

wrote later that in this period "a spirit of secret murder stalked abroad among the people, and many of the 'undesirables' lost their lives by being murdered by unknown assassins, unknown so far as the general public were concerned." And Peter wrote, "I know from my experience in Mormonism that to give it [the church] the power it would rewrite the world's history with the blood of its inhabitants. This you may think is strong language but it is in accord with the spirit of the leaders of the Mormon Church when I was in Utah." In his letter to Robert Salmon written the year after leaving Utah, he gave a succinct summary: "The Mormons do intertain doctrins [that] when they are put in force are destructive of the rights of there fellow man."[6]

In Salt Lake City at the end of April, with Governor Alfred Cumming now nominally in charge, President Young called off sending pioneer families to White Mountain. No refuge had yet been found, and perhaps Young began to hope that with the help of Thomas L. Kane, war might be averted and the people allowed to return home. Young did not stop the exploring parties, however, or the Move South. Cumming and Kane traveled to Provo, Springville, and the Spanish Fork Indian Farm to allay the fears of the people. On the way back on May 6, they met eight hundred wagons going south, which distressed Cumming: "I regret to have been an eye-witness . . . to scenes of great trial and suffering." By May 11, Salt Lake City and the northern settlements were nearly vacated. One church estimate reported that in the previous two weeks, an average of six hundred wagons passed through the city daily. By the end of May, meetings were no longer held in the Tabernacle, and by June 7, Charles L. Walker wrote, "Every house is fastened up. And the windows boarded over and everything still and quiet. In fact the city seems quiet deserted. No women to be seen and very few men. And those on guard." Sixty miles south in Spanish Fork, however, all was not quiet, for young women and men were still racing horses around the streets at night. The bishop's counselor reproved them in a ward meeting and "commended mothers to take care of their daughters after night."[7]

[6] Hicks, "History of Spanish Fork," 14; Peter McAuslan to Arthur Maxwell, Jr., [1886] (#37 McAuslan Papers), 26; Peter McAuslan to Robert Salmon, December 1860 (#14 McAuslan Papers), 2.

[7] Brigham Young to George W. Bean, April 28, 1858, as given in Stott, *Search for Sanctuary*, 129; "Letter from Gov. Cumming to Secretary Cass, May 12, 1858," *New York Times*, June 24, 1858, 1; Church Historian's Office, *History of Brigham Young*, 232; Larson and Larson, *Diary of Charles Lowell Walker*, 1:33, 34; Record of Members, Spanish Fork Ward, May 23, 1858, 39.

Unbeknownst to Governor Cumming, President Buchanan decided in early April to send commissioners to Utah to force peace on the Mormons. The two commissioners, Lazarus W. Powell and Ben McCulloch, arrived in Salt Lake City on June 7, 1858, and on June 10, President Young and other leaders left Provo to meet them. Talks ensued, but the commissioners were not there to negotiate.[8] Buchanan's proclamation, written in April and brought by the commissioners, was presented:

> The great mass of these [Mormon] settlers, acting under the influence of leaders to whom they seem to have surrendered their judgment, refuse to be controlled by any other authority. . . . Their hostility to the lawful government of the country has at length become so violent that no officer bearing a commission from the chief magistrate of the union can enter the territory or remain there with safety. . . . Such is believed to be the condition to which a strange system of terrorism has brought the inhabitants of that region, that no one among them could express an opinion favorable to this government, or even propose to obey its laws, without exposing his life and property to peril.[9]

His words matched Peter's sentiments. But fellow Scot Henry Hamilton read Buchanan's proclamation in Spanish Fork a few days later and declared that "the most of it is lies."[10]

"Peace" was reached on June 11, 1858. The Mormons agreed to allow the army to enter their valley and they, in turn, would be granted "a free pardon for the seditions and treason heretofore by them committed." Proclamations from General Albert Sidney Johnston and Governor Alfred Cumming followed, and then the peace commissioners traveled to Provo, where Powell addressed about four thousand people in the bowery—the outdoor meeting structure covered with branches—on June 16. In this speech he announced the end of hostilities between the Mormons and the United States, praised the people for their industriousness, and mentioned their substantial contribution to the Mexican War when they had raised the Mormon Battalion, which had marched from the Missouri River to southern California. Although Powell's speech marked the turning of the tide, many no doubt still agreed with Charles L. Walker, who wrote that Commissioner Powell said that "all things

[8] Furniss, *Mormon Conflict*, 192–203.
[9] "By James Buchanan, A Proclamation," *Deseret News*, June 16, 1858, 2.
[10] Hamilton, Journals, June 22, 1858.

The U.S. Army marching past Brigham Young's houses on June 26, 1858.
From T. B. H. Stenhouse, The Rocky Mountain Saints, *388.*

were peaceably settled &c we might return to our homes and a lot more of such like gas, but he lied in his heart and he knew it."[11]

On June 26, the army—consisting of about 2,400 men plus 800 civilian army employees and a number of military wives, some with servants—marched peacefully through Salt Lake City and across the Jordan River. It took them more than eleven hours to traverse the city. Legend has it that when Colonel Philip St. George Cooke, leading his regiment of dragoons, passed Young's houses, he doffed his cap in honor of the Mormon Battalion, of which he had been the commanding officer. And when the band passed the same houses, they struck up "One-Eyed Riley," a popular bawdy song. Mormon residences were not violated, nor were their gardens destroyed by the army's stock. On June 30, President Young announced that the Saints might move back to their homes, and to set the example, he started back with his families the same day. Once at home, but afraid of assassins, Young had all the doors locked and bolted

---

[11] Roberts, *Comprehensive History of the Church,* 4:419–43; Larson and Larson, *Diary of Charles Lowell Walker,* 1:35.

and allowed access only by the east door, which was guarded by two men. The move back north took all of July, for some people did not have wagons or teams and had to wait until someone could return and help them.[12]

In the next couple of weeks, the army moved slowly south on the west side of the Jordan River so as to interfere as little as possible with the people going north on the east side. The troops eventually camped in the foothills at the head of Cedar Valley while their permanent base at the town of Fairfield was built. Not until early September did they fully move into Camp Floyd, named for John B. Floyd, secretary of war. In spite of initial warnings by the church leaders to have nothing to do with the soldiers, it was not long before commerce was thriving. The army needed hay, cordwood, lumber, shingles, and adobe bricks. The troops also wanted whatever fresh produce, butter, and cheese the Mormons would sell. On July 19, 1858, one entrepreneur established an express service to convey passengers and mail between Salt Lake City and the camp.[13]

Also on July 19, Indian agent Garland Hurt, who had come in with the army, returned to the Indian Farm at Spanish Fork. Before Hurt left Salt Lake City to return to his post, President Young—perhaps mindful of the succession of murders in Utah County—wrote to Governor Cumming to inform him that "if Dr. Hurt returned to the farm he would not be responsible for his safety, and that he did not deem it prudent at present for him to go." George A. Hicks in Spanish Fork, however, wrote, "As soon [as] the army was barely in, Hurt came back and took possession of the Indian Farm and proceeded to 'teach the Indians the arts of peace' and everything went on as though nothing had happened." President Buchanan had appointed a new superintendent of Indian Affairs, Jacob Forney, to replace Young in that role, and Hurt conducted Forney on a tour of the various Indian farms.[14] Hurt, however, wanted to plant

---

[12] The number who marched through Salt Lake City is based on the army muster roll taken four days later on June 30, 1858. The size of the Utah Expedition fluctuated wildly with units not yet arrived, others departing within days of each other, and desertions. R. B. Nielson, *Roll Call at Old Camp Floyd*, iii, 256, 269, 271; William P. MacKinnon, e-mail messages to the author, January 17 and 18, 2008; Auerbach, "Utah War," 26–28; Furniss, *Mormon Conflict*, 201–202; Church Historian's Office, *History of Brigham Young*, 242. For Young's fear of assassins, see Church Historian's Office, History of the Church, November 18, 28:1084. Young dreamed of being attacked; see Church Historian's Office, Journal, September 25, 1858, 21:200. For an example of those who had to wait for help before going north again, see Poulter, "Life," 148–49.

[13] R. B. Neilson, *Roll Call at Old Camp Floyd*, vii–viii; Church Historian's Office, *History of Brigham Young*, 243–44.

[14] In the closing days of his administration, President Franklin Pierce had signed a law splitting the roles of governor and superintendent of Indian Affairs in Utah and other territories.

some crops at the Spanish Fork farm before summer was over and so returned while Forney continued his tour. Hurt disagreed with Forney's philosophy of handing out gifts and making promises to the different tribes that Forney would find difficult to keep. He thus kept his distance and stayed at home on the farm. Besides supervising the planting of crops, he oversaw improvements, including the construction of a "Spanish" wall of baked mud and straw around the fields, a well, and two large corrals.[15]

The Mormon settlements now experienced a new kind of disruption. On August 1, Henry Hamilton went to the Spanish Fork Seventies Quorum. He wrote that it was so poorly attended that the meetings were suspended until further notice. Instead of meetings and community projects to build fences, mills, or bridges, people individually or in small groups went to Camp Floyd to work. Hamilton noted in his journal for August 15, "I find that there is a great many of the Brethern gone to make dobbies [adobe bricks] for the solders as they have a great demand for them at a $1 per hunder [hundred]. It is said that they require 1400000 dobbies." The army needed adobe bricks for the barracks and other buildings at Camp Floyd. James Ririe, a Scot then living in Springville, wrote, "As they were building and digging wells [at Camp Floyd], I got a job hauling rock for their wells at $4.50 a load. I hauled one load a day. But I found they were giving one dollar a hundred for adobes. I . . . took to making adobes. I made fifty hundred in ten days. That was fifty dollars."[16]

Spanish Fork's bishop, John L. Butler, was not pleased to see so many going to Camp Floyd, for they seemed to quickly lose their faith: "When they were here they seemed to be pretty good Saints but when they went over there they drank in the spirit that was there, and they soon went by the board." George A. Hicks, however, saw a brighter side: "A great benefit they proved to be for we were very destitute and they gave us employment and paid us well. They purchased our surplus produce and gave us gold in exchange. In fact, I do not know what the poor of the country would have done for the common necessaries of life if the army had not have come to Utah."[17]

The people who benefited most were those living in Utah County, close

[15] "Utah. Condition of Mormon Affairs," *New York Times*, August 24, 1858, 1; Hicks, "History of George Armstrong Hicks," 32; Beeton, "Teach Them to Till the Soil," 307.

[16] Hamilton, Journals, August 1, 15; Ririe, [Autobiography], 9:366.

[17] Butler, "Autobiography," 433; Hicks, "History of George Armstrong Hicks," 30.

to Camp Floyd. Nearly every man in Springville went to work at the camp, and probably the same was true for all the communities in the area. Peter, his brothers, and uncles were likely among them. With money now available and merchant wagon trains beginning to arrive from the East, people could once more buy clothing and cast off their patched rags. George W. Brimhall from Ogden decided to go to the army's camp before heading north after the Move South: "As I had not seen money for a long time, I thought I, too, would go, for our clothes were wearing out. In fact, the people were almost entirely destitute of clothing. . . . We sold squash pies to the officers, buttermilk and dried fish to the privates, doing a splendid thing for ourselves and patrons, until we had replenished our clothing."[18]

The late summer of 1858 brought a new harassment in Springville. Zephaniah Warren believed he had nearly been killed the summer before for having spoken out about the Parrish murders. Now ward teachers came to visit and asked how often he prayed. He said he did not pray, for he "did not believe in bothering God about such a little matter as blessing a meal of victuals." A few nights later a policeman came to his door and asked him to come outside. Suddenly he found himself surrounded by ward teachers who were also policemen. The men made mysterious signs, then led him out of the city through the east gate and into a melon patch. One of the men cut a large melon off the vine and sliced it open, and all of them, including Warren, seated themselves around it. The leader asked him to say the blessing. Fearing for his life, he prayed as he had never before. They then ate the melon, and afterward, in silence, the men escorted Warren back to his home. The policemen considered it an amusing joke, but the experience thoroughly shook Warren, and he left the next summer for California with his family.[19]

On September 10, Spanish Fork residents Anna Maria Markham and her nine-year-old daughter were alone in an open field near the town when three young Indian men from the farm approached on horseback. Perhaps spurred on by alcohol, two of the men attacked the mother and daughter, brutally raping them both. The outrage in the Mormon communities and the army was immediate. Governor Cumming asked General Johnston

---

[18] D. C. Johnson, *Brief History of Springville*, 50; [Brimhall], "Making a Living in 1858," 2:32–33.

[19] Affidavit of Zephaniah J. Warren, March 26, 1859, *Valley Tan*, April 19, 1859, 2; D. C. Johnson, *Brief History of Springville*, 48–49; 1860 United States Federal Census, San Salvador, San Bernardino, Calif., roll M653-64, 652.

for troops as a posse comitatus to apprehend the Indians. On October 1, Johnston sent two hundred mounted men to surround the Indian Farm. Most of the Utes had fled to the mountains upon hearing that the soldiers were on the march, but two chiefs were still present. One refused to be taken and, in fleeing, was shot and killed. The other chief and some of his men were held until the guilty Utes were brought in. The Indians were then released except for the two offenders, who were taken to Camp Floyd. Garland Hurt, fearing Indian revenge for the killing of the chief and seeing the terror of the local people, asked for soldiers to be stationed nearby. General Johnston responded by keeping a detachment at the farm and sending a hundred to Springville and another hundred to Pondtown for a few weeks.[20] The army had thus ironically become the Mormons' temporary protector, as well as supplier of work, clothing, and money.

In Salt Lake City, President Young remained secluded, and the usual Sunday meetings had not resumed since the Move South. Instead of holding the semiannual fall conference, Young and the Twelve Apostles decided on a private meeting of the church authorities. Letters were sent to all the bishops on September 26, 1858, requesting them, their counselors, and the presidents of the various quorums with their counselors to attend the special conference on October 6. When the day arrived and the men had gathered in the Tabernacle, Daniel H. Wells, counselor to President Young, remarked, "Perhaps the brethren might suppose there was going to be some awful secrets advanced, but he did not know of any. We have met to transact business, pertaining to the Church, and get instructions, and to find out how things are through the territory, so far as this notice has had a chance to spread itself." Neither President Young nor Heber C. Kimball were able to attend, said Wells, because they were ill. Wells continued: "This is the kingdom of God and He has his eye upon us, and has preserved, and is protecting us continually. We have met to discuss the interest and welfare of Zion and give each other our views . . . and see if we cannot fill ourselves with the spirit of God, that we may infuse it into the people."[21]

---

[20] A. Cumming to A. S. Johnston, September 25, 1858; A. Cumming to Garland Hurt, September 25, 1858; G. R. Paul to F. J. Porter, October 3 and 17, 1858; and A. S. Johnston to Irvin McDowell, October 12, 1858, all in *Message from the President of the United States*, 35th Cong., 2nd sess., 152–53, 158–60; Moorman and Sessions, *Camp Floyd*, 197–203.

[21] Larson and Larson, *Diary of Charles Lowell Walker*, 1:38, 41, 44, 50; Church Historian's Office, Journal, September 26, 1858, 21:201; Brigham Young, Letterpress Copybook Transcriptions, 418; Church Historian's Office, History of the Church, October 6, 1858, 28:993–95.

Wells then addressed the commerce the members had with the soldiers: "There is no sin in selling grain to the army, but the sin is in disposing of it for less than it is worth, and depriving the poor of obtaining sufficient for their wants." He was referring to the meager harvest that year, since the Move South had disrupted the planting season in the northern settlements. He added, "No censure should be passed upon the brethren for going to work and getting means, so long as they take care of themselves, live their religion and pay their tithing."[22]

Then Apostle George A. Smith spoke; he "felt that the present was the dawning of a glorious era upon the saints. Quoted Matthew 13 chapter, 41st verse, 'the son of man shall send forth his angels, and they shall gather out of his kingdom all things that offend and them which do iniquity,' and said he conceived the sieve was at work to sift out those who were not pure before God. Spoke powerfully on the necessity of cleansing from our midst all hypocrisy and iniquity." Besides concern about grain, the second purpose of the meeting was now clear: to rid themselves of the impurities in the church. Wells then mentioned that not all the presidents of Seventies had been notified of this meeting and said they would like to have as full an attendance of the authorities as possible. He ended with "It is time for the quorums to trim themselves . . . and see that Israel is cleansed." The afternoon session was adjourned until November 13, when President Young and Heber C. Kimball would have recovered from their colds and could meet with them. On October 8, Brigham Young wrote letters of invitation to the November meeting, this time mentioning that all the presidencies of the Seventies and all other quorums were included.[23]

On November 10 in the Spanish Fork Seventies Quorum meeting, President Dorrity "made some remarks on some of the brethern leaving off the faith of the Saints and exhorted the Quor. to hold fast to the word of God." The next day, Dorrity left for Salt Lake City to attend the special conference. It convened in the Tabernacle on November 13, and this time Heber C. Kimball and Daniel H. Wells were present, along with nine of the Twelve Apostles. After the opening prayer, Kimball said, "I feel quite particular about the doors being guarded. . . . There are a great

22 Church Historian's Office, History of the Church, October 6, 1858, 28:995.
23 Ibid., 28:995–1001; Church Historian's Office, Journal, September 26, 1858, 21:201; Our Correspondent, "Utah. Condition of Mormon Affairs," *New York Times*, August 24, 1858, 1; Brigham Young, Letterpress Copybook Transcriptions, 431–35.

many men in these mountains, who would assassinate Pres. Young at any moment, if they had the opportunity; and they would be perfectly willing to die, if they could accomplish the deed; therefore I want the brethren to watch the doors."[24]

Kimball continued, "Right at this time we have what some call trials. We have entered into the order of heaven, for the express purpose of becoming saviors of men." He then spoke of the Kingdom of God as being temporal as well as spiritual: "Our duties do not consist in praying and preaching only, but we have to do this and that, and in short, to do just as we are told to do. Save your wheat, your corn, barley, potatoes and everything else that is good, just as Joseph did in Egypt, and you know he became the savior of a great nation, by laying up grain." President Young arrived just before noon and spoke for the first time since the army had come through the city. His words, however, were not recorded except that he "gave much good teaching instruction & reproof."[25]

In the afternoon, Apostle Orson Hyde settled down to business: "If the brethren from the settlements or this City knew of any who had apostatized in their feelings, acts or speeches they should let it be known, that we may act upon their cases as the Spirit may direct." The rest of the afternoon was spent hearing evidence for Saints who had fallen away and severing them from the church. A counselor from the Quorum of Seventies in Salt Lake City's Sixteenth Ward was in attendance and reported, "Meny that had left for the States of [or] California & had gon to the Solders Camp & have spoken agenst the Church & its Athoreties wer Cut off from the Church." The meeting then adjourned until the next morning.[26]

The following day Heber C. Kimball "reproved the Bishops and presiding Elders for not cutting off the dead limbs from the church, but [they] have presented them at this Conference for Prest. Young to bear the responsibility of cutting them off & thereby putting his life in jeopardy." Daniel H. Wells then requested "the Bishops & Presidents to present the names of those persons who had apostatized or were worthy

[24] Record of Fiftieth Quorum of Seventies, November 10, 1858; Church Historian's Office, History of the Church, November 13, 1858, 28:1083–84.

[25] Church Historian's Office, History of the Church, November 13, 1858, 28:1083–95; Kenney, *Wilford Woodruff's Journal*, 5:237.

[26] Church Historian's Office, Journal, November 13, 1858, 21:312–13; Tripp, Journal, 4:32.

to be cut off from the Church." When the pruning commenced, "a larger number than on yesterday" were sheared off. Young then spoke and rhetorically asked if all had been removed who ought to be: "I tell you no. If all should be Cut off that ought to be[,] there would be many more than there is to day." He explained that any man who willfully broke the law of God should be excommunicated. In the early afternoon the special session was closed, with the next meeting scheduled for April 6 at the regular annual conference.[27]

Kirk Anderson, editor of the *Valley Tan*, a newly established non-Mormon newspaper, reported that he had tried to attend the meetings but had been turned away. "We understand however, that the Guillotine was busily at work," he wrote, "and many heads went off—that the act of decapitation was very brisk for a while, and that two hundred and fifty spiritual heads were knifed, and fell into the basket of the vulgar world." One those heads belonged to Peter McAuslan.[28]

---

[27] Church Historian's Office, Journal, November 14, 1858, 21:315; Kenney, *Wilford Woodruff's Journal*, 5:238–39; Thomas, *Elias Smith's Journal*, November 14, 1858.

[28] Samuel Pitchforth said the number was more than two hundred; Pitchforth, Diary, November 14, 1858. Brigham Young wrote that it was about a hundred; see, e.g., Brigham Young to J. M. Bernhisel, November 20, 1858, Brigham Young, Letterpress Copybook Transcriptions, 544–45. *Valley Tan*, November 19, 1858, 2; Record of the Fiftieth Quorum of Seventies, 4–5.

16

Cradlebaugh's Court

PETER NEVER REFERRED TO HIS EXCOMMUNICATION. IT SIMPLY confirmed what he already knew: he was no longer a Latter-day Saint. The church leaders' insistence that members do what they were told, whether right or wrong, he wrote, "was most strongly urged the last year or two that I was thare, so much so that I could not believe it, and of course I found out that I could not be consistently a Mormon."[1]

Peter was not alone, for three others in his Seventies Quorum were cut off at the same special conference: James A. Riley, thirty-two, from Tennessee; Thomas Watters, twenty-four, a coal miner from Scotland; and Amos Stiles, thirty-five, from New Brunswick, Canada.[2] The men began to discuss how they might leave Utah, for they knew it was not safe to stay with the label of "apostate." They remembered only too clearly what had happened to the Parrishes when they tried to leave for California after losing their faith. Peter decided to go to California also, as that was where Agnes's brother John McAuslin, who had traveled with them from Glasgow, was now living, having left Utah in the spring of 1855 for the gold fields.[3] Peter discussed his determination with his family. His parents, his brother William and his wife, Mary, and two younger unmarried brothers decided to go with him. His brother-in-law and old

---

[1] Peter McAuslan to Robert Salmon, December 1860 (#14 McAuslan Papers), 1.

[2] Record of Fiftieth Quorum of Seventies, 4–5.

[3] Among Peter's papers is a note dated August 1, 1860 (i.e., about eleven months after they arrived in California), seeking information about John McAuslin, who "was last heard of from Jackson, Ammattor [Amador] Co., August 1857. He was then working at the diggins." (#13 McAuslan Papers). This was no doubt a draft for a newspaper advertisement and shows that John, while still in Utah, had sent the McAuslans at least one letter.

friend John Allan, however, was not ready to give up on Mormonism, nor were his young uncles, Sandy and Dougal Adamson. In spite of all the difficulties of the past few years, this was their holy religion. Although the McAuslans' departure would split the family, Peter stayed in touch with his sister Agnes Allan for the next thirty years.

Winter was upon them, which barred any chance of leaving. Their thoughts turned toward the next spring. Agnes was pregnant again, due to be confined in April, so they would wait until after she had delivered. In the meantime, early December 1858 brought extreme cold and a violent windstorm. Henry Hamilton in Spanish Fork wrote, "There was some very severe wither in the beginning of this mounth which caused some to get badly frozen & 1 man in S.L.C. was got dead." A friend of John and Agnes Allan, William Carruth, wrote that in addition to the man frozen to death, a great many cattle died, especially those that had come across the plains that season, as they were already worn down. John Allan spent much of that winter hauling wood to Camp Floyd, crossing Utah Lake on the ice. Peter and his brothers needed money too if they were to leave Utah, and Camp Floyd was the place to make it.[4]

January 1, 1859, brought a "grand" review of the military forces at Camp Floyd, which now numbered about three thousand.[5] Although in mid-December President Young had gone on a sleigh ride with his counselor Daniel H. Wells, he mostly kept close to home. At night, besides two guards at the east gate, he had five guards sleep in his office—not far from his bedroom—"in case of surprise"; in addition a bell was installed on the gate opposite the door to his office, which would sound the alarm if someone came through it.[6] In spite of the continuing fear these arrangements represented, George A. Smith, one of the apostles, wrote in the journal of the Church Historian's Office on New Year's Day,

> The year 1858 has been a year long to be remembered upon the pages of the history of the Saints. The wrath of a great nation, lashed, as it were, into a perfect frenzy, was ready to be exerted to the uttermost to destroy the people of God, but that Allwise Being who declared, through the Prophet Joseph, that it was his business to provide for his Saints, has caused the whole to be overruled in an astonishing manner.[7]

---

[4] Hamilton, Journals, December 19, 1858; Carruth, Autobiography and Journal, 33; Allan, "John Allan," 3.

[5] Ackley, "Across the Plains in 1858," 223.

[6] Church Historian's Office, Journal, December 15, 1858, and January 1, 1859, 22:12, 55.

[7] Ibid., January 1, 1859, 22:62.

Smith concluded, "We here record our thanks and gratitude to our Heavenly Father for the great and mighty miracles by which he has preserved the Latter Day Saints from b[l]oodshed, distress and destruction, trusting in Him for a continuance of His protection. We hail 1859 as a happy new year."[8]

On Sunday, January 2, the Tabernacle was once more opened for public meetings, the first time in six months. Orson Pratt preached that day on the authenticity of the Book of Mormon. The departure in the fall of "a great many rowdies"—teamsters and others discharged from army service—and the return of Tabernacle meetings gave a renewed sense of normalcy. President Young ventured out for rides more often. Apostle John Taylor wrote of him, "He enjoys a tolerable degree of health, but looks rather pale, probably from his close confinement."[9]

In early February 1859, John Allan sold five acres of land in Spanish Fork to Henry Hamilton, for he had decided to move back to Cottonwood with his wives (Peter's sisters) Agnes and Janet. In Spanish Fork the former spirit of community and faith seemed fractured. On February 10, Henry Hamilton complained that only eight or nine attended the ward meeting, for "it seamed that the people had not time to spair for this some time past for to come to meetings." Four days later a city election was held in Spanish Fork, and Hamilton expressed surprise that some of the city officials proposed by the bishop were not unanimously sustained as in the usual Mormon practice: "The people was voting for the city officers. [T]his is the first time that ever I seen the saints voting against thease who were nominated by the authorite of the church but the Bishop gained the day."[10] He did not explain how the bishop "gained the day," but the independent-minded voters must have included those who had been cut off or were otherwise dissatisfied.

In most ways, however, the community ignored those who were no longer members. In the Spanish Fork Seventies Quorum, President Dennis Dorrity wanted to fill the vacancies: "Prest. Dorrity then spoke of the 4 that had apostatized and that he wished the Quorum to be kept full according to instructions and as there is 4 Brethern here with recommends from the Bishop & there Presidents it was moved and Secd. that they be received into the Quorum & carried."[11]

[8] Ibid.

[9] Church Historian's Office, Journal, January 2, 1859, 22:65; John Taylor to George Q. Cannon, January 12, 1859, Church Historian's Office, History of the Church, 29:118–19.

[10] Hamilton, Journals, February 3, 10, and 14, 1859.

Early March proved to be of great interest to Peter. The last of the federal judges to arrive in Utah Territory was John Cradlebaugh, an Ohio lawyer and state senator. President Buchanan had chosen him after his first choice, Emery Davis Potter, declined the appointment. Buchanan's interest in Cradlebaugh stemmed from a speech Buchanan liked that the latter had given in early 1858 on the Missouri Compromise of 1820. Although appointed as associate justice in early June 1858, Cradlebaugh did not leave for Utah until the fall. His wife and baby had died in child-birth, leaving him with the care of two young sons. It appears he waited until the end of summer, when the older one entered boarding school and arrangements were made for the care of the younger one.[12]

Judge Cradlebaugh arrived in Salt Lake City on November 4 in a manner that would exemplify his character. Along the journey west he had picked up a Mormon woman who "wished to go to Zion." On their final night, they camped on the top of Big Mountain, where the temperature dropped so low that all of Cradlebaugh's fingers were frostbitten. The next day at noon they arrived at Mountain Dell, about thirteen miles from Salt Lake City. There at the stage station Cradlebaugh told the manager, Ephraim Hanks, that he was very tired and wished to spend the night. He sent his driver and the woman with his carriage on to the city. Hanks, a notoriously tough character and one of "Brigham's boys," the next day related to the men in President Young's office that Cradle-baugh "has the appearance of being an ox driver; he was very roughly dressed." He added that Cradlebaugh "has but one eye and that is a very good one." Hanks had treated the judge's frozen hands, and the next morning Cradlebaugh had set off on foot for the city. Hanks on horse-back later caught up with him and found him hitching a ride on the back of a wagon piled with wood. Hanks told him that a carriage driven by the U.S. surveyor, David H. Burr, and his son had come out to meet him. Cradlebaugh replied, "I do not want any of those airs, I have come here to do my duty." As March 1859 was to demonstrate, carrying out his duty would not be easy.[13]

---

[11] Record of Fiftieth Quorum of Seventies, February 20, 1859.

[12] 1850 United States Federal Census, Washington, Pickaway, Ohio, roll M432–720, 217–18; Cradle-baugh gravestone, Art Inventories Catalog; Biographical Directory of the United States Con-gress; Howe, *Historical Collections of Ohio*, 3:78.

[13] Church Historian's Office, History of the Church, November 4, 1858, 28:1065–67.

During the winter months, Cradlebaugh heard of the recent murders, particularly those of the Parrishes when General Albert Sidney Johnston forwarded a letter from Mrs. Parrish asking for the perpetrators to be punished. He also took an interest in the Mountain Meadows massacre and the murders of Henry Forbes, the Aiken party, Henry Jones, and Jones's mother. By early March he had decided to hold a grand jury in Provo, the main town of the Second Judicial District, which included Utah Valley and south. Because there was no courthouse, the proceedings were to be held in a schoolhouse called the Provo Seminary, and because there was no jail, Judge Cradlebaugh asked for troops to bring prisoners from Camp Floyd, to guard them and others until called for by the court, and to "preserve the peace." One hundred and ten soldiers under the command of Captain Henry Heth arrived in Provo on March 7, 1859. Although Heth been ordered to establish quarters outside the city limits, he discovered that these limits extended for several miles beyond the town. Finally, at the suggestion of the U.S. deputy marshal, they set up camp in a corral adjacent to the seminary, to which the city marshal said he had no objection. The troops brought with them from Camp Floyd six or eight prisoners, including the two Indians, Moze and Looking Glass, accused of assaulting Anna Maria Markham and her daughter near Spanish Fork; the others were accused of crimes committed at Camp Floyd.[14]

The outcry from the Mormons was immediate, for this was exactly what they feared—the stationing of soldiers in their midst. It brought vividly to memory the specter of mob violence and all they had experienced in the Midwest, where local civil authorities often joined the persecution. On March 10, a petition to Cradlebaugh, signed by fifty-six people in Provo, began, "We the undersigned feeling ourselves aggrieved and outraged by the appearance of a military force in our peaceful city, surrounding the court and investing the halls of justice." The petition went on to say that the troops' presence was "an attack upon the fidelity of our civil officers," who, the petitioners stated, could easily secure and take care of prisoners. The petition conjectured that Judge Cradlebaugh intended to "intimidate private citizens, witnesses and jurors, and to pre-

---

[14] Furniss, *Mormon Conflict*, 215. Judges had been given the right to request troops by the original orders for the Utah Expedition: "Instructions to General W. S. Harney," in Hafen and Hafen, *Utah Expedition*, 31. John Cradlebaugh to F. J. Porter, March 5, and Henry Heth to F. J. Porter, March 10, 1859, *Report of the Secretary of War, December 1, 1859*, 140–41.

vent justice," and finally that the proceeding was "judicial terrorism" meant "to coerce a grand jury to find presentments under fear of bristling bayonets." It ended by requesting that the troops be removed. Mayor B. K. Bullock and the city council of Provo added their own statements, asserting that Judge Cradlebaugh had failed to ask the city's permission to use the seminary lot for the troops and that their presence tended "directly to intimidate those persons who have occasion to attend the District Court."[15]

To this Cradlebaugh replied that moving a company of infantry into the city was "well considered" before it was decided upon, and that it was necessary because there was no jail or other place of confinement and no provision had been made for feeding or caring for the prisoners. "So soon as I can dispense with their [the army's] most useful services, I shall do so," the judge noted. He continued, "When, where, or in what manner these soldiers have annoyed or interfered with the citizens of Provo, I challenge you to show. . . . As to your remark about intimidation, allow me to say that good American citizens have no cause to fear American troops." The city fathers wrote to Cradlebaugh again, complaining that the people saw the soldiers' presence as making the court "a military inquisition," repeated the charge of intimidation, and added an intent of "espionage." They further noted, "We have reason to fear that the time is not far distant when witnesses will be sworn at the point of the bayonet, and the law executed by the sword."[16]

Thus commenced several weeks in which the bitterness of the Mormons against the federal imposition of troops on their land nearly brought the two sides to armed conflict. The "peace" imposed on the territory in 1858 was tentative at best. The Utah War did not end with the peaceful arrival of the army or the establishment of Camp Floyd, for the final chapter was still to come.

[15] "Petition of the citizens of Provo to City Council" and "Petition of Provo City Council to Judge Cradlebaugh," *Message of the President of the United States*, 36th Cong., 1st sess., 7–9; "United States District Court, United States Troops," *Deseret News*, March 30, 1859, 1. The petition in the government document lists fifty-six signers ("True copy. A. Cumming"); the *Deseret News* article said it was signed by "over 500" citizens but did not list them, and it also recorded the petition as saying to "pervert justice" rather than "prevent."

[16] "Reply of Judge Cradlebaugh to Provo City Council," March 12, 1858, and "Rejoinder of Provo City Council to Judge Cradlebaugh," March 15, 1859, *Message of the President of the United States*, 36th Cong., 1st sess., 9–12.

More petitions of protest came to the judge. One from Spanish Fork had 57 signatures and another from Payson had 120. There were also letters to Cradlebaugh from smaller groups, defending the presence of the troops. One was signed by eight of the grand jury witnesses, who said they had "witnessed no act, nor heard any expression, either from officers or troops, that would be calculated to intimidate any one, not even the most fastidious." They went on: "Their presence is far from being disagreeable to us, as we have been frequently menaced here, as elsewhere, by citizens of this district, with threats and acts of intimidation, and for no cause that we can conceive of but that of having expressed our disapprobation of their criminal conduct." An affidavit by six other men called to testify in the Parrish-Potter murders said that "from the Mormon community we have received threats of intimidation, in case we should divulge the facts concerning said crimes . . . which threats we believe would have been carried into execution but for the timely aid afforded by the Commanding General in the stationing of troops." A third petition asking for the army to remain in Provo was signed by ten citizens, including Zehpaniah Warren, who had twice felt menaced by leading men in Springville.[17]

Petitions were sent to General Johnston as well. One from Springville residents—probably the same ten who petitioned Cradlebaugh—asserted that "a despotic ecclesiastical law has been substituted for the civil." The man who gave Johnston the letter said that "many others would have signed it but were restrained from doing so by fear, and if the names of the signers are made public they will be made special objects of persecution." Johnston replied that he could not legally interfere to relieve any oppression under which they might be suffering. To army headquarters he wrote,

> You must not suppose that there are any disturbances here, far from it, all is smooth on the surface; but I fear there is an undertow that sweeps away every principle of liberty and the basis of our own code of morals. Many poor persons, heads of families, have at various times applied to me for means of transportation to take themselves out of the territory and away

17 "Petition of the citizens of Spanish Fork City to Judge Cradlebaugh," *Message of the President of the United States*, 36th Cong., 1st sess., 12–14; "To Judge Cradlebaugh," March 14, 1859, *Report of the Secretary of War, December 1, 1859*, 144; "Second Judicial Court," *Valley Tan*, April 5, 1859, 3; Church Historian's Office, History of the Church, March 18, 1859, 29:344.

from an association which they say has become distasteful to them; of course I can do nothing of the kind.[18]

The situation worsened on March 18, when U.S. marshal Peter K. Dotson arrested men implicated in the Parrish murders, including the mayor of Provo and two citizens from Springville. Aaron Johnson, bishop of Springville, was also subpoenaed but could not be found. The protest was immediate. The marshal of Provo, fearing a riot, added two hundred men to the police force. Captain Heth, alarmed that the police with some of the local people might try to storm his camp to rescue the prisoners, sent a message by express rider to General Johnston, describing his fears. The next day, Johnston, in an effort to quell any outbreak, ordered out eight companies of infantry, one of artillery, and one of cavalry under Major Gabriel R. Paul of the Seventh Regiment, totaling nearly nine hundred soldiers. By March 22 they were encamped near the mouth of the Provo River, about four miles from the city, ready to help Captain Heth if the Mormons interfered with him. Cradlebaugh released Mayor Bullock after one day for lack of evidence, but the feeling of outrage grew as Marshal Dotson set out to arrest many of the leading men implicated in the Parrish, Aiken, Forbes, and Jones murders. On the night of March 26, some men, hiding behind buildings, threw a volley of stones that struck the soldier standing guard at the temporary jail.[19]

On March 25, 1859, several thousand citizens of the territory petitioned Governor Cumming, questioning the legality of Cradlebaugh's court and his having ordered troops under instructions of "an ancient date." It claimed that those same instructions gave the governor "the superior authority" in calling for a posse comitatus, and it requested that Cumming use his influence and authority to have all the soldiers removed. Cumming in response wrote a proclamation protesting "this present military movement" as incompatible with the letter and spirit of the instructions given him as the "chief executive magistrate of the Territory." On March 30, Judge Cradlebaugh commented in open court that rather than

[18] Albert Sidney Johnston to Col. Lorenzo Thomas, March 10, 1859, Letters Sent, HQ, Department of Utah.

[19] Henry Heth to Col. C. F. Smith, March 18; A. S. Johnston to John Cradlebaugh, March 19, 1859; F. J. Porter to Maj. G. R. Paul, March 19; Henry Heth to General Johnston, March 27, 1859, all in *Report of the Secretary of War, December 1, 1859*, 143–44, 147–49, 159; Editorial, *Valley Tan*, April 5, 1859, 2.

a proclamation, as it was titled, it was a protest, and rather than being addressed to the commanding officer of the army in Utah, it was written to the public at large. He pointed out that rather than being afraid of the military detachment stationed at the courthouse, people by the hundreds crowded in when the court was in session. And he added that as far as the troops being there without his having consulted with the governor, "the Court has yet to learn that it is subservient to, and cannot act except under Executive dictation."[20]

Beneath the uproar and fear over the troops stationed in Provo was fear of the court itself—the subject of much interest to Peter. Judge Cradlebaugh wanted to bring to justice those who had committed the crimes of the previous two years, especially in the case of the murder of the Parrishes. He was there to do his duty, but in Mormon eyes he was far too zealous. He found himself stymied from the start. "There is no place but what has a provision of law that persons found committing crimes can be arrested, brought before tribunals, committed to prison and detained until the court having jurisdiction can try them. Such provision does not seem to be made here," Cradlebaugh said in his charge to the grand jury. He added that the legislature had given criminal jurisdiction to the probate courts, which was illegal under the Organic Act by which Utah had been made a territory.[21]

Six weeks before the start of the court session, the Territorial Legislature had passed other laws intended to prevent Cradlebaugh from punishing the perpetrators of the crimes. The acts included requiring jurors to have lived in the territory for a year before being called and to be taxpaying property owners, thus keeping non-Mormons such as soldiers or teamsters from being eligible. Another act stipulated that jurors were to be selected by the all-Mormon county courts. Four days after the start of the session, Cradlebaugh discovered that one of the jurors, Wilber J. Earl, was involved in two of the cases and so excused him from the grand

---

[20] "Memorial and Petition," *Deseret News*, March 30, 1859, 2; Church Historian's Office, Journal, March 25, 1859, 22:235; "By Alfred Cumming, Governor, Utah Territory. A Proclamation," *Deseret News*, March 30, 1859, 4; "Judge Cradlebaugh's Remarks on the Governor's Proclamation," *Deseret News*, April 6, 1859, 2. To calm the situation, President Buchanan sided with Cumming and reprimanded Judges Cradlebaugh and Sinclair, saying that Governor Cumming was the supreme executive in the territory; J. S. Black to J. Cradlebaugh and Chas. E. Sinclair, May 17, 1859, *Message of the President of the United States*, 36th Cong., 1st sess., 2–4.

[21] "Charge," *Deseret News*, March 16, 1859, 1.

jury. Still no progress was made. As all the jurors were Mormon and those implicated in the murders were local church leaders, the grand jury refused to bring indictments.[22]

After two weeks, on March 21, 1859, Cradlebaugh dismissed them, saying, "There seems to be a combined effort on the part of the community to screen the murderers from the punishment due them for the murder they have committed. . . . If it is the desire of this community that persons guilty of crimes shall be screened, and that high, notorious crimes shall be covered up, it will have to be done without the aid of this court." He told the jurors that they could not use the courts simply to protect themselves from gentiles and Indians. If they refused to punish crimes committed by church members, then no one would be punished. The court, he said, "will do justice to all, or it will do nothing." And with that he ordered the release of Moze and Looking Glass and two non-Mormons, one accused of stealing a soldier's coat and the other charged with shooting a soldier in the knee.[23]

Judge Cradlebaugh then set about to act as a sitting magistrate, to take affidavits and issue bench warrants. The day after he dismissed the grand jury, he issued twenty-five subpoenas for witnesses in connection with the Parrish murders and sent U.S. marshal Dotson to serve them. The men being sought fled to the mountains. After five or six attempts to find them, Dotson wrote to General Johnston, asking for two hundred troops: "The criminals have either fled or secreted themselves. I have reason to believe that this whole community is engaged in aiding these offenders to elude the process of the court and vigilance of the officers of the law. . . . I find it impossible with the means now at my command to execute the process of the court, and I am therefore constrained to call upon you for military aid." General Johnston offered troops from Paul's command outside Provo. Governor Cumming was immediately critical: "It cannot . . . excite surprise that so many of the people have fled, preferring to be branded as criminals to being dragged to camp, and confined in a guard-house, until it shall please the judge to release them

---

[22] "An Act," *Deseret News*, January 26, 1859, 4; "An Act," *Deseret News*, February 2, 1859, 3; "District Court, 2nd Judicial District," *Deseret News*, March 16, 1859, 8.

[23] "Discharge of the Grand Jury," *Deseret News*, March 30, 1859, 2; Alexander Wilson to J. S. Black, November 15, 1859, *Message of the President of the United States*, 36th Cong., 1st sess., 27; "Court Doings at Provo," *Deseret News*, April 6, 1859, 1.

or to give them a trial." Nevertheless, on March 29, Dotson and a company of dragoons left Provo at about 1 A.M. for Springville to surprise the wanted men, but he found no one left to serve a warrant to, as all the leading men had taken refuge in the snowy mountains.[24]

Two days before Dotson's foray into Springville, President Young's counselor Daniel H. Wells and two others called on Governor Cumming to ask him to republish his proclamation of the previous June "pardoning all offenses before a certain date." Cumming's proclamation had stated that President Buchanan pardoned the Mormon people for "all treasons and seditions heretofore committed" and that "all criminal offences associated with, or growing out of, the overt acts of sedition and treason are merged in them, and are embraced in the 'free and full pardon' of the President." The pardon, however, was not republished, presumably because none of the crimes taken up by Judge Cradlebaugh's court could be construed as related to treason.[25]

On March 23, shortly after Cradlebaugh had dismissed the grand jury, Peter, his father, and his brother William came to Provo to declare their intention of becoming U.S. citizens. The military detachments under Major Paul had arrived at the mouth of the Provo River the day before, and Judge Cradlebaugh and Attorney General Alexander Wilson were hearing testimonies about the murder of Henry Jones and his mother. On that day two men became citizens and ten, including the three McAuslans, took oaths of intention before Cradlebaugh. Throughout the court session, many had come with the same purpose, mostly instructed by their bishops in another effort to have the territory qualify for statehood. A Danish resident of Sanpete Valley confidentially told Colonel Daniel Ruggles, who was guarding army horses and mules grazing in the area, that many of the men hiding in the mountains were willing and eager to fight against the United States. Ruggles summarized the resident's report: "Not long since, he had, with many others, taken the oaths of naturalization to support the Constitution and the laws of the United States, before a United States judge, and . . . the same night

---

[24] P. K. Dotson to A. S. Johnston, March 24, 1859, *Report of the Secretary of War, December 1, 1859*, 155; A. Cumming to Lewis Cass, *Message of the President of the United States*, 36th Cong., 1st sess., 22–23; "The Court and the Army," *Deseret News*, April 6, 1859, 2.

[25] Church Historian's Office, Journal, March 27, 1859, 22:240; "A. Cumming, Governor of Utah Territory," *Deseret News*, July 7, 1858, 3. The *Deseret News* ("News by the Eastern Mail," June 8, 1859, 4), confirmed that the president's amnesty extended only to political offenses.

they [the Mormon leaders] had counted the Mormons to see whether there were enough to make a State, as then, whence once admitted as such, they were assured that they would be entirely independent of the United States." The McAuslans had no interest in helping Utah become a state, but because they planned to settle in California, they took the opportunity to begin the naturalization process.[26]

On April 1, Judge Cradlebaugh summed up the case of the Parrish murders:

> Until I commenced the examination of the testimony in this case, I always supposed, that I lived in a land of civil and religious liberty, in which we were secured by the Constitution of our country, the right to remove at pleasure, from one portion of our domain to another, and also that we enjoyed the privilege of "worshipping God according to dictates of our own conscience." But I regret to say, that the evidence in this case, clearly proves, that so far as Utah is concerned, I have been mistaken in such supposition.[27]

Peter, now determined to leave Utah, was only too aware of the truth of the judge's statement.

Cradlebaugh adjourned his court on April 4, 1859. Captain Heth, afraid that Mormons might try to liberate the four prisoners, all of whom were connected with the Parrish murders, requested reinforcements. Major Paul responded, quickly moving his troops into town to join those of Heth. Thus, Judge Cradlebaugh, Marshal Dotson, who was in charge of the prisoners, and more than nine hundred soldiers marched the thirty-six miles back to Camp Floyd.[28]

Three weeks later in Spanish Fork, on April 24, Agnes gave birth to the couple's second daughter, whom they named Bethia after Peter's mother. Although delighted, Peter and Agnes were aware that traveling with a newborn would add to their difficulties. Spring was late, but it would not be long before the travel season and their chance to escape Utah would be upon them. They must start planning in earnest.

---

[26] Minute Book and Naturalization Record "C," 158; Todd, Autobiography, 7; Daniel Ruggles to F. J. Porter, June 2, 1859, *Report of the Secretary of War, December 1, 1859,* 187.

[27] "Incident in Court at Provo," *Valley Tan,* April 12, 1859, 2.

[28] Auerbach, "Utah War," April 4, 1859, 64–66.

17

Shaking the Dust from Their Feet

WHILE THE COMMOTIONS IN THE COURT AND IN THE TOWNS OF Utah County were taking place, Salt Lake City was rife with rumors that the army was headed in their direction. On March 22 Daniel H. Wells, commander of the Nauvoo Legion, ordered men "to have their arms and ammunition in readiness." On March 27 Wells told Governor Cumming that army officers and others had made threats that they intended to storm Salt Lake City and assassinate Brigham Young.[1]

On April 1 President Young told the men in the Church Historian's Office that he thought the present trouble with Cradlebaugh and the army would "fizzle out," but that they ought to search again for "some good hiding places," lay up grain there, "and prepare for another war." The Utah correspondent to the *New York Herald* wrote that on April 18 an express rider from Camp Floyd brought word that two regiments were coming to Salt Lake City to make arrests. He also reported that the Nauvoo Legion had five thousand men ready and armed. On April 26 Charles L. Walker said that he heard army troops were to come to Salt Lake City by May 1.[2]

Two days later, on April 28, President Young wrote that "affairs are very quiet at present." But in Spanish Fork they were not: men were being called up for a new duty. Peter no longer attended meetings and thus did not know what instructions were handed out, but now, labeled an "apostate,"

---

[1] Larson and Larson, *Diary of Charles Lowell Walker*, 1:63; Church Historian's Office, Journal, March 27, 1859, 22:240.

[2] Church Historian's Office, History of the Church, April 1, 1859, 29:302; "Our Salt Lake City Correspondence," *New York Herald*, May 25, 1859, reprinted in the *Millennial Star* 21 (June 25, 1859): 408; Larson and Larson, *Diary of Charles Lowell Walker*, 1:68.

he more than ever was alert to what was happening. On the morning of April 30, 1859, Peter's brother William, who may have been employed on the Spanish Fork Indian Farm, sought out U.S. Indian agent Garland Hurt in one of the fields. William reported that during the two previous nights, armed men had secretly left the town—at least fifty on the second night—heading, he thought, to Salt Lake City. Hurt conveyed this information in a letter to F. J. Porter, the assistant adjutant to General Johnston, adding that William felt "confident that there is secret mischief brewing" and "the pretext is that General Johnston designs capturing Salt Lake City." Hurt, thinking the movements might be to prevent another military posse from attending Judge Charles E. Sinclair's upcoming court session in the city, asked William to give him a list of those who had left. Hurt added, "He desires his name to be kept secret."[3]

The next night, Peter and Thomas Watters, who had also been excommunicated the previous November, went to the farmhouse where Hurt lived. They waited in the shadows until Hurt stepped out of the house at about nine o'clock, then told him they wanted to speak to him privately. After walking about a hundred yards away, Peter and Thomas told Hurt that more men had left the previous night, making it the third night in a row for such activity. Hurt reported, "They insist that there must be some secret military service on foot, but they seem to be afraid to inquire into the matter. They say there is no security for them if they are known to oppose the Mormons except in the immediate vicinity of the army." Hurt said he could not take notice of the rumors unless they supplied him with names, which they promised to do. Peter told Hurt that one of the men had borrowed bullets from him and had shared a bed with William the previous night, and that "on the report of a pistol just before midnight [he] rose, took his gun and blankets and left."[4]

Hurt added in his letter that the McAuslans and Thomas Watters had returned the following evening, May 1, with names, but that they were "only able to give the names of some of their neighbours." The group, they said, was headed by A. K. Thurber. They listed thirteen men, several of them Scots, including James Laird, one of the parties to the Seventies Quorum trial that had marked the end of Peter's faith in Mormonism. Hurt went on, "They say that an expedition has been made out

---

[3] Brigham Young to A. Calkin, April 28, 1859, *Millennial Star* 21 (July 2, 1859): 431; Garland Hurt to
    F. J. Porter, May 1, 1859, Letters Sent, Letters Received, Army Headquarters, Utah Territory.
[4] Ibid.

and started for 4 nights in succession and they know of some men who have been ordered out who refused to go. I think myself that there must be some movement on foot, and towards Salt Lake." Seven of the men they mentioned reported to A. K. Thurber in the Nauvoo Legion, suggesting an official militia movement.[5]

Garland Hurt wrote two other letters about the McAuslans' reports, one to General Johnston directly and another again to F. J. Porter on May 2. These contained essentially the same information as the first letter but included one more name and also mentioned, "They say that a party has been dispatched for four nights in succession, and have learned that a fifth one will be fitted out to night. They think that more than 100 men have already equiped [sic] themselves and left." The letter of May 2 added, "Peter McCoslin comes this morning and informs me that he has learned that they are rendezvousing in the hills east or south east of Mogo's Brewery. He insists that there is no doubt about the matter." Mogo's Brewery, also called Hot Springs Brewery, was a rest stop serving food and beer halfway between Camp Floyd and Salt Lake City at Point of the Mountain. Hurt continued, "They . . . say that most of the church authorities have assembled there, and that they have sentinels placed on the surrounding heights to watch the movements of the gentiles—and especially the Army."[6]

One of the men the McAuslans listed was Lewis Barney. In his autobiography, Barney described these secret maneuvers:

> It was not long after they located them selves at Campfloid before the goverment judges comenced their vexatious prosecutions against . . . President Young in particular. Making arangements for his arrest by Sending a force to take him and drag him into prison and to death. We had witnessed the slaughter and robery of our people for nearly 30 years and we did not intend to Stand Still and let him [them] cut our throats and Shoot down our best men with out resistance. Consequently there was many Companies Secreted in the mountains ready to make a dash into Salt Lake City with a sufficient force to repel the force sent by them for the Capture of president Young and at the same time rush into Campfloid and Capture it and take possession of there Stores. I was caled on as one of these minute men and left my home in the night with Bishop Bulten [Butler] and hid ourselves in a canion waiting the arival of an express with orders to march.[7]

---

[5] Ibid.; Utah County Military District, 1850–1866, Utah Territorial Militia Muster Rolls, roll for April 20, 1857, 11.

[6] Garland Hurt to A. S. Johnston, May 1; and Garland Hurt to F. J. Porter, May 2, 1859, Letters Sent, Letters Received, Army Headquarters, Utah Territory.

[7] Barney, Autobiography, 81.

The secret maneuvers of the men from Spanish Fork were only part of an elaborate network of armed Mormon "minutemen" stationed from Utah County up through the settlements north of Salt Lake City, "ready to make a dash" into the city if the troops started moving in that direction. At the northeast end of the Oquirrh Mountains, directly south of the Great Salt Lake, men were stationed on a high peak. They planned to light a large pile of wood as a signal as soon as they saw the army, for the signal would be visible—smoke by day, fire by night—to people in Salt Lake City and a long way north. Above City Creek in the northern part of the city, two mail contractors herding their mules came upon a cannon hidden behind a screen of scrub oaks. When Marshal Dotson heard of this, he informed Governor Cumming, who asked Dotson to go and check on it. Dotson found the place where the cannon had been hidden, but only the tracks of its carriage remained.[8]

Governor Cumming learned of more armed parties, this time at the south end of Utah Lake. He wrote to U.S. secretary of state Lewis Cass that he believed the men stationed around in the mountains were the "consequence of a feverish anxiety" created by a report that Judge Sinclair was coming to Salt Lake City with a large number of troops, and that the men were sentinels ready to alert the "minutemen" to rally to the defense of Brigham Young.[9]

Fearing an armed conflict, Cumming issued an order on May 9, 1859, to disperse: "I now hereby order and command that all persons so associated, and assembled together shall immediately disperse and return to their homes and usual avocations; and that all and every of such persons who shall refuse immediately to obey this command and injunction are hereby declared disturbers of the public peace of this Territory and, as such . . . shall be arrested and dealt with according to law." He commissioned John Kay, the territorial marshal and a Mormon, to enforce this executive order and had it published in both the *Deseret News* and the *Valley Tan*. Kay reported back on May 16 that he had found no one in the mountains except men cutting timber or searching for cattle preparatory to the spring drive to higher pastures. Whatever the reason, the

---

[8] David H. Burr to Charles E. Sinclair, May 5, 1859, Letters Sent, Letters Received, Army Headquarters, Utah Territory.

[9] A. Cumming to Lewis Cass, May 12, 1859, Utah Territory, *Message of the President of the United States*, 25.

minutemen in the mountains did disperse, and the army did not march on Salt Lake City.[10]

Spring was upon them, and Peter and his family and the other excommunicated men made plans to leave. Fearing for their safety, they wrote to Governor Cumming to request an army escort out of Utah. On May 9, 1859, Cumming, responding to them and probably others, addressed a letter to General Johnston, "Sir: The public interest requires that a military force should be furnished for the protection of persons and property on the northern route to California. . . . Many persons who contemplate leaving this Territory would probably prefer accompanying the command. You will therefore oblige me by giving me an early notice of the probable time of the departure of the troops, that I may notify the parties."[11]

Johnston replied on May 11 that he would "place a force on the northern route to California for the protection of travelers." Protecting emigrants from Indians on the route to California was a regular duty of the army. There had been several incidents with different tribes in the previous few years, and more were expected in the summer of 1859. Johnston's letter continued, however, expanding the army's role and giving a new type of protection: to safeguard refugees from Mormonism and help them leave Utah without interference. "If persons desirous of emigrating from this Territory could assemble at a given time and place, with their families, trains, stock, &c.," Johnston wrote, "complete protection by a special escort could be given them; and should I be notified by any considerable number of such intentions, I will furnish the force for their protection."[12]

On May 17 the *Valley Tan* advertised a meeting at the aptly named "California House" in Salt Lake City to be held on May 21 for those wishing to emigrate with the army escort, so that they could discuss a starting date and a place to gather. The California House was a hotel belonging to William H. Rogers, an old Californian and a frontier scout in western Utah Territory known familiarly as "Uncle Billy." More

---

[10] "By the Governor," *Deseret News*, May 11, 1859, 8; "Affairs in this Territory," *Valley Tan*, May 10, 1859, 2; "Report of Marshal Kay," *Deseret News*, May 18, 1859, 1.

[11] A. Cumming to A. S. Johnston, May 9, 1859, *Report of the Secretary of War, December 1, 1859*, 175.

[12] A. S. Johnston to A. Cumming, May 11, 1859, *Report of the Secretary of War, December 1, 1859*, 176. For problems with Indians in 1858, see Jacob Forney to E. E. Mix, September 6, 1858, "Utah Superintendency," *Report of the Secretary of the Interior, December 2, 1858*, 565. For troubles expected in 1859, see F. Dodge to Jacob Forney, January 4, 1859, "Utah Superintendency," *Report of the Secretary of the Interior, December 1, 1859*, 744.

recently he had been made a deputy U.S. marshal during Cradlebaugh's court.[13]

On May 18, Cumming asked the *Deseret News* to print the last part of Johnston's letter to advertise the military escort. The paper complied and then ran it again in the advertising section for the next two weeks. The second week, however, Albert Carrington, the editor, questioned the need for an escort: "That there is, or will be any danger of persons being molested on leaving the Territory we do not for a moment believe."[14]

On May 24, Governor Cumming again wrote General Johnston to forward a note from D. W. Bayliss, a non-Mormon watchmaker and "chairman of an emigration meeting," and James E. D. Jester, "meeting secretary." Bayliss's letter specified the emigrants' plans for awaiting the military escort: "We will use every endeavor to assemble our families and gather our stock and effects at or near the crossing of Bear river, on the north route, on or before the 1st day of June." He ended the letter by estimating that "we will number about forty families, with considerable loose stock." Johnston replied to Cumming that he had ordered a detachment of troops to leave Camp Floyd on June 12 "to accompany the emigrants and afford to them the needful protection." They could not leave any earlier, he noted, because the rivers were too high. The previous winter had brought unusually heavy snow in the mountains, and a late spring resulted in high runoff as the snow melted.[15]

The McAuslans and others left Spanish Fork for Camp Floyd in mid- to late May. It was the first leg of their trip out of Utah. One can only imagine the sad partings with family members who were not leaving: Agnes and Janet, married to John Allan; Jane, recently married to George B. Ogilvie; Ann, married to Dougal Adamson, her uncle; and Christina, married to Joseph Romney. In addition, they were leaving Peter's uncles, Sandy and Dougal Adamson; and Elizabeth McAuslin Maxwell, the sister of Peter's wife, Agnes. The McAuslans' desire to cut their ties with Utah and Mormonism prevailed over family attachments. Perhaps they harbored hopes that one day the others would follow. After all, they had

---

[13] "Attention, Emigrants!" *Valley Tan*, May 17, 1859, 2; "California House," *Valley Tan*, December 10, 1858, 2; Rogers, "Statement," 271.

[14] "Now's the Time for Emigrants," *Deseret News*, May 18, 1859, 1; "The Military Escort," *Deseret News*, May 25, 1859, 1. For a detailed account of the escort, see Aird, "Escape from Zion."

[15] A. Cumming to A. S. Johnston, May 24; D. W. Bayliss to A. Cumming, May 21; and A. S. Johnston to A. Cumming, May 27, 1859, *Report of the Secretary of War, December 1, 1859*, 182–83.

come to Utah in waves, and maybe they would leave the same way. But there could be no dreams about one thing: they could not hope to once more visit the grave of their little boy, Peter Alexander, or that of Peter's grandmother, both in the Salt Lake Cemetery.[16]

Those who traveled together out of Spanish Fork numbered at least seven families, consisting of twenty-nine people. They thus made a large enough group to ward off any problems with the Mormons, there being safety in numbers. After a two- or three-day journey, they reached Camp Floyd and set up their own camp nearby. Brigham Young's office noted on May 28 that a Mormon looking for his horse had "found many camps in the low hills in Rush Valley, supposed to be emigrants fitting out for the States or California."[17]

Besides Peter and Agnes with their little girl and new baby, the McAuslans consisted of Peter's parents and their two youngest sons, Frank, almost twenty-three, and David, sixteen; and Peter's brother William, his pregnant wife, Mary, and their two young daughters. Their travel companions included Thomas Watters, who had gone with Peter to see Garland Hurt, with his pregnant wife; and three others, all former members of the Spanish Fork Seventies Quorum: Edmund Ellis, his wife, and two young children; Joseph Howell, his wife, and four children; and Morris Jenkins, his wife, and three children. All in this group were originally from Great Britain.[18]

Other families from Spanish Fork may have joined those going with the army escort. And some are known to have left Utah by the southern

---

[16] Their hopes that others would follow were not entirely in vain. In the mid-1860s, Janet left her husband, John Allan, and two young sons to be raised by her sister Agnes. In 1867 she came by stagecoach to California to rejoin the family. Jane and George B. Ogilvie left the church in 1859 but did not leave Utah until 1869. Intending to join the McAuslans, they found the area around Elko, Nevada, lush after an unusually wet spring and so settled there to ranch. Peter's other sisters, Agnes Allan, Ann Adamson, and Christina Romney, remained faithful Mormons.

[17] Church Historian's Office, History of the Church, May 28, 1859, 29:458.

[18] Mary Muir McAuslan, the wife of Peter's brother William, was leaving her parents, two brothers, and a sister. Edmund Ellis and Morris Jenkins settled near Placerville: 1860 United States Census, Cosumnes, El Dorado, Calif., roll M653-58, 1175 and 1167. Thomas Watters, 1860 United States Census, Sacramento Ward 4, Sacramento, Calif., roll M653-63, 559; and Joseph Howell, 1860 United States Census, Township 3, Amador, Calif., roll M653-55, 405. The two others who had been cut off in November 1858 with Peter—James A. Riley and Amos Stiles—took the southern route to California with another excommunicated seventy, John J. Sassnette. The three settled in San Bernardino: 1860 United States Census, San Bernardino, San Bernardino, Calif., roll M653-64, 615, 619, and 628.

route to California, and still others to have gone east to the "States." It was a time of upheaval in Spanish Fork, with Thomas Todd, a fellow Scot and resident of Spanish Fork who had sailed with Peter and Agnes on the *John M. Wood,* commenting in his autobiography, "About this time, a good many fell away from the Church and went their own way."[19] The 1860 census shows a third of the houses empty. The occupied ones averaged three and a half persons per house. Applying the same average to the unoccupied ones, one can estimate that more than three hundred individuals had gone. How many actually left the territory is unknown. Many of those who remained in Utah, like Peter's brother-in-law John Allan and his uncles, Dougal and Sandy Adamson, moved their families back to where they had lived before the Move South. Lewis Barney, one of the "minutemen" in the secret maneuvers, moved to Springville, where houses cost little. On April 20, Brigham Young's office journal recorded a visit from George W. Bean, the leader of the 1858 White Mountain expedition. He told Young, "There are many persons in Utah County who are uneasy, some had openly apostatized; others who wished to move to other parts of the Territory; town property can be bought cheap, especially at Springville."[20]

On June 19, after the McAuslans and others had left, the Spanish Fork Ward meeting noted that one man spoke of "the apostacy now going on among the people," and on July 24, John W. Berry, the new bishop of Spanish Fork, called out the "names of those that had left the Country, and had been disfellowshipped by their Quorums." Among them was Peter's brother Frank, who had left with his parents.[21]

Some wishing to go with the army escort came from other towns in Utah County or farther south. Benjamin L. Clapp from Fort Ephraim in Sanpete County was probably one of them. An early convert from Alabama, a member of the First Council of the Seventy, and a polygamist, he had come to Utah in 1850. An outspoken man, he had run into

---

[19] Todd, Autobiography, 7.

[20] Barney, *One Side by Himself,* 179–80; Church Historian's Office, Journal, April 20, 1859, 22:291. Ronald O. Barney (*One Side by Himself,* 179) gives another reason for leaving: the soil in the bottomlands had become saturated with mineral deposits, making it unsuitable for crops. What proportion of the population lived in those low areas is unknown, but in general the land around Spanish Fork was unusually fertile. See Hurt, "Appendix N," 453.

[21] George B. Ogilvie, the husband of Peter's sister Jane, was also named as being cut off. Genealogical and Minute Book, Spanish Fork Ward, June 19 and July 24, 1859.

trouble with church authorities before. Warren Snow, bishop of nearby Manti, and others reported to President Young's office that Clapp had allowed two hundred soldiers and camp followers to be stationed in Fort Ephraim: "Clap said they had as good a right to admit them into the fort as Brigham, to admit them into the Territory." The men also complained that Clapp was encouraging members to sell hay and grain too cheaply—a topic emphasized in the special conference the previous November when Peter was excommunicated. After calling Bishop Snow an "oppressor" and saying that the price at which they were selling was fair, Clapp "then left the council in a rage and went to the soldiers and asked for protection." He traveled to California with his second wife and her five children.[22]

General Johnston had ordered two companies for the escort of the McAuslans and other families, one infantry and one dragoon, making a total of 162 military men, with rations for eighty days. On June 5, in a letter of instruction to Major Isaac Lynde, who was to lead the escort, he wrote, "A considerable number of defenseless families, (principally women and children,) wishing to leave this Territory for California, have asked that the strong arm of the government may be specially extended over them." He continued: "Some of the families have come to this camp, where they will stay till you march, to obtain, they say, in the vicinity of the army, security against marauders and persecutors, which the laws of the Territory and the sentiment of the community will not give. Many families will join you near Salt Lake City, some will fall in with your column as you pass their respective homes, and others will await your arrival on Bear river." Johnston's final instructions to Lynde said to go no farther than Humboldt Sink, near present-day Reno, unless he was convinced that the emigrants needed further protection.[23]

---

[22] Bishop Snow and the others also reported Clapp's actions at a meeting of the Seventies Council in Salt Lake City; the council quickly voted to cut him off. At the annual Conference of the Church on April 7, 1859, Clapp was officially excommunicated. Jenson, *Latter-day Saint Biographical Encyclopedia*, 1:195–96; Church Historian's Office, History of the Church, December 25, 1858, 28:1199–1202; "Minutes of the Annual Conference," *Deseret News*, April 13, 1859, 1; 1860 United States Census, Elkhorn, San Joaquin, Calif., roll M653-64, 980. Bishop Snow of Manti was another local church leader who had taken it upon himself to cleanse the town of impurities. In the spring of 1857 he had ordered a young man—not Henry Jones—castrated for alleged sexual improprieties; Bigler, *Forgotten Kingdom*, 132.

[23] A. S. Johnston to C. F. Smith, May 27; A. S. Johnston to I. Lynde, June 5, 1859, *Report of the Secretary of War, December 1, 1859*, 184, 189–90.

Camp Floyd, established less than a year before in Cedar Valley west of Utah Lake, was a substantial town with three to four hundred small adobe buildings lining wide streets, and a large parade ground. In the late spring of 1859, about twenty-eight hundred military men were stationed there, with almost as many civilians working for the army in some capacity, many of whom lived in adjacent "Frogtown" or "Dobietown" (Fairfield). Together they formed a community of more than five thousand people, making it the second-largest city in Utah.[24]

By June 10 an army captain reported that "a considerable number of Mormons are collected near camp to go to California with Major Lynde." On Sunday, June 12, the convoy with the McAuslans started. Another army captain wrote that it was an unpleasant day: "Existence is almost unendurable with the dust and stifling. There is no nook or cranny but the dust will reach it." Lynde, in his final report on the trip, wrote, "Eight wagons with ox teams left the vicinity of this camp under my protection, which caused my progress to be slow at first. These emigrants avowed themselves to be seceders from the Mormon faith, and stated that they had reason to fear molestation from the Mormons, and for that reason they sought the protection of the troops."[25]

Moving north, the company stayed on the west side of the Jordan River, away from the main route of Mormon travel between Provo and Salt Lake City. Two days later they crossed the Jordan to enter Salt Lake City from the west. The *Deseret News* reported that "eight or nine" wagons of emigrants were with the escort as the group came through the city. The next September Brigham Young wrote to Thomas L. Kane that "when they [Major Lynde's troops] came to muster, the detachment had only 9 wagons to escort on a track wherein at the time there was no known danger." Danger or not—and certainly the perception of danger was real to the emigrants—a number of others joined the caravan as they traveled north. Assuming the emigrants followed the pattern established when they came to Utah, two or more families, or eight to ten people, shared a wagon.[26]

[24] Alexander and Arrington, "Camp in the Sagebrush" 6; "From Camp Floyd," *San Francisco Herald*, May 1, 1859, 3.

[25] Phelps, Diaries, June 10, 1859; Auerbach, "Utah War," June 12, 1859, 68; I. Lynde to F. J. Porter, October 24, 1859, *Report of the Secretary of War, December 1, 1859*, 240.

[26] "Return of Troops," *Deseret News*, June 15, 1859, 4; "Troops for the Humboldt," *Deseret News*, June 22, 1859, 4. Brigham Young to Thomas L. Kane, September 17, 1859, Brigham Young, Letterpress Copybook Transcriptions, 5:251 (my thanks to William P. MacKinnon for alerting me to this letter); Taylor, "Mormon Crossing," 326n23.

Camp Floyd.
Drawing by Captain Albert Tracy.
Used by permission, Utah State Historical Society, all rights reserved.

On the night of June 14, Major Lynde's command and the emigrants camped on the bench east of the penitentiary near Sugar House, not far from Salt Lake City. The *Deseret News* reported that about twenty soldiers came into the city and became "disorderly." The next day, according to a statement sworn to by Jacob Hamblin, a well-known Mormon visiting from southern Utah, Lynde went to the office of Jacob Forney, the superintendent of Indian Affairs, and there said that "he believed that Brigham Young had ordered every one of the murders which had been committed in the . . . Territory and God damn him." Nevertheless, the *Deseret News* noted that when the escort left the city and traveled through the northern Mormon settlements, they were "very careful not to encamp in the wheat fields, nor trespass in any way upon the citizens."[27]

That Peter and his parents and brothers were among those escorted

27 "Troops for the Humboldt," 4; Church Historian's Office, History of the Church, June 16, 1859, 29:512–13. Both sources refer to Major Lynde as Major Lyon or Lyons.

is known from records in California.[28] Although no list of families who left has been discovered, the names of some can be surmised, such as those who are known to have been excommunicated or who left some record of wishing to leave, and who also appear in northern California in the U.S. census taken less than a year later, in June 1860. At least two joined the escort in Salt Lake City: D. W. Bayliss, the non-Mormon who addressed the letter to Governor Cumming from the "emigration committee," was certainly one, along with his wife and two children, but James E. D. Jester, the secretary for the committee, stayed and took over Bayliss's watchmaking business in Salt Lake City. Joseph V. Vernon, his wife, and young daughter probably also went with the escort. Judge Delana R. Eckels, chief justice for Utah Territory, had written to Secretary of State Lewis Cass on January 1, 1859, while on a trip east. He enclosed a letter from Vernon, whom Eckels described as a former "high Priest in the Mormon Church," noting that "he heads the party of inhabitants called by the Mormons 'Apostates' and is also a leading monogamist." Vernon, writing "for Self and friends" the previous September, listed the problems in Utah, particularly the continuing all-encompassing power of Brigham Young and the fear experienced by dissenters. Vernon ended the letter by stating, "If you do not return early in spring we intend to leave the Territory, our lives are in jeopardy every hour while we remain here." The names of his friends are unknown, but most likely some of them joined the escort as well.[29]

From Salt Lake City the expedition moved north past the hot springs just outside the city and then kept to the "upper road" at the base of the mountains, as the lower one was still too wet. When the expedition passed west of Ogden—the largest city north of Salt Lake City—they found the bridge over the Weber River "out of repair" and the road "miry." On May 25 the Salt Lake correspondent for the *San Francisco Herald* reported, "Already a large company is gathering on Bear river, where they have

---

[28] J. M. Guinn, *History of the State of California*, 660; "Sutter Pioneer Goes to His Reward," *Daily Appeal*, December 22, 1908, 5; "Death of Peter McAuslan," *Sutter County Farmer*, December 25, 1908, 7; "Laid to Rest," *Hayward Journal*, 3.

[29] "Jas. E. D. Jester, Watch-maker & Jeweler," *Valley Tan*, June 29, 1859, 4; D. R. Eckels to Lewis Cass, January 18, 1859; and J. V. Vernon to Judge Eckels, September 25, 1858, Department of State, Territorial Papers, Utah Series, 316–21. Bayliss settled in Sacramento near Thomas Watters, and Vernon in San Francisco: 1860 United States Census, Sacramento Ward 4, Sacramento, Calif., roll M653-63, 569; and San Francisco District 10, San Francisco, Calif., roll M653-67, 296.

appointed a rendezvous to await the escort promised them, and they expect to take a final leave of the 'kingdom' about the first of next month." But it was not until June 18 that the escort reached Brigham City, the northernmost Mormon settlement, and the Bear River. How many emigrants had now joined the escort is unknown. The only estimate comes from D. W. Bayliss at the time of the May meeting in Salt Lake City. He wrote then that about forty families would go. If one assumes four to a family, then approximately 160 individuals were in the departing group, or about the same number as the soldiers who accompanied them.[30]

Bear River was six feet higher than ever seen before—too high to ford—so Lynde had to use the ferry to get the company across. It took a day and a half to get all the people, wagons, and animals over. On one trip, the ferry broke and four mules drowned. From there the route went a hundred miles northwest to the City of Rocks, a landmark (now in southern Idaho) of jumbled, eroded granite where many left their names. Here the Salt Lake road met the California Trail. About twelve miles farther along, the expedition began the climb over the Goose Creek Mountains.[31]

On the other side near today's Nevada border, Thomas Poulter, who had sailed on the *John M. Wood* and steamed up the Mississippi River with Peter and Agnes, was camping in a hilly area. He, his wife, the twins born on the ship and now five years old, and a younger child were also leaving the Mormons. Working for the firm Carlisle and Davis, Poulter was in charge of the provision wagon for a company driving cattle to California. That evening a band of Bannock Indians came into their camp to see what they had. Suddenly a bugle sounded. "The Indians flew off like a clap of thunder," wrote Poulter. It was then that the cattle drivers discovered that the army escort was also camped in the vicinity. "We found that they were sent to protect our train as far as 300 miles," Poulter noted. That night fifteen of their herd boys left to work for the troops. He does not mention whether the two families met again, for Peter and Agnes were with the army camping nearby.[32]

[30] Major Lynde's Itinerary, *Report of the Secretary of War, December 1, 1859*, 245–55; "Our Salt Lake Correspondence, May 25, 1859," *San Francisco Herald*, June 8, 1859, 3.

[31] Lynde to Porter, October 24, 1859, 240–41; *Valley Tan*, June 29, 1859, 2. For a more detailed account of the itinerary and events, see Aird, "Escape from Zion."

[32] Poulter, "Life," 44:150–51. The Goose Creek Mountains were in the territory of the Northwestern Shoshones. The Bannocks lived around Fort Hall in today's eastern Idaho. The emigrant trails, however, attracted various tribes as profitable places to beg for food or to steal from the emigrants. Madsen, *Shoshoni Frontier*, 110.

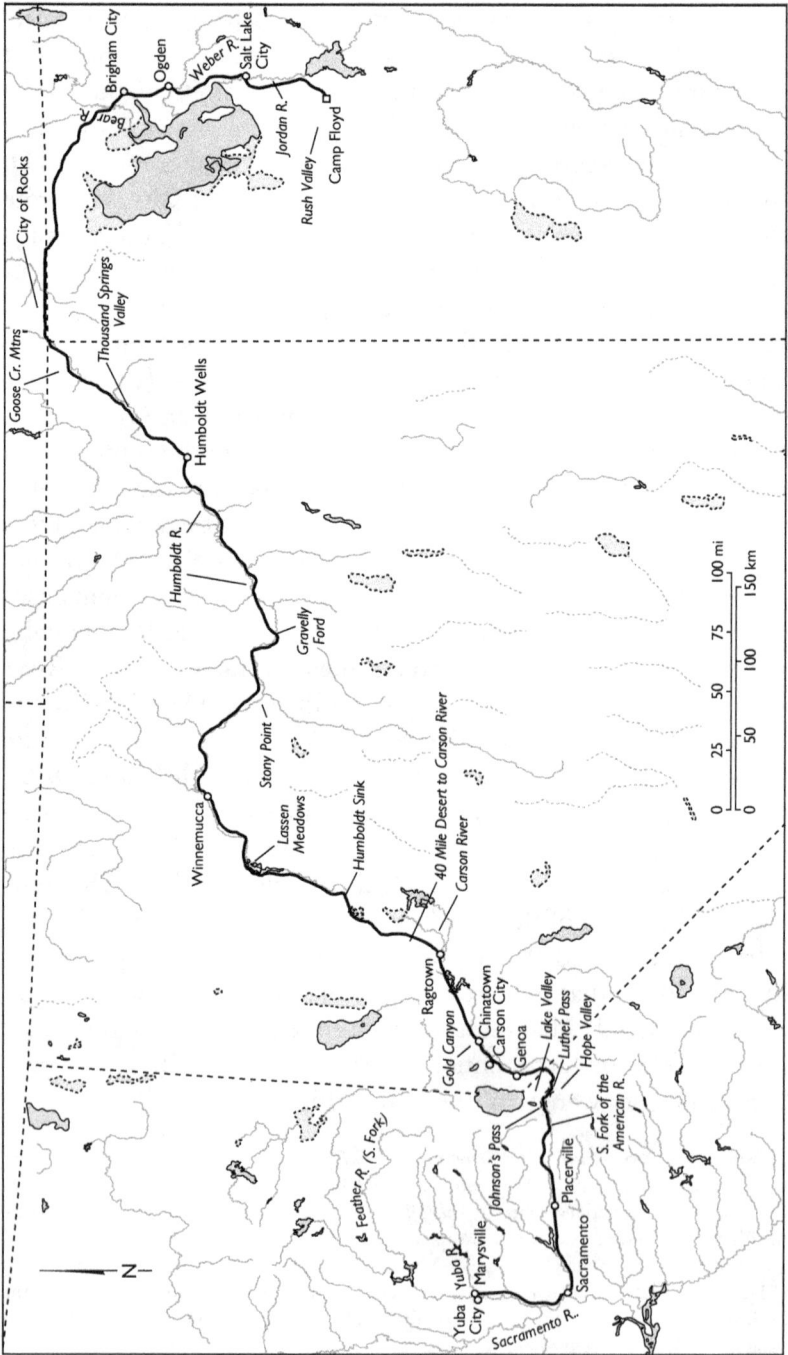

The McAuslans' route from Camp Floyd to Marysville, California.
Map by Bill Nelson.

In the same general area, Hozial Baker, a seventy-year-old emigrant from Seneca Falls, New York, and his small party "passed soldiers' encampment,—two companies, designed as a guard for the Mormon emigrants." Baker described meeting Indians there as well: "We have calls from Sho-Shone Indians about every meal, for biscuits. They are great beggars, yet always seem pleased." He continued, "Now on again, over hills and through gulches, the sun burning our feet over the heated gravel and stones." Baker, whose party stopped to let the cattle graze, soon met the army group again: "Passed those soldiers, in camp at the so-called Thousand Springs. They were slaughtering an ox."[33]

From there it was eighty miles to the headwaters of the Humboldt River. On July 4, instead of stopping to celebrate Independence Day, the group traveled steadily. Near Humboldt Wells (now Wells, Nevada), the flies became thick and annoying. Here the travelers had their first view of the Humboldt River, which they would follow for the next three hundred miles. They knew they needed the river and yet they dreaded it, for the minerals in the water would make it increasingly unfit to drink.[34]

The Humboldt was overflowing. Lynde wrote:

> I found that the stream was so high that I could not travel by the usually traveled road, which passes down the north side of the stream and near its banks. I had to take the road on the south side, which runs along the base of a chain of mountains, which I found very rough and hilly, but the road was tolerably good as far as the south fork of the Humboldt river, a distance of about seventy miles.[35]

The weather turned cloudy and cool, often with rain in the evenings, a welcome relief from the hot dusty days since leaving Camp Floyd. After crossing the South Fork of the Humboldt, Lynde noted, "The mountains close in upon the river, and the road passes over a mountainous country, and does not again touch the valley of the Humboldt for a distance of about fifty miles, near Gravelly Ford. This distance is over some of the worst hills and the worst road I ever saw." Midway on this section, Captain Lafayette McLaws, second in command of the escort, reported that they came upon disappointed gold seekers returning from Pikes Peak who were "the most destitute" of men. The emigrants traveling with the escort,

[33] Baker, June 30, July 2 and 3, 1859, *Overland Journey*, 45–46.

[34] Lynde to Porter, October 24, 1859, 241; Lynde's Itinerary, 248.

[35] Lynde to Porter, October 24, 1859, 241.

he said, gave them milk and beef in exchange for driving their cattle. By then the summer heat had returned.[36]

At Gravelly Ford they found a mail station. Lynde noted that the few Indians there were "miserably poor, nearly naked, and subsisting on squirrels and nuts that they dig from the ground," and that "they beg from the emigrants the cattle that die from disease, and eat them." He added that the "musquitos and flies became very troublesome to the men and animals, and the water very much impregnated with alkali."[37]

After a day of rest, Lynde's convoy left Gravelly Ford on July 14 and followed the river to Stony Point (near present-day Battle Mountain), where they found a second mail station. When they camped there, Dr. Edward Covey, the army medical officer, reported to Lynde that one private was so ill that "it would endanger his life to move him," and the doctor could not estimate how long it would take before he would be well enough to travel. Lynde decided to leave the majority of his command there under Captain McLaws while he went on with the emigrants and a detachment of fifty men and three officers. For the next ninety-six miles, the river valley was "covered with water, and deep sloughs running parallel to the river render[ed] it impossible to reach the main stream except at long intervals." The water had a high concentration of alkali, which made it dangerous for the animals, and "the musquitos and flies worse than I ever saw them before."[38]

Near today's Winnemucca, they came to another mail station and a trading post. Lynde decided that the need for his protection was over: "The persons at the mail stations reported that no Indians were in the valley, and I had seen none since leaving Gravelly Ford, except a few individuals employed about the mail stations. Believing that it was useless for me to proceed further, I determined to return." It was July 19, and he had brought the emigrants almost six hundred miles.[39] From here the McAuslans and the others in their party were on their own. No longer branded "Mormon apostates," they became simply emigrants eager to reach California.

---

[36] Lynde's Itinerary, 248–49. McLaws, Diary, July 9, 1859. For a list and short biographies of the officers of the escort, see Aird, "Escape from Zion," 222–24.

[37] Lynde to Porter, October 24, 1859, 241.

[38] Ibid., 241–42.

[39] Lynde's Itinerary, 250; Lynde to Porter, October 24, 1859, 242.

18

A New Life, a New Vision

THE ARMY ESCORT HAD TAKEN THEM TWO-THIRDS OF THE WAY
to Sacramento. After the soldiers left them, the McAuslans and their
companions most likely stayed together for at least part of the more than
three hundred miles still to go.[1] Travel became progressively difficult as
the Humboldt River water and the grass deteriorated in quality, the road
became sandier, and the people and animals grew increasingly parched
and worn down. At last they came to Lassen Meadows (now Rye Patch
Reservoir), a true oasis of good grass and willows, where the emigrants
stopped to rest the animals and harvest grass to see them across the bar-
ren stretch to the Great Meadows at the Humboldt Sink. By now the
heat was so intense that the emigrants traveled at night, leaving little
time for sleep.[2]

When the emigrants reached Great Meadows, where the Humboldt
River disappears into sand and reeds, they cut more grass and filled all
available vessels with water. Before them lay the hardest segment of all,
the dreaded Forty Mile Desert. Parties usually started in the late afternoon, and if the oxen did not die on the way, they could hope to be across
by the middle of the next day. Hozial Baker, the seventy-year-old emigrant from New York who had passed them before and was now about
a week ahead of Peter and Agnes, commented on seeing not only many
cattle bones but also a number of graves, one with a headboard for "Mar-

---

[1] The size of the emigration in 1859 was perhaps the largest of any pre–Civil War year. The McAuslans and others leaving Utah were on the front end of the main body of emigrants. For details,
see Aird, "Escape from Zion," 197.

[2] Williams, Diary, July 29, 1859.

garet" who had died in 1853. Baker mused that she "sleeps quietly; no prowling wolf has molested her, nor the other graves. So far from the white settlements!"[3]

The McAuslans and their party apparently made it through the Forty Mile Desert without major incident. When at last the emigrants pulled off the desert into the valley along the Carson River, they came to the first settlement they'd encountered since Brigham City: Ragtown. It was not much. One emigrant that summer found a store and several families living there. Animals continued to die, however, for no sooner had they begun to recover from the trying trek through the desert than they were confronted with another. This one was usually negotiated in a single night, but the sand was deep, making it hard to pull the wagons.[4]

After crossing this second desert stretch, the emigrants came to Chinatown (today's Dayton) and the mouth of Gold Canyon. The rich ores in the region had only just been discovered. It would be another three years after the McAuslans passed by for the Comstock Lode to begin to pay. Captain James Simpson, an army topographical engineer whom General Albert Sidney Johnston had sent to explore a shorter route directly west of Camp Floyd, visited Chinatown two months before the McAuslans passed it. He found two stores, twelve houses, and fifty Chinese living there. About 150 men, white and Chinese, were engaged in mining in the area. Simpson visited an opium den and a gambling room and reported that no women lived in the town.[5]

About twelve miles west of Chinatown, the McAuslans came to Carson City, a settlement approximately the same size as Chinatown but with aspirations of becoming the capital of a hoped-for state separated from Utah. From there, they headed southwest through the lush Carson Valley to Mormon Station, or Genoa. First established by Mormons in 1849 as a trading post for those headed to California, it lay close to the mouth of Carson Canyon, a major gateway to the Sierra Nevada. On account of the approach of the army to Utah's eastern border, the Mormon settlers were called back to the faith's heartland in September

---

[3] Baker, *Overland Journey*, July 18, 1859, 51.

[4] Williams, Diary, July 31, 1859.

[5] Simpson did find a shorter route west that saved 250 miles. The next year, it was used by the Pony Express, the telegraph, the mail, and many emigrants. For his description of Chinatown, see Simpson, *Report of Explorations*, 90–91.

1857. Although the Mormon settlers had not returned from the Wasatch front, Genoa had grown to become the largest settlement in Nevada; in June 1859 it had twenty-eight houses, two stores, two hotels, a newspaper, a telegraph office, and a population of between 150 and 200.[6]

After resting themselves and the animals a few days in Carson Valley, the McAuslans started the strenuous pull up the Sierra Nevada. The first part up Carson Canyon—described by all emigrants as the worst of the whole route and especially hard on wagons—was a twelve-mile steep, rough track between high perpendicular walls and around and over a chaotic tumble of granite boulders. Nevertheless, a hard day's pull up more than two thousand feet brought them to Hope Valley, a welcome grassy flatland. Following a route that had been opened as a "road" since 1852, they turned northwest to go up Luther Pass, at almost eight thousand feet, and then down to Lake Valley (now Lake Tahoe Valley). From there they turned west again to climb Johnson's Pass (7,382 feet). Finally on the more gradual western slope of the Sierra, they followed the South Fork of the American River and then a ridge to Placerville and at last Sacramento.[7]

It was mid-August before the exhausting journey was over. Horace Greeley, the influential editor of the *New York Tribune*, had arrived by stagecoach a week or two before the McAuslans. They would have agreed with his sentiment: "Right glad was I to find myself once more . . . surrounded by the comforts of civilization, and with a prospect of occasional rest. I cannot conscientiously recommend the route I have traveled to summer tourists in quest of pleasure, but it is a balm for many bruises to know that I am at last in CALIFORNIA."[8]

The McAuslans soon moved north to Marysville. in Yuba County, Marysville was the chief town of northern California, rivaling Stockton as the third-largest city after San Francisco and Sacramento. The center for the northern counties, the area was known for its fruit orchards and other produce. Greeley went there in September to attend the agricultural fair and wrote to his paper, the *New York Tribune*: "The wonderful productiveness of the Sacramento and Yuba valleys . . . could hardly be surpassed

---

[6] Nevada became a territory in 1861, with Carson City as its capital. At the time the McAuslans passed that way, the telegraph had been completed only between San Francisco and Genoa; it did not reach Salt Lake City until 1861. Greeley, *Overland Journey*, 234–35; Simpson, *Report of Explorations*, 93.

[7] Howard, *Sierra Crossing*, 62–65, 139–56.

[8] Greeley, *Overland Journey*, 239.

anywhere." He added that although the population in Marysville was probably a little over fifteen thousand, "it expects to be soon connected by railroad with Sacramento and San Francisco, which will give a new and strong impulse to its already rapid growth." Located at the junction of the Yuba and Feather rivers just above where they join the Sacramento River, Marysville was already the terminus for steamboats headed for the northern gold mines. "It needs but the railroad connections aforesaid to render it a formidable rival to Sacramento herself," wrote Greeley.[9]

Peter and Agnes spent the rest of their lives in the northern Sacramento Valley west of Marysville.[10] Initially Peter and his family homesteaded 160 acres about three miles to the northwest of Yuba City in Sutter County, not far from where his parents, Peter and Betsy McAuslan, had settled on a farm. Situated on the natural floodplain of the Feather River, Peter and Agnes contracted malaria. In December 1866, Peter sold his farm, and the next February and March, he and his brother William searched nearer the coast for better land and a healthier climate.[11]

William decided to move his family to Hayward, in Alameda County on the east side of San Francisco Bay, but Peter returned to Sutter County. There he homestead 160 acres near Live Oak, just east of the Sutter Buttes, ancient and highly eroded volcanic peaks that rise abruptly out of the valley floor. His new farm was eight miles northwest of Yuba City and close to that of Agnes's brother John McAuslin. It was unimproved and had to be cleared of live oak stumps and underbrush before it could be plowed. "Mighty hard work," wrote Peter to his sister Jane McAuslan Ogilvie in Nevada. Eventually it became a good farm, with wheat, fruit trees, and grapevines. Peter and Agnes had two young daughters when they left Utah, and in California the couple had seven more children, three boys (one of whom was stillborn) and four girls. In 1863 Peter became a naturalized citizen.[12]

[9] Ibid., 282–83.

[10] Sources for Peter's life in California: Guinn, *History of the State of California*, 660–61; Delay, *History of Yuba and Sutter Counties*, 246; Chamberlain, *History of Sutter County*, 119; 1860 United States Census, Yuba, Sutter, Calif., roll M653-70, 763; 1870 United States Census, Butte, Sutter, Calif., roll M593-92, 102; 1880 United States Census, Yuba, Sutter, Calif., roll T9-84, 426.

[11] Peter McAuslan to Agnes McAuslin McAuslan, February 28 and March 6, 1867 (#19 McAuslan Papers).

[12] Peter McAuslan Land Grant, Scrip #684, U.S. Land Office, Sutter County, Calif., June 3, 1874, 369 (#25 McAuslan Papers); Peter McAuslan to Jane McAuslan Ogilvie, December 28, 1870 (#22 McAuslan Papers); Certificate of Citizenship for Peter McAuslan, United States of America, May 18, 1863 (#16 McAuslan Papers).

Sutter Buttes, near where the McAuslans homesteaded.
From William C. Bryant, *Picturesque America*, 1:413.
Courtesy of Historic Images.

Agnes's brother John McAuslin, who had traveled with Peter and Agnes from Glasgow to Salt Lake City in 1854, had left in the spring of 1855 for the gold fields in California. For eleven years he mined in the gold regions of California, on the Fraser River in British Columbia, and near Idaho City. In 1866 he married his Scottish sweetheart, and they bought 160 acres close to where Peter and Agnes a year later homesteaded a farm. Although John had left the Mormons and their religion in 1855, he had done so without bitterness. Writing ten years later, he said that he did not "see any use in offending them. . . . People have a perfeact right to believe any thing they have a mind to." Peter's younger brothers, Frank and David, lived with their parents and managed their farm near Yuba City; his sister Janet, who had divorced John Allan, arrived in 1867 to join the household. Almost ten years after arriving in California, the elder Peter died, and two years later Betsy followed.[13]

---

[13] Chamberlain, *History of Sutter County*, 119; John McAuslin to Agnes and Peter McAuslan, February 19, [1865] (#17 McAuslan Papers), 1. Betsey McAuslan Land Grant, Certificate #4336, U.S. Land Office, Sutter County, Calif., November 2, 1872, 44 (#23 McAuslan Papers); 1860 United States Census, Marysville Ward 1, Yuba, Calif., roll M653-72, 856; McAuslan to Ogilvie, December 28, 1870 (#22 McAuslan Papers); "Estate of Betsey McAusland," Probate Records, April 17, 1872, Sutter County, Calif., vol. A, 47–48.

Peter saved drafts of letters and scraps on which he recorded his thoughts. From these it is possible to piece together his experiences and thinking after leaving Utah. Many of the letters were to his sister Agnes McAuslan Allan. In the mid-1880s she and her husband, John Allan, and his plural wife, Jane Fleming Ferguson Shaw Allan, settled in Bluff, Utah. In one letter Peter tried to dissuade Agnes from Mormonism: "As I was to some extent the cause of you being a Mormon, I would like to undo the evil I have done." In that letter and a seventy-six-page one written a year earlier, he tried to convince her that the Bible—and thus Mormonism, Christianity, Judaism, and Islam—could not be from God. He cited numerous examples of biblical contradictions to prove his point. The following will illustrate his arguments.[14]

Peter pointed out that although God in the Ten Commandments had told the Israelites, "Thou shalt not kill," he had ordered them time and again to go out and slay whole groups, including the Canaanites, Amorites, Hittites, and Midianites. Reading the Bible literally, Peter showed that God condoned not only murder but slavery, adultery, theft, and polygamy. Such acts and institutions were completely incompatible with a God of love, mercy, justice, and wisdom, he reasoned. But God could not be inconsistent, and therefore the Bible could not have been inspired by him. But for all his arguments and logic, Peter had no success with Agnes, who remained a faithful Mormon.

For himself, Peter never regretted leaving the Mormon faith. "I have no desire to return and swim in the muddy watters [*sic*] of Mormonism nor any other sect or system upon earth," he wrote. Yet he did not dwell on his experiences in Utah that made him leave the religion, nor did he speak out in books or lectures in an effort to expose the crimes he believed the church hierarchy had authorized. Instead he focused on his own spiritual experiences and his belief in spiritual progression. In an undated draft, Peter described his 1848 vision and told how he later came to view that experience. He said it had given him great confidence in the truth of Mormonism, "until I got to learn that the Mormon Church was not the only class of people that had spiritual manifestations." Nevertheless, he acknowledged the blessings of the spirit among the Saints, for his letter continued, "I am quite well aware that the Mormon people have had

---

[14] Peter McAuslan to Agnes McAuslan Allan, March 1, 1884, and ca. 1885 (#34 and #35 McAuslan Papers).

a great deal of expearence of a spiritual nature. . . . [That] healing through prayer and the laying on of hands has often occurred is not questioned by me, and further that they are honest in their opinions and motives."[15]

About 1886 Peter wrote a letter to his nephew Arthur Maxwell, Jr., who was the son of Agnes's sister, Elizabeth McAuslin Maxwell. Arthur, a faithful Mormon, lived in Peoa, Summit County, Utah. Much of this thirty-nine-page letter, like those he wrote to his sister Agnes, consisted of arguments for why the Bible and the Book of Mormon could not be inspired by God. In addition he maintained that priests did not have a claim to higher knowledge of spiritual matters and certainly did not have the authority to carry out God's judgments.[16]

In one section of the letter he commented again on his 1848 vision: "After sincere prayer I received a demonstration from an intelligent source or power which I to this day can say was not of man. With my limited knowledge at that time I accepted it as a confirmation by God and so bore testimony to that effect until I found out I was mistaken." Peter then commented that he was sure Arthur was thinking that he should have said, "untill my mind got darkened by disobedience." This was "the Mormon reply to all such in my position," he wrote. "That to the honest faithfull and simple will appear to be a clincher, but to me it is far otherwise."[17]

Continuing his letter, Peter observed that throughout history there have been individuals "highly developed in the spiritual faculties, just as we find some highly developed in the poetical, musical, and mathematical faculties." He then told of an experience he had had two years after leaving Utah: "In the year 1861 I received a most marvelous manifestation of spirit power. I will only say this about it now—it came spontaineous[ly], or in other words it was not sought for on my part."[18] It took him another twenty-five pages of discussion about the attributes of God and the nature of the Bible before he finally gave a description of this vision, which is quoted here in its entirety:

---

[15] McAuslan to McAuslan Allan, March 1, 1884 (#34 McAuslan Papers), 1 of transcription; Peter McAuslan to [Arthur Maxwell Jr.], undated (#61 McAuslan Papers).

[16] Peter McAuslan to Arthur Maxwell, Jr., ca. 1886 (#37 McAuslan Papers), 28A. Peter did not change Maxwell's views; Maxwell became bishop of Peoa in 1913.

[17] Ibid., 7–8. Compare Peter's comment on "disobedience" causing "darkness" of the mind to statements in the 1869 church trial of the Godbeite leaders. Brigham Young's counselor, Daniel H. Wells, said, "We have no proof that . . . you have committed any sin, but then you *must* have done something of the kind or you could not be in the dark as you are today." To this, Brigham Young had reportedly replied, "Yes, and it will come to light in due time." Walker, *Wayward Saints*, 166.

[18] McAuslan to Maxwell (#37 McAuslan Papers), 8, 10.

After having retired to rest and meditating upon the current events of the times, I seemed to be emersed in an atmosphere of spiritual light. All my faculties became quickened in a high degree, my spiritual senses became opened, I could see without my natural eyes, I could hear without my natural ears. I felt calm and serene in a high degree, with an awful [i.e., full of awe] sense of security, also with a sense of a powerful and sublime spiritual presence. It commenced on my part with unusual heavy breathings automatic in their nature. After three full inhalations I would be addressed by the intelligence, not audible but impressional. It was the same to me as if it had been spoken aloud. I asked mental questions and received answers.

Now I will relate some of the sayings. In answer to the question who was communicating with me, the likenesses of Joseph Smith and Hyrum passed slowly before my spiritual vision just the same as I had seen them in the Old Country. I will pass over a vision in regard to the negro, and many other sayings—it would take too long to relate them—and commence with the saying: Joseph Smith and Hyrum are prophets to the Glory of God. Brigham Young and his confederates are imposters to their own destruction and all that shall follow them. Polygamy is wrong. Daniteism is wrong. The prophecy of Joseph Smith in regard to the rebellion commenceing at South Carolina [i.e., the Civil War] is a true prophecy and is about to commence to be fulfilled, and would be fulfiled to the very letter. The prophecy in regard to the building of the Temple in Jackson County, Missouri, is also a true prophecy, and this generation would not all pass away until it would be fulfiled. Mormonism is sent and is permited for a purpose and will fulfil that purpose.

Arnold spiritualism, the common Spiritualism of to day, and all other sects and systems upon Earth are permited and sent for a purpose and would fulfil the purpose for which they were sent. All sects and systems have centers arround which they revolve. Jesus Christ will come again in the flesh. He will bring in the reign of peace, love, and good will to all mankind. All is right! All is right! There is nothing wrong. Yea, there is nothing wrong in all the world. All sects and systems when they have served their purpose will become as a nut in the hand of the Allmighty which he can crush to powder and scatter to the four winds of heaven. All light and all truth are centered in him.[19]

---

[19] Ibid., 35–38. None of Peter's surviving writings mention seeing likenesses of Joseph and Hyrum Smith in the "Old Country." "Daniteism" (Danitism) refers to the widespread belief that Brigham Young had a secret group of henchmen to carry out special orders, including murder and other crimes. Arnold spiritualism appears to have been popular in the mid-nineteenth century; Charles Lowell Walker noted in his diary for April 13, 1859, that his father was reading a book by "Mr. Arnold, a spiritualist pretending to be under the influence of Jesus Christ"; Larson and Larson, *Diary of Charles Lowell Walker*, 66.

When Peter saw Joseph and Hyrum Smith after asking who was communicating with him, he meant that they were the spirits through whom the pronouncements were relayed, for after describing this spiritual experience, he spoke of the unknown source of what he had heard: "If I could not identify the personnel of that intelligence that communicated with me, how could I or any other human being identify the Supreme Being, he being so infinitely above our comprehension that we can form no estimate of him whatever?" He then noted that it is an easy thing to be led to believe that one can know the Supreme Being, but to know the impossible is a very different thing.[20]

The prediction that Brigham Young and his followers would be destroyed obviously did not come true. From Peter's perspective of 1861, however, it must have looked possible, perhaps even probable, as Young was continuing to maintain a wall of silence about the Mountain Meadows massacre and other murders of the period. How long would the U.S. government tolerate his defiance of outside investigations or his theocratic despotism in the midst of the country's democracy?

Joseph Smith's prophecy that war between the North and the South would begin in South Carolina was true in referring to the Civil War, but Smith had further predicted that it would extend until it involved all nations on earth (D&C 87:1–5). Mormons in that period believed that this would be the punishment meted out to the United States for persecuting their faith. This latter part was not "fulfilled to the very letter." Nor was Smith's prophecy that a temple would be built in Jackson County, Missouri—considered by the LDS church to be the site of the New Jerusalem—and "this generation would not all pass away" until it was fulfilled (D&C 84:1–5).

That these predictions proved wrong does not lessen the obvious significance this vision had for Peter. It was the defining spiritual experience of his post-Mormon years. It showed his continuing belief in Joseph Smith as having received revelations from a higher source. It confirmed that leaving Brigham Young, Mormonism, and Utah was the right course for him and part of the Supreme Being's plan. To Peter, the vision was empirical

---

[20] McAuslan to Maxwell (#37 McAuslan Papers), 38–39. T. B. H. Stenhouse, who left the Mormons in 1870 and had spiritualist leanings, also concluded that Joseph Smith "was but the vehicle of 'spirit communication.'" See Stenhouse, *Rocky Mountain Saints*, 520n, 521–22, 546; and Walker, *Wayward Saints*, 296–97.

evidence of the truth of spiritualism, the belief that dead spirits can communicate with the living, and thereafter Peter became an ardent believer.

Like Mormonism, modern spiritualism began in upstate New York and claimed direct revelation from beyond the material world.[21] Many famous figures became converts, including Horace Greeley, the editor of the *New York Tribune*; Robert Dale Owen, son of the social reformer; and Nathaniel P. Tallmadge, former U.S. senator from New York and governor of Wisconsin Territory. Others took a serious view of it, including James Fenimore Cooper, George Bancroft, William Cullen Bryant, and Harriet Beecher Stowe. In the 1870s, when spiritualism reached its peak, it could claim somewhere between one and eleven million followers.[22] The Civil War contributed to its growth as increasing numbers of people wished to contact their loved ones who had died in the war. Peter's interest may likewise have been sharpened by the loss of his first son in 1856.

Peter believed spiritualism was superior to any religion because revelation could come without the intermediacy of a hierarchical organization. From his experience in Utah, he had become convinced that the priesthood—in Mormonism or any religion—kept people from receiving the truth directly: "No high priest (so called) has any right to monopolize spiritual things, but . . . the heavens and the earth are open books for all mankind to read. It has been the aim of priestcraft ever to keep those books sealed."[23] It was the experience of encountering God through visions, healings, and direct revelation that had seemed conclusive evidence of the truth of Mormonism. Believing the faith was truly from

---

[21] The roots of spiritualism date to at least Old Testament times. King Saul, facing battle with the Philistines, consulted a medium in Endor who contacted the dead spirit of the prophet Samuel. Samuel predicted Saul's defeat and death. See I Samuel 28:3–25. Modern spiritualism began with the sisters Margaret and Catherine Fox in 1848 in Hydesville, New York. In 1856, Margaret secretly married Elisha Kent Kane, a famous Arctic explorer and brother of Thomas L. Kane, the friend of the Mormons who helped effect peace between them and the army in 1858. Weisberg, *Talking to the Dead*, chapters 11 and 12. In spiritualism a group gathers for a séance. The leader is a "medium," someone with a special ability to communicate with the spirits of the dead. The participants, usually sitting around a table and holding or touching hands, concentrate their thoughts on contacting a particular spirit. The medium then relays either in words or writing what the spirit said.

[22] *Banner of Light* (November 24, 1888), as cited in Weisberg, *Talking to the Dead*, 304n2; Ahlstron, *Religious History*, 488–90. The number of followers is impossible to pin down, for without a formal organization until 1893 (when the National Spiritualist Association was formed), records are nonexistent. Additionally, it was a wide-spreading umbrella that encompassed varying aspects of spirit communication and varying degrees of committed investigators; thus the number depends on what aspects are included or how "follower" is defined. See Hazen, *Village Enlightenment*, 80–81, 167n48.

[23] McAuslan to Maxwell (#37 McAuslan Papers), alternate draft, 28.

God, Peter had then expected to find a holy life with the chosen people in Zion. But instead he found that Brigham Young had abandoned spirituality in favor of priesthood control and the practicalities of building the Mormon kingdom. Priesthood meetings were often more concerned with irrigation ditches than with matters of the spirit.

Peter's views closely matched those of a group of estranged British Mormons called the Godbeites, who organized in Utah ten years after the McAuslans left. They too believed in spiritualism and held that Joseph Smith's revelations had come through spirit manifestations. They too concluded that Brigham Young was misusing his power. Ronald W. Walker, the historian of the Godbeites, summed up the attraction: "Spiritualism had a rakish, revolutionary quality that especially suited British converts. It questioned and challenged staid thought, just as their brand of British Mormonism had done. In short, spiritualism had many enticing parallels to Mormonism: it had intellectual appeal; it had phenomena; and it carried the banner of revolution."[24]

But more than that, spiritualism had scientific appeal and seemed worthy of investigation by the best minds. To the "common sense" ideas of the Scottish Enlightenment—that reason was the measure of all things and the only reliable path to knowledge and understanding—was added the need for evidence from the senses. Spiritualism offered many kinds of empirical proofs of life after death and immortality. Mediums welcomed skeptics to public demonstrations. Daniel Douglas Home, a Scot and early medium, displayed in his séances a repertoire of rappings, table turnings, and other spirit manifestations such as phantom hands that would appear and disappear. He could levitate, handle fire, and change his height. His séances in London were popular with high society there and from the Continent. In particular they attracted the interest of Sir William Crookes of Oxford University, the foremost authority on the uses of chemistry in industry. One British convert was the naturalist Alfred Russel Wallace, who published a book on spiritualism in 1881 and whom Peter described as "the great Scientist, who has declared that Spiritualism is as much an established fact as any other fact established by Science." The French astronomer Camille Flammarion of the Paris Observatory was likewise persuaded. In the United States, Robert Hare, a professor of chemistry at the University of Pennsylvania, an outstanding experimenter and scien-

24 Walker, *Wayward Saints*, 112, 119–20. The quotation is on page 112.

tific debater, and the country's expert in theories of electricity, magnetism, and matter, was convinced and wrote a 460-page examination of spirit manifestations. Thomas A. Edison hoped to build a device that would facilitate communication with the spirits. Even the American psychologist William James, who studied the case of a woman who experienced hypnotic trances, decided to keep an open mind about spiritualism.[25]

With all the new discoveries of the period—evolution, genetics, microbiology, the relationship between the physiology of the nervous system and human behavior—spiritualism appeared to be one more frontier ripe for exploration. It was a "sublime subject," Peter wrote, "treading upon the margin or boundary of another world." Scientific discoveries might well offer real proof of religion. Many scientists took spiritualism seriously. For those untrained in science, many natural phenomena such as gravity, magnetism, electricity, and the propagation of light, as well as the telegraph lines recently strung across the country, appeared equally mysterious. That spirits "beyond the veil" could communicate with the living did not seem an unreasonable stretch. Peter expressed it this way: "Thank God man is indowed with the Spirit to think, investigate, search. He seeks and he finds. He knocks and Nature opens up her treasure house to him. The denizens of the most dismal of all vaults, the grave, has given forth light. They have spoken and we have heard."[26]

Applying the scientific method to spiritual beliefs was basic to Peter, who wanted evidence based on God-given reason. He wrote, "All who have approached this subject with an unbiased mind, free from supercilious, positive pride & know-it-all-ness, have had as good and satisfactory reasons and proofs to believe that those occult forces are what they profess to be, namely our spirit-friends who have passed through the change called death. As a hunter has, who comes upon the footprints of a deer in the snow, to know that it was in reality a deer and not a buffalo which produced those foot prints."[27]

---

[25] Hazen, *Village Enlightenment*, chapter 2; Weisberg, *Talking to the Dead*, 261; Peter McAuslan to the editor of the *Sacramento Bee*, April 8, 1888 (#40 McAuslan Papers), 3 of transcription; James, *Varieties of Religious Experience*, 395. Among his many books on spiritualism, Peter owned Home's two-volume autobiography, *Incidents of My Life*, published first in 1863. From its wear, Peter read it frequently.

[26] Peter McAuslan, essay on spiritualism, n.d. (#59 McAuslan Papers), 1 of transcription; Peter McAuslan to the editor of the *San Francisco Golden Gate*, November 22, 1889 (#41 McAuslan Papers), 7 of transcription.

[27] McAuslan, essay on spiritualism (#40), 2 of transcription.

The ideas behind spiritualism seemed not that distant from Mormon concepts like healing practices, the bestowal of the Holy Spirit through the laying on of hands, or belief in spiritual communication between minds. Orson Pratt, who had been so influential in Peter's conversion to Mormonism, and his brother Parley P. Pratt believed there was more in the world than the senses could discover. According to them, the Holy Spirit worked as a "spiritual telegraph"; it was a phrase also common among spiritualists, and the *Spiritual Telegraph* was the name of one of their newspapers. In 1889 Peter expressed a similar idea: "There is the telegraph, and telephon[e], and there are human organisms who are mediums through which are conveyed intelligent communications between the so called dead and their friends on earth."[28]

Spiritualism was likewise closely connected to social reform, fitting perfectly with Peter's leanings. Spirit messages regularly expressed concern about the direction society was taking, and they invariably pointed toward reform in labor laws, marriage laws, and women's rights. They also supported abolition, communitarianism, and living the healthy life. The ideal was harmony in all things and progress as a natural law. With this came the concept that there was correspondence between our earthly world and the spheres of the spirits, with everything in the former also in the latter, but in a refined state.[29]

In an undated note headed "What does Spiritualism teach?" Peter expressed how he understood the cosmos and our place and purpose in it:

Earth is . . . on it's passage way from chaos to a condition of beauty, order, and harmony. . . . Man as an outgrowth of Earth is first germination, growth, maturity, old age, and decay. So Earth itself will follow the same law. But man being endowed with an immortal spirit, the aim and purpose of his being here on Earth is that he might gain experience and become individualized, self poised, and in harmony with the great Over Soul of the Universe. By coming in contact and passing through the crude and dark conditions of physical life, man is being taught by the contrasts of the evil and the good the great importance of conforming to the laws of nature in the lives of physical, mental, and spiritual being. This is what is meant by partakeing of the tree of knowledge of good and evil.[30]

---

[28] Hazen, *Village Enlightenment*, 56–58; McAuslan to the editor of the *Sacramento Bee*, 1 of transcription.

[29] Hazen, *Village Enlightenment*, 82, 95–112.

[30] Peter McAuslan, "What Does Spiritualism Teach?" undated note (#64 McAuslan Papers).

Two themes run through Peter's writings of his later years: the beauty and truth of spiritualism and the injustices still meted out to the working classes by capitalism. Peter's interest in labor problems and his wish for better treatment of workers were a logical outcome of both his views about our ultimate purpose here on earth and his own experiences in Scotland.

In early 1898, just before his seventy-fourth birthday, Peter outlined in a letter to his sister Agnes what he had come to believe. Having mellowed over the years, he wrote that he did not wish to disturb her in her religious belief, but that he would state his:

> I believe in a great Supreme power that rules the Universe, that all his works are good. That all life has come upon this earth in accord with the will and purpose of that Supreme Power. That the sorrows and pains, the evils and inharmonys that we see arround us and [that we] are passing through are esential for our education and the progress of the real "I am" or entity, the spirit that is within these bodies of ours. That when we lay down our bodies, it is not a calamity so much so as it apears to be, but it is passing from this physical state to a more interior or spiritual condition.
>
> I believe that God is impartial, that he has no favorites, that he is no respecter of persons, that he never did nor never will ordain a priesthood composed of man to proclame his will and . . . condemn him to everlasting darkness and misery if they fail to believe it.
>
> The human spirit after it leaves the body is under spiritual law, and when we who are living comply with certain conditions, we can communacate with the departed. . . . If Jesus was here to day, he would be recognised as a clarvoint and healing medium. The last 50 years has produced a great many such mediums and many other spiritual gifts have been developed in different parts of the world. . . .
>
> I have found out that man is a very selfish animal and the present structure of society tends to foster that principle in man. Man in olden times as well as now were very crafty—hence the effort of the cunning and crafty to monopalize not only the good things of this life, but the spiritual gifts allso.[31]

Peter had changed in his thinking. He no longer believed in Zion as a state of glory ushered in by the coming of Christ. Rather, he believed that each person, if aware, gained peace, harmony, and God's wisdom through life's experiences, and after death each would continue to develop on a spiritual plane. For Peter now, Zion was a process, not a time or a place.

[31] Peter McAuslan to Agnes McAuslan Allan, January 17 and 18, 1898, originals in possession of Ada Redd Rigby, Blanding, Utah (#47 and #48 McAuslan Papers). Peter's "50 years" is precise, as spiritualism had spread widely since 1848.

WHAT ROLE AGNES PLAYED IN PETER'S INTELLECTUAL AND spiritual life is unknown. Letters have survived that Agnes wrote to her sister, Elizabeth McAuslin Maxwell, between 1872 and 1900 (the year Agnes died), but they are about the expected crop, the children, or relatives in Scotland, with nothing referring to their earlier life. One letter, however, gives a glimpse into her thinking and faith. Elizabeth's husband, Arthur Maxwell, Sr., had died two and a half months before, and Agnes wrote to Elizabeth that she hoped "God will give you health and strength so that you may be able to bear up under your afflictions." Agnes went on: "Let us strive to do the best we can so that when our tur[n] comes, as come it must, we will be able to greet the ones that have gone before with a certinty of aprovel, knowing that we have made the best of this world's experience we possably could do." Agnes died on August 14, 1900, after being taken ill the day before, during a visit to her daughter Margaret in San Francisco.[32]

Peter died eight years later, on December 21, 1908, a month before his eighty-fifth birthday.[33] When he died, several articles about him appeared in the local papers. The most descriptive said,

> Uncle Peter McAuslan, who had been seriously ill with pneumonia at his home near Encinal [a district near Live Oak, California], died on Monday, Dec. 21st. Mr. McAuslan was the third oldest man in this precinct. He was a man of more than ordinary intelligence, a great reader and a writer of much ability. He was a devout and honest believer in Spiritualism and while he was not aggressive he was frequently more than a match for his opponents in an argument. He was a pioneer of this county and will long be remembered as an accomplished neighbor, a kind husband and father, whose creed was honesty and brotherly love.[34]

Almost half a century had passed since the McAuslans had left Utah and the religion that had brought them to America. Although Peter no longer believed in the faith, he never lost his feelings for the Mormon people; no doubt this was partly because he still had Mormon family

---

[32] Agnes McAuslin McAuslan to Elizabeth McAuslin Maxwell, January 5, 1872 (McAuslan Papers), 1–2. The only mention of her earlier life is in two letters (March 11, 1882, and March 9, 1888), when she laments not having seen a coal fire since she left Scotland. "Death of Mrs. McAuslan," *Sutter County Farmer*, August 17, 1900, 2.

[33] "Death of Peter McAuslan," *Sutter County Farmer*, December 25, 1908, 6, 7; "Sutter Pioneer Goes to His Reward," *Daily Appeal*, December 22, 1908, 5.

[34] *Sutter County Farmer*, December 25, 1908, 6.

Peter McAuslan with two of his daughters, Margaret (*center*) and Agnes (*right*).
Taken on the McAuslan farm near Live Oak, California,
in the 1890s when Peter was in his seventies.
Courtesy of Jean Williston Heilmann, Grass Valley, California.

members. His nephew Arthur Maxwell, Jr., continued to send him the
Deseret News. Referring to congressional efforts in the 1880s to abolish
polygamy and the consequent persecution of church leaders, Peter wrote
in one letter, "I feel very much interested in the events that are taking
place in Utah. My sympathies always flow out towards the oppressed
and suffering. . . . I have no sympathy with the present crusade against
your most prominent men because they believe polygamy to be the
revealed command of God to certain men in the Mormon Church."[35]
Thus his feelings of charity extended even to the leaders whose over-
weening authority in the past had led to the killing of innocent people.

---

[35] McAuslan to Maxwell (#37 McAuslan Papers), 1–2.

Peter had hoped to find Zion in the New World, where there would be peace among the people and God's wisdom would flow down upon them. But Utah was not the Promised Land for him. Nevertheless, he came to believe that what happened there and all through his life contributed to his spiritual growth. "I have no regrets," he wrote, "about my experience as a Mormon, as I do know that I was sincere and honest in my belief as a Mormon and am now in my belief and knowledge of the facts I have acquired." Recognizing that human beings can never fully know God, he nevertheless felt he knew enough to say, "In the absence of an absolute knowledge of the Supreme Being, I hold that . . . God is a God of love, and that all that transpires here on Earth will ultimate [i.e., end] in good, for God is good."[36]

Peter's life encompassed a panorama of events and experiences: his training and skill as a calico pattern designer; the bitter labor struggles in industrializing Scotland; the appeal of Mormonism and his feelings of brotherhood among God's people after his conversion; the epic but tedious journey to Utah; the pioneer life there battling locust plagues, drought, and severe winters; the misuse of power by church leaders that had led to murder; the family's escape with an army escort; the dust and deserts of the Great Basin and the hard haul over the Sierra Nevada; and finally a modest life in the Sacramento Valley. He had journeyed in faith from Scottish Presbyterianism to Mormonism to spiritualism. His empathy for the laboring masses and the unfortunate individual ran like a thread throughout. If Peter were here to conclude this account, he would probably end with the affirmation he received in his 1861 vision. The words make no sense, he conceded, unless looked at from some point of view far beyond our limited human understanding: "All is right! All is right! There is nothing wrong. Yea, there is nothing wrong in all the world."[37]

---

[35] McAuslan to Maxwell (#37 McAuslan Papers), 1–2.

[36] Ibid., 30; McAuslan to McAuslan Allan, March 1, 1884 (#34 McAuslan Papers), 34 of the transcription.

[37] Peter McAuslan, undated note (#63 McAuslan Papers).

The first page of Peter McAuslan's draft letter to Robert Salmon, December 1860. *Courtesy Donna Miller Forguson, Live Oak, California.*

Epilogue: "I Was Sorrowfully Disappointed"

IN DECEMBER 1860, JUST OVER A YEAR AFTER ARRIVING IN California, Peter wrote to Robert Salmon, his old friend in Scotland. In 1848–49 they had shared a room in Denny, and Peter had preached Mormonism to him. On March 3, 1849, Robert and his wife became the first people Peter baptized after being ordained a priest.[1] Peter wrote the 1860 letter in response to Salmon's having asked him why he had left the church.

The letter, a draft, is written on pale-blue ledger paper, folded so as to make four pages. It was discovered among McAuslan's papers and books in Live Oak, California, where he had settled.[2] Scribbling, as if he were trying out his pen, appears at the top of the first page, as does the word "Splendure," as if he were unsure how to spell it (he used "splender" in the letter). The last page also has a few scribbles at the bottom and numerical calculations at both top and bottom. The letter ends abruptly.

Robert Salmon was born in 1812 in Balloch, Dunbartonshire, Scotland. The Salmon and McAuslan families had known each other in Kirkintilloch, Denny, and Barrhead, where both successively moved to find work in calico printing factories. Salmon was still in Barrhead when Peter wrote to him, and Peter and his family were living in Marysville, California, shortly before they homesteaded their first farm close to Yuba City.

Besides giving his reasons for leaving the church, the letter reveals much about Peter's character. Always on the side of the powerless, he

---

[1] Record of Members, Falkirk and Barrhead Branches; Peter McAuslan to Agnes McAuslan Allan, March 1, 1884 (#33 McAuslan Papers), 5.

[2] Peter McAuslan to Robert Salmon, December 1860 (#14 McAuslan Papers). I am grateful to Donna Forguson, great-great-granddaughter of Peter McAuslan, for a photocopy of the letter.

respected the Mormon people. He found individual Mormons to be as good as anyone he had known anywhere. He said he knew that many had had experiences that made them stronger in their faith. He was not writing to persuade Robert to leave the church, but asked him only to judge from his own experiences. Maintaining that God meant for people to grow in knowledge, Peter expressed feelings of charity toward believers in Mormonism, saying he expected that in time their understanding would develop and they would outgrow the church's doctrines. He thanked Robert for being concerned about him and took it as a "token of the magnaminity of your Soul towards me."

Mary'sville [California], Dec[r] 1860

Mr. Robart Salmon

Dear Brother

I received your letter some time ago and was happy to learn that you were all well and in good spirits. I am happy to inform you that we are also well and in as good spirits now as I ever was, and I might add, better than I ever was in the Mormon Church, but I know that you cannot believe that according to your present faith, but no matter, all is right.

I still intertain the same faith in regard to the First principles of the Gosple of Christ, that is, as farr as *Faith, Hope* and *Charity* is concerned. Or in other words, I believe and do know that I injoy the Spirit of God more so then ever. And that Spirit leads me to have faith, hope and charity, and to follow after truth wherever I may find it, Independent of Churches with there Dogmas or Prophets and Priests that preach that your Salvation depends on Paying up your Tithing that they might live in ease and Splender and in the injoyment of all the pleasure that this world can bestow![3]

More particularly I will state a few of the reasons I had for leaving Salt Lake and the Mormon Church. ~~First~~ I was taught to believe when I was in the Old Cuntry that when I got to ~~the So-called~~ Zion I would have the pleasure of seeing and hearing a Prophet, Seer, and Revelator of the *Lord*. I was sorrowfully dissapointed after being there over 5 years. I was forsed to come to the conclusion that Brigham Young is no more inspired by the Allmighty then many other men are, who are out of the Pale of Mormondom.

Of course you say I have no right to judge the Servent of the Lord. Well I have not time to discuss this subject at this time, but would mearly say

---

[3] When he left Utah, Peter owed $91.77 in combined labor and produce tithing. Although others in Spanish Fork were also in arrears, this amount was greater than average. Local Unit Financial Records, Spanish Fork, 102.

that I clame [claim] it as a right to judge all things for myself, feeling as I do that I shall have to give an account for *myself* of the course I persue in this life. If I take a right course, I shall receive the reward. If I take a wrong course, I shall suffer the Penality anexed thereunto, and of course I would consider myself a fool or a dupe to expect any man to be responceable for my actions. ~~Hence you can see at once from these few remarks that that~~

The Doctrin of doing as you are told, whither it appears to you to be right or wrong, was most strongly urged the last year or two that I was thare, so much so that I could not believe it, and of course I found out that I could not be consistently a Mormon.[4] Such a doctrin as that in the hands of uninspired men, even suppose them to be of Spotless Character, would in my estamation lead to most fearfull consequences.

[p. 2] What do I suppose those consequences to be, you might ask? In my humble oppion it requires no Prophetic Eye to See what those conciquences would be. Firstly, instead of man excercising those reasonable [reasoning] facculities that God has indowed him with for the discovery of truth, they would lie in a dorment condition. Hence an end to progression and the expansion of his intellect, and insteed of God's purposes ~~being~~ towards man being aided (which are in my oppion man's development phisically, intelectully and morally), they would be retarded.[5]

Therefore, you see, I desided for myself—after earnest Prayer to the Allmighty to aide me in the discovry of truth and it's addoption, and the renouncement of error—that such a doctrin could never come from the

---

[4] Charles Derry, an English convert, came on the same ship as Peter in 1854, lived in Ogden, and also left Utah and the Mormons in 1859, but to go east. He similarly complained, "It seemed to me that the leading men were set upon crushing out what manhood there was in the people by their oppressions, and at the same time the burden of their teaching was, 'obedience to counsel,' 'follow your leaders,' 'do as you are told,' 'heed the counsel of the living oracles.' " Derry, *Autobiography*, 33.

Articles on obedience appeared in the *Deseret News* with fair regularity, for instance: "Blessings of Obedience" on June 16, 1858; "Salvation Attending Obedience" on July 28, 1858; and "Effects of Intimacy with the Priesthood," which admonished members to obey God's servants even if they were flawed men, on August 11, 1858. Church leaders often preached obedience. One example will give the flavor: On November 8, 1857, Heber C. Kimball exhorted, "Learn to do as you are told . . . if you are told by your leader to do a thing, do it. None of your business whether it is right or wrong." *Journal of Discourses*, 6:32.

[5] Sociologist Thomas F. O'Dea made a similar observation: "The emphasis upon the free agency of man, upon man's development through his own effort, and upon the possibility of the individual's achieving Godlike status" contradicted the "church claiming descent from the rule of a specially chosen prophet-founder and embodying a hierarchy of office and decision-making." The result is an inherent conflict between individual effort and obedience; and although the church has made an accommodation for individual participation within the authoritarian structure, "it remains a potential source of strain, and for the intellectuals it is an actual source of difficulty." O'Dea, *Mormons*, 242–43.

Allmighty, and of course must have been concocted by man for the sub-jugation and inslavement of his fellow man, both Soul and body. Such is the ultimate [fate] of the faithfull followers of Brigham Young.

As I know from expearience that I cannot affect your faith in Mor-monism or, in other words, what you understand to be Mormonizm in Scotland, neither do I wish to, but would ask you to go ahead and prove it for your self and not depend upon my expearience in Mormonizm. I am of the many but one (judging from my own past expearience) [and] am convinced that you will do that anyway, but as you have asked my reasion's for leaving Mormonism, I shall give you a few of the most prominent of them, without going into detail.

That I might put no Stumbling Block in your path, I might add that I do know that there are many just as good men as I would wish to asco-caite with whose expearience in Mormonizm has made them Stronger in the Faith. And I must say that my feelings are very charityable towards them as a people, that is to those who are honest in the faith.[6] And although such do intertain absurd doctrins, they are not to blame. It requires time and expearience to develop them; then they shall get rid of there [their] absurdities just as I as one of the many have down [done] before them.

But I think I here you exclame, "Poor fellow! I am vexed for you. You have got into darkness, but I hope and Pray that you might be brought back to the light again, yea to the glorious light of the latter day Gosple." I am thankful to you for such feelings and accept them as a token of the magnaminity of your Soul towards me.

But to return to my reasons. The Mormons do intertain doctrins [that] when they are put in force are destructive of the rights of there fellow man.[7] Do I know this? Yes I do. What are they? When the Celestial law is fully put in force there shall no one leave the Mormon church and go over to the

---

[6] Others who left in the late 1850s expressed similar sentiments. Charles Derry wrote, "I have no desire to create the impression that the mass of the people of Utah were bad. On the contrary, I am satisfied there were many God-fearing people who had made great sacrifices for the truth." John Hyde, an English convert who had left Utah in 1856, remarked in a letter addressed to Brigham Young: "I admire the industry of your people, their notable labors and their general sincerity." Stephen Forsdick, another Englishman who left Utah in 1856, echoed the others: "As a whole, I consider the Mormon people a kind-hearted and generous class of people. They were sincere in their belief, which is shown by the sufferings they endured in crossing the plains and settling up of the valley." Derry, *Autobiography*, 38; Hyde, *Mormonism*, 333; Forsdick, "On the Oregon Trail to Zion," 49.

[7] Compare with Thomas G. Alexander's statement: "Although the Mormons suffered and fought for their religious rights in the Midwest, they disregarded the rights of those who differed with them in Utah. In Utah, the property and, in some cases, the lives of dissidents and non-Mormons were clearly not secure." Alexander, *Utah*, 133.

enemy.[8] The enemy here alluded to is the world or all who do not believe in Mormonism—"all who are not for us are against us" and of course enemies.[9] How do they mean to accomplish this? The Angel of the Lord shall [p. 3] destroy them, or in other words, the dannits shall slay them. The dannits are a well disipled branch of the Preisthood organized with captains over Tens and Fifties to exacute a very prominent part of gods judgments upon the Earth.[10] Who did I hear preach these doctrins? John Young, Head Patriarch ~~of the Church~~, and many other dignatrys of the church.[11] In fact I do not mean to write any thing in this letter but what I do know and can vouch for as being doctrins entertained by the Mormon Church in Salt Lake. I heard the Bishop of the 19 Ward declare that if the Celestial Law was put in force, they the people of the Lord would be cutting one another's throats.[12]

We were also taught—that our minds might be prepared for coming events—to beware of Sympathy, as that feeling would destroy a great many in this Church. How that to beware of sympathy? Because when that time comes and is at hand you may see the dead Bodys of your Fathers, your

---

[8] "Celestial law" refers to all the laws of God. These laws were often spoken of separately, such as the celestial law of tithing, of consecration, or of marriage (i.e., plural marriage). McAuslan here is referring to blood atonement. This law taught that a person must have his own blood spilled on the ground through someone slitting his throat to atone for certain egregious sins such as apostasy and adultery. See Brigham Young's sermon of February 8, 1857, *Journal of Discourses*, 4:220.

[9] Although many examples might be given of this kind of preaching, a sermon given by Orson Hyde on October 25, 1857 serves here: "When that day comes, . . . those who are not right and pure will be devoured and destroyed. . . . Why have they not yielded obedience to the laws of the kingdom of God and taken upon them the yoke of Christ? . . . Persons holding that position are ready to turn to the enemy. . . . 'He that is not for us is against us.'" *Journal of Discourses*, 5:355–56.

[10] This description of the Danites comes from the "History of Joseph Smith," dated October 1838, which was published in the *Millennial Star* the year McAuslan emigrated to Utah: "He," referring to Sampson Avard, "proceeded to administer to the few under his control, an oath, binding them to everlasting secresy [*sic*] to everything which should be communicated to them by himself. Thus Avard initiated members into his band, . . . which *he* named *Danites*. . . . [H]e held meetings to organize his men into companies of tens and fifties, appointing a captain over each company." Emphasis in original. *Millennial Star* 16 (July 22, 1854): 458–59. It seems likely that Peter, not knowing who authorized the murders of the Parrishes, Henry Forbes, or Henry Jones and his mother, assumed it must be the Danites about whom rumors had spread across the territory.

[11] John Smith, the oldest son of Hyrum Smith, was the presiding church patriarch in this period. However, at the semiannual conference in Salt Lake City on October 8, 1853, President Young's eldest brother, John Young, was voted a church patriarch, i.e., a local patriarch. *Deseret News*, October 15, 1853, 2. McAuslan heard John Young on November 26, 1856, when he preached in Salt Lake City's Nineteenth Ward, where McAuslan was then living. Record of Members, Nineteenth Ward, 116.

[12] Alonzo H. Raleigh, then bishop of the Nineteenth Ward, recorded in his journal on December 1, 1856, "I declared my intentions to carry out the law of God, to the verry letter in Sanctifying Israel & cleanzing the inside of the Platter by wiping out inniquity from our midst." Raleigh, Journal, 151–52.

Brothers, or your nearest, dearest relatives and friends lying upon the Streets, and if you should pass by, say not a word to anybody, nither ask the cause, just conduct yourself as if nothing had happened. All is right, it was done by athority.[13]

But I wish to inform you that it is not so. Those who renounce the faith and who have courage enough to speek what he dose think and know would meet with such a fate faster than a murderer or an adulterer. Do I know of any such cases? Yess I do. Not that I saw the deed commited with my own eyes, but this deed that I am going to relate was commited at the Town of Springville only 6 miles from Spanish Fork where I resided at that time, and the people not being atall prepared to act by the above council, "pass by and not say a word about it," there secret deeds were published upon the house tops. So I got to know as much about it as if I had seen it with mine eyes, a day or so after it was done.[14]

A Father and Two sons had renounced the Faith and desided on leaving the Territory. A few days before they desided to start, there carriage and horses were stolen out of ther stable by night. There was another man, a Dannit, acting in consort with them with the pretended intention of leaving at the same time.[15] The time appointed came; they left the town at a time when they thought they would be least suspected, prepared with laraets to captured their own horses as they knew the field that they were in.[16] They had not proceeded far when they came to where other Dannits were lieing in waite. The work of death commenced. In the struggle the Traitor Dannit fell with the Father and one son. The other son, making his escape unhurt, went straight back to town [where a] public metting

---

[13] George A. Hicks, who lived in Spanish Fork before and during the time that McAuslan lived there, described John Young's visit on September 27–29, 1856, in a similar way: "It was during the Reformation that that liable doctrine known as 'blood atonement' was first preached in Utah. John Young . . . said there were hypocrites in Zion and that [they] were not fit to live and the time had come that their blood would have to be shed to save them and he continued, 'If you should find your fathers or your mothers by the way side with their throats cut go on about your business and say nothing about it for it would be all right. Zion must be purified.'" Hicks, "History of George Armstrong Hicks," chapter 10.

[14] George A. Hicks wrote, "This [Reformation] preaching soon began to have an effect throughout the country and many were the victims that fell by the hand of the destroyer. . . . My wife and myself both saw the blood of the Parishes at Springville two days after the murder. Those were truly perilous times such as only fanatic[s] know how to bring on a country." Hicks, "History of George Armstrong Hicks," chapter 10.

[15] There were actually two men, Gardiner G. "Duff" Potter and Abraham Durfee, who had been sent by Bishop Aaron Johnson to find out when the Parrishes were planning to go. They told the father, William Parrish, that they too wished to leave. Both men betrayed the Parrishes, but to call them Danites is probably inaccurate. The sons were Beason and Orrin Parrish.

[16] They did know that two of the four horses were in Provo. See note 19 below, on debt. Abraham Durfee twice mentioned that the Parrishes had a bridle with them, but neither it nor a lariat was found with the corpses. "Property Found on the Bodies," Hosea Stout Miscellaneous Papers.

[meeting] [was] going on at the time. He entered the metting and plead[ed] for protection. The Bishop promised him protection upon the condition that he remaind and behaved himself.[17]

I have not the lest doubt but that you have heard of this case. Nither do I doubt but that it has had the approprate coloring to suite the tastes of honnest and [p. 4] faithful but to[o] credulous Saints at home [i.e., in Scotland] put upon it by some faithfull Elder from Zion.[18] But I have only to say I have given you a simple unvarnished statement of the facts as they occurred and would mearly add that they were men of good moral carac-ter, had commited no crime and were in debt to no body.[19]

---

[17] Orrin, the younger son, told a different story: "Witness ran to his uncle's house; some ten or twelve men were standing in the street to the left. Witness [Orrin] got in so quick they could not catch him." A guard was set over the house that night, and the next day he was taken before Justice of the Peace John M. Stewart and examined in a court of inquiry. "Testimony of Orrin E. Par-rish," *Valley Tan*, April 19, 1859, 1. Also in Cradlebaugh, *Utah and the Mormons*, 45–47.

[18] This slaying became known as the Parrish-Potter murders, Duff Potter being the betrayer who was killed by mistake. In 1857 the *Millennial Star*, the LDS newspaper published for the British Saints, did not mention any of the happenings in Springville in mid-March 1857 or six months later at Mountain Meadows. In 1858 the paper was filled with news of the army's imminent arrival and the Move South. In 1859, when U.S. associate justice John Cradlebaugh opened his court for a grand jury to consider the Parrish murders and others, the *Millennial Star* first gave notice of it on May 28 but failed to mention what crimes were being investigated. Almost a month later the editor, Asa Calkin, wrote that "the thirst for blood, rapine, and plunder is as strong as ever in the breasts of those corrupt and profligate judges. . . . The charge brought against the citizens, and which was made the excuse for the crusade against them, is false and utterly groundless." But still no explanation of the charges was published. "Passing Events," *Millennial Star* 21 (May 28, 1859): 355; Editorial, *Millennial Star* 21 (June 25, 1859): 411.

[19] They may actually have been in debt. Durfee described what had been said in a meeting in Bishop Johnson's council room about three weeks before the murders: "There was something mentioned at this meeting about the Parrishes—that they were going to leave the Territory. The Bishop said there were some demands against them, for debts that they were owing; he did not state the debts." Shortly before the murders, the Parrishes' four horses and carriage were stolen. The next day, Duff Potter and William Parrish applied to Justice of the Peace John M. Stewart for a search warrant. They found two of the horses in the possession of B. K. Bullock, the mayor of Provo. Potter and Parrish returned to Springville without the horses. That evening Potter attended another council meeting at Bishop Aaron Johnson's house. According to Durfee, "the Bishop told him [Potter] that Parrish or his son was owing Bullock something in regard to an order that Parrish's son had traded to Bullock, and that he (the Bishop) wanted those horses placed where they belonged to answer the demand." Thomas O'Bannion, in whose house the Parrishes lived, stated in his affidavit that "Moses Daley came to me a few days before the murder, and told me to tell Parrish if he did not settle that matter between Beason [Parrish] and Bullock his blood would pay the debt." Thus the Parrishes may have owed some sort of debt, but the bishop appears to have enforced payment for it by taking the horses and carriage. Raising some doubt as to the idea of debt is the fact that the horses in Bullock's possession were returned to William Parrish's widow the next summer. Even if the debt was legitimate, there were courts to settle such mat-ters. "Testimony of Orrin E. Parrish," "Confession of Abraham Durfee," and "Affidavit of Thomas O'Bannion," *Valley Tan*, April 19, 1859, 1, 4; Brigham Young to Aaron Johnson, July 30, 1857, Brigham Young, Letterpress Copybook Transcriptions, 730. The testimonies, affidavits, and Durfee's confession are also in Cradlebaugh, *Utah and the Mormons*, 43–61.

This act occurred during the reformation excitement, and it was expected that the Celestial laws were gowing to be put in forse right straite. And as they had allready declaired there independence from the United States,[20] they had full faith that the lord would fight there Battles and sustain them as an independent Kingdom to the dismay and overthrow of all there enemies, even the Prophet himself declaring that with Ten men of the right stripe he could defie all the armies of the U.S.[21] But the enemies from within were more to be feared, hence the necessity of cleansing the inside of the Platter first.[22]

As it is not attall according to my feelings to write on this subject and [I] would not have troubled you now with this expos[t]ulation on Mormonizm had you not, allong with others, requested me to write you on this subject. I have a few more remarks to make and then I shall close for the present.

A few words about polligamy or celestial marriage. There is no such a thing as revelation from the Lord required in order to get more wifes. Previous to the Mormon rebellion, there was generall teaching to all to go ahead and get more wifes as they could to receive a Celestiall Salvation with it.[23] That coupled allong with consecration of all your property to the Lord— that is, Brigham, the only Lord they may ever expect to see,—that down there Celestial Salvation is about sure, or as I would speek it, they are bound hand and foot, and must remain slaves to Lord Brigham during there natural lives. You must see at once that a man after he has got two or three wives and they have children by him, natural affection, even if he should lose faith

---

[20] Two examples of such preaching: On August 31, 1856, Brigham Young declared, "We are bound to become a sovereign State in the Union, or an independent nation by ourselves" (*Journal of Discourses*, 4:40). On September 6, 1857, when the U.S. Army was on its way to Utah, Young "declared that the thred [*sic*] was cut between us and the U.S. and that the Almighty recognized us as a free and independent people and that no officer appointed by the government should come and rule over us from this time forth" (Brooks, *On the Mormon Frontier*, 2:636).

[21] Brigham Young made this declaration several times in the fall of 1857 when the army was on its way to Utah. "Our enemies will not be able to come within a hundred miles of us. I know that ten men, such as I could name and select, could stop them before they got to Laramie. . . . I count five such men equal to twenty-five thousand, and believe that two of them could put ten thousand to flight." October 8, 1857, *Journal of Discourses*, 5:339. See also statements on October 25, 1857, ibid., 5:353; and November 15, 1857, ibid., 6:41.

[22] This scriptural metaphor (Matthew 23:25 and Alma 60:23–24) was applied frequently to eliminating apostates during the Reformation. For example, on November 2, 1856, Jedediah Grant preached, "Let every Elder throw the arrows of God Almighty through the sinner and pierce their loins, and penetrate their vitals, until the banner of Christ shall wave triumphantly over Israel. Shall we give up, and let the wicked and ungodly overcome us? No, in the name and by the power of God we will overcome them. We will cleanse the inside of the platter and have Israel saved." *Journal of Discourses*, 4:75.

[23] Church leaders promoted polygamy during the Reformation. The general belief was that the more wives a man had, the greater the glory in heaven for himself and his wives. The "Mormon rebellion" is the reason President Buchanan gave for sending the army to Utah.

in Mormonism, binds him to his children, and as the saying amongst them is, "if he should appostatize[,] his property won't."[24] Thus you see the Trap is well planed and it's hard to get out of, and the reasion of them being so anxious to get them into it, before the expected fight with *Uncle Sam* [in the Utah War], for if a man will fight for anything it will be for his wives and children coupled with a fanicial [fanatical?] religion. As is to be expected, the women live very unhappy lives with but few exceptions.

The present prospect for Joseph Smith's prophesy in regard to South Carolina being fullfilled is at present exciting much interest at Salt Lake with the Saints.[25] I learn this from the pappers.[26] (Such a prophesy even though it should come to pass) looses much of its weight when the fact is known that S.C. has possessed the ellements of disunion as far back as the [early] 1800[s] and has manifested itself less or more ever since.[27]

Unlike apostates—individuals who renounce and then actively battle against their former religion—Peter never worked to destroy the Mormon church. Although his letter to Robert Salmon did not mince words about how blind obedience had led to murder, Peter held that each must judge the faith for himself or herself. In the end, the letter did not dissuade Salmon from Mormonism. Instead, Salmon came to Utah six years later in 1866 with his wife, nine children, and a daughter-in-law. They settled on a farm in Coalville, Summit County, Utah, next to that of Peter's sister Agnes and brother-in-law John Allan. In 1877, when Summit Stake was organized, Salmon was appointed bishop and continued in that capacity until 1889, when he was ordained a local patriarch. In his secular life, Salmon was county clerk and a justice of the peace. He died in 1891 at age seventy-eight.[28]

---

[24] John Hyde quoted Brigham Young as saying, "If you tie up the calf the cow will stay." Hyde, *Mormonism*, 38.

[25] Peter was referring to Joseph Smith's prediction of a war between the North and the South that would begin in South Carolina and in which all nations on earth would become involved (D&C 87). By this means, Mormons of the time believed, the United States would be punished for acting against Mormonism. Paul Peterson commented, "When the Civil War failed to lead to the consummation of all things, a re-reading of historical processes was made necessary." Peterson, "Mormon Reformation of 1856–1857," 80.

[26] Peter's nephew, Arthur Maxwell Jr. (the son of Peter's wife's sister, Elizabeth McAuslin Maxwell), regularly sent the *Deseret News* to him in California. Peter McAuslan to Arthur Maxwell Jr., circa 1886 (#37 McAuslan Papers), 1.

[27] South Carolina supported states' rights and free trade, and the people had resisted federal tariffs on their trade with Europe since 1819. The state passed the Ordinance of Nullification in 1832 that declared the federal tariff acts of 1828 and 1832 to be "null and void."

[28] Mormon Pioneer Overland Travel, 1847–68. Salmon's son, Robert, Jr. (1836–71), emigrated to Utah before his father and family, arriving there in 1861. He farmed on John Allen's land on shares. Salmon's daughter Ann (1837–1920), who came with the main part of the family in 1866, lived with John and Agnes Allen, at least for a time. Agnes and John Allan to Peter McAuslan, July 20, 1869 (#20 McAuslan Papers); "Death of Robert Salmon," *Deseret News*, February 28, 1891, 23.

Bibliography

ARCHIVAL SOURCES

1841 Scotland Census. General Register Office, Edinburgh.

1851 Scotland Census. General Register Office, Edinburgh.

1856 Utah Census Returns. LDS Church Archives.

Aird, Emily McAuslan. "The Family History." 1950. In author's collection.

Allan, Peter. "John Allan." N.d. In author's collection.

Ancestral File of the Family History Library. Church of Jesus Christ of Latter-day Saints, Salt Lake City.

Anderson, H. Reese, ed. "Extracts from the Journal of Alexander Adamson and Other Notes Giving an Account of the Trip to America of Agnes Baird Adamson and Her Sons Alexander and Dougal Adamson." Copy in author's collection.

Andrew, Frederick Chadwick. Diary. LDS Church Archives.

Barney, Lewis. Autobiography. Utah State Historical Society.

Beck, Eva Pearl Elder. "History of Joseph Ellison Beck." 1966. Special Collections, Harold B. Lee Library, Brigham Young University.

Bishop's Records 1850–77. Nineteenth Ward, Salt Lake City, LDS Church Archives (extracted by Church Archives staff).

Carruth, William. Autobiography and Journal. LDS Church Archives.

Church Historian's Office. History of the Church. LDS Church Archives.

———. Journal. LDS Church Archives.

"Coroner's Inquest [of the Parrish-Potter Murders]." Hosea Stout Papers, 1844–70, Letters and Miscellaneous, Utah State Historical Society.

Cradlebaugh gravestone. Art Inventories Catalog, Smithsonian American Art Museum, Smithsonian Institution Research Information System (database).

Crow, Julina Markham. "History of the Life of Stephen Markham." Works Progress Administration, Utah State Historical Society.

Davies, John J. Diary. Federal Writers Project, Works Progress Administration, Utah State Historical Society.

Eldredge, Horace S. Journal, September 1852–April 1854. LDS Church Archives.

Empey, William A. Diary, September 1852–April 1854. LDS Church Archives.

Ferguson, Andrew. Diaries and Autobiography, 1852–80. Special Collections, Harold B. Lee Library, Brigham Young University.

Genealogical and Minute Book, 1859–69. Spanish Fork Ward, Utah Stake. LDS Church Archives.

Gibson, William. Journal. 3 vols. LDS Church Archives.

———. Journal #150. LDS Church Archives.

Hamilton, Henry. Journals, [1851]–1900. LDS Church Archives.

Harmon, Appleton. Autobiography and Diary, 1850–53. Special Collections, Harold B. Lee Library, Brigham Young University.

Hicks, George Armstrong. "History of George Armstrong Hicks." 1878. Typescript by Kent V. Marvin, Mary Anne Loveless, and Karen Kenison.

———. "History of Spanish Fork." 1913. Special Collections, Harold B. Lee Library, Brigham Young University.

Hoth, Hans. Diary. Translated by Peter Gulbrandsen. Bancroft Library, University of California, Berkeley.

Jensen, Andrew, comp. Manuscript History and Historical Reports, Spanish Fork, Utah County. LDS Church Archives.

Journal History of the Church of Jesus Christ of Latter-day Saints. Chronological scrapbook. LDS Church Archives.

King, Hannah Tapfield. Journals. Typescript by Frank T. Watkins. LDS Church Archives.

Larsen, Christian J. Journal excerpts. Journal History, October 5, 1854. LDS Church Archives.

Lindsay, William. Autobiography. Utah State Historical Society.

"List of £13 Compy. and Per. Emig. Fund passengers on the 'John M. Wood' March 7th 1854," followed by "List of deaths in the company of the ship John M. Wood." Empey File, Mormon File, March–August 1854, Huntington Library, Pasadena, Calif.

"List of deaths in the company of the ship John M. Wood." *See* "List of £13 Compy."

Local Unit Financial Records, 1844–1963. Nineteenth Ward, Salt Lake Stake. LDS Church Archives.

———. Spanish Fork, Utah County. LDS Church Archives.

Lyon, John. Notebook with diary of voyage on the ship *International* in 1853. Copy courtesy of T. Edgar Lyon, Jr.

MacDonald, Elizabeth Graham. Autobiography. LDS Church Archives.

MacMaster, William Athole. Diaries, 1848–87. LDS Church Archives.

Manuscript History of the British Mission. LDS Church Archives.

Martin, Edward. Journal, August 1852–May 1855. LDS Church Archives.

McAuslan, Peter. Papers in author's collection.

McIntyre, Alistair. "Place Names: Row Parish" and "Place Names: Luss Parish." Dumbarton Library, Dumbarton, Scotland.

McLaws, Lafayette. Diary. Utah State Historical Society.

Mitchell, Hezekiah. Journal. June–September 1854. LDS Church Archives.

Mormon Pioneer Overland Travel, 1847–68. LDS Church Archives. In lds.org/churchhistory/library (database).

Moyle, James. Reminiscences. LDS Church Archives.

"Odds and Ends about Kirkintilloch, Chiefly in the Forties." N.d. William Patrick Library, Kirkintilloch, Dunbartonshire.

Old Parish Registers (OPR). Church of Scotland baptisms, marriages, and burials, 1553–1854. General Register Office, Edinburgh.

Particular Registers of Sasines. Scottish Record Office, Edinburgh.

Phelps, John Wolcott. Diaries. John Wolcott Phelps Papers, 1857–59. Utah State Historical Society.

Pitchforth, Samuel. Diary, February 1857–July 1861. LDS Church Archives.

"Property Found on the Bodies." Hosea Stout Miscellaneous Papers. Utah State Historical Society.

Raleigh, Alonzo Hazelton. Journal, September 1853–February 1861. LDS Church Archives.

Rampton, Henry. Diary. LDS Church Archives.

Receipts for Smith's ferry and toll bridges at Cross Creek and St. Mary's Mission. Empey File, Mormon File, March–August 1854. Huntington Library, Pasadena, Calif.

Receipts for transportation. Empey file, Mormon File, March–August 1854. Huntington Library, Pasadena, Calif.

Record of Fiftieth Quorum of Seventies. Spanish Fork, Utah County. LDS Church Archives.

Record of Members. 1851–53. Baillieston Branch, Glasgow Conference, British Mission. LDS Church Archives.

———. 1840–54. Glasgow Branch, Glasgow Conference, British Mission. LDS Church Archives.

———. 1844–1909. Kilmarnock Branch, Glasgow Conference, British Mission. LDS Church Archives.

———. 1847–51. Barrhead Branch, Glasgow Conference, British Mission. LDS Church Archives.

———. 1848–49. Tollcross Branch, Glasgow Conference, British Mission. LDS Church Archives.

———. 1848–50. Falkirk Branch, Edinburgh Conference, British Mission. LDS Church Archives.

———. 1848–55. Paisley Branch, Glasgow Conference, British Mission. LDS Church Archives.

———. 1850–56. Nineteenth Ward, Salt Lake City. LDS Church Archives.

———. 1852–91. Spanish Fork Ward. LDS Church Archives.

Register of the ship *International*. Emigration Records of the Liverpool Office of the British Mission, 1851–1855. LDS Church Archives.

Register of the ship *John M. Wood*. Emigration Records of the Liverpool Office of the British Mission, 1851–55. LDS Church Archives.

Richards, Franklin D. Journal, 1844–54. LDS Church Archives.

Richards, Samuel W. Journals, 1839–1909. LDS Church Archives.

Richardson, William. Diaries, 1884–94. LDS Church Archives.

Rowan, Matthew. "A Concise Historical Account of the Rowan Family." Utah State Historical Society.

Sexton's Internment Records. Salt Lake City Cemetery. LDS Church Archives.

Sinclair, Peter. Journal, 1853–54. LDS Church Archives.

Smith, Job. Diary and Autobiography, 1849–77. Special Collections, Harold B. Lee Library, Brigham Young University.

Sons of Utah Pioneers. Utah Pioneer Card Index.

Sproul, Andrew. Diary, 1841–47. Federal Writers' Project, Works Progress Administration, 1936, Utah State Historical Society.

Squires, John Fell. Autobiography. LDS Church Archives.

Sutherland, Thomas. Journal. LDS Church Archives.

Sutton, John Allen. Autobiography. LDS Church Archives.

Temple Records Index Bureau. LDS Church Archives.

Todd, Thomas. Autobiography. Circa 1895. Special Collections, Harold B. Lee Library, Brigham Young University.

"Transfers of City Lots." Salt Lake County, County Recorder, Land Deeds, Book A, February 1855–April 1859. LDS Church Archives.

Tripp, Enoch B. Journal. 18 vols. Special Collections, Harold B. Lee Library, Brigham Young University.

Trustee-in-Trust. Raleigh's Time Book A. LDS Church Archives.

———. Raleigh's Time Book B. LDS Church Archives.

Utah County Military District, 1850–66. Utah Territorial Militia Muster Rolls, 1849–70. LDS Church Archives.

Whipple, Nelson Wheeler. Autobiography. Mormon File, Huntington Library, Pasadena, Calif.

Williams, Howard. Diary. Utah State Historical Society.

Woodruff, Wilford. Journal. As given in Church Historian's Office, History of the Church 1839–circa 1882. LDS Church Archives.

Young, Brigham. Office Files, 1832–78. LDS Church Archives.

———. Letterpress Copybook Transcriptions. LDS Church Archives.

Young, Franklin W. "A Record of the Early Settlement of Payson, Utah County, Utah Territory." 1861. LDS Church Archives.

GOVERNMENT DOCUMENTS

Biographical Directory of the United States Congress. 1774–present. In bioguide.congress.gov (database).

Cradlebaugh, John. *Utah and the Mormons: Speech of Hon. John Cradlebaugh, of Nevada, on the Admission of Utah as a State; Delivered in the House of Represen-tatives, February 7, 1863.* Washington, D.C.: L. Tower and Co., ca. 1863.

"Criminal Cases in District Courts of Utah." *Letter from the Attorney General,* 42nd Cong., 2nd sess., House Exec. Doc. 256. Washington, D.C.: Government Printing Office, 1872.

Letters Sent, HQ, Department of Utah, 1858–61. Records of the United States Army Continental Commands, 1821–1920. RG 393, National Archives.

Letters Sent, Letters Received, 1859–61. Army Headquarters, Utah Territory, War Department, Records of the Adjutant General's Office, 1780s–1917. RG 94, National Archives. Copy in the Utah State Historical Society.

Message from the President of the United States. 35th Cong., 2nd sess., House Exec. Doc. 2, serial set 998. Washington, D.C.: James B. Steedman, 1858.

Message of the President of the United States. 36th Cong., 1st sess., Senate Exec. Doc. 32, serial set 1031. Washington, D.C.: George W. Bowman, 1860.

Minute Book and Naturalization Record "C." November 13, 1855–January 6, 1865. Utah County, 2nd Judicial District Court. LDS Church Archives.

Probate Court, Salt Lake County. Utah Civil and Criminal Case Files, 1852–87. Utah State Archives.

Probate Records, 1872–1926. Sutter County, Calif., vol. A. California State Archives.

Report of the Secretary of War, 1855. 34th Cong., 1st sess., Senate Exec. Doc. 1, part 2, serial set 811. Washington, D.C.: Beverley Tucker, 1855.

Report of the Secretary of War, December 1, 1859. 36th Cong., 1st sess., Senate Exec. Doc. 2, serial set 1024. Washington, D.C.: George W. Bowman, 1860.

U.S. Department of State. Territorial Papers, Utah Series. RG 59, National Archives.

U.S. Federal Census for 1850, 1860, 1870, and 1880.

U.S. Land Office, Sutter County, Calif. Patent Records of Sutter County, Book C. California State Archives.

"The Utah Expedition." 35th Cong., 1st sess., House Exec. Doc. 71, serial set 956. Washington, D.C.: James B. Steedman, 1858.

"Utah Superintendency." *Report of the Secretary of the Interior, November 29, 1856.* 34th Cong., 3rd sess., Senate Exec. Doc., vol. 2, no. 5, serial set 875. Washington, D.C.: A. O. P. Nicholson, 1856.

———. *Report of the Secretary of the Interior, December 3, 1857.* 35th Cong., 1st sess., House Exec. Doc. 2, serial set 942. Washington, D.C.: William A. Harris, 1858.

————. *Report of the Secretary of the Interior, December 2, 1858.* 35th Cong., 2nd sess., Senate Exec. Doc. 1, serial set 974. Washington, D.C.: William A. Harris, 1859.

————. *Report of the Secretary of the Interior, December 1, 1859.* 36th Cong., 1st sess., Senate Exec. Doc. 2, serial set 1023. Washington, D.C.: George W. Bowman, 1860.

Utah Territory. *Message of the President of the United States.* 36th Cong., 1st sess., House Exec. Doc. 78, serial set 1056. Washington, D.C.: Thomas H. Ford, 1860.

NEWSPAPERS

Daily Appeal (Marysville, Calif.)
Deseret News (Salt Lake City)
Harper's Weekly (New York City)
Hayward Journal (Hayward, Calif.)
Illustrated London News
Millennial Star, Latter-day Saints' (Liverpool, England)
Mormon (New York City)
New York Herald
New York Times
San Francisco Herald
Stirling Journal and Advertiser (Stirling, Scotland)
Sutter County Farmer (Yuba City, Calif.)
Valley Tan (Salt Lake City)
Western Standard (San Francisco)

BOOKS AND PAMPHLETS

Ahlstron, Sydney E. *A Religious History of the American People.* New Haven, Conn., and London: Yale University Press, 1972.

Alexander, Thomas G. *Utah: The Right Place.* Salt Lake City: Gibbs Smith, 1995.

Allred, LaNora P. *Spanish Fork: City on the Rio de Aguas Calientes.* Spanish Fork, Utah: J-Mart, 1981.

Arrington, Leonard J. *Brigham Young, American Moses.* Urbana and Chicago: University of Illinois Press, 1986.

————. *Great Basin Kingdom: Economic History of the Latter-day Saints, 1830–1900.* Lincoln: University of Nebraska Press, 1966.

Alter, J. Cecil. *Jim Bridger.* Norman: University of Oklahoma Press, 1962.

Bagley, Will. *Blood of the Prophets: Brigham Young and the Massacre at Mountain Meadows.* Norman: University of Oklahoma Press, 2002.

Baines, Dudley. *Emigration from Europe, 1815–1930.* Cambridge: Cambridge University Press, 1995.

Baker, Hozial H. *Overland Journey to Carson Valley and California.* San Francisco: Book Club of California, 1973.

Barney, Ronald O. *The Mormon Vanguard Brigade of 1847: Norton Jacob's Record.* Logan: Utah State University Press, 2005.

———. *One Side by Himself: The Life and Times of Lewis Barney, 1808–1894.* Logan: Utah State University Press, 2001.

Barr, James. *Balloch and Around: Life in Balloch, the Vale of Leven and Loch Lomondside, 1820–45.* Compiled by Graham Hopner. Dumbarton, Scotland: Dumbarton Public Libraries, 1992.

Bartholomew, Rebecca, and Leonard J. Arrington. *Rescue of the 1856 Handcart Companies.* Provo, Utah: Charles Redd Center for Western Studies, 1992.

Bergera, Gary James. *Conflict in the Quorum: Orson Pratt, Brigham Young, Joseph Smith.* Salt Lake City: Signature Books, 2002.

Bigler, David L. *Forgotten Kingdom: The Mormon Theocracy in the American West, 1847–1896.* Spokane, Wash.: Arthur H. Clark, 1998.

———. *Fort Limhi: The Mormon Adventure in Oregon Territory, 1855–1858.* Spokane, Wash.: Arthur H. Clark, 2003.

Black, Susan Easton, and Larry C. Porter, eds. *Lion of the Lord: Essays on the Life and Service of Brigham Young.* Salt Lake City: Deseret Book Co., 1995.

Bloxham, V. Ben, James R. Moss, and Larry C. Porter. *Truth Will Prevail: The Rise of the Church of Jesus Christ of Latter-day Saints in the British Isles, 1837–1987.* Solihull, West Midlands, England: Church of Jesus Christ of Latter-day Saints, 1987.

Bremner, David, *The Industries of Scotland: Their Rise, Progress, and Present Condition*, 1869, reprinted Newton Abbot, England: David & Charles Reprints, 1969.

Brockbank, Isaac. *Autobiography.* Salt Lake City: BIRMA, 1997.

Brooks, Juanita. *John D. Lee: Zealot, Pioneer Builder, Scapegoat.* Glendale, Calif.: Arthur H. Clark, 1972.

———. *The Mountain Meadow Massacre.* Norman: University of Oklahoma Press, 1970.

———, ed. *On the Mormon Frontier: The Diary of Hosea Stout.* 2 vols. Salt Lake City: University of Utah Press, 1964.

Brown, Callum G. *Religion and Society in Scotland since 1707.* Edinburgh: Edinburgh University Press, 1997.

Brown, Stewart J., and Michael Fry, eds. *Scotland in the Age of the Disruption.* Edinburgh: Edinburgh University Press, 1993.

Bryant, William C. *Picturesque America.* 2 vols. New York: D. Appleton, 1872.

Buchanan of Auchmar, William. *A Historical and Genealogical Essay upon the Family and Surname of Buchanan.* 1723; reprint, Glasgow: J. Wylie and Co., 1820; facsimile reprint, Bowie, Md.: Heritage Books, 1994.

Burton, Richard F. *The City of the Saints.* Edited by Fawn M. Brodie. New York: Alfred A. Knopf, 1963.

Campbell, Alan B. *The Lanarkshire Miners: A Social History of Their Trade Unions, 1775–1974.* Edinburgh: John Donald, 1979.

Campbell, Eugene E. *Establishing Zion: The Mormon Church in the American West, 1847–1869.* Salt Lake City: Signature Books, 1988.

Carwardine, Richard. *Trans-atlantic Revivalism: Popular Evangelicalism in Britain and America, 1790–1865.* Westport, Conn., and London: Greenwood Press, 1978.

Chamberlain, William Henry. *History of Sutter County, California.* Oakland, Calif.: Thompson and West, 1879.

Cheyne, A. C. *The Transforming of the Kirk: Victorian Scotland's Religious Revolution.* Edinburgh: Saint Andrew Press, 1983.

Church Historian's Office, Church of Jesus Christ of Latter-day Saints. *History of Brigham Young, 1847–1867.* Edited by William L. Knecht and Peter L. Crawley. Berkeley, Calif.: MassCal Associates, 1964.

Clark, Anna. *The Struggle for the Breeches: Gender and the Making of the British Working Class.* Berkeley: University of California Press, 1995.

Clayton, W. *The Latter-day Saints' Emigrants' Guide.* Edited by Stanley B. Kimball. Gerald, Mo.: Patrice Press, 1983.

Coleman, Terry. *Going to America.* New York: Pantheon Books, 1972.

Collier, Fred C., comp. and ed. *The Teachings of President Brigham Young*, vol. 3: *1852–1854.* Salt Lake City: Collier's Publishing Co., 1987.

Conybeare, William John. *Mormonism.* Traveller's Library, vol. 25, 1856. Reprinted from *Edinburgh Review* 202 (April 1854).

Cook, Lyndon W., ed. *Aaron Johnson Correspondence.* Orem, Utah: Center for Research of Mormon Origins, 1990.

Cooley, Everett L., ed. *Diary of Brigham Young, 1857.* Salt Lake City: Tanner Trust Fund, University of Utah Library, 1980.

Cornaby, Hannah. *Autobiography and Poems.* Salt Lake City: J. C. Graham and Co., 1881.

Culverwell, Robert James. *The Marriage Contract. Happy and Fruitful Marriages . . . When and Whom to Marry: A Popular Medical Sketch.* London: self-published, 1848.

Delay, Peter J. *History of Yuba and Sutter Counties, California.* Los Angeles: Historical Record Co., 1924.

Derry, Charles. *Autobiography of Elder Charles Derry.* 1908–16; republished, Independence, Mo.: Price, 1997.

Devine, T. M. *The Scottish Nation: A History, 1700–2000.* New York: Viking, 1999.

Doctrine and Covenants (D&C) of the Church of Jesus Christ of Latter-day Saints.

Eldredge, John. *Illustrated Emigrants' Guide to the Historic Sites along the Hastings/Mormon Trail, Fort Bridger to the Salt Lake Valley*. Salt Lake City: Trail-Buff.com Press, 2005.

England, Breck. *The Life and Thought of Orson Pratt*. Salt Lake City: University of Utah Press, 1985.

Evans, Richard L. *A Century of "Mormonism" in Great Britain*. Salt Lake City: Publishers Press, 1937.

Falkirk Council Archives. *Guide to Archives—Churches*. Callendar House, Callendar Park, Falkirk, Scotland, n.d.

Firmage, Edwin Brown, and Richard Collin Mangrum. *Zion in the Courts: A Legal History of the Church of Jesus Christ of Latter-day Saints, 1830–1900*. Urbana and Chicago: University of Illinois Press, 1988.

Flinn, Michael, Judith Gillespie, Nancy Hill, Ailsa Maxwell, Rosalind Mitchison, and Christopher Smout. *Scottish Population History from the 17th Century to the 1930s*. Cambridge: Cambridge University Press: 1977.

Fowler, L. N. *Marriage: Its History and Ceremonies; with a Phrenological and Physiological Exposition of the Functions and Qualifications for Happy Marriages*. New York: Fowler and Wells, 1847.

Franzwa, Gregory M. *The Oregon Trail Revisited*. Tucson: Patrice Press, 1988.

Fraser, W. Hamish, and R. J. Morris, eds. *People and Society in Scotland, Volume II, 1830–1914*. Edinburgh: John Donald, 1990.

Fraser, William. *The Chiefs of Colquhoun and Their Country*. 2 vols. Edinburgh: privately printed, 1869.

Furniss, Norman F. *The Mormon Conflict, 1850–1859*. New Haven, Conn.: Yale University Press, 1960.

Gordon, Sarah Barringer. *The Mormon Question: Polygamy and Constitutional Conflict in Nineteenth Century America*. Chapel Hill: University of North Carolina Press, 2002.

Graham, Henry Gray. *The Social Life of Scotland in the Eighteenth Century*. 2 vols. London: Adam and Charles Black, 1900.

Greeley, Horace. *An Overland Journey from New York to San Francisco in the Summer of 1859*. Edited by Charles T. Duncan. New York: Alfred A. Knopf, 1964.

Guinn, J. M. *History of the State of California and Biographical Record of the Sacramento Valley, California*. Chicago: Chapman Publishing Co., 1906.

Hafen, LeRoy R., and Ann W. Hafen. *Handcarts to Zion: The Story of a Unique Western Migration, 1856–1860*. Lincoln: University of Nebraska Press, 1960.

———. *The Utah Expedition, 1857–1858: A Documentary Account*. Glendale, Calif.: Arthur H. Clark, 1982.

Hafen, LeRoy R., and Francis Marion Young. *Fort Laramie and the Pageant of the West, 1834–1890*. Lincoln: University of Nebraska Press, 1984.

Haines, Aubrey L. *Historic Sites along the Oregon Trail*. Tucson: Patrice Press, 1994.

Hamilton, Janet. *Poems, Essays, and Sketches: Comprising the Principal Pieces from Her Complete Works.* Glasgow: James Maclehose, 1880.

Hartley, William G. *My Best for the Kingdom: History and Autobiography of John Lowe Butler, a Mormon Frontiersman.* Salt Lake City: Aspen Books, 1993.

Hazen, Craig James. *The Village Enlightenment in America: Popular Religion and Science in the Nineteenth Century.* Urbana and Chicago: University of Illinois Press, 2000.

Hedren, Paul L. *Fort Laramie and the Great Sioux War.* Norman: University of Oklahoma Press, 1998.

Heywood, Martha Spence. *Not by Bread Alone: The Journal of Martha Spence Heywood, 1850–1856.* Edited by Juanita Brooks. Salt Lake City: Utah State Historical Society, 1978.

Hodgert, Robert. *Journal of Robert Hodgert: Elder of the Church of Jesus Christ of Latter-day Saints.* Salt Lake City: filmed by Genealogical Society of Utah, 1982.

Home, D. D. [Daniel Douglas]. *Incidents of My Life.* London: Tinsley, 1863.

Howard, Thomas Frederick. *Sierra Crossing: First Roads to California.* Berkeley: University of California Press, 1998.

Howe, Henry. *Historical Collections of Ohio.* 3 vols. Columbus, Ohio: Henry Howe and Son, 1891.

Hunter, Louis C. *Steamboats on the Western Rivers: An Economic and Technological History.* New York: Dover, 1993.

Hyde, John, Jr. *Mormonism: Its Leaders and Designs.* New York: W. P. Fetridge., 1857.

James, William, *Varieties of Religious Experience.* New York: New American Library, 1958.

Jarvis, Bill. *Corsets in Stripeside.* Falkirk, Scotland: Falkirk District Libraries, 1990.

Jensen, Richard L., and Malcolm R. Thorp, eds. *Mormons in Early Victorian Britain.* Salt Lake City: University of Utah Press, 1989.

Jenson, Andrew, comp. *Church Chronology.* Salt Lake City: Deseret News, 1899.
———. *Latter-day Saint Biographical Encyclopedia.* 4 vols. Salt Lake City: Andrew Jenson History Co., 1901.

Johnson, Alan P. *Aaron Johnson, Faithful Steward.* Salt Lake City: Publishers Press, 1991.

Johnson, Don Carlos. *A Brief History of Springville, Utah.* Springville, Utah: William F. Gibson, 1900.

Johnston, Thomas. *The History of the Working Classes in Scotland.* 1946; reprint, Wakefield, England: EP Publishing, 1974.

Journal of Discourses. 26 vols. London and Liverpool: LDS Booksellers Depot, 1854–86.

Kenney, Scott G., ed. *Wilford Woodruff's Journal.* 9 vols. Midvale, Utah: Signature Books, 1984.

King, Elspeth. *Scotland Sober and Free: The Temperance Movement 1829–1979.* Glasgow: Glasgow Museums and Art Galleries, 1979.

Knox, W. W. *Industrial Nation: Work, Culture and Society in Scotland, 1800–Present.* Edinburgh: Edinburgh University Press, 1999.

Lamar, Howard Roberts. *The Far Southwest, 1846–1912: A Territorial History.* New York: W. W. Norton and Co., 1970.

Larson, A. Karl, and Katharine Miles Larson, eds. *Diary of Charles Lowell Walker.* 2 vols. Logan: Utah State University Press, 1980.

Levitt, Ian, and Christopher Smout. *The State of the Scottish Working-Class in 1843: A Statistical and Spatial Enquiry Based on the Data from the Poor Law Commission Report of 1844.* Edinburgh: Scottish Academic Press, 1979.

Lewis, Samuel. *A Topographical Dictionary of Scotland.* 2 vols. London: S. Lewis, 1849.

Lloyd, James T. *Lloyd's Steamboat Directory.* Cincinnati: James T. Lloyd, 1856.

Lockwood, Jeffrey A. *Locust: The Devastating Rise and Mysterious Disappearance of the Insect That Shaped the American Frontier.* New York: Basic Books, 2004.

Lyman, Edward Leo. *Political Deliverance: The Mormon Quest for Utah Statehood.* Urbana and Chicago: University of Illinois Press, 1986.

Lyon, T. Edgar. *John Lyon: The Life of a Pioneer Poet.* Provo, Utah: Religious Studies Center, Brigham Young University, 1989.

MacDonald, Hugh. *Rambles Round Glasgow.* 1854; reprint, Glasgow: John Smith and Son, 1910.

Mackay, Charles. *The Mormons: or Latter-day Saints; A Contemporary History.* London: National Illustrated Library, 1851.

Mackenzie, Peter. *Reminiscences of Glasgow and the West of Scotland.* 3 vols. Glasgow: John Tweed, 1866.

MacKinnon, William P. *At Sword's Point, Part 1: A Documentary History of the Utah War to 1858.* Norman, Okla.: Arthur H. Clark, 2008.

Madsen, Brigham D. *The Shoshoni Frontier and the Bear River Massacre.* Salt Lake City: University of Utah Press, 1985.

Mattes, Merrill J. *The Great Platte River Road.* Lincoln: University of Nebraska Press, 1969.

May, Dean. *Three Frontiers: Family, Land, and Society in the American West, 1850–1900.* Cambridge: Cambridge University Press, 1994.

McCaffrey, John F. *Scotland in the Nineteenth Century.* New York: St. Martin's Press, 1998.

McChristian, Douglas C. *Fort Laramie and the U.S. Army on the High Plains, 1849–1890.* National Park Service, February 2003. http://www.cr.nps.gov/history/online_books/fola/high_plains.pdf.

McKay, Archibald. *The History of Kilmarnock.* Kilmarnock, Scotland: Archibald McKay, 1864.

McWhirter, James. *Mine Ain Grey Toon.* Barrhead, Scotland: W. Neilly, 1970.

Moorman, Donald R., and Gene A. Sessions. *Camp Floyd and the Mormons: The Utah War.* Salt Lake City: University of Utah Press, 1992.

Morgan, Dale L. *Shoshonean Peoples and the Overland Trails: Frontiers of the Utah Superintendency of Indian Affairs, 1849–1869.* Edited by Richard L. Saunders. Logan: Utah State University Press, 2007.

Mortimer, William James, comp. and ed. *How Beautiful upon the Mountains: A Centennial History of Wasatch County.* Salt Lake City: Wasatch County Chapter of Daughters of Utah Pioneers, 1963.

Mulder, William, and Russell Mortensen, eds., *Among the Mormons: Historic Accounts by Contemporary Observers.* New York: Alfred A. Knopf, 1958.

Murray, Norman. *The Scottish Hand Loom Weavers, 1790–1850: A Social History.* Edinburgh: John Donald, 1978.

Murray, Robert. *Annals of Barrhead.* 1942; reprint, Thurso, Caithness, Scotland: Barrhead Community Council, 1994.

Neill, John. *Records and Reminiscences of Bonhill Parish.* 1912; reprint, Herts, England: Layston Litho, 1979.

Nielson, Carol Holindrake. *The Salt Lake City 14th Ward Album Quilt, 1857: Stories of the Relief Society Women and Their Quilt.* Salt Lake City: University of Utah Press, 2004.

Nielson, Roger B. *Roll Call at Old Camp Floyd, Utah Territory: Soldiers of Johnston's Army at the Upper Camp, 8 July to 8 September 1858.* [Springville, Utah]: privately printed, 2006.

Oakley, C. A. *Our Illustrious Forbears.* Glasgow: Blackie and Sons, 1980.

O'Dea, Thomas F. *The Mormons.* Chicago: University of Chicago Press, 1957.

Papanikolas, Helen Z. *The Peoples of Utah.* Salt Lake City: Utah State Historical Society, 1976.

Paul, R. Eli. *Blue Water Creek and the First Sioux War, 1854–1856.* Norman: University of Oklahoma Press, 2004.

Piercy, Frederick Hawkins. *Route from Liverpool to Great Salt Lake Valley.* Edited by Fawn M. Brodie. Cambridge, Mass.: Belknap Press of Harvard University, 1962.

Pratt, Orson. *A Series of Pamphlets.* Liverpool: R. James, 1851.

Quarterly Report of the Edinburgh Conference of the Church of Jesus Christ of Latter-day Saints, Held in Whitefield Chapel, Carrubber's Close, High Street, Edinburgh, September 5, 1852. LDS Church Archives.

Reinders, Robert C. *End of an Era: New Orleans, 1850–1860.* Gretna, La.: Pelican, 1998.

Rémy, Jules, and Julius Brenchley. *Voyage au Pays des Mormons.* Paris: E. Dentu, 1860.

Report of the Glasgow Conference of the Church of Jesus Christ of Latter-Day Saints, Held in the Mechanic's Institution Hall, Canning Street, Calton, Glasgow, 1st January, 1852. LDS Church Archives.

Report of the Glasgow Conference of the Church of Jesus Christ of Latter-day Saints, Held in the Mechanics' Institution Hall, Canning Street, Calton, Glasgow, 3d July, 1853. Special Collections, Harold B. Lee Library, Brigham Young University.

Report of the Glasgow Quarterly Conference, Held in the Mechanics' Institution, Canning St., Calton, 1st January, 1850. LDS Church Archives.

Report of the Glasgow Quarterly Conference, Held in the Mechanics' Institution, Canning Street, Calton, Glasgow, March 24 and 25, 1849. LDS Church Archives.

Report of the Glasgow Quarterly Conference, Held in the Merchants' Hall, Hutchinson Street, Glasgow, June 24, 1849. LDS Church Archives.

Report of the Glasgow Quarterly Conference of the Church of Jesus Christ of Latter-day Saints, Held in the Mechanics' Hall, Canning Street, Calton, Glasgow, on 1st January, 1851. Special Collections, Harold B. Lee Library, Brigham Young University.

Roberts, B. H. *A Comprehensive History of the Church of Jesus Christ of Latter-day Saints, Century I*. 6 vols. Provo, Utah: Brigham Young University Press, 1965.

Robinson, Stuart. *A History of Printed Textiles*. Cambridge, Mass.: MIT Press, 1969.

Rose, Jonathan. *The Intellectual Life of the British Working Classes*. New Haven, Conn.: Yale University Press, 2001.

Rosenberg, Charles E. *The Cholera Years: The United States in 1832, 1849, and 1866*. Chicago: University of Chicago Press, 1962.

Simpson, James H. *Report of Explorations across the Great Basin in 1859*. 1876; reprint, Reno: University of Nevada Press, 1983.

Slaven, Anthony. *The Development of the West of Scotland: 1750–1960*. London: Routledge and Kegan Paul, 1975.

Sonne, Conway B. *Saints on the Seas: A Maritime History of Mormon Migration, 1830–1890*. Salt Lake City: University of Utah Press, 1983.

———. *Ships, Saints, and Mariners: A Maritime Encyclopedia of Mormon Migration, 1830–1890*. Salt Lake City: University of Utah Press, 1987.

Spencer, Clarissa Young, and Mabel Harmer. *Brigham Young at Home*. Salt Lake City: Deseret Book Co., 1940.

Stampp, Kenneth M. *America in 1857*. New York: Oxford University Press, 1990.

Stenhouse, T. B. H. *The Rocky Mountain Saints*. Salt Lake City: Shepard Book Co., 1904.

Storey, Joyce. *The Thames and Hudson Manual of Textile Printing*. London: Thames and Hudson, 1974.

Stott, Clifford L. *Search for Sanctuary: Brigham Young and the White Mountain Expedition*. Salt Lake City: University of Utah Press, 1984.

Taylor, P. A. M. *Expectations Westward: The Mormons and the Emigration of Their British Converts in the Nineteenth Century.* Ithaca, N.Y.: Cornell University Press, 1966.

Thomas, Sarah S. Castle, comp. *Elias Smith's Journal.* 3 vols. N.p.: Sarah S. Castle Thomas, 1984.

The Topographical, Statistical, and Historical Gazetteer of Scotland. 2 vols. Glasgow: A. Fullarton, 1842.

Treble, James H. *Urban Poverty in Britain, 1830–1914.* New York: St. Martin's Press, 1979.

Tullidge, Edward W. *Tullidge's Histories.* Vol. 2. Salt Lake City: Juvenile Instructor, 1889.

Turnbull, Geoffrey. *A History of the Calico Printing Industry of Great Britain.* Altrincham, England: John Sherratt and Son, 1951.

Unruh, John D., Jr. *The Plains Across: The Overland Emigrants and the Trans-Mississippi West, 1840–60.* Urbana and Chicago: University of Illinois Press, 1993.

Useful Arts and Manufactures of Great Britain. London: Society for Promoting Christian Knowledge, 1848.

Walker, Ronald W. *Wayward Saints: The Godbeites and Brigham Young.* Urbana and Chicago: University of Illinois Press, 1998.

Walker, Ronald W., Richard E. Turley, and Glen M. Leonard. *Massacre at Mountain Meadows: An American Tragedy.* New York: Oxford University Press, 2008.

Warner, Elisha. *The History of Spanish Fork.* Spanish Fork, Utah: Press Publishing Co., 1930.

Weisberg, Barbara. *Talking to the Dead: Kate and Maggie Fox and the Rise of Spiritualism.* New York: HarperCollins, 2004.

Wharton, Thomas K. *Queen of the South: New Orleans, 1853–1862: The Journal of Thomas K. Wharton.* Edited by Samuel Wilson, Jr., Patricia Brady, and Lynn D. Adams. New Orleans: Historic New Orleans Collection, 1999.

Whatley, Christopher A. *The Industrial Revolution in Scotland.* Cambridge: Cambridge University Press, 1997.

Whyte, Ian D. *Scotland before the Industrial Revolution: An Economic and Social History, c. 1050–c.1750.* New York: Longman, 1995.

Wilson, John Marius. *The Imperial Gazetteer of Scotland of Dictionary of Scottish Topography.* 2 vols. London and Edinburgh: A. Fullarton and Co., [1857].

Winskill, P. T. *The Temperance Movement and Its Workers: A Record of Social, Moral, Religious, and Political Progress.* 4 vols. London and Glasgow: Blackie and Son, 1892.

ARTICLES AND BOOK CHAPTERS

Ackley, Richard Thomas. "Across the Plains in 1858." *Utah Historical Quarterly* 9 (July–October 1941): 190–228.

Aird, Polly. "Bound for Zion: The Ten- and Thirteen-Pound Emigrating Companies" *Utah Historical Quarterly* 70:4 (Fall 2002): 300–25.

———. "Escape from Zion: The United States Army Escort of Mormon Apostates, 1859." *Nevada Historical Society Quarterly* 44 (Fall 2001): 196–237.

———. "Why Did the Scots Convert?" *Journal of Mormon History* 26 (Spring 2000): 91–122.

———. "'You Nasty Apostates, Clear Out': Reasons for Disaffection in the Late 1850s." *Journal of Mormon History* 30 (Fall 2004): 129–207.

Alexander, Thomas G., and Leonard J. Arrington. "Camp in the Sagebrush: Camp Floyd, Utah, 1858–1861." *Utah Historical Quarterly* 34 (Winter 1966): 3–21.

Allan, John. "Parish of Row." In *The Statistical Account of Scotland*, edited by John Sinclair, 9:123–27. 1791–99; reprint, Wakefield, England: EP Publishing, 1978.

Arrington, Leonard J. "Charles Mackay and His 'True and Impartial History' of the Mormons." *Utah Historical Quarterly* 36 (Winter 1968): 25–40.

Auerbach, Herbert S., ed. "The Utah War: Journal of Capt. Albert Tracy, 1858–1860." *Utah Historical Quarterly* 13 (1945): 1–119.

Bagley, John. "Reminiscences." In *Bear Lake Pioneers*, compiled by Edith Parker Haddock and Dorothy Hardy Matthews. [Paris, Idaho?]: Daughters of Utah Pioneers, 1974.

Beeton, Beverly. "Teach Them to Till the Soil: An Experiment with Indian Farms 1850–1862." *American Indian Quarterly* 3 (Winter 1977–78): 299–320.

Bennett, Richard E. "'My Idea Is to Go Right Through Right Side Up with Care': The Exodus as Reformation." In *The Collected Leonard J. Arrington Mormon History Lectures*, 55–70. Logan: Utah State University, 2005.

Bigler, David L. "The Aiken Party Executions and the Utah War, 1857–1858." *Western Historical Quarterly* 38 (Winter 2007): 457–76.

Bitton, Davis. "Mormonism's Encounter with Spiritualism." In *The Ritualization of Mormon History and Other Essays*, 83–97. Urbana and Chicago: University of Illinois Press, 1994.

———. "Zion's Rowdies: Growing Up on the Mormon Frontier." In *The Ritualization of Mormon History and Other Essays*, 54–68. Urbana and Chicago: University of Illinois Press, 1994.

Bitton, Davis, and Linda P. Wilcox. "Pestiferous Ironclads: The Grasshopper Problem in Pioneer Utah." *Utah Historical Quarterly* 46 (Fall 1978): 336–55.

[Brimhall, George W.]. "Making a Living in 1858." In *Our Pioneer Heritage*, compiled by Kate B. Carter, 2:31–33. Salt Lake City: Daughters of Utah Pioneers, 1966.

Brown, Callum G. "Religion, Class and Church Growth." In *People and Society in Scotland, Volume II, 1830–1914*, edited by W. Hamish Fraser and R. J. Morris, 310–35. Edinburgh: John Donald Publishers, 1990.

Brown, Stewart J. "The Ten Years' Conflict and the Disruption of 1843." In *Scotland in the Age of the Disruption*, edited by Stewart J. Brown and Michael Fry, 1–27. Edinburgh: Edinburgh University Press, 1993.

Buchanan, Frederick S. "From the Missouri to the Clyde: Samuel W. Richards in Scotland, 1846–1848." *Nauvoo Journal* 7 (Fall 1995): 24–38.

Buchanan, H. "Parish of Strathblane." In *The New Statistical Account of Scotland*, 8:71–88. Edinburgh and London: William Blackwood and Sons, 1845.

Buice, David. "When the Saints Came Marching In: The Mormon Experience in Antebellum New Orleans, 1840–1855." *Louisiana History* 23 (Summer 1982): 221–37.

Burns, John. "Parish of Barony of Glasgow." In *The Statistical Account of Scotland*, edited by John Sinclair, 7:338–55. 1791–99; reprint, Wakefield, England: EP Publishing, 1978.

Butler, John Lowe. "Autobiography." In *My Best for the Kingdom: History and Autobiography of John Lowe Butler, a Mormon Frontiersman*, by William G. Hartley, 369–434. Salt Lake City: Aspen Books, 1993.

Cage, R. A. "Health in Glasgow." In *The Working Class in Glasgow, 1750–1914*, edited by R. A. Cage, 56–76. London: Croom Helm, 1987.

———. "Population and Employment Characteristics." In *The Working Class in Glasgow, 1750–1914*, edited by R. A. Cage, 1–28. London: Croom Helm, 1987.

Cameron, John. "Calico Printing in Campsie." In *The Parish of Campsie: A Series of Biographical, Ecclesiastical, Historical, Genealogical, and Industrial Sketches and Incidents*, appendix 5–52. Kirkintilloch, Scotland: D. Macleod, 1892.

Carter, D. Robert. "Fish and the Famine of 1855–56." *Journal of Mormon History* 27 (Fall 2001): 92–124.

Crowther, M. A. "Poverty, Health and Welfare." In *People and Society in Scotland, Volume II, 1830–1914*, edited by W. Hamish Fraser and R. J. Morris, 265–89. Edinburgh: John Donald Publishers, 1990.

Dempster, John. "Parish of Denny." In *The New Statistical Account of Scotland*, 8:115–38. Edinburgh and London: William Blackwood and Sons, 1845.

Dilts, Bryan Lee. "Historical Background." In *1856 Utah Census Index, An Every-Name Index*, iii. Salt Lake City: Index Publishing, 1983

Evans, Thomas D. "Thomas D. Evans, and His Wife, Pricilla." In *Our Pioneer Heritage*, 14:267–78. Salt Lake City: Daughters of Utah Pioneers, 1971.

Forman, Adam. "Parish of Kirkintilloch." In *The New Statistical Account of Scotland*, 8:168–211. Edinburgh and London: William Blackwood and Sons, 1845.

Forsdick, Stephen. "On the Oregon Trail to Zion in 1853: Memoirs of Stephen Forsdick." *Brand Book of the Denver Westerners* 9 (1953): 31–55.

Graehl, Louise. "Story of Louse Graehl." In *Treasures of Pioneer History*, compiled by Kate B. Carter, 4:56–57. Salt Lake City: Daughters of Utah Pioneers, 1955.

Harrison, John F. C. "The Popular History of Early Victorian Britain: A Mormon Contribution." *Journal of Mormon History* 14 (1988): 3–15.

Hartley, William G. "'Don't Go Aboard the *Saluda*!': William Dunbar, LDS Emigrants, and Disaster on the Missouri." *Mormon Historical Studies* 4 (Spring 2003): 41–70.

———. "From Men to Boys: LDS Aaronic Priesthood Offices, 1829–1996." *Journal of Mormon History* 22 (Spring 1996): 80–136.

———. "Ordained and Acting Teachers in the Lesser Priesthood, 1851–1883." *Brigham Young University Studies* 16 (Spring 1976): 375–98.

———. "Ward Bishops and the Localizing of LDS Tithing, 1847–1856." In *New Views of Mormon History: A Collection of Essays in Honor of Leonard J. Arrington*, edited by David Bitton and Maureen Ursenbach Beecher, 83–97. Salt Lake City: University of Utah Press, 1987.

Hillis, P. L. M. "The Sociology of the Disruption." In *Scotland in the Age of the Disruption*, edited by Stewart J. Brown and Michael Fry, 44–62. Edinburgh: Edinburgh University Press, 1993.

Horne, William A. "Health." In *The Third Statistical Account of Scotland: Glasgow*, edited by J. Cunnison and J. B. S. Gilfillan, 5:475–77. Glasgow: Collins, 1958.

Hurt, Garland. "Appendix N: Population and Resources of the Territory of Utah." In *Report of Explorations across the Great Basin in 1859*, by James H. Simpson, 451–55. 1876; reprint, Reno: University of Nevada Press, 1983.

Janetski, Joel C. "The Ute of Utah Lake." *Anthropological Papers of the University of Utah* 116 (1991): 17–67.

King, Elspeth. "Popular Culture in Glasgow." In *The Working Class in Glasgow, 1750–1914*, edited by R. A. Cage, 142–83. London: Croom Helm, 1987.

Knox, W. "The Political and Workplace Culture of the Scottish Working Class, 1832–1914." In *People and Society in Scotland, Volume II, 1830–1914*, edited by W. Hamish Fraser and R. J. Morris, 138–66. Edinburgh: John Donald Publishers, 1990.

Laurie, John. "Parish of Row." In *The New Statistical Account of Scotland*, 8:65–83. Edinburgh and London: William Blackwood and Sons, 1845.

Lingren, John. "Autobiography." In *Treasures of Pioneer History*, compiled by Kate B. Carter, 1:233–72. Salt Lake City: Daughters of Utah Pioneers, 1952.

MacKinnon, William P. "And the War Came: James Buchanan, the Utah Expedition, and the Decision to Intervene." *Utah Historical Quarterly* 76 (Winter 2008): 22–37.

———. "'Lonely Bones': Leadership and Utah War Violence." *Journal of Mormon History* 33 (Spring 2007): 121–78.

———. "Sex, Subalterns, and Steptoe." *Utah Historical Quarterly* 76 (Summer 2008): 227–46.

MacLaren, A. Allan. "Bourgeois Ideology and Victorian Philanthropy: The Contradictions of Cholera." In *Social Class in Scotland: Past and Present*, edited by A. Allan MacLaren, 36–54. Edinburgh: John Donald Publishers, [1976].

MacPhail, I. M. M. Introduction to *The Statistical Account of Scotland*, edited by John Sinclair, 9:ix–lv. 1791–99; reprint, Wakefield, England: EP Publishing, 1978.

Martin, John. "Industrial Advancement." In *Kirkintilloch*, edited by John Horne, 165–200. Kirkintilloch, Scotland: D. Macleod, 1910.

May, Dean L. "Rites of Passage: The Gathering as Cultural Credo." *Journal of Mormon History* 29 (Spring 2003): 2–41.

McCann, Lloyd E. "The Grattan Massacre." Booklet reprinted from *Nebraska History* 37 (March 1956).

Morgan, Dale L. "The Administration of Indian Affairs in Utah, 1851–1858." *Pacific Historical Review* 17 (November 1948): 383–409.

[Naisbitt, Henry W.]. "Leaves from the Life of a Man, by a 'Mormon' Elder." *Millennial Star* 40 (April 29–August 5, 1878): 259–61, 276–77, 292–94, 326–27, 340–41, 356–58, 371–73, 386–88, 403–405, 434–36, 451–53, 467–68, 483–84.

Naisbitt, Henry W. "Recollections of Our Zionward Journey." *Juvenile Instructor* 38 (April 15, 1903): 230–33.

Parshall, Ardis. "'Pursue, Retake and Punish': The 1857 Santa Clara Ambush." *Utah Historical Quarterly* 73 (Winter 2005): 64–86.

Peterson, Paul H. "The Mormon Reformation of 1856–1857: The Rhetoric and the Reality." *Journal of Mormon History* 15 (1989): 59–87.

Poll, Richard D. "The Move South." *BYU Studies* 29 (Fall 1989): 65–88.

Poll, Richard D., and William P. MacKinnon. "Causes of the Utah War Reconsidered." *Journal of Mormon History* 20 (Fall 1994): 16–44.

Poulter, Thomas A. "Life of Thomas Ambrose Poulter from His Diary." In *Utah Pioneer Biographies*, 44:94–165. Salt Lake City: Genealogical Society of Utah, 1964.

Ririe, James. [Autobiography]. In *Our Pioneer Heritage*, compiled by Kate B. Carter, 9:338–75. Salt Lake City: Daughters of Utah Pioneers, 1966.

Rogers, Wm. H. "Statement." Appendix II in *The Mountain Meadows Massacre*, by Juanita Brooks, 265–78. Norman: University of Oklahoma Press, 1962.

Smith, J. V. "Manners, Morals and Mentalities: Reflections on the Popular Enlightenment of Early Nineteenth-Century Scotland." In *Scottish Culture and Scottish Education, 1800–1980*, edited by Walter M. Humes and Hamish M. Paterson, 25–54. Edinburgh: John Donald, 1983.

Sunter, William. "Ecclesiastical History." In *Kirkintilloch*, edited by John Horne, 78–136. Kirkintilloch, Scotland: D. Macleod, 1910.

Taylor, Philip A. M. "The Mormon Crossing of the United States, 1840–1870." *Utah Historical Quarterly* 25 (1957): 319–37.

Thorp, Malcolm R. "Sectarian Violence in Early Victorian Britain: The Mormon Experience, 1837–1860." *Bulletin of the John Rylands Library* (Autumn 1988): 135–47.

Treble, J. H. "The Occupied Male Labour Force." In *People and Society in Scotland, Volume II, 1830–1914*, edited by W. Hamish Fraser and R. J. Morris, 167–205. Edinburgh: John Donald, 1990.

[Tullidge, E. W.]. "History of Spanish Fork." *Tullidge's Quarterly* 3 (April 1884): 137–70; (July 1884): 300–302.

Van Ravensway, Charles. "Character and History of the Mississippi." In *Mississippi Panorama*, edited by Perry T. Rathbone, 17–26. St. Louis: City Art Museum, 1950.

Walker, Ronald W. "Raining Pitchforks: Brigham Young as Preacher." *Sunstone* 39 (May–June 1983): 5–9.

Watson, R. "Parish of Dunipace." In *The New Statistical Account of Scotland*, 8:379–89. Edinburgh and London: William Blackwood and Sons, 1845.

Whatley, Christopher. "Crucible of the Modern World." In *In Search of Scotland*, edited by Gordon Menzies, 160–83. Edinburgh: Polygon, 2001.

Whittaker, David J. "The Bone in the Throat: Orson Pratt and the Public Announcement of Plural Marriage." *Western Historical Quarterly* 18 (July 1987): 293–314.

Withrington, Donald J. "'Scotland a Half-Educated Nation' in 1834? Reliable Critique or Persuasive Polemic?" In *Scottish Culture and Scottish Education, 1800–1980*, edited by Walter M. Humes and Hamish M. Paterson, 55–74. Edinburgh: John Donald, 1983.

Theses and Dissertations

Buchanan, Frederick Stewart. "The Emigration of Scottish Mormons to Utah, 1849–1900." Master's thesis, University of Utah, 1961.

Bullert, Bette Jean. "Ethical Individualism and Religious Divisions in Enlightenment Scotland: The Case of Adam Smith." Master's thesis, University of Oxford, 1980.

Peterson, Paul H. "The Mormon Reformation." PhD diss., Brigham Young University, 1981. Provo, Utah: Joseph Fielding Smith Institute for Latter-day Saint History and BYU Studies, Dissertations in LDS History Series, 2002.

Whittaker, David J. "Early Mormon Pamphleteering." PhD diss., Brigham Young University, 1982. Provo, Utah: Joseph Fielding Smith Institute for Latter-day Saint History and BYU Studies, Dissertations in LDS History Series, 2003.

Index

CPSIA information can be obtained
at www.ICGtesting.com
Printed in the USA
LVHW030550130323
741479LV00003B/329

9 780806 192123